Also by Alexander Stille

Excellent Cadavers: The Mafia and the Death of the First Italian Republic

The Future of the Past

Benevolence and Betrayal: Five Italian Jewish Families Under Fascism

*The Sack of Rome: How a Beautiful European Country with
a Fabled History and a Storied Culture Was Taken Over by a
Man Named Silvio Berlusconi*

THE FORCE OF THINGS

THE
FORCE
OF
THINGS

A MARRIAGE IN WAR AND PEACE

ALEXANDER
STILLE

FARRAR, STRAUS AND GIROUX   NEW YORK

To Lucy
(who knows)
and to Sam
(that he may know)

Farrar, Straus and Giroux
18 West 18th Street, New York 10011

Copyright © 2013 by Alexander Stille
All rights reserved
Printed in the United States of America
First edition, 2013

Grateful acknowledgment is made for permission to reprint an excerpt
from "Non chiederci la parola" by Eugenio Montale, copyright © Arnoldo
Mondadori Editore S.p.A., Milano, Italy. Reprinted by permission. All
rights reserved. Translation by Alexander Stille.

Library of Congress Cataloging-in-Publication Data
Stille, Alexander.
   The force of things : a marriage in war and peace / Alexander Stille. — 1st ed.
      p.   cm.
   ISBN 978-0-374-15742-5 (alk. paper)
   1. Stille, Alexander—Family relationships.   2. Journalists—United States—Biography.
   3. Authors, American—Family relationships.   I. Title.

PN4874 .S68835 F67 2013
070.92—dc23

2012021272

Designed by Abby Kagan
Photographs courtesy of Alexander Stille

www.fsgbooks.com
www.twitter.com/fsgbooks • www.facebook.com/fsgbooks

1   3   5   7   9   10   8   6   4   2

Contents

THE FORCE OF THINGS

The Force of Things

I. LISTS

Most of her life my mother made lists. Laundry lists, grocery lists, lists of errands, of Scrabble scores, of vices and virtues, New Year's resolutions and household repairs. For a number of years, early in her marriage, she kept careful accounts of her monthly expenses in various bound ledger books:

> *groceries $9.25*
> *dry cleaning $1.75*
> *maid $12*
> *liquor $3.00*
> *cigarettes $1.50*
> *Lucy's jacket $10.00*

These ledger books are mostly blank. Good intentions tended to run out by mid-month. My father, during these years, kept her on a pretty tight leash, with a monthly allowance she considered entirely unreasonable. They would often argue about money, along with other things. Perhaps in order to mollify my father and justify herself, she would begin to keep careful accounts, nickel by nickel, dollar by dollar. But these efforts at household economy would soon fall by the wayside, as she would revert to her generous, free-spending ways.

Throughout her life, she woke early, long before everyone else in the house, sat in bed, and drew up lists. After her death, I found many of them, by her bedside table, by the phone downstairs, tucked into drawers. Unlike her monthly budget, she followed through on these rigorously, crossing out errand after errand as the day went by.

She was neat and fastidious, and—perhaps in reaction to my father's tendencies—kept as little paper around as possible. What she kept was important. In the back of one drawer, I found a faded, yellowing list that had been made by her college boyfriend, Clinton Rossiter, probably in the late 1930s, when they were both at Cornell. Perhaps she got her passion for lists from Rossiter, or perhaps she gave it to him, asking him to draw up a list of what he did and did not like about her.

ELIZA IS:

1. A snob.
2. too dramatic.
3. ignorant of her possibilities and responsibilities.
4. ———[crossed out]
5. naturally lazy.
6. often dumb.
7. no puritan.
8. a lover of lots of suitors.
9. a coed. [underlined three times]

1. refined and fine looking.
2. natural and without airs.
3. intelligent, if and when she wants to be.
4. loyal.
5. sweet.
6. good-dresser.
7. no hypocrite.
8. my girl, and my fortress in the storm.
9. and wow! what legs. (How do you know, Rossiter?)

signed: Clinton Rossiter, III, President of USA.

Despite its irritatingly condescending tone, this list of faults and virtues contains some elements of truth: "no puritan, a lover of lots of suitors, a coed, refined and fine looking, good-dresser, no hypocrite, and wow! what legs." My mother was something of a wild, rebellious girl. She bucked against the restrictions of her loving but decidedly puritanical mother. Her girlhood letters are full of fast cars and "swell" boys. To discipline her coltish daughter, my grandmother sent my mother to a Quaker boarding school in distant Pennsylvania. While high-minded, the school was coed, and my mother seemed to have little difficulty finding trouble. She was always being disciplined for wearing lipstick and smoking cigarettes and staying out late. My grandmother must not have been that strict or disapproving, because my mother is remarkably confiding about her various romantic adventures in her many letters home.

One letter—partly in the form of a list—written when she was sixteen begins:

Sunday
Dear Mummy,

I'm sorry I haven't written you sooner but, you see, I've gone and fallen in love again. I'll tell you all about him,

Name—Charles Edward Lippincott—commonly known as Ted.
Age—Seventeen
Class—Senior
Occupations—waiter on tables, collector of stamps and pigeons.
Looks—Black hair, brown eyes, marvelous semi-snub nose, very white teeth, tall, medium weight, about 5'10"1/2

The first lists I've found also date from this period. In a letter from boarding school she lays out exactly what money she will need to get home when school ends in the spring:

$8.25—Pullman
$2.00—trunks lugged to Paoli
$1.60—transportation to Philly
$3.00—meals and tips
$14.85

Another of my mother's lists I found, unexpectedly, among my father's things. Unlike my mother, he kept reams and reams of paper so indiscriminately that important papers could easily got tossed out with last month's newspapers or six-year-old junk mail. I almost threw out, in a suitcase full of old bank statements from the early 1960s, a partially torn envelope with a long list of words on it in my mother's unmistakable handwriting.

It didn't take more than a second to understand that the list referred to my father.

nagging
suspicious
pettiness
anxiety
cruelty
recrimination
selfishness
coldness
disorganization
stinginess +
other forms of ungenerousness

complete lack of:
gentleness
humor
tolerance
consideration
common sense
generosity

On the back side of the envelope, in pencil, was a second, shorter list that I am certain referred to herself:

lack of confidence
easily influenced
easily confused
weak-minded, in other words.

But this list appears to have been lost and forgotten. I wonder whether my father intended to keep it or if it ended up among his bank statements by chance.

There was another list I only heard about but didn't see, which she made after the fire at my parents' New York apartment. The fire took place in 1981, when I was living in Italy. My father worked at home in his pajamas, smoking and drinking coffee until about four o'clock in the afternoon, when he would send his daily story to his newspaper in Milan. His office was filled with enormous piles of newspapers and magazines. He received several daily papers and subscribed to at least a few dozen magazines, in some cases keeping every issue from 1946. The office—and his messiness—was everything my mother hated, a kind of jungle of wild, irrational disorder she tried to keep at bay with her lists. He smoked a pipe and routinely emptied it in a wastebasket full of paper. He had started a few fires, but never one this serious. He had gone downstairs after filing his story, walked around in his pajamas, and began rummaging through the refrigerator. My mother had gone out to run some errands. He was talking on the phone to his paper in Italy when the firemen burst through the front door with their axes. His office had gone up in flames; a neighbor had seen the fire from across the street and called the fire department. Most everything in his office was burned and the upper floor was flooded with water. When my mother returned, she found the fire trucks outside, smoke everywhere, doors broken in, glass shattered, phones melted in the heat, water pouring from the upper floor through the ceiling of the living room. Many of my father's books upstairs had been burned or singed with smoke; the ones downstairs, the best, were now in danger of being destroyed by water. My father was still in his pajamas, walking around moaning, but not doing anything. "Oh, my god, what an idiot I am!" he said. "I might as well kill myself!" "Don't you think you've done enough damage for one day?" my mother said, with her characteristic deadpan humor. She immediately set to placing garbage bins, wash pails, and pots and pans underneath the leaks in the ceiling to catch the flooding water. By sheer happenstance, my sister, Lucy, and her boyfriend turned up in the afternoon and immediately began helping my mother as my father moaned on. Then two friends of my parents stopped by for a drink. They had all arranged to go to a party of mutual friends. My parents, in the midst of the fire, had forgotten about the appointment. "Please, take Misha," my mother told them. "He's of no use to us here." And so my father went off to the party, while my mother, my sister, and her boyfriend cleaned up the house.

Afterward, they went out to dinner and my mother started writing a list.

Insurance company
Window repair
Carpenter
Locksmith
Plastic bags
Cleaning service
Divorce?

When she died, she left very few papers behind. Only a few letters, photographs, and the Rossiter list in the drawer of her bedside table. She traveled light and died light. All her bills were paid, her will written, signed, and with the lawyers, nothing much for us to do. Lucy and I were surprised by her death, even though she had been very sick for nearly two years. She never told us how ill she was at the end and she never asked us to come. I was in Rome, Lucy in Los Angeles. My mother had taken care of it all in advance, as if her goal was to be as little trouble as possible. She was like a guest in this world, who didn't want to be a bother and slipped away before the rest of the household awoke. I did find a list by the side of her bed that she had been keeping in the days before she died—

Take vitamins
Call Doctor R.
Get cash
Pay Lillian
Write check to Bruno
Check on oil heater in Great Barrington

Everything on the list had been meticulously marked off.

2. NAMES, DATES, AND PLACES

My father died, as he lived, surrounded by newspapers.

They piled up like snowbanks in a blizzard in a world where it snowed newsprint every day.

While my mother was alive, she had tried to confine his mess to his office-bedroom, but after she died, the newspapers gradually crept down the stairs and began taking over the apartment like tropical vegetation reclaiming land that had been painstakingly cleared, the fragile progress of civilization returning to jungle. As the months passed, piles of newspapers took over the downstairs coffee table, colonized the surfaces of the living room cabinets, spread out and made themselves comfortable on the two living room sofas, drifted to the dining room, first covering one end of the table and then half the table, so when you joined my father for dinner, you would sit at one end and stare at a growing stack of papers. If you suggested moving them (even temporarily) he became agitated. The chairs at that end were gradually converted into newspaper storage devices. My father had always slept in the bed in his office, but the bed was swallowed up by papers and he moved down the hall to what had been my mother's bedroom, an inner sanctum that had always been kept inviolate of any clutter—and the newspapers and books and magazines invariably followed. When he failed to answer the doorbell and we had to call the fire department to break down the door to his apartment, we found him in his pajamas (as he had lived and worked for most of his life) on my mother's bed, newspapers and books on the bedside table and a few scattered on the bed next to his body. His heart had given out before the newspapers could complete their work and bury him.

A refugee of two countries—first Russia and then Italy—whose family had been forced to flee with only what they could carry, my father could not bring himself to throw anything away. His closet was a kind of rest home for retired clothing: shoes that had curled in half with age, whose leather was hard and cracked and brittle; ties with irremovable stains and visible burn holes from the embers of his pipe; moth-eaten sweaters and shirts frayed almost to rags. There were strange and wildly improbable items—purple suede chukka boots, a camel's hair Nehru jacket, a debonair sailor's cap—that were impossible to imagine on my father, a short and stout European intellectual with thick black glasses, without laughing out loud. Clearly they represented fashion fads that had mercifully passed or moments of temporary consumer insanity that had been quickly regretted and consigned to oblivion but never thrown out. There were suits that were literally six sizes too big or too small, but nothing—not all my mother's entreaties—could convince my father to give them to the Salvation Army or throw them out.

And yet, paradoxically, through diametrically opposite means—the one through the rigorous paring away of everything nonessential, the other through the inability to throw anything out—my parents ended up in the same place: each preserved surprisingly few personal papers. My father's need to keep everything meant that he kept track of nothing. His own personal documents, letters from friends and family, his own stories, all got mixed up together with the piles of newsprint that took over his office. He knew and had received letters from many of the leading Italian writers and journalists and politicians of his generation, but he made no effort to save them. They disappeared invariably into one of the stacks in his room and were eventually swept away in the tide of paper that flowed in and out of his study. The important things were carried away with the junk mail like topsoil washed away in a flood. Others must have been consumed in the fire.

Among the few papers my father did make an effort to conserve was a single half-piece of cheap, yellowing typing paper containing just two lines:

Ilya Kamenetzki, May 19, 1884, Kreutzburg, Latvia
Sara Altschuler, April 17, 1886, Moscow, Russia.

These were his parents' names, the dates and places of their birth in my father's own handwriting.

Why would he have needed to copy out such basic information about his parents—surely everyone knows his own parents' names and birthdates by heart—and keep it tucked away in a cardboard shoebox in the bottom of a closet together with the deeds to our house and other important legal and financial documents?

The seemingly simple fixing of names and dates and places was a highly complex matter for Jews of my father's and his parents' generations, who were almost inevitably born in one country with one name and died in another under another name—often with multiple passages and mutations in between.

Perhaps the most notable thing about the piece of paper my father kept in the shoebox is that one of its principal facts is wrong. My grandfather was not born in Kreutzburg, Latvia; he was (as far as we know) born in Mir, a town near the Russian-Polish border in what is now Belarus. But when Mussolini allied himself with Hitler and passed anti-Semitic laws in 1938, and my father's family was forced to leave Italy and tried to get into the United States, he refashioned his identity as a Latvian.

At the time, the American government was working hard to limit immigration—it had adopted a strict quota system specifying how many people it would admit from each country. The quota to which you were assigned depended on birthplace. My grandfather had been born as a Russian subject, but his native village, Mir, now belonged to Poland, and so my grandfather would have had to apply under the Polish quota, which was massively oversubscribed. The Latvian quota, however, was still open: after all, Latvia had existed for only a heartbeat. It was created in 1920 and would be occupied by the Nazis in 1941. Stuck between the hammer and the anvil, Hitler's Germany to the west and Soviet Russia to the east, many real Latvians found it difficult to emigrate, leaving room for an imaginary Latvian, my grandfather.

In Italy, my grandfather survived a dizzying series of legal and semi-legal *escamotages*. As a non-Italian whose degrees were not initially recognized in Italy, he practiced dentistry at the beginning through a typically Italian formula, using a *prestanome* (literally someone who lends his name) under whose name my grandfather's dentistry office was registered.

It is typical of these lives, with their documents of false or questionable information, that we do not know when my grandfather entered Italy or exactly when my grandmother and their two children joined him.

In keeping with this family tradition of malleable names and dates, my father's own name changed numerous times over his lifetime. He was born as Mikhail Kamenetzki in Moscow and died as Michael U. Stille in New York. In the family and to many friends he was known as Misha, sometimes written as Mischa or Miscia. Throughout his writing life he was known as Ugo Stille. And there were people who called him Misha, Michael, Ugo, and even, most improbably, Mike.

Like many of my grandfather's fictions, the name Stille was invented during the Fascist period at the time of Mussolini's racial laws. One of the many provisions of these laws was that Jews were no longer allowed to publish in Italian newspapers. At the time, my father was a university student and had the opportunity to write for a magazine, *Oggi*, which was as close to being independent as something could be under Fascism. But, being Jewish, he needed to write under an assumed name. My father ended up writing a column, together with his best friend, Giaime Pintor, under the name Ugo Stille. "*Stille*" means silence in German, and it seemed a good name for a pseudonym. They wrote separate stories on alternate weeks but using the same name, which suited the fact that they had become inseparable friends.

My father left for the United States in 1941, and Giaime (a Sardinian variation of James, pronounced "Jai-may"), who was not Jewish, remained behind. When resistance to Nazism organized in 1943, Pintor used Ugo Stille as his *nome di battaglia*, his partisan code name. My father—both to honor his friend and because he had become known writing under his assumed name—made Stille his legal last name, becoming in effect Mr. Silence. Thus, he always published under the name Ugo Stille and became, under American law, Michael Ugo Stille. Although adopting the name Stille was an act of remembering his bond with Giaime, it was also, at the same time, a way of erasing important parts of his past and identity. Kamenetzki, the name under which he had been born and left Russia, the name under which his family had been persecuted in Italy, was gone. Stille, as a name, is hard to place. To some degree, I suspect, it was an act of camouflage and self-invention.

I remember one day in the early 1980s, my mother and father came to visit me in Italy and we met the writer Antonio Tabucchi at a party. Tabucchi was fascinated by my father's multiple names and the fact that he had known him for years exclusively by his pseudonymous byline in the newspaper *Corriere della Sera*. Tabucchi had translated into Italian the great Portuguese poet Fernando Pessoa, who wrote under more than a dozen different names, each "writer" having a distinct style and literary persona, one an ardent modernist, another a formal poet rooted in the nineteenth century, a third a surrealist, another writing in English, and so on. These figures conducted debates in Portuguese literary journals and published for years under their fictional names. Tabucchi was equally drawn to other writers, such as Borges and Pirandello, who played with multiple identities and the fragile, fictional, and provisional nature of identity. And so, when Tabucchi was presented with my father, he suddenly exclaimed: "And so, Ugo Stille really exists!" "Of course I exist," my father replied gruffly with evident irritation—he had been ill-tempered about everything during that trip—but I think Tabucchi's remark also hit a raw nerve. My father was a realist, a man with both feet planted firmly on the ground, and had little patience with what he would have considered nothing more than a literary parlor game, confusing curious literary speculation with the serious business of reality.

To demolish this sort of nonsense, he liked to repeat the following story about Samuel Johnson and James Boswell during their trip to the Hebrides. Ever the follower of intellectual fashion, Boswell was spouting the latest theories of the philosopher David Hume that cast doubt on the existence of external reality. Johnson approached a large boulder and gave it a kick, saying, "Thus, sir, I refute Mr. Hume!" My father might have wanted to liquidate Tabucchi's bit of literary cleverness and assert his existence by kicking Tabucchi in the shins. My father had, after all, lived through some of the main events of the twentieth century—the Russian Revolution, Fascism, World War II, the Holocaust—and these were not literary inventions or fictive events. But Tabucchi's remark, although nothing more than a playful greeting, touched on something real, namely that my father was a man who had, to some extent, made and remade himself at different points in his life and that much about his history and identity was unstable—had his father been born in Kreutzberg or Mir? Did he come to Italy for the first time in 1908 or 1919 or 1922? Was my father Russian, Italian, or American? He had spoken Russian and German before settling on Italian as his preferred language. Which, then, was his native tongue? Between the passage of the racial laws in 1938 and his arrival in the United States three years later, he was essentially a man without a country, and in this time, he became the pseudonymous Ugo Stille, whose fictional existence seemed to express this stateless condition. He then became Michael Kamenetzki, Americanizing it. For a time, he spelled his name Cameneschi. After the war, he then became Michael U. Stille, an American citizen whose past as a Russian and a Jew is nowhere in evidence. It was a legitimate choice but one that killed off various alternate identities—aspects of himself that, under other circumstances, he perhaps might have chosen to emphasize. They represented traumatic moments in his life and he closed them off as one cauterizes a wound, stopping further bleeding but leaving numb scar tissue in its place. At the same time, as if in some other parallel universe, he resumed his journalistic career under the name of Ugo Stille, who was closely related to but rather different from Michael U. Stille of 46 West Eleventh Street or 218 East Sixty-First Street, New York City. Ugo Stille, his journalistic persona, was an idealized self, a figure of hard logic and crystalline mental clarity, of Olympian distance and dispassionate, clear-eyed perspective on the confused human drama below. And at home, the man in his pajamas was Misha—far from Mount Olympus, surrounded by his stacks of newspapers—highly irascible and highly irrational, storming and thundering about my mother's latest spending spree or some magazine he suspected she had thrown out.

3. CROSS-POLLINATION

How these two very different people came together and, more incredibly, how they stayed together was perhaps the central mystery of my early life.

My parents were opposites in almost all ways, not only in matters of neatness. My mother loved vegetables; my father hated them—unless they were deep-fried breaded zucchini (an honorary carbohydrate, essentially French fries masquerading as a vegetable)—and considered the appearance of broccoli or Brussels sprouts at our family table a personal affront, to which he reacted with fury. My mother hated arguments; my father started them. My mother almost never raised her voice; my father could shout and keep on conducting an entire argument at full volume like a tenor singing his way through an opera. My mother liked eating by candlelight; my father didn't trust restaurants with candlelight—what were they trying to hide? He insisted on turning up all the lights as if he were performing surgery when he ate—he wanted to see what he was eating. My mother loved flowers; my father considered them a useless waste of money. My mother was extremely decisive; my father agonized over every decision and then immediately regretted whatever decision he had taken. At restaurants, she never took more than thirty seconds to order and never sent anything back. My father would often change his order and then change it back again without giving a thought to whether he was inconveniencing the cook or the waiter. My mother was a big tipper; my father tipped so stingily that one of us would sometimes linger behind and leave a few more dollars on the table.

My father regarded bathing as optional. The obligation of bathing every day, which for my mother was a sacred tenet, he viewed as something of a small-minded bourgeois convention. A person, he felt, should bathe if and when he felt like it. My father was terrified of doctors and was deeply convinced that as long as he stayed away from them, he could not, technically, be sick. My mother believed religiously in modern medicine and faithfully went to every routine checkup and follow-up visit. And her faith seemed repaid: she survived four different cancers. But in the end they both lived to almost exactly the same age and died within two years of each other. My father managed to avoid seeing a dentist for a good forty years—something of a feat worthy of *The Guinness Book of World Records* for a relatively prosperous citizen of late-twentieth-century America. Luckily for him, he had an iron constitution, and, miraculously, his teeth—though brown from decades of cigarettes and black espresso—stayed with him until the end, while my mother endured the torment of endless root canal surgeries and periodontal operations.

My mother loved gardening and being out in the country; my father felt lost outside of any city with fewer than three million people. My mother drove; my father was driven. My mother would never arrive at a friend's house without a bottle of wine or a bouquet of flowers; my father considered his presence more than sufficient. "Why are you so afraid people won't like you?" my father would say disdainfully. My father, a chain smoker, gave up cigarettes in a day when the doctor told him to stop; my mother kept smoking through a thirty-year war with cancer. My father generally drank only at parties; my mother drank every evening. My father was usually a happy and good-natured drunk; my mother became gloomy and lugubrious when she drank. My father loved large parties full of interesting people—whether he knew them or not; my mother generally preferred intimate dinner parties and the company of family and old friends. My mother was a gracious hostess and believed in making people feel at ease; my father enjoyed challenging people and freely insulted people who said things he thought were foolish, especially if they were my mother's friends. My mother almost always spoke ill of my father; my father almost invariably sang my mother's praises.

As marriages go, it was a stormy one. They fought constantly—over money, over throwing out and keeping newspapers, over politics, over food, over how to behave, over friends and relatives. I recall very precisely my sister teaching me the word "divorce" after a particularly brutal battle between my parents. Because of the tumult in the house, I had been granted the special dispensation of sleeping with Lucy. I must have been very small, because I remember sitting on her bed struggling with and repeating the word, which I pronounced "di-worce," and struggling more with its meaning, which I found terrifying. Some years ago, I ran into some old family friends who had fallen out of touch with my parents years before. They had last seen one another at a dinner at my parents' house that had ended abruptly after my mother had thrown a glass ashtray at my father and opened a gash on the side of his head. They had assumed that my parents had gotten divorced shortly after this incident and were greatly surprised to learn that they had stayed together until the bitter end.

My parents' union was, among other things, a marrying—or clash—of civilizations. It was the result of one of the great, perhaps the greatest, brain drains in human history: the migration of a huge chunk of educated Europe in response to the rise of Fascism and Nazism. Entire university departments—most of the great minds that conceived of and built the atomic bomb, from Albert Einstein and Enrico Fermi to Edward Teller and Hans Bethe—moved en masse. The entire Frankfurt School of philosophy, including Theodor Adorno, Herbert Marcuse, and Max Horkheimer, transferred itself to Southern California, along with anti-Fascist writers such as Thomas Mann and Bertolt Brecht and the great avant-garde composer Arnold Schoenberg. The New School for Social Research in New York was originally named the University in Exile and was loaded with stars of Europe's best universities, including the philosophers Hannah Arendt and Jacques Maritain, the linguist Roman Jakobson, and the great French anthropologist Claude Lévi-Strauss—all figures who changed their respective fields in the United States and around the world. The University in Exile even established something called the École Libre des Hautes Études (the Free School of Advanced Studies), where the luminaries of French intellectual life who had fled Nazi-occupied France lectured in French on West Eleventh Street in New York (across the street from where I grew up). It was here that Lévi-Strauss, encountering Jakobson, began to apply the theories of structuralism to anthropology.

This massive injection of talent into the collective bloodstream of this country invigorated and transformed American life. The look of major American cities was altered by the skyscrapers of Walter Gropius and Ludwig Mies van der Rohe. Exiled movie directors like Billy Wilder, Ernst Lubitsch, and Fritz Lang made an impact on popular culture through films such as *Sunset Boulevard*, *The Apartment*, *Ninotchka*, *To Be or Not to Be*, *Scarlet Street*, and *The Big Heat*.

It is a credit to the United States that it was so open and welcomed such a large influx into its midst and integrated it into its national life. America was not a blank slate. It already had a vibrant, important culture, but what happened in the middle of the twentieth century was a genuine cross-pollination in which old met new and produced new forms. European-born artists such as Josef Albers, Arshile Gorky, and Willem de Kooning exerted a huge influence on American artists such as Robert Rauschenberg, Cy Twombly, and Jackson Pollock, helping to create what became known as "abstract expressionism" and making New York and not Paris or Berlin the center of the art world. This relationship between Europe and America was not without its complexities. Vladimir Nabokov's classic American novel *Lolita*—another great product of the mid-century brain drain—although ostensibly about the love affair between a middle-aged European man and an American teenager, is also a kind of metaphor for Nabokov's own relationship with the American language and culture, whose vitality and vulgarity he was passionately, hopelessly, and ambivalently in love with.

A certain amount of the difficulties of my parents' marriage were the result of deep cultural differences. My mother came from a midwestern white Anglo-Saxon Protestant world where people did not scream at one another. If they raised their voices, it meant they were getting divorced. My father came from a much more operatic culture in which people's yelling at one another was considered fairly normal. My mother came from a position of relative security in a society that, even at the height of the Depression, was rich, optimistic, and confident. My father had the deep anxieties of someone who had been twice uprooted, twice a refugee, always in a legally precarious position, persecuted as a Jew, and hounded out of a Europe that was literally destroying itself when he and his family left it in 1941. My mother's instinct was to trust and give people the benefit of the doubt. My father's experience gave him a much darker, more suspicious attitude toward people.

An incident that occurred in their later years illustrates their different views of human nature. My mother had her wallet stolen while shopping at the supermarket. My father was furious and gave my mother an earful. "*Eleezabet*, how could you be so foolish, so trusting? I can just see you trotting around the supermarket with your purse unzipped!" A couple of hours later, the doorbell rang. It was a taxi driver who explained that he had found my mother's wallet in the back of his cab. The thief had evidently taken the wallet, jumped in a taxi, took the money, and abandoned the rest. My mother was delighted to have the wallet and credit cards back and touched that the cabdriver had gone to the trouble to bring it to her at the end of his shift. For my mother, this episode reconfirmed her faith in the essential goodness of man. She—not without some difficulty—convinced my father to give her money for a generous tip for the driver.

My father, on the other hand, suspected that the driver might be in on an elaborate con scheme both to steal the wallet and to get more money out of my mother. He might have come here, my father suggested, to case the joint.

From my mother's point of view, her marriage was a kind of epic struggle, like a battle between Order and Chaos or a science fiction horror film like *The Blob*, in which the protagonists combat extraterrestrial ooze that threatens to swallow up an entire town. She had studied art, had a keen, highly refined visual sense, and had absorbed the Bauhaus school's pared-down, minimalist aesthetic. My mother's physical surroundings were fundamental to her sense of well-being. Creating a beautiful space with clean surfaces was an expression of her deepest self, like making a flower arrangement for a Buddhist monk. A glass left on a table or a dish left in the sink made her uncomfortable in her skin and in her soul, as if the universe itself was off-kilter and the planets had strayed from their orbits; she could not rest until things were put right. For my mother, my father's mess was everything she hated, was much more than mere disorder. It was a spiritual condition, a disease of the soul: entropy, despair, confusion, the weight of dusty history, the tragedy of Europe and the crippling past, the love of needless complication, useless speculation, regret, equivocation, the inability to decide and live in the present. Throwing out meant choosing, looking forward, getting on with things, having a positive attitude toward life.

At the same time, my mother's battle for order had its element of mania, too. At a certain point, she became obsessed with throwing out a collection of magazines my father had stored in the attic of our country house in Massachusetts. My father had an extraordinary set of the leading cultural-intellectual magazines of the post–World War II period. He had every single issue of *Partisan Review*; *Commentary and Dissent*; Dwight Macdonald's *Politics*; Jean-Paul Sartre's *Les Temps Modernes*; the British review *Encounter*, edited by Cyril Connelly; the Italian magazine *Tempo Presente*, founded by Ignazio Silone—the principal journals of opinion in four countries during the same period. But at a certain point, my mother was no longer satisfied that she had succeeded in relegating these to the attic of a house 120 miles from our New York apartment. The fact that they just sat there, piles of paper, clogging up the attic, began to burn a hole in her mind, to become an obsession. "We've got to get rid of those magazines!" she would tell me, banking on the fact that my father would never notice. I tried to talk her out of it, explaining that these were rare and valuable documents. "But this isn't a library." I made her promise she would give them to a library rather than throw them out. She placed a call to Berkshire Community College, and when they said they didn't want the magazines, she consigned the collection to the county dump.

In the fourth circle of Hell, Dante encounters a mass of people who are locked for eternity in a struggle, pushing a heavy weight back and forth and yelling: "Why do you spend?" "Why do you save?" It is the punishment for those guilty of the sins of avarice and prodigality. Somewhere nearby, I suspect, is a corner where my parents are wrestling over a pile of newspapers, saying: "Why do you have to throw this out?" "Why do you have to keep it?"

Losing everything twice left my father with a kind of *horror vacui*— fear of empty spaces, the irresistible tendency to fill every corner and surface. Yet, curiously, he was not an accumulator of things in general. Virtually every object, every chair, table, couch, ottoman, every painting or object on the walls, every vase, plate, dish, pot, pan, or serving spoon was brought into the house by my mother. For my father all that counted was the accumulation of printed matter. Along with the newspapers were the books.

My father was a product of that Eastern European Jewish civilization that Hitler succeeded in effectively destroying. Books and learning held a sacred place in this culture, where everything else in life could (and probably would) be taken from you.

Books were a virtual obsession with my father. His two libraries, the one in the city and the other in the country, comprised about ten thousand books. He continued collecting the best books in virtually every field up until the time of his death, from philosophy, physics, and literature to world history and, of course, politics. He was the scourge of publicity departments on both sides of the Atlantic, whom he hounded mercilessly for free books. Even now, years later, I still run into people who used to work for this or that publisher who remember my father distinctly. Sometimes in the late afternoon, after he had sent his daily story, he would, paper bag in hand like a homeless person, make the rounds of Midtown publishers, cadging books from the amiable young college graduates who generally worked in the entry-level jobs at publicity departments. He was not averse to buying books when he had to: he never made a trip to France without coming home with a suitcase full of Pléiade editions, the beautiful volumes of French classics with leather bindings and fine onionskin paper.

While he was careless with his papers, he was meticulously precise with his books. Every one of the ten thousand books had its place, and he knew exactly where it was. If you took one down from the shelf and read it, he would notice within twenty-four hours and begin hounding you about it. "What have you done with that copy of Dickens?" My mother would occasionally lend a book to a friend. My father was invariably furious and would make her keep a list of who had borrowed what and then badger her to get them back. "What's the point of having all these books if no one is allowed to read them?" my mother would ask. "You understand nothing!" he would reply with a contemptuous wave of his hand. "But you've never even read most of these books," she replied. "Have you ever read this book about ancient Chinese technology or medieval warfare?" "Idiot, you understand nothing!" Collecting, of course, is a pleasure in and of itself. For my father, a great collection of books had to have both depth and balance, meaning he had to keep up with seminal works in fields he had little background in—anthropology, linguistics, art history, Renaissance philology, contemporary fiction. The building up of his library—in the midst of the piles of newspapers—meant the creation and maintenance of his own world of order and logic against the chaotic foreground of contemporary events, as messy and ephemeral as the piles of newsprint that crowded the house. He knew ancient Greek and Latin and had studied philosophy at university until his life was blown off course by Mussolini and Hitler. The pressure of events and the catastrophe of history had made him a journalist. What mattered about the books was not just what he had read or would read; it was about constructing a perfect world, the collection that he *might* read, or that someone else—some perfect scholar or polymath, the ideal man—might read. In an ideal world in which there was sufficient time and peace of mind. It was the victory of reason against the forces of darkness and chaos. And so the library was like the creation of an alternate universe, in which he was gradually creating the person that he never got to be.

These things were opaque to my pragmatic American mother ("What's the point of having a book if you're not going to read it?"), who saw the world as linear and rational and did not understand the ravings of a King Lear who insisted on his full retinue of knights: "Reason not the need!" And yet, after the fire he started, my mother made paper covers for the books that had been damaged by smoke and by the firemen's hose. Some books were actually burned beyond hope; others were simply blackened on the outside. But my mother helped my father keep them by carefully making new, clean covers for them, writing the title and author's name on the front. My father appreciated my mother's aesthetic sensibility. He liked the beautiful places she created, but at the same time he considered her ideas about clutter and cleanliness little more than simpleminded midwestern philistinism, the triumph of superficial middle-class American Babbittry.

My father cited, approvingly, a passage from *The Leviathan*, in which Hobbes wrote that fear was the dominant human emotion and that he had absorbed fear along with his mother's milk, since he had been born as the Spanish Armada was making its way toward British shores. This was certainly the case for my father, whose early life was dominated by violent change and displacement. He was born in the middle of the Russian Revolution and absorbed insecurity along with his own mother's milk. My grandmother's family—wealthy Russian Jewish capitalists— had their factories and their house expropriated; with great difficulty, my father still an infant, they moved from Moscow to Germany, then to Naples and then Rome. After reestablishing themselves in Italy, they were wiped out again and had to find a way out of Europe. No sooner did my father arrive in the United States than he was drafted and sent back to Italy with the U.S. Army.

All the change and forced moves in the first twenty-five years of his life left my father with a profound desire to experience as little change and movement as possible during the rest of his life. In practical terms, this meant that he would spend as much time as possible in the next fifty years in his pajamas on the living room couch reading books and newspapers, smoking and drinking black espresso. He elevated immobility to a metaphysical level: one of his favorite novels was *Oblomov*, whose main character doesn't leave his bed for the first 150 pages of the book and then does so only to move to the couch.

He would have happily remained for the rest of his life in the apartment in Greenwich Village where they were living when I was born, had the building not been sold and my parents forced to move. He experienced the act of changing apartments not as a practical problem but as a cataclysmic event that threatened his existence (as if the Bolsheviks were again about to storm the Winter Palace or the Wehrmacht was again on the move). Once installed in the new house, he never wanted to leave—and, indeed, never did; it was there that we found him unconscious. He always took credit for finding their second apartment, and he seemed convinced that thanks only to his alacrity and foresight, the family had narrowly avoided a fate of homelessness. "*Eleezabet*, if it had been up to you, we'd be living in a tent in Central Park!" he would repeat often, recalling that traumatic move with a visible shiver of horror, imagining, no doubt, his beloved books scattered on the sidewalk for bystanders to pick among.

He was immobile but not inactive. He probably wrote something like six thousand to seven thousand newspaper stories in his lifetime, becoming a mythic figure in Italian journalism—courted by prime ministers and billionaire industrialists as the man who really understood America. In his younger days, it was not uncommon for him to write two stories a day. I would often wake up in the night and hear him clattering away on his ancient Royal typewriter, which had never been cleaned; some keys were inoperative or virtually illegible, punching holes in the paper instead of printing letters. Very often, though, the stories had to be dragged out of him. The newspaper would call repeatedly, urging him to write something. "But *theess* is of no importance!" he would say with utter disdain after putting down the phone. They would call back twenty minutes later and resume. Finally, at about three in the afternoon, he would get off the couch and you could hear from upstairs the sound—like machine-gun fire—of his banging out a story. He would then read the piece aloud to a stenographer in Milan. The phone lines were not nearly as good back then, and so he would often scream. *"Pronto!? Pronto! Mi senti?!"* ("Hello? Can you hear me?") He would then finally get dressed, eat something, and go out.

Many Italians were convinced that he had fabulous inside sources at the CIA or the White House, because he seemed to know what was going to happen before it happened. While he did know many people, most of his best ideas came to him during his hours on the couch reading or in his pajamas and slippers in his office clipping and filing newspapers, listening to the radio or television. Many of his "scoops" were based on pure logical analysis. A bit immodestly, he liked to compare himself to Agatha Christie's detective Hercule Poirot, who relied principally on his brain—"the little gray cells"—rather than the gumshoe detectives who exerted more external effort but rarely ever solved the case. He was a great believer in what he called "*la forza delle cose*," the force of things. Writing about daily ephemeral events, he was always looking for the underlying movement of deeper historical forces. He was very good at not being distracted by public declarations, press conferences, or individual intentions, realizing that the outcome of events is generally determined by the inner logic of the force of things.

4. UNHISTORIC ACTS

What remains of someone who has led a purely private life? My mother did not leave her mark on the world, nor did she try to. Although she had always worked, she insisted she did it for the money. Unlike the men in her life, she did not see herself as building a career that, like a monument, would represent a lifetime of achievement. (Her father's portrait hangs in the lobby of the University of Chicago Law School.) My father left thousands of newspaper articles and is still remembered by millions of readers, and a photograph of him hangs on the walls of the *Corriere della Sera* offices along with portraits of other past editors, a little Pantheon of Italian journalism. My mother's influence was limited to several dozen people whose lives she had touched in important ways. She had been a housewife, mother, sister, friend, and colleague. She had probably cooked twelve thousand dinners over forty years of marriage, washed hundreds of thousands of dishes, made tens of thousands of beds, and folded innumerable pairs of socks. Like the vast majority of people, she had led an anonymous life, not even imagining in her wildest private dreams that she might leave a legacy the rest of the world need concern itself with. She had not nursed unfulfilled literary or artistic ambitions, did not leave a sheaf of poems or the draft of an unfinished novel in a drawer for us to find after her death. If someone had asked her what her greatest achievement was, I expect she would have responded without hesitation: raising two children.

It was true of my mother, as George Eliot wrote of her imperfect heroine Dorothea Brooke at the end of her great novel *Middlemarch*:

> Many who knew her, thought it a pity that so substantive and rare a creature should have been absorbed into the life of another, and be only known in a certain circle as a wife and mother . . . Her

finely touched spirit had still its fine issues, though they were not widely visible. Her full nature . . . spent itself in channels which had no great name on the earth. But the effect of her being on those around her was incalculably diffusive: for the growing good of the world is partly dependent on unhistoric acts; and that things are not so ill with you and me as they might have been, is half owing to the number who lived faithfully a hidden life, and rest in unvisited tombs.

For the most part my mother's fragile claim on immortality lay in the memories of friends and relatives, all destined to vanish sooner or later, most of them—those of her generation—very soon. Her best energies had gone into ephemeral things: a number of deep, lifelong friendships; the intimacy of long Scrabble games on summer afternoons; flower beds and vegetable gardens; tea and conversation following an afternoon of shopping or a visit to a museum; her impeccable wardrobe and a very natural, graceful sense of style; the rooms and houses she had occupied; a table beautifully set; the right arrangement of flowers; her wry, understated wit; a thousand small human connections; several thousand considerate gestures; a very genuine, unfeigned kindness to both friends and strangers; a natural empathy and curiosity that allowed her to connect with a surprisingly wide range of people. Her legacy was like that of the countless good dinner parties she gave: the warm feeling created by the excellent food and lively conversation lingered in the mind for years, though the exact content of what was said or eaten dissipated almost immediately with the aroma of the roast lamb and the taste of the chocolate mousse. It is the magical nature of beauty to be evanescent: the sudden feeling of ease between two friends who understand each other, the contagious hilarity of someone's expression in the telling of a story—which is never as funny in the retelling—the softness of the air and the clarity of light on a particular day.

As my mother's own life drew to a close, the fragility and evanescence of her life struck me with increasing poignancy and I decided to interview her, to capture a few scraps of memory while I could.

She had been diagnosed with six inoperable brain tumors in early 1992, when she and my father were living in Milan. The Italian doctor had given her only a few weeks to live, and I flew to Milan to bring her back to New York to see if doctors there felt anything could be done for her—if only to hold the cancer at bay for a little longer. Her death seemed imminent—as it happened, she lived for another year, but death hung over us; its presence affected everything we did and said and yet it was a presence we could not name or acknowledge.

Under these very unusual circumstances, interviewing my mother seemed to offer a way—a kind of fiction or cover story—for us to talk about a lot of important things we wanted to talk about without coming out and saying: "Before you die, there are a number of things I want to discuss." It wasn't necessary to convince her. She was always candid and forthright and flattered by the attention. She had expressed some jealousy that I had shown a great deal of interest in my father's family history while working on a book about Italian Jews during Fascism. "You seem to find the Italian Jewish part of your background extremely exotic and interesting and you're not interested in the boring old midwestern Wasp half of you," she said. Now, in this odd situation, with her confined to bed, I got out my tape recorder and we began a series of interviews over a period of a couple of weeks. She was on cortisone at the time in order to relieve the swelling of the tumors in her brain that were making it hard for her to walk and see, but the cortisone also made her excitable and extremely talkative. My mother could be brutally honest under normal circumstances, but on cortisone she had no brakes and no censors and sometimes told me more of the nitty-gritty of her life than I had bargained on. It worked almost like a truth serum, under which she dredged up detailed recollections she hadn't talked about (or perhaps even thought about) in years: elaborate descriptions of my own birth and of her wedding day with my father, and an unvarnished narration of an extramarital affair (among other things) came tumbling out in surprisingly minute detail.

Gradually, in the years after her death, I began collecting family papers and letters, some found in the back of drawers, others in the attic of my grandparents' farm in Michigan, where they had been left in the care of the mice but had been kept by the farmer who bought the place and passed them on to my uncle, who kindly gave many of them to me. As I put them into order and transcribed the tapes of my mother's and father's interviews, I began to learn a surprising amount about their lives, and something of the dense weave of their lived experience began to emerge.

While it was personally satisfying to learn that far more remained of my mother's unhistoric life than I had imagined possible, could it have meaning for anyone other than those of us who knew her? Sifting through the thousands of pages of documents, which were like an enormous jig-saw puzzle, I began to regard my parents and their closest relations a bit like figures I had encountered in the archives doing historical research, many of whom were as obscure as my parents—or more. The famous and the unknown partake of the times in which they live. Whether we know it or not, we are born into history and pass through a stretch of it. The zeitgeist rubs off on us and leaves its telling signs like the carpet fibers at a crime scene. Like pollen in springtime, or the fine, almost invisible dust that has covered the furniture when you return home after a long absence, history attaches itself to everything, affects the way we think and talk, the possibilities we imagine for ourselves, the choices we make or fail to make. Our lives have meaning—above and beyond our individual qualities—because we are part of and express the times in which we live.

PART I

BOGERTS

The Father and Mother of Lists

I. THE FATHER OF LISTS

On an October evening in 1911 in a rooming house in Ithaca, New York, a young man of twenty-seven set about writing carefully in a lined notebook with a black ink pen. He was at a crucial turning point—beginning his first semester of teaching at Cornell Law School—and starting a journal marked the start of his new life.

> Oct. 10. Worked at office 8:30 to 11: class in property 11–12; loafing, walking about and at room and at lunch 12–1:45. at work at office 1:45–5: getting stamps, postcards, hair cut and collars 5–6: dinner and chat with Marsh and Andrews 6 to 8:45. That schedule means just about 8¾ hours work in class and preparation and I should say is as fair an average of my days so far. Laborers work 8 to 9 hours. Lawyers (as in Elmira) work 7 to 8. Probably my quota is made out by 8¾ hours. That leaves 15¼ hours in the day unaccounted for. An hour is taken each morning in shaving, bathing and dressing. Meals take about 1½ hours. That means 12¾ hours. Of this 8 goes to sleep. We thus have 4¾ hours unaccounted for. It is spent principally in three ways—miscellaneous reading and writing letters, and walking for exercise or pleasure. All in all, not much time is wasted, except that it would be well to read a newspaper after lunch for a half hour and to devise some certain way of spending the time from 12 to 1. I am in want of outdoor activity. It seems hard to do anything in the office except mechanical detail. The evenings after 9 can well be used for reading for pleasure and profit outside of law. One or two evenings a week ought to be

given to social recreation. Matters of immediate attention are 1.) a newspaper—*New York Sun*. 2.) Occupation at hour from 12 to 1.

The young man was my grandfather, my mother's father, George Gleason Bogert.

My mother's lists, it turns out, had a pedigree.

I remember my grandfather, whom I knew only as a child, as a man of silence. He was remote and irascible. Noise got on his nerves and the noise of small children got on his nerves exceedingly. My grandparents gathered many of their grandchildren on their farm in Michigan for most of the summer—they even built a guesthouse so that we could stay for long periods of time, albeit out of earshot—but my grandfather often found us an intolerable nuisance. Suddenly, in the middle of dinner on the screened porch, he would begin tapping a knife on a glass or banging his fist on the dinner table—"Can we please have some adult conversation around here!" he would say with great irritation when we children had begun to make a ruckus. As the youngest of the grandchildren present, I was generally the worst offender—frequently guilty of, along with talking, humming at the table. I was banished to the laundry porch and forced to finish my meals out there contemplating the washer-dryer, the spare freezer, a large mound of black walnuts, walls of my grandmother's canned fruits and vegetables, and the pencil markings on one wall on which my grandmother had measured each grandchild's height and age at various stages of our lives.

My grandfather had the somewhat unusual habit of watching Chicago White Sox games on an old, grainy black-and-white television set with the sound completely off. We were supposed to stay clear of or tiptoe quietly past the room where he was watching. A game normally played at a loud stadium in the presence of tens of thousands of cheering and screaming fans, my grandfather enjoyed in solitude and cloistered silence.

Grammie and Grampie (as we called them) had separate bedrooms, not unusual for married couples of the day, but he also had his own little hideaway on the farm property, known as "the Doghouse," a little two-room shack, with an office and an air conditioner (very rare for that day) and a second bedroom, giving him an even more remote place to sleep than his private bedroom in the main house. He spent long hours there—

with the air conditioner serving more to block out noise than to ease the heat—working on legal publications of one kind or another. He went bald at a fairly young age, so that he looked like an old man, with just a few wisps of white hair, early in life and remained one for what seemed like forever. He generally wore a straw hat in the form of a baseball cap, with a white handkerchief hanging down from the back to keep the summer sun from burning his neck. The cap with the handkerchief made him look like photographs I had seen of soldiers in the French Foreign Legion whose funny hats with flaps in the back were meant to protect them against the desert sun of their colonial possessions.

Grampie, who kept on working into his eighties, was the highly respected author of a thirteen-volume textbook (that later grew to eighteen volumes) known as *Bogert on Trusts*—the ultimate product of the hard work and efficient use of time that began that fall in Ithaca. The very name—*Bogert on Trusts*—suggested unimpeachable authority, and indeed, it became the standard reference and textbook in the field of trusts and estates law for three generations of lawyers. (It remains in print today, with a new coauthor.) Occupying its own shelf, like a one-man *Encyclopaedia Britannica*, it was, I believe, the first textbook to compile and interpret virtually every case bearing on trusts (literally thousands of cases from courts around the country)—a colossal and impressive undertaking in the age before the computer. It spoke of a highly disciplined and orderly mind, as well as a dogged spirit of unusual determination and thoroughness. Trusts were not the most scintillating specialty, although my grandfather had enjoyed a brief flirtation with the sexier field of aviation law in his youth before making his reputation with *Bogert on Trusts*. On the strength of his solid scholarship, he went on to become the dean of Cornell Law School, was hired away by the very prestigious University of Chicago Law School, and was elected president of the Association of American Law Schools. The short-tempered old man with the funny cap with a handkerchief was a gray (or bald) eminence in his field.

Grampie's irascibility and need for silence were not, apparently, products of old age. My mother claimed that when she was a small child living in Ithaca, my grandfather took a gun and shot a neighborhood cat that was yowling within earshot of the house and disturbing his peace and quiet. When they moved to their house on Greenwood Avenue in Chicago, near the University of Chicago, he had his bedroom up on the attic floor, away from the rest of the family, where it was most quiet. When he came home from work, he would often shut himself up in the living room, crank up the gramophone, close the glass doors behind him, put on a record of classical music, and lie down on the couch. It was understood that no one was supposed to enter the room and disturb him.

But along with his irascibility, he had a subtle, understated sense of humor that came out from time to time when he spoke to us mysteriously about Fred the Snake, who lived down in the ravine near their house, or a made-up word he used, "chumma," which sounded like a cough and meant "excuse me." Poking fun at the general level of conversation among his Michigan neighbors, he would frequently say: "Sure hope the rain don't hurt the rhubarb." He had a good ear for mimicry and would, according to my mother, often echo the accent of whomever he was speaking with, suddenly sounding like a Southerner when speaking with a Southerner and sounding like a Frenchman when talking with a Frenchman. It was hard to tell whether he was making fun of someone or doing it unconsciously.

I don't recall him touching or playing with us, but there is a photograph of me as a child sitting on his knee.

I was just a teenager when he and my grandmother sold their farm and moved down to Florida full-time, where he lived and died in virtual solitude.

Since I'd known him only when I was a small boy and he was an old man, the discovery of a diary that he kept while still young promised the possibility of getting beyond the formal, public facade of a reserved old lawyer and discovering the real, private person my grandfather may have been. But what is most striking is that the private and public voices of my grandfather were virtually the same. Behind the facade was another facade, the same facade—or the possibility that it was not a facade at all. My grandfather's notebook is generally dry and impersonal, the diary of a self-disciplined young man determined to make something of himself.

Oct. 3, 1911
Today has been a bright, pleasant day, with cool air. I think coffee has played too large a part in my diet lately, since I have had a peculiar feeling of heaviness in the head and of nervousness of the stomach. I resolved tonight to stop the drink beginning tomorrow. Teaching is still such a novel work that I can think of little

else but the responsibility of it and am taking things too seriously to make it comfortable for my second self, who would like a little leisure recreation. I have felt the strain of classroom work—the nervous tension from keeping things going for fifty minutes in such fashion that no breaks occur. Dr. Andrews of the German department and I bowled two sad exhibitions at McCallister alleys tonight. He is, however, a peacefully cheerful and clear minded person who lends a restful feeling to one in conversation—not a bad companion. I must decide the question of a newspaper soon. Shall it be the *New York Sun* or only the *Cornell Sun* or both? I'm desirous of becoming more observing in my walks. What pleasure can be had from forming an interest in trifles and getting to know something of them? Franklin's autobiography has stimulated me somewhat in that respect.

Keeping a diary, for my grandfather, was not a literary activity or an effort at developing his inner life. It was very practical in its aims: to lay out a program of self-improvement and record the extent to which he was able to stick to it. This was clearly very much part of the zeitgeist in this age of self-made men, Horatio Alger rags-to-riches stories, and a frontier world of rugged individualism. It is a tradition, apparently, that goes back almost to the beginnings of the Protestant Reformation—the writing of journals as a means of keeping a person on the straight and narrow path to salvation and of rooting out sin and evil. By my grandfather's time, this old Protestant tradition had mingled with the popular genre of self-help and self-improvement.

At the end of *The Great Gatsby*, Nick Carraway arranges the funeral of his mysterious dead friend. One of the only people to show up is Gatsby's father, whose actual name is Henry C. Gatz. The old man arrives clutching a notebook that shows how the young James Gatz planned his brilliant future by creating a schedule that would place him on the path to self-improvement.

The Great Gatsby was published in 1925 (although the fictional notebook of the young Gatz is dated 1906)—fourteen years after young George Gleason Bogert began to put pen to paper in his diary. They both, of course, owe a lot to the autobiography of Benjamin Franklin (as my grandfather explicitly acknowledged), who may be credited with founding the genre of the self-help book in America. Franklin carefully listed what he regarded as the thirteen principal virtues: Temperance, Silence, Order, Resolution, Frugality, Industry, Sincerity, Justice, Moderation, Cleanliness, Tranquillity, Chastity, and Humility.

Clearly my grandfather was following some of Franklin's cherished principles—Silence (avoid trifling conversation); Order (let all things have their places); Industry (lose no time; be always employed in something useful).

Although the form was out of Ben Franklin, the tone of my grandfather's diary reminds me of the novel *The Remains of the Day*, by Kazuo Ishiguro, the narrative of an English butler who is so tightly buttoned, so conventional and under such tight control, that he seems entirely unaware of the emotional current that is stirring underneath the surface of the narrative—a story of loneliness and failed love. My grandfather's diary is remarkably dull—full of entries such as:

> Oct. 11. Rain, fog and clouds all day. Class . . . went finely this morning—all reciting and being attentive. Have done nothing but work and bowl a game with Andrews tonight. No mail except a notice of a faculty gym. Club meeting tomorrow night.

But it is dull in an interesting way. There are occasional mentions of young women he meets, something that clearly stirs an interest in him, but nothing ever seems to lead to anything and these brief items are subsumed in the details of his work as a young law professor. He makes an intriguing reference to his "second self who would like a little leisure recreation," but decides that the duties of his new career allow very little room for it.

It would be easy to make fun of his earnest tone of self-improvement: *"I'm desirous of becoming more observing in my walks. What pleasure can be had from forming an interest in trifles and getting to know something of them?"*

But this rather rigid, scripted, programmatic, orderly approach to life is more understandable when placed against the background of the time. My grandfather had grown up in the late nineteenth century, born in 1884 in Dakota Territory (before North and South Dakota became states). The area had only recently been opened up by the Union Pacific Railroad and pacified by the war waged by people such as General George Custer against the Sioux Indians. During my grandfather's youth, the frontier was still open, with all the promise and uncertainty of making or losing a fortune. In fact, his father ran a bank in Scotland, North Dakota, but then lost all his money (and that of several of his closest relatives) in a mining venture that failed, according to my grandfather, in part because of the unscrupulous conduct of his business associates. (There was, of course, at this time, no protection against this sort of thing, no federally insured bank deposits, no Federal Reserve, and no Securities and Exchange Commission.) After this business disgrace, my great-grandfather moved the family to Bolivar, Missouri, where, rather than running a bank, he worked as a cashier in one and tried to save money to pay back the relatives to whom he owed money. Although only forty-nine and of normally robust health, Taylor O. Bogert, my grandfather's father, came down with the "grippe," as the flu was known then, and, ten days later, was dead. His flu had turned into pneumonia—now easily treatable with antibiotics, but often fatal at that time, when influenza epidemics could kill millions or tens of millions worldwide in a single year.

On January 31, 1902, the *Bolivar Herald* published an obituary with the following headline:

HON. T. O. BOGERT

CASHIER OF BANK OF BOLIVAR PASSES AWAY

THE CITY IN GLOOM

. . . His death came as a shock to the community. His physique was remarked as one of singular strength and robustness. When the news flashed over the town that T. O. Bogert was dead, men stood aghast: exclamations of surprise were uttered and all had great difficulty in realizing that the death angel had made a visit in so unexpected a manner. Truly this ends a comparatively short earthly life, yet one of great usefulness. Our brother lived earnestly and accomplished his work very quickly and was summoned to "come up higher."

When a young man, he gave his heart to Christ and never forgot his allegiance. Ardently did he throw himself into the service of his Master. In all the walks of life, he made his influence felt. While at Scotland he labored for the uplift of town and community and lent his instrumentality to the founding of an academy. He was ever ready with his purse to help a struggling young man or woman to get an education.

My grandfather was only sixteen at the time and his sister twelve. There was no Social Security and no safety net, and the loss of the family breadwinner frequently had the effect of reducing a family to instant poverty. My great-grandmother was forced to move back to her own father's house in Gouverneur, New York, near Lake Ontario at the Canadian border. Her father had once been perhaps the leading citizen of the town but had, too, suffered some major reversals of fortune that had reduced him to precarious financial and physical health. Indeed, he died later that same year, leaving the family in deep trouble. They stayed in Gouverneur for one more year as my grandfather completed high school. Young George G. Bogert took New York State scholarships examinations in the summer of 1902, and won a scholarship and free admission to Cornell University. At Cornell, he took another set of examinations and won four hundred dollars a year of scholarship money to help with his education during the first two years of college. At the same time, his mother followed her son to Ithaca, rented a house, and sublet most of the rooms out to boarders to keep the family afloat. My grandfather, unlike most college boys, did not join a fraternity at Cornell. Instead, he worked at a student laundry (for which he earned an extra six dollars a week) and as the rent collector for the family boardinghouse. He studied typing, typed other students' theses for money, and eventually got an office job as secretary to the president of Cornell. His money-making jobs did not prevent him from graduating Phi Beta Kappa, among the top students in his class, becoming as well the star of the university's debating club, "winning," as he later wrote, "an intercollegiate oratorical contest at the University of Virginia and being elected Class Orator for the commencement exercises in 1906."

If young George Bogert's diary seems excessively serious, earnest, and goal oriented—like the resolves of a hero of a Horatio Alger novel—it was also because he had encountered and overcome genuine hardship and had done so through a mix of extraordinary self-discipline, hard work, and intelligence. He had forgone many of the pleasures of a typical youth— social life, sports, dances, fraternity life—and pulled himself up by his bootstraps. Before he had finished Cornell, his mother also died, leaving him entirely an orphan, working his way through school but also taking care of and helping to support his sister, who was four years younger than himself and became one of the first women to obtain a PhD from Yale, in chemistry.

If my grandfather's orderly approach to life was rigid, programmatic, and a bit dull, it was surely because in his experience life was so unpredictable, precarious, and dangerous. He exercised enormous self-control perhaps because so much else in his life—illness, death, financial disaster— was beyond his control. And to hold himself together under considerable adversity, to suffer the loss of first his father and then his mother, and not to waver in his sense of purpose, he may have needed to make himself somewhat hard and cold inside.

Later in life my grandfather wrote a lengthy genealogy of his family, meticulously tracing the two sides back to the seventeenth century, when they arrived in this country. Genealogy was an apt activity for my grandfather. It played to his strengths—great thoroughness and dogged determination in hunting down thousands of tiny pieces of information, as he had done in composing his masterwork on trust law. It was, in some ways, the ultimate family list in keeping with the lists contained in his early diary. Even the entry on himself was written in the neutral-seeming third person. It was a search for meaning and origins and identity that did not require introspection. And yet the careful compilation of external facts still added up to some form of indirect self-understanding and a reckoning with the past. Pursued doggedly over many years, the genealogy responded to some deep personal impulse. But underneath the dry accumulation of dates and names and facts, one detects a certain covert passion.

What comes through most strongly in his depiction of our ancestors is the extreme hardship of their lives and the perseverance they showed in the face of it. Both sides of his family were among the settlers of a remote part of northern New York State, close to the Canadian border, farther north than Toronto, a harsh, unaccommodating landscape dense with woods, with a short growing season and a bitter six-month winter, thin soil on rocky, wooded terrain that had to be cleared before it could be farmed. These Bogerts and Gleasons eked out a living on this inhospitable land, raising large families they could barely feed.

Life in Alexandria Township in 1831 when David Bogert and his family arrived there must have been difficult and full of hardships. The country was in large part covered with timber. Much of the land was rocky. Clearings had to be made and log houses constructed. During the long, hard winters, fireplaces were the only source of heat. The growing season was short. It was a struggle to

fit the land for agriculture and to save enough to make the pay-
ments which were due on it, small as they were. These pioneers
deserve great credit for overcoming such hardships, raising large
families, and eventually accumulating a modest competence.

Some entries, giving only a list of names and dates, tell stories of infant mortality, with many of the children dying before the age of ten and
many of the women dying in childbirth or dying suddenly in their twenties or thirties.

James Carnegie, Henry [Bogert]'s father-in-law, lived from 1782 to
1857, 75 years. He is buried in Plessis cemetery, with his four wives,
Abigail who died in 1813 at the age of 29; Elizabeth who died in
1826 at the age of 44; Phoebe who died in 1828 at the age of 38; and
Sally who died in 1848 at the age of 60.

Death, illness, and economic ruin hang over our ancestors' lives like
specters. Of one relative who fought in the Civil War but nearly died of
typhoid fever, my grandfather wrote: "He went to the war a stalwart man
and during the weeks of his illness, was reduced in weight to almost one
hundred pounds."

Like my grandfather himself, some of them left scraps of information
about themselves in an effort to make sense of their difficult lives. Levi
Wheeler Gleason (1797–1875), at his death, dictated a page-long statement about his life. Most of it is occupied with telling a notable episode
from his early years: as a young man he and two friends set out from home
to seek their fortune but lost their small stake after being drawn into a
card game by a pair of gamblers.

"He made a vow that he never would play another game of cards as
long as he lived, which vow he faithfully kept," Levi wrote, also using
the third person. The rest of his life he summarized in two sentences:
"At the age of 25 he married Miss Eliza R. Dickinson by whom he had
9 children, 5 girls and 4 boys, the youngest of whom died at the age of
one year. For more than 50 years he was a faithful servant of the Lord
Jesus."

These were my grandfather's great-grandfather and grandmother.

"They were persons of very modest means living in poverty and raising a large family by farming poor, sandy soil in or near Pitcairn," my grandfather wrote. "I have never heard any comment on the characteristics of Levi, but have been told that his wife, Eliza, was a person of great strength of character and fine personality. Levi W. and Eliza Gleason are buried in the Gleason lot in the cemetery at Gouverneur, New York. On Mrs. Gleason's tombstone, the following words are inscribed: 'Our Mother, she cared for us and she labored for us.' "

There are glimpses of the great uncertainty that haunted my grandfather's early life. In the entry on his own grandfather, George M. Gleason (after whom he was named), his mother's father, he suddenly and surprisingly breaks into the first person, allowing a surprising degree of emotion to creep into the text.

> He suffered a great deal mentally and in a financial way from the wayward life led by his only son, George Harris Gleason, who got into many scrapes, wasted money, and failed to support himself. The great disappointment felt over the very unsuccessful life led by his son undoubtedly caused both him and his wife great worry and anxiety. Another unfortunate feature of Mr. Gleason's later life was that some of his investments proved unsuccessful and his financial condition became weaker as his health began to fail . . . Not withstanding his distressed financial condition and failing health, in the year 1901 when my father died he immediately offered to take my mother, sister and myself into his home in Gouverneur, where we were furnished a very welcome haven during the year needed to complete my preparation for college.

My grandfather omitted that among George M. Gleason's misfortunes was a conviction for bribery while acting as a member of the New York State Assembly—perhaps from a sense of personal loyalty and affection toward his own grandfather.

Despite his travails, George M. Gleason "had a dry sense of humor and loved to joke," my grandfather wrote, a description that would apply equally well to himself, as he probably realized.

2. THE MOTHER OF LISTS

1933—

8/12
Padlocks for garage $1.50
Poison ivy weed killer $3.00
Oil stain and alcohol, floors $1.49
One gallon ivory paint $3.01
Black paint, signs $0.41
Putty knife $0.23
String $0.10
Glass candlestick $0.10
Set 25 pitchers and glasses $1.00

My grandmother wrote diligently in a red-leather-bound account book, noting every penny spent and earned at their Michigan farm for years. Although my grandparents lived very comfortably on a law professor's salary and the farm was not a money-making proposition, the meticulous day-by-day accounting was an act of virtue and responsibility that was important in and of itself. She, too, was a child of Benjamin Franklin and a careful keeper and compiler of lists.

And yet, my grandmother was, in important ways, quite different from her husband. She shared his Franklinian virtues of frugality and industry—reflected in the red leather notebook and in countless entreaties to my mother to live within her means—but she was more of a dreamer, with a powerfully idealistic, romantic, and utopian streak. The very enterprise she was keeping such close practical accounts of—their farm in Michigan—was in and of itself wildly unpractical. She treated it as a going concern, rising early in the morning to plow and staying out late on the tractor to reap, carting baskets of peaches to market and noting every item of profit and loss in her account book, but it made no financial sense. She had pushed to buy the place in the country because she wanted to farm. She had notions about returning to the land, about having a relationship with nature, about organic farming and diet, which would, she felt, greatly lessen the tensions and anxieties of modern life and lead to a healthier, better world—perhaps even world peace.

My own memories—and those of my cousins—are childhood memories of a stout, energetic old woman who wore frilly, old-fashioned dresses and ungainly black orthopedic shoes, who bustled around her kitchen, baking biscuits and blackberry pies, and drove a tractor around her Michigan farm. Although comfortably well off, she wasted nothing, canning all her excess fruit and vegetables and making her own soap out of tar and lard, derived mainly from leftover bacon fat from our morning breakfasts. It seemed impossible to imagine that black tar soap could get you clean, but it did.

She was an extremely high-minded person and, like many high-minded people, somewhat lacking in irony and humor. I remember her getting up from the dinner table a few times in high dudgeon after my grandfather had made some sarcastic remark, and storming off in a huff, saying something like "Why, I've never been so insulted in my entire life!" But my grandmother was good-natured and affectionate with us grandchildren. She hummed as she worked around the house with a kind of operatic tremolo in her voice and, unlike her husband, took pleasure in her grandchildren's antics.

Unfortunately, by the time I was about ten or twelve years old, my grandmother began to suffer from the symptoms of Alzheimer's disease, and within a relatively short time, she was reduced to a shadow of her former self. We knew something was drastically wrong when she thriftily packed up the butter from her fridge in Michigan in a suitcase of clothes bound for Florida, wherein it melted everywhere and ruined everything. Eventually, she was an external shell without a mind, incapable of speech, a body in a bed being turned a few times a day to avoid bedsores. These images of an old woman with a beautiful face and a vacant stare crowded out even the childish images of the woman in the frumpy dresses on the tractor or the black soap she made from lard. There was virtually no evidence for us that she had once been a formidable and remarkable woman, something of a pioneer of her time, active in politics, a kind of proto-feminist who became president of the Illinois League of Women Voters, something of a force in Chicago politics, and a person intensely interested in organic farming, food, and returning to the land back in the late 1930s and early 1940s, when this movement was just beginning and long before these became staples of American counterculture.

My grandmother's deterioration was extraordinarily painful for my mother, who adored and idolized her own mother and tried to explain to

Lucy and me that her mother was not the Alzheimer's patient with the glassy-eyed gaze.

If my grandfather's early journal entries are indicative of methodical cast of mind, my grandmother's very different spirit is reflected in a curious document I found among her papers, in which she earnestly lays out her own approach to life.

LOLITA BOGERT PHILOSOPHY

We are all endowed at birth with a varying degree of creative power. The most primitive manifestation as we mature is in procreation, but it permeates every other phase of living as well. When it is applied constructively, for good use it is religion. This can take many forms, humble or exalted: creating beauty where there was ugliness, order where there was disorder, understanding where there was bewilderment, health where there was disease.

All that is good is God, and the religious life is the one that seeks in its own way to establish the kingdom of God on earth.

The measure of greatness of any individual is in the vastness and quality of his creative power, and the effectiveness with which he applies it.

Love is divine in so far as it lifts one up to a higher plane of existence than he has known before . . .

My grandfather was high-minded, too, but in a much more practical way. Rather than trying to save the entire world, he worked on trying to harmonize the patchwork of conflicting statutes across the vast, fragmented United States. As he put it in his family history, in which he refers to himself in the third person,

Bogert has had a long and pleasant connection with the National Conference of Commissioners on Uniform State Laws, an organization founded by the American Bar Association in 1892 for the purpose of drafting and securing the adoption of statutes which would improve and make uniform the law of the several states.

My grandparents met in 1918, just as the United States was preparing to enter World War I. My grandfather had continued toiling away in Ithaca, publishing his book on "sales law" and earning tenure. The "second self" he referred to in his journal—the Dionysian part of himself that "would like a little leisure recreation," as he put it—remained largely buried until he met my grandmother. My grandfather had volunteered for and become an officer in the judicial branch of the army known as the Judge Advocate General's Corps. Based in Fort Dix, New Jersey, waiting to be shipped off to France, he took leave to visit the Jersey Shore. There, at an officers' dance, he met my grandmother, whose family, the Metzgers (second-generation German immigrants), had a house in Atlantic City, where they spent their vacations away from their principal residence in Brooklyn. If my grandfather was a highly practical man, my grandmother and her family were a bit less so. Her mother, Nina Elizabeth Metzger, had rather romantic ideas about life. She clothed her two daughters in elaborate, flowing, and diaphanous dresses and insisted that they take singing lessons, with hope that they might become opera singers— something neither had a great aptitude for. She gave my grandmother the unusual and romantic name of Lolita. My great-grandfather—my grandmother's father—although a business executive, was a man of artistic temperament who spent all his free time making architectural drawings of buildings he would never build. My great-grandparents sent both of their daughters to college. My grandmother was a student at Adelphi College in Brooklyn when she met my grandfather at the Jersey Shore. My grandmother was the far prettier (and brighter) of the two daughters and had an assiduous young suitor when she met my grandfather in 1918. She was twenty at the time, and her suitor appears to have been about her age. My grandfather, although inexperienced in matters of love, was in a different category: he was thirty-four, a respected law school professor, a captain in the Judge Advocate General's Corps—a man who already cut something of a figure in the world. He evidently was able to trump the bid of Grammie's young suitor with relative ease. We have a photograph of the three of them sitting on the sand of the Jersey Shore, my grandfather in a funny-looking early-twentieth-century men's bathing suit, with tank top and shorts; my grandmother, in one of her diaphanous dresses; and the young rival suitor, fully clothed with white trousers, buck shoes, and a bowler hat. My grandfather has clearly already won the contest for my grandmother's hand: he wears a "cat that just ate the canary" grin and is sitting nestled close to Lolita, with a proprietary hand on her shoulder, while the younger suitor   a diminutive boy with big ears—sits a respectful distance away but looks at the camera with a good-natured smile, seemingly resigned to his position as odd man out.

My grandparents married after just a few weeks' engagement—haste dictated by the war and my grandfather's imminent departure. (It was not that unusual to marry a person you had known such a short time back then.) In a world of uncertainty, it was often prudent to act quickly rather than put things off. They took a brief honeymoon in North Carolina and had just enough time, before my grandfather sailed for France, to conceive my mother, who was born on January 6, 1919, almost nine months after the day of their marriage in April 1918. With her husband overseas, my grandmother moved back in with her parents in Brooklyn, where her father was a high-level manager with the United Shoe Machinery Company, where he earned an annual salary of five thousand dollars. This was clearly a good sum at the time, enough to permit a man to own two houses and maintain a wife who did not work and wore fur coats, as well as two daughters in college with diaphanous dresses and no career plans.

"So I was born into their household, with Gramma, Granpa, and Aunt Louise, in Brooklyn Heights and they thought I was just the cat's pajamas," my mother said. "They took pictures of me like crazy. I was quite old—maybe six months old—by the time my father got back from France and saw me."

Because my grandfather had been away throughout his wife's pregnancy, at the time of my mother's birth, and for the first six months or so of her life, there was tension in their relationship that never entirely went away. "Mother always had the theory that he never really accepted me as his child because he hadn't been there when I was born and he was very jealous. And he just thought I was something that happened when his back was turned. It was my mother's theory."

After all, my grandfather, despite being a mature, grown man of thirty-six at this point, had extremely little experience of this side of life; he had never had a serious relationship with a woman, had spent all his time assiduously building his legal career, and was, like his wife (according to my mother, who learned this from her mother), a virgin at the time of his marriage. My grandfather's almost nonexistent personal life before marriage meant that he had little or nothing to fall back on to help him deal with his feelings of jealousy and anger.

He and my grandmother had two more children in relatively short order, my uncle George and my aunt Virginia, known as Ginny. My grandfather always picked on her. "If he heard us making trouble, he would assume it was my fault and hit me," my mother said. But my grandfather was not a bad father to his other two children. His favorite was the youngest, Ginny; and his son, also named George, admired his father enough to follow him into trusts and estate law and eventually become the coauthor of *Bogert on Trusts*. Ginny has a very different recollection of her father than my mother did. She remembers him being quite paternal and even affectionate, taking her hand and walking her and a classmate to school every day.

At one point, during their early years in Ithaca, someone—a soap company in some promotional scheme—designated the Bogerts "the most attractive family in New York State."

In 1928, my grandfather was hired away from Cornell by the University of Chicago Law School, which was busy transforming itself into one of the great intellectual centers in the United States. In Chicago, they led a comfortable and privileged life and moved in social circles that included Nobel Prize winners and prominent scholars. My grandfather was president of the Quadrangle Club, a University of Chicago faculty club.

"It was a distinguished community of people, but they were just Tom, Dick, and Harry to me," my mother said. "Some of these people were brilliant and very good at what they did, but not so brilliant in other ways." There was a fairly high level of discussion at the family dinner table "interspersed with nonsense," my mother said.

My mother knew her father mainly as a grouchy, ill-tempered man who wanted to be left alone to do his work and who seemed particularly annoyed at her. But, once, she got to glimpse another side of him when, as a child, she sat in on one of his lectures. "I was supposed to meet him after class, but I arrived early and slipped into the back of the lecture hall. He was like an entirely different person. It was a lecture with about fifty or sixty people and he put on a real performance. He lectured very well. He knew how to project his voice, was very clear, very aggressive. I was impressed even as a child. I never got to see that side of him. When he came home, he became a grump. So I only caught glimpses of what a potent person he was."

My grandfather's annual salary when he began teaching at Chicago in the 1920s was ten thousand dollars. The family had a large, handsome three-story house in Chicago, the country's second-largest city, owned a second home in the country, and had a staff of three or four people to help run them. They had a live-in maid named Marie, who was black. Marie's sister came to do the laundry twice a week, and a third person, Marie's sister's husband, did the heavy cleaning. Coal, of course, was the principal fuel in Chicago at the time: the air was sooty and gritty and gray with coal dust, which collected on the windowsills and in the folds of curtains and in between the cushions on the couch. And when the wind blew the wrong way, the air was also filled with the stench of decaying meat from the slaughterhouses, which had earned Chicago the title "hog butcher for the world."

"My parents had a rather rich social life," my mother said. They went out a lot and gave what seemed to their children like rather grand parties. "When they would give a big dinner they hired a cook—two cooks—who started cooking two or three days beforehand," my mother said. "We were not allowed anywhere within striking distance of it. We had to eat in the kitchen. And the guests arrived in what we thought were very glamorous clothes, which were put up on Mother's bed, and we would sit on the stairs and watch them. And they had a butler serving drinks. It was Prohibition at the time—Daddy didn't believe in Prohibition. And he would always serve one drink. They lived high, wide, and handsome in a funny kind of way." The children's social lives were also rather formal, composed of dancing classes and cotillions. Their lives, too, had a high-minded component. They were sent to the University of Chicago Lab School, which was meant to be an educational laboratory in which the theories of John Dewey were put into practice at the elementary school level. "It was a progressive school," my mother said. "They didn't believe in the standard curriculum. They had things like shop and cooking. Boys learned to cook. We used to raise white mice and see if their teeth fell out if you didn't give them milk—things like that. We also had good basic training in things like Latin and music."

The stock market crash of 1929 and the Great Depression made a great impression on the family immediately. "When there was the run on the banks, my mother came home and asked us kids how much money we had in our piggy banks. Of course we had about thirty-six cents, so that was ridiculous but it was the feeling of the time." They were relatively cushioned from the effects of the Depression. They had a steady professor's salary to fall back on. The University of Chicago faculty was asked to accept a 10 percent pay cut. Because of the income generated by *Bogert on Trusts*, my grandparents lived a cut above most faculty members. At one point, my grandfather's colleagues put on a little skit at the Quadrangle Club showing a couple of down-and-out unemployed professors sitting on a park bench as a smartly dressed George Bogert strolls by twirling a cane. "Well, Bogert, how come you're looking so chipper?" they asked. "You forget. I have my royalties!" And this became a standing joke in the house for years. "Whenever anybody showed any evidence of spending money, we would say, 'You forget! I have my royalties,'" Aunt Ginny explained. I imagine my mother, who had the biggest reputation for fine dressing and personal extravagance, would have used that line a lot.

The crowds of unemployed men gathered downtown, far from the Hyde Park area where the University of Chicago was and where my mother and her family lived. From time to time, someone would knock on the door asking if they could wash windows or shovel snow for a little money.

My grandfather appears to have been affected by the armies of unemployed, 25 percent of the workforce at the time, and wrote a plea for a program in Chicago designed to create jobs for the jobless. His proposal was a mix of compassion and old-fashioned Protestant work ethic, worrying about destroying "the morale and self-respect" of the unemployed by giving them money for nothing.

September 14, 1931
Tasks for the Unemployed

I write to urge that you use your influence to see to it that as many of the unemployed are put to work this fall and winter on work for community benefit.

The citizens who have jobs will gladly contribute the $8,000,000 to provide food, shelter and clothing for the unemployed but this money should not be given to the able-bodied jobless as charity or the dole if it can be helped.

In order to keep up the morale and self-respect of those who have to accept this help as many as possible should be put to work on tasks that benefit Chicago and Cook County . . .

Let's not condemn the jobless to a winter of demoralizing idleness if any work of a public nature can be found for them.

George G. Bogert
Professor of Law, University of Chicago.

"They were very liberal for the circles they moved in," my mother said. "Mother and Daddy were considered radical because they were for Roosevelt while most everybody else they knew was for Hoover. And I was always very much that way. All the kids in the family were."

In the midst of the Depression, in 1933, my grandparents bought a sixty-three-acre farm in Three Oaks, Michigan, about a two-hour train ride from Chicago. It cost a mere $3,350, only about a third of a law professor's annual salary, and it cost even less to build a house there. My grandmother, although a mother, housewife, and professor's spouse, threw herself into turning the property into a working farm, combining it with her utopian ideas of organic farming and healthy eating as the road to a sound, good life. They soon bought another forty acres. My mother referred to the farm—acres and acres of flat cornfields and peach orchards in the middle of hundreds and hundreds of miles of flat midwestern farmland—as "the dump." As a teenager who longed to be charging around Chicago with her friends in convertible cars or being courted by various beaux, my mother regarded it as a form of servitude to be dragged each weekend—and all summer—out to Three Oaks to lend a hand while my grandmother drove her tractor and mulched and weeded until it got dark at night.

In some ways, my grandmother was a strict and conventional woman with a rather old-fashioned, Victorian worldview. She never had a career or even a job. She wore frumpy clothes and sensible shoes and was relatively strict. She insisted that children must eat everything on their plates and would have them sit at table for hours until they did. (My uncle George and my mother were known for stuffing food he didn't like into a teapot in the dining room, and once my mother threw a fried egg she didn't want out the window into a snowbank. With Chicago's cold climate, the egg remained there frozen until spring, when it suddenly appeared in the grass.) My grandmother believed that children needed plenty of cold air, and so the children often slept out on a porch—even in winter, with lots of blankets. When my mother became a teenager, my grandmother believed in strict curfews and no lipstick—restrictions my mother rebelled against constantly.

But she also had a highly unconventional and broad-minded side. As the president of the Illinois League of Women Voters, she became something of a power in local politics, making frequent trips to Springfield and Washington. Women had only just gained the right to vote in 1919, and so she was an early activist for women's issues long before there was an official feminist movement. "Her name was in the paper all the time, to the point where my father used to joke that he had become the husband of Lolita Bogert," my mother said. My mother inherited her mother's political passion—all her children did to some degree—and admired her idealism enormously.

"With her it was never a question of accepting conventional wisdom in matters large and small—of doing or thinking as others did because that's the way the world goes—but of searching afresh for the just and honorable solution. Once she had found it, there was no budging her," my mother said of my grandmother at the time of her death in 1983.

She championed organic agriculture, women's rights, and civil rights long before those became popular causes. She moved against the grain of most people in her social circle by becoming an ardent New Dealer and Roosevelt supporter in the 1930s. But when she felt that Roosevelt had disappointed her—by being too cautious, too much of a politician on rights for black Americans—she actually deserted him in the 1940 election. Alone even in her own family, she supported Wendell Willkie, a liberal Republican who was more outspoken on certain issues, such as racial discrimination: "The Constitution does not provide for first and second class citizens," Willkie said. "Freedom is an indivisible word. If we want to enjoy it, and fight for it, we must be prepared to extend it to everyone, whether they are rich or poor, whether they agree with us or not, no matter what their race or the color of their skin."

In this period, my grandmother actually wrote a short story about an interracial marriage called "Sometimes Yvonne Grows Tired of Waiting." The main character was a French-American dressmaker named Yvonne who worked in a fancy apparel shop.

> There she had met the uniformed colored doorman, a man considerably her senior, and had come to regard him as a "quiet fine Christian gentleman." Being fresh from France where color lines are drawn not so sharply as here, she had not hesitated to marry him. The marital relationship proved a happy one. One child was born of the union, a brown-skinned boy with delicately chiseled features.

The couple live in relative peace for a number of years in a mixed neighborhood until they suddenly find themselves the object of various persecutions large and small.

When finally her electric lines were cut so that she might no longer use the sewing machine that was her sole source of livelihood, she concluded at last that they would have to move.

Yvonne and her family wind up in a filthy rooming house that is crawling with cockroaches and unsavory characters. Then Yvonne finds a house that someone is prepared to rent to them, but on the day she and her family show up with all their furniture, they are turned away. "I had a conference with the owner of the building last night," the rental agent tells her. "There was some question whether the building should go white or colored, and the owner has decided it should go white. Here is your deposit back."

At the end of the story—it is only five pages—Yvonne has reached a condition of near despair: "People have forgotten God . . . Some day they will turn to Him again. But meantime . . . some of us get very tired waiting."

My grandmother had a brief secret life writing fiction—she wrote only a couple of stories. But I was enormously impressed that my grandmother would write a short story about racial prejudice and miscegenation in the 1940s, well before civil rights became a major national issue.

There is also the letter—a stirring call to arms—with which she begins her tenure as the president of the Illinois League of Women Voters:

September 3, 1937
Dear League Colleague:

You and I are embarked on high adventure, adventure that will tax our abilities to the utmost, that will weary us often, that will discourage us sometimes; but one that will more than square the balance by an occasional thrill of quick and brilliant achievement and by the unspectacular but enduring satisfaction of slow accomplishment.

Ours is the task of holding people up to their birthright of democratic government, and even when they would be lulled into false security by "bread and circuses." Ours is the task of quietly leading women into fulfillment of their full stature, even though the old idea dies hard, in practice if not in words, that women are chattel, forever condemned to mediocrity. Ours is the administrative task of bringing out the best in every individual we deal with even though understanding of human minds and emotions is still scientifically in its infancy.

I count it a privilege to be embarked on this high adventure with you. Let us learn together.

Sincerely yours,
Lolita Bogert
(Mrs. George G. Bogert)
President

As a reform-minded Democrat in a city dominated by the corrupt political machine of Mayor Edward Joseph Kelly, my grandmother was always fighting City Hall and conducting (usually) losing battles for extremely worthy causes. She succeeded in helping elect to the city council the former University of Chicago economist Paul Douglas, who went on to have a long, distinguished career in the United States Senate. On the city council, Douglas generally found himself outvoted and outmaneuvered in political struggle by the tough but uneducated machine politicians. "I have three degrees," Douglas once said. "I have been associated with intelligent and intellectual people for many years. Some of these aldermen haven't gone through the fifth grade. But they're the smartest bunch of bastards I ever saw grouped together." My grandmother evidently played a role in getting him to run for the U.S. Senate in 1942, a race in which he was defeated by the Kelly machine but did well enough to lay the ground for a successful bid in 1948.

On Senate stationery, he wrote to my grandmother insisting that without her support he might not have made it there. "I shall never forget the way you stood behind me and rallied the forces in our 1942 primary campaign. Without that, 1948 would have never been possible."

She married when she was only twenty; it wasn't until she was in her thirties that she really came into her own and began to develop a strong, independent identity and a highly developed political consciousness. As she began to assert herself in various ways, she entered increasingly into conflict with her husband.

"I became a bone of contention between them," my mother told me. "My father beat up on me all the time. He would come into a room full of junk that we were playing in and he would automatically hit me, assume that I had made the mess. I got very sad and discouraged and I became anemic . . . He spanked all of us. Physical punishment was no disgrace in those days. We all had to lower our pants and he put us on his knee and whacked us with a hairbrush, something that really hurt. What he did with me was hit out. The first thing when he walked in the room he would hit me." My mother developed anemia in this period and, after having skipped a year in school because she was a precocious early reader, had to be held back a year. My grandmother was convinced that my mother's anemia was the result of being picked on by her father.

At a certain point, however, my grandfather's aggression toward my mother threw his marriage into crisis. "She told him, 'If you ever strike that child again, I am going to leave you,'" my mother said. My grandmother appears to have compensated for her husband's hostility toward my mother by drawing particularly close to her. They formed a curious alliance against my grandfather. "She made me her confidante," my mother said. My grandmother told my mother about her battles with her husband. In the early to mid-1930s, my grandparents' marriage went through something of a crisis. "He was not very pleasant to her. He was very insecure despite his professional success. He was very dependent on her but he treated her very badly. She would get up from the dining table in tears all the time when he would say something mean."

Moreover, there was a lot of tension over the fact that my grandfather paid too much attention to other women. My grandmother, although fourteen years younger than my grandfather, had become rather overweight by her thirties. "Grammie broke her ankle, it had been set very badly and she had trouble with her legs and feet after that. She had been quite slim and beautiful before that, but after the ankle she didn't move around so much, and in those days women were supposed to eat all the whipped cream and fattening stuff they could. So, although she remained very pretty, she was definitely overweight."

Sometimes my grandmother would get extremely angry (my mother and both her siblings recalled) over the way my grandfather behaved at parties. "My father had always been a flirt. He was always latching on to other women and pinching them and dancing too close. Mother would get furious and tell me that Grampie had misbehaved himself with Mrs. So-

and-so. One in particular was Mrs. Sears, the wife of another professor, a much older and more serious man. She was a very snappy-looking dame and very flirtatious—Grammie was really furious about that."

My uncle George recalls his mother coming home one evening from a party at the Quadrangle Club in tears. When he asked what the matter was, she replied, "Men are capable of such great heights, but when they sink they sink lower than any woman!" Apparently, Grampie had ignored Grammie at the party and flirted outrageously with Mrs. Sears.

Then, at a certain point, my grandparents entered into a complex, platonic *ménage à quatre* with another professor at the law school, Harold Shepherd, and his wife, who were younger than my grandparents but had no children and became fixtures in my grandparents' house for a period of time. "He was rather good-looking and she was cute and vivacious," my mother said. "Grampie liked the wife and Grammie fell in love with the husband. We didn't know it then. They had no children. He would dance with us—Ginny and me. They became great pals of the family. Mother was secretly in love with him. He pretended to be in love with her. I think he did this with a number of women. She was naive enough to believe—because of a little pressure of the hand or a look—that he was madly in love with her, too. This went on for quite a long time. Once, when Grampie was especially nasty to me, she told me about this great love she had for Mr. Shepherd. I was about fourteen then. He would write her a letter and she would interpret it the way she wanted. So she used to show me his letters. They were friendly letters. You could read them as simply friendly letters, but she read all kinds of things into them. He would ask her to dance and she read that as a love declaration."

At least according to my mother, there doesn't appear to have been a lot of infidelity in my grandparents' circle, but rather a lot of wandering libido, barely suppressed passion, sexual tension, and unfulfilled longing.

Among my grandmother's papers, I found a series of letters from a man named Lee, who was clearly in love with my grandmother but never actually came out and said so. The man in question, Lee Rainey, was a neighbor of theirs who was a librarian at the University of Chicago, a friend of the Chicago poet Carl Sandburg, and a (bad) would-be poet himself. His letters are incredibly flowery, with a kind of excessive, sugary romanticism in which he expresses his passion through metaphor— torrential streams rushing through dark glades, glistening dewdrops illuminated by beautiful dawns and sunsets, and so forth.

In 1933, in a letter full of talk of "earth and poesy," of Peter Pan and the land of the Faeries, there is a wild metaphor in which he writes:

> I must have perished long ago . . . and become Lolita in the twilight of his eyes, has sometime seemed to be dreaming of that some island, I am tonight overtaking her at the little wicket of the New Year, to share a secret. I tried a sign, but it was too cryptic to carry clearly.

The letter seems to say everything and nothing. It appears to be a declaration of love, but read another way it's just a lot of highfalutin literary nonsense.

Two years later, he is still at the same game, saying and not saying.

> And then again
>   dear Lolita,
>   it may have been a footfall in the wood that brought you to your blessed hour. Long ago, one who shared a heavenly evening with you when June was four days short of zenith and had banned the drabness of the wake of dawn. Indeed, when your toes first touched the earth . . . he was beneath a cherry tree in a Kentucky garden reading Homer there, both *Iliad* and *Odyssey*, in the brush. Little did he dream between hexameters how that tiny bundle of a maid would one day at her end of a Ridge hear his call from the far-away Vermont end, or with basket and trowel he gathered greenery for a wave at his wistful window. But she did, and how dear was her reply.

This is Rainey's way of thanking her for a letter he had received from her at his vacation home in Vermont, where he spent the summer—and by all accounts, at this point in her life, my grandmother was not a "tiny bundle of a maid." My grandmother had absolutely no romantic interest in her neighbor, and it is quite likely that he did not have a real interest in her. He was what my aunt and uncle described as an extremely effeminate man. Although one did not use the word then, everyone suspected that he was homosexual, whether he acted on it or not. If this is true, he may have pretended to be or imagined himself to be in love with my grandmother—an unavailable married woman—knowing she was an entirely safe object of his passion, which was entirely verbal. Rainey was also married, and my grandmother would sometimes go over to his house in the evenings and listen to him read poetry. For a married woman to visit, unaccompanied, another man might have raised a few eyebrows in the Chicago of that time, but my grandmother, confident of her innocent and high-minded intent, paid no mind to convention.

And so my grandparents' world would seem to have been something of a turmoil of misplaced passions and urges: Lee Rainey writing his flowery sentences to my grandmother; my grandmother reading and rereading the ambiguous letters of Professor Shepherd for secret signs of passion; Shepherd leading various women on but loving (perhaps) none of them; my grandfather chasing after various Mrs. Searses and Mrs. Shepherds— enough to infuriate my grandmother but not enough to satisfy himself.

In the midst of all this, my mother came of age. She was born in 1919 and hit adolescence as these various romantic scenarios were playing out. My mother was precocious and very pretty, and as she developed into an extremely striking young woman, she began to attract a lot of sexual attention—not least of all from her own father.

"As I got older, I became quite pretty. And he would ask me to dance," my mother said. "I had become very frivolous and very popular with the boys at University High, riding around in cars and staying out too late. I always thought I was in love with somebody. I was a giddy girl. There was no drinking or drugs in those days. It was very innocent stuff. The occasional mash note and kisses in the dark, but that was about it. But you were able to drive a car when you were about fourteen years old. We were out with the Herschel gang. The gang would drive up and down Lakeshore Drive. The Herschels were a very neighborly family that lived on the way home. They had a big backyard and quite a lot of money. And they had a basketball court in their backyard. It was where everyone congregated after school."

In the midst of this, her father began to show an unhealthy interest in his pretty elder daughter. "He tried to dance with me after dinner and held me tight. I didn't know much about sex, but I could tell that there was something going on. I knew that if he had an erection, instinctively there was something wrong with that. My mother saw what was going on and took me into my room and said, 'If your father ever tries to get in bed with you, you kill him!' He never did but . . . I think that's when my mother decided to send me to boarding school."

It was also at some point during this time (although it might have been a bit earlier) that my grandfather—the master of self-control who had budgeted and used his time so well for so long—suffered something of a nervous breakdown. Doctors recommended that he take a leave of absence, and he spent a period of months taking the sun out in Arizona. "He was away for quite a while," my mother said. "Grammie stayed with the kids and they tried to keep us in the dark about the whole thing. When he came back he had a sun lamp installed in his room, and he used to go up and take sunbaths all the time."

Although the exact chronology of events—and the possible causal relations between them—was fuzzy in my mother's head when we talked about it nearly sixty years later, it was clear that there was a cluster of episodes in a period of a few years that seemed to characterize a phase of crisis in the family's life: my grandfather's hitting my mother; my grandmother's threatening to leave him; my grandfather's flirtations with other women; my grandmother's falling in love with someone else or imagining that she had fallen in love with someone else; my mother's adolescence; my grandfather's inappropriate interest in my mother; my grandfather's nervous breakdown; and my grandmother's decision to send my mother away to boarding school.

"I think it may have been connected to her 'love affair' and she threatened to leave him and that may have sent him into a state of depression," my mother said.

My mother was clearly very preoccupied with this episode with her father as she lay on her deathbed high on cortisone. She had talked about it with both Lucy and me in the past as well as with some of her closest friends, but it seemed to be something she wanted to clear up before dying. On the one hand, her returning to it repeatedly was a sign of its importance, and she called it "a serious factor in my life"; on the other, she kept insisting that her mother had made more of the incident than was warranted. She seemed to blame her mother for creating an excessively negative picture of her father and traumatizing my mother in the process. "I want to clear up this business about Grampie because he's been unfairly marred by my mother," she said, returning again to the subject. "It's not true that my father ever tried to seduce me. And what happened between us, although a little unfortunate, was certainly not incest. He tried to dance with me after dinner. I was a teenager, starting to be pretty, and he was in his late forties perhaps and still lusty. He liked to dance with me and hold me too tight and I could tell, although I didn't really know what an erection was, that there was something funny going on. But he didn't keep it up. He didn't fondle my bosoms, he didn't peep on me, he didn't do anything. That was it. And my mother took me into my room and she said, 'If your father tries to get in bed with you, you kill him.' And this is what led me to believe all my life that I was the victim of—if not incest—incestuous feelings. My father was also very ashamed of this."

And yet a certain amount of bad blood remained between them. My grandfather, even in his extreme old age, talked to my uncle about cutting my mother out of his will. And my mother (although she knew nothing of that) refused to attend his burial service after he died. Grampie died in Florida but wanted his ashes buried in the Gleason family plot in Gouverneur, New York. Although my mother had the shortest distance to travel, she, alone among his three kids, chose not to go. The reason she gave my aunt Ginny—who heard about it for the first time after my grandfather's death in 1977—was that she had not forgiven her father for his unwanted sexual attention.

To protect her daughter—whether from her own wildness or from anything further happening between father and daughter—my grandmother sent my mother to a Quaker boarding school in Pennsylvania called Westtown.

This appears to have strengthened my grandmother's feeling that my mother was *her* child and her child alone. "She made it plain that she was in charge of any decisions regarding me. My father had no control over me whatsoever. She decided that life in Chicago was too wild for me." My mother fought going away but gave in. "I adored my mother as a child—I mean I thought everything she did was perfect and believed everything she said. I argued with and disagreed with her a lot, but underneath it all, I thought she was right about everything—everything. And I was her ally, her confidante, her best friend, I guess. She adored me, too. I was her favorite child by far. She liked the others, but I was adored. She thought I was beautiful, talented—you name it. No matter how wicked and how silly I was."

PART II

KAMENETZKIS

The D'Annunzio Letter, or the
Last of the Kamenetzkis

It all started with the D'Annunzio letter.

One day, my aunt Lally, my father's sister, mentioned casually, in passing, that she had a letter written by the great Italian poet Gabriele D'Annunzio addressed to her father—as if there was nothing unusual about my grandfather, a Russian Jewish dentist from the shtetl of Mir, having been in epistolary contact with the "poet-soldier" of Italian Fascism. The content of the letter was even more surprising: it was a personal testimonial declaring that my grandfather, Ilya Israel Kamenetzki, had provided important help to D'Annunzio's soldiers in 1919–1920 during the occupation of Fiume, a crucial event in the history of Fascism.

Fiume is a town on the coast of Croatia that had once been part of the Venetian Empire and had a population that was closely divided between speakers of Italian, Hungarian, and Serbo-Croatian. At the end of World War I, with the dismemberment of the Austro-Hungarian Empire, control of Fiume (Rijeka in Serbo-Croatian) was hotly contested by both Italy and the newly created Yugoslavia. The solution was to make Fiume an independent city-state. Even though Italy won significant territorial concessions in the Treaty of Versailles, D'Annunzio denounced the Fiume compromise as a vile betrayal that left Italy with a "mutilated victory." Acting on his own initiative, D'Annunzio in 1919 led a private expedition of about 2,600 former soldiers and took the city by force.

For over a year, D'Annunzio lived out the fantasy of ruling over his own tiny country; he and his men—a bizarre collection of extreme nationalists, syndicalists, socialists, and a leader of Italy's nudist movement—engaged in a prolonged bacchanalia and acts of piracy and drew up a utopian program for a radical egalitarian-nationalist state. D'Annunzio held drunken orgies in his princely residence and would then emerge onto the balcony, entertaining crowds below with long ecstatic speeches. After a fifteen-month standoff, the Italian Army finally ousted D'Annunzio's legionnaires with ease. Although it had elements of farce and proved that D'Annunzio was supremely unsuited to governing, Fiume had extremely serious consequences. Carried out in defiance of Italy's elected government and of international treaties, the occupation of Fiume was the first crack in the new international order that was set up after World War I—the war that was supposed to end all wars. In many ways, this small coup d'état was a dress rehearsal for Mussolini's March on Rome three years later. It was also the first pure expression of Fascist doctrine, showing that, in the hands of the determined man of action, the treaties and laws of democratically elected governments were mere pieces of paper to be shredded by his powerful will. Mussolini and his nascent Fascist movement took note and borrowed liberally from the rhetoric and pageantry of D'Annunzio and his legionnaires. When Mussolini took power, one of his first transgressive acts was to retake Fiume and make it part of Italy, in violation of international law. D'Annunzio's occupation of Fiume went on to assume a mythic place in Fascist culture—like the battle of Bunker Hill in the American Revolution or the storming of the Bastille in the French Revolution—and those who had participated in it enjoyed patriotic merits, and considerable privileges, during the twenty-year reign of Fascism.

The letter suggested an intriguing but wildly improbable scenario: that my Russian dentist grandfather had had some role in this troubling yet crucial historical episode in the beginning of the Fascist revolution that had earned the recognition of one of its founding fathers. I asked my father about it. He shrugged. He knew all about the letter but had never thought to mention it, as if it was simply a fixture of his childhood of no particular importance, like the color of the wallpaper in his parents' apartment in Rome. The letter, in fact, it gradually emerged, had been a critically important document that had served the family as a kind of passe-partout, opening many doors in Fascist Italy. It had helped the family, which had been living in a kind of semi-legal limbo, to obtain Italian citizenship. They had used it to blunt the full effects of the racial laws and again to help them leave the country and get to America. "How did your father end up in Fiume and what did he do there?" I asked my father. "Probably he wasn't actually there," he said with nonchalance, lying on his living room couch and chomping at a piece of Italian bread slathered with butter and marmalade and spilling crumbs on his sweater vest. He then explained that one of my grandfather's dental patients was a well-known Italian actress named Elena Sangro, who was one of D'Annunzio's last mistresses. It was she who had gotten D'Annunzio to write the letter on my grandfather's behalf. Perhaps my grandfather had stopped in Fiume on his way to Italy, but more likely D'Annunzio's mistress had put him up to it in order to grease the wheels for my grandfather with the Fascist bureaucracy. "This is unbelievable," I said to my father. "So there are two possibilities: that your father, a dentist from Byelorussia, participated in the dawn of the Fascist revolution, or that he and Gabriele D'Annunzio, the unofficial poet laureate of Fascist Italy, perpetrated a fraud against the government by passing your father off as a patriotic hero for his nonexistent contributions to the Fascist revolution. Either way, it's incredible."

"I find it much less incredible than you do," my father said drily. "That's the way life under Fascism was." He brushed the crumbs from his chest onto the couch and changed the subject.

The desire to get to the bottom of this mystery became a consuming passion. I had already begun trying to learn as much as I could about my father's family by talking to my aunt, who was much more forthcoming than her brother. Getting anything out of my father was like pulling teeth (to extend the dentistry metaphor), except when, usually without prompting, he would come out with some incredible story. Then, when I'd press him for more details, he would clam up.

My aunt Lally, by contrast, was the living repository of the Kamenetzki family history. She had never married and had lived with her parents until they died—when they were in their eighties and she was nearly fifty. Her life revolved around theirs; after their deaths, she remained surrounded by their things, by family memorabilia, books, papers, and photographs, as well as the growing rows of bottles of medicine they needed as their health deteriorated. She was particularly close to her mother and absorbed from her all of the family lore and stories. My aunt was never happier than when reminiscing about her parents' lives, describing with vividness and passion events long before she was born. She could tell you what courses my grandmother took at Moscow University, the names of her professors, and what performances she had seen at the Moscow theater before the revolution. She knew about the character and political dispositions of my grandmother's various sisters, whom she had never met.

(Biba was a Bolshevik, while Clara, Rosa, Masha, and my grandmother were all in favor of the Constitutional Democratic Party.)

If the Kamenetzki family home was the center of my aunt's world, my father, by contrast, had already begun to make a name for himself when he was still a teenager in Italy. After World War II, he moved even further out of the family orbit. He was consumed by his work and by his role as a rising star of Italian journalism: interviewing presidents and secretaries of state, going to parties, covering stories, and meeting interesting new people. He remade his life in the United States, married my mother, and created his own American family. He had little time or patience for looking backward.

Although we all lived in New York, we saw very little of the Kamenetzkis during my childhood. They came to our house perhaps once a year on Christmas day, which, as highly assimilated Jews, they were quite happy to celebrate. Every once in a while, we would make our way up from our apartment in Greenwich Village to their apartment on West End Avenue and 106th Street, which, though only about five miles from our house, seemed light-years away. White Russians who had first fled the Soviet Union, then settled in Paris, and then fled the Nazis could be seen occupying the benches lining the island in the middle of upper Broadway and chatting in Russian as traffic whizzed by on either side of them. Full of aging refugees from Eastern Europe, the Upper West Side at that time was home to Alexander Kerensky, briefly the leader of Russia after the fall of the czar and before the October Revolution of the Bolsheviks, and Isaac Bashevis Singer, along with many much more humble souls who populated Singer's stories of the life in the shtetl. In the United States of the early 1960s—the era of John and Bobby Kennedy—my grandparents seemed like relics of another century, holdovers from czarist Russia, with old, ill-fitting clothes, speaking broken English, their fourth- or fifth-best language. Their apartment was dusty and cluttered with old furniture that was heavy and uncomfortable, some of which they had dragged from Russia and Italy, including the large old wooden grandfather clock brought all the way from Russia in the middle of the civil war, with elaborate chains and pulleys, which had stopped telling time. There was a musty sadness to the place, of people who had been uprooted again and again and who—through no particular fault of their own—had run out of gas trying to start over one last time. My grandmother Sara ("Mumi") had grown very fat and walked with a cane. They lived a precarious and marginal life, making ends meet with a little money from Social Security and a little from my aunt's jobs. My grandfather had been forced to give up a lucrative and successful dentistry practice in Rome; his various dentistry certificates were not recognized in this country, and so for a time he practiced out of the apartment illegally. Lucy and I would play in the dark, gloomy room that had served as his dental studio, climbing up on the swiveling dental chair, playing with the plaster molds of the teeth and palates of former patients.

We were not sorry to leave their apartment, to return to the bright sunshine outside, to our much larger and much more attractive home in the Village, to my mother's much more orderly, spick-and-span world. Perhaps because we saw them so infrequently, I always sensed that my father was ashamed of his family—or perhaps that was just me. I recall one day coming home to our house on Eleventh Street with a friend of mine as my Kamenetzki grandparents were making their way up the front steps of our house, two rumpled refugees moving slowly with the help of canes. "*Those* are your grandparents?" my friend said with a disapproving tone. I felt ashamed, and ashamed of myself for feeling ashamed.

My grandfather died when I was nine and my grandmother when I was eleven, so I never had a proper conversation with them that I can recall. I remember liking my grandmother more than my grandfather. She was fat but had a generous and affectionate manner. "Sandro, *vieni kvi*" (come here), she would say to me (using my family nickname) in Russian-accented Italian, a language I didn't speak at the time. My grandfather I recall as having a square, protruding jaw and a scowling countenance and a somewhat pompous, self-important demeanor that reminded me of pictures of Mussolini.

When they died, the last of the Kamenetzkis was my aunt, whom we all knew as Lally, but whose formal name was Myra.

She was short and fat, about five feet tall and two hundred pounds, with a small, pale face and an enormous shelf of breasts that shook when she laughed. She wore ungainly plastic glasses and had an unfortunate taste in clothes, favoring formfitting wool outfits that accentuated all the wrong things, turning her figure into a rippling set of curves: double chin, breasts, belly, hips, and buttocks. My aunt had often been treated, rather unfairly, as the butt of jokes in our house. She was sweet and good-natured but talked constantly, and my father complained—generally in her earshot—about her "insufferable chatter." (In fact, he was more likely to make fun of her in her presence and defend her when she wasn't around.) She was far from stupid and in fact was very well educated. But she was highly developed in some areas, and completely childlike in others. If you asked her about Schiller's poetry, which of Flaubert's novels she preferred, or her favorite cantos of Dante, she could give you a well-reasoned, well-informed disquisition about each of them, but she lacked all sense of proportion and would go on too long in minute detail or talk at equal length and perhaps even greater passion about the virtues of her dog, Ciao, or the merits of the her favorite New York City buses. She had grown up in a household with servants and had never learned to do anything domestic, such as cooking or housework, and she was blessed or cursed with a kind of good-natured obliviousness to the practical dimension of life. When she made some token effort at help—circling around the kitchen for a couple of minutes trying to figure out what to do with a dirty plate, finally placing it precariously on the edge of a counter—we soon realized it was best for everyone if she didn't try to help at all.

Most people would consider her life a series of disasters and missed opportunities. She was born, dangerously small and underweight, in Riga in 1921, as my grandparents were trying to make their way out of the Soviet Union during the Russian civil war. After they moved to Rome, her education was interrupted by the passage of Mussolini's racial laws. Among the many contradictions of these anti-Jewish laws was that young Jews who had started university were allowed to finish while those who had not yet begun were not allowed to enter or even to continue at their secondary school. So my father, who was two years older than my aunt, continued his university career in the middle of the anti-Jewish campaign and was able to graduate even after Italy's entrance into World War II, but my aunt was forced out of her Italian *liceo*. And while she was able to get her high school degree at an improvised Jewish school, she was unable to proceed on to college. When our family came to New York, my father was almost immediately drafted into the U.S. Army and my aunt was left to bear a large share of the burden of supporting her parents, initially working as a messenger and errand girl while taking university courses at night. She later ran the New York office of an Italian pharmaceutical company—a job she loved and insisted she was very good at—but then the company closed down its American operation. Working full-time, she was in her thirties before she got her college degree. She then started working as an Italian teacher. After my grandfather was hit with a paralytic stroke and spent nearly two years unable to move, she lived a hellish life dividing her time among a full-time job, nighttime nursing duties, and her own stop-and-go university career. She soldiered on in obscurity toward a PhD in Italian literature for years, and those years eventually turned into decades. When I was an adult and she was nearly sixty and I got to know her better, she was still nominally at it and spoke of finishing—even though by this point it was clear she would never do so.

Her mother's death, which meant relatively little to us, was for her the end of the world. I remember when she came to stay with us after her mother died. I was forced to vacate my bedroom and would watch her fat, bathrobed figure pacing up and down the hall at night. At one point, she suggested that we play chess. "All right, chess champ, let's see how good you are!" she said with a kind of forced joviality. My father had taught me chess, and I played with the dogged single-mindedness of a child. At a certain point, she made a critical blunder, leaving her queen unprotected. As soon as I swooped in to take it, she wailed in protest and snatched the piece from my hand. "No, that isn't the move I meant to make!" she protested with real heat and passion. "You can't do that," I said. "You took your hand off the piece. That's how the rules of chess work. As soon as you move and take your hand off a piece, you have made your move!" "But I was still thinking. I meant to do something else!" She refused to budge and wouldn't give me the piece back. "That's cheating," I yelled. "It's not cheating!" she insisted. "I should have my turn back." Even as a eleven-year-old child I realized that there was something strangely childish about her behavior, that it meant as much or more to her to win this chess game than it did to me. But I felt offended: I would never have bent the rules to win. And so I walked away, even though I knew, under the circumstances, I should have relented and let her have her way. Even then I felt as if there was something metaphorical about the situation: that she had made some wrong move in life that she regretted and desperately wanted to take back.

And yet for a person who had lived such a difficult life, she was remarkably good-natured, optimistic, and uncomplaining. She was something of a Holy Fool out of a Russian novel, a person almost free of guile or malice, who was incredibly appreciative of whatever good things came her way. Her small face with its upturned nose and excited expression reminded me of the drawing on the cover of a paperback edition of

Voltaire's *Candide* we had read in school. She seemed to believe that she lived in the best and most interesting of all possible worlds—even though she had led a life that most people would consider a long, uninterrupted string of tragedies. *"A me piacciono i contratempi!"* ("I like misadventures"), she said, telling me about a ski trip she had taken as a young woman during which the bus had broken down, leaving everyone stranded in the cold for hours. When we gave her gifts, she literally oohhed and ahhed, with a thrilled tone of voice. "Oohh, how beauuutifull," she would say. "Liz," she would say to my mother, "you know exactly what my taste is! I adore this kind of wool." I remember her saying on a couple of occasions when I served her dinner, "You know, I think this is the best pasta I've ever tasted!" Highly unlikely, given the tens of thousands of plates of pasta she must have eaten, but indicative of her attitude of making the best out of things.

As children, we dreaded receiving her Christmas gifts. She considered herself "very creative" while also having very little money and, as a result, insisted on making her presents. There was a period when she started fashioning unspeakable jewelry out of plastic beads that was taken off and consigned to the trash as soon as she left. Then there was a period in which she started giving us misshapen knitted articles of clothing that never saw the outside of any of our closets. There was another period when she started giving us rocks—not exotic, brilliantly colored, or special stones, just the kind of rock you might dig up in a garden.

She was nonetheless convinced, with a streak of naive arrogance, that she was simply ahead of her time. "Ten years before it became fashionable, I had the idea of wearing shoes of a different color on my feet. I tried to get the salesgirl to let me buy one green shoe and one yellow one, but she refused and now it's all the rage! And so you see," she would continue, in case someone had failed to see the point, "that I was simply ahead of my time." And then for further emphasis she would repeat the key facts of the story.

For many years she taught Italian at Hunter College and also gave private lessons to individuals. She had endless enthusiasm for teaching and formed lasting bonds with many of her students. The people wanting to learn Italian were generally an unusual lot, some of them opera singers who needed Italian for their careers. She got very involved and would happily tell anyone everything about the joys and vicissitudes of her students' lives and careers for as long as they were prepared to listen. The students, in turn, were enormously devoted to her.

I became closer to her after I got out of college and decided to work on my rudimentary Italian in order to try to go live and work in Italy for a period of time. She was a good teacher, and some of her more annoying qualities—her didactic tendency of repeating herself, explaining every point again and again—could be turned to good use in teaching a language. She knew the language extremely well and continued to express genuine wonder at the unorthodox behavior of Italian words of Greek derivation, even though she had explained it ten thousand times before. She had, after all, studied both ancient Greek and Latin in her Italian high school. She was an unabashed Italian chauvinist, considering it clearly the most beautiful and expressive language in the world. "You know the Italian language is very visual," she would say; "I think it's more visual than English. For example, in English, we say 'upside down,' whereas in Italian we say 'sotto-sopra,' downside up. If you think about it, what you see when you see something upside down is the underside, so the Italian describes what you actually see: the *downside up*." She was convinced that the best Italian was Tuscan dialect, spoken, however, with Roman pronunciation. "*Lingua toscana in bocca romana*" (the Tuscan tongue spoken by a Roman mouth), she would repeat over and over, which just happened to be what she spoke.

The hours and hours of Italian conversation helped me get to know her better, and I came to appreciate her virtues, in contrast to her more irritating or laughable faults. All her lessons took place in coffee shops or anywhere else other than her apartment, which she refused to let anyone enter since her mother's death many years earlier. As a result, she led an itinerant life, moving around the city with a series of shopping bags, looking like a homeless person. The one other person who had been inside her apartment was my father, who had a key in case of emergency. Although he avoided his sister's company, he was attached to her and became very agitated and worried when he couldn't reach her. She kept odd hours, often staying up late at night and sleeping late, and since she led this peripatetic existence during the day, she was often not around to receive or return phone calls. "That idiot! She's probably trotting around the city like a fool, completely unaware of what she's doing! Of course it never occurs to her to call—that would be too sensible! But, frankly, I'm getting a little worried. I haven't heard from her in four days. Idiot! Do you think she might be sick?" Once, when this happened, he took the unprecedented step of taking her key and going over to the apartment to see if she was there. He came back utterly and uncharacteristically silent and pale as chalk. All he could do was repeat things like "It's unbeliev-able. It's unbelievable. It's a nightmare, a nightmare." He sounded like Mr. Kurtz at the end of *Heart of Darkness*, repeating "the horror, the hor-ror." To shock my father, the messiest person I had ever met, with the state of an apartment was something quite extraordinary, and so we knew that whatever was going on in Lally's apartment must have been pretty awful. After this, my father, when he became exasperated with her, would mention the apartment. "Why don't you, instead of going on and on about this nonsense, clean up that apartment of yours! Unbeliev-able. You live like an animal!" She would take it with good nature and titter a nervous laugh. When we met, I began to suggest that she let us help clean up her apartment. She would always agree in principle but de-lay and avoid. "Yes, but I need to do some preparation beforehand. Then perhaps we can do it."

Normally meek and mild-mannered, she could become stubborn and even surprisingly fierce when pressed about her apartment, suddenly rais-ing her voice and showing her fangs. But in 1989, she was diagnosed with cancer and the moment to do something about the apartment arrived.

Getting her to a doctor was already a major concession. As best as we could figure out, she hadn't been to a doctor in about forty years—following in the Kamenetzki tradition that a person cannot be sick if she or he does not see a doctor. But after a week of vaginal bleeding, which at the age of sixty-seven she recognized as being abnormal, she agreed, at the urging of a friend, to see a doctor. She was diagnosed with a tumor in her uterus.

Living in the specter of a major operation, she suddenly became rather docile and we decided to push her on cleaning up the apartment. I worked hard to convince her, arguing that it was a very bad idea for her to recuperate in a dirty apartment that no one else could enter. Although I genuinely believed this, I confess that I had an ulterior motive: laying my hands on the D'Annunzio letter and the other family documents. My father had to call from Milan (where he was working at the time) to con-vince her, and she finally agreed—on the condition that only I and my girlfriend, Sarah, to whom she had also taught Italian, handle the cleanup and that she be spared the shame of having my mother see her apartment.

She tried to cancel our visit at the last moment, offering vague pretexts for delay, but we arrived dressed in our most worn jeans and with a carful of garbage bags, mops, brooms, cleaning liquids and sprays, rags and paper towels. I was worried that when we arrived she might have fled or would decide not to let us in.

We rang Lally's doorbell, and after a long delay the front door opened slowly, giving us a first glimpse of the apartment. As in many old Upper West Side apartments, there was a long corridor leading in from the entryway. The corridor itself was filled with trash and paper—not piles of trash, but a high, compact wall of trash that was several feet tall and a couple of feet wide, filling more than half the corridor and reaching all the way to the front door, making it impossible to open the door fully and difficult to pass along the corridor. We determined not to make any comments about the mess so as not to discourage Lally, but the apartment was well beyond what I had imagined or could have imagined. What had been a fairly large apartment had become a series of corridors or passageways through walls of junk, a labyrinthine maze leading from room to room.

The various walls of trash were composed of different materials: books, magazines, pieces of furniture, cardboard boxes, plastic bags, articles of clothing, mail, napkins, old lottery tickets, household objects, all mixed together rising in piles up above the head and sometimes almost to the ceiling. (How did such a short woman get this stuff up there? I wondered.) These walls reminded me of something organic, like the nests of magpies or mice, who will use any sort of found material to make their homes. At the same time, the walls were all-encompassing, almost as if she had set about burrowing for herself a set of tunnels and we had entered into some kind of science fiction movie: *The World of the Mole People*.

Although it was an intensely physical, material environment—it was, after all, nothing but stuff: objects, dirt, grime, endless scraps of yellowing paper—it almost didn't seem like a real place. The wild extravagance of the mess, mess on a scale that I had never seen or even imagined, had something mythic about it, like the Augean stables that were among the labors of Hercules. It seemed as much a metaphor as a place, a vision of life spun totally out of control: the final scene of an episode of *The Twilight Zone*, in which a character who tries to keep everything in her life is finally crushed under the accumulation of stuff.

It was not really an apartment, since virtually none of the rooms performed the functions for which they had been intended—there was no table visible at which to eat in the dining room; there were no couches or chairs to sit on in the living room, no beds that could be used to sleep in either of the bedrooms. Everything had been engulfed by these mountainous piles of junk.

I felt in crossing the threshold that rather than entering my aunt's apartment I had unwittingly entered into the dark, claustrophobic interior of my aunt's mind, and it was the mind of madness.

There was no functioning closet, no open space or even a clear surface onto which Sarah and I could put our coats. We eventually put them on top of a kitchen cabinet, the only free space we could find. The kitchen was filthy and had no floor, just an unwashed slab of concrete and an ancient rolled-up strip of ugly brown linoleum that she had bought once with the idea of covering the floor. But a decade or two later, the heavy roll of linoleum still sat there, like an incomplete thought, growing curled and brittle and discolored at the edges. Sarah began to work on the kitchen and told me to keep Lally busy out in the dining room—ironically named, since in all likelihood no one had actually ever been able to eat a sit-down meal there during the Kamenetzkis' tenure in the apartment.

All the cleaning materials we had brought would clearly be of no use for several days or possibly weeks, since we could not see the floor, let alone clean it. The only thing to do was to get out the garbage bags and begin throwing things out. I had decided to simply start with what was plainly rubbish before getting into any arguments with Lally about what belongings should be kept or thrown out. And there was enough rubbish to keep us busy for several days. The place had not been cleaned or painted in twenty years and there was a layer of soot, dirt, and grime on everything. My hands became black in five minutes. But, fortunately for us, there was virtually no wet garbage, just an endless supply of every other sort: crumbled old copies of *The New York Times*, years of junk mail, years of Christmas boxes, paper, and ribbons, knitting magazines, countless travel brochures of trips not taken. There were literally a couple of thousand lottery tickets strewn everywhere, like confetti through the ruins. This was part of my aunt's mad, unreasonable optimism: believing that, in the midst of her squalor, she was always a ticket away from the multimillion-dollar jackpot.

As I went through the piles of stuff, I began to perceive a logic of sorts. The apartment was like an archeological dig whose pattern I gradually began to grasp. The most recent piles—her coat, the clothing she wore last week, the books she needed for work—were stored on top, by the front door. As we gradually dug through the piles, we could actually date them. Here was Christmas 1988, the presents we gave her carefully put back in their boxes, the wrapping paper and ribbons not far away. Two feet farther down, Christmas 1987. There was probably every electricity and phone bill she had received and paid over twenty years, not together in a pile but wherever she happened to put them down when she paid them, so that often the layers of the archeological dig could be dated by months as well as years. Just as the size of the rings of a tree can tell you about specific years in the tree's life (whether it was a dry or a wet year), the number of feet between years in Lally's piles could tell us something about whether they had been particularly busy years. Because she had literally not thrown anything out, you could document her whole life: sometimes day by day and week by week. Here was the receipt for $2.15 from the Korean fruit stand. Nearby, a brochure for a trip to Russia she thought about taking that same week. It was a record of comic-tragic futility. I would find an extension cord inside its original paper bag. And then, six or ten inches farther down, I would find another, identical extension cord in an identical paper bag. She obviously had decided she needed an extension cord for something, had gone out and bought one, and then lost it under the accumulation of junk. Went out and bought another one. Then it, too, was buried in the rubble. As I saw these futile repetitions, my aunt's life appeared like the tale of Sisyphus in a minor key. Instead of pushing the boulder up the hill over and over, my aunt was out shopping for the same extension cord or lightbulb over and over again.

In some ways, the state of the apartment was a bit like her conversation. In the piles of stuff, her most precious things were mingled hopelessly with junk of no possible interest, just as in her conversation, remarks of genuine interest were lost amid streams of trivial chatter. In both areas, she was strangely lacking in a sense of proportion, of being able to tell the forest from the trees, the difference between a useless object or an entirely unnecessary explanation and something truly important.

Along with throwing out nothing that she had ever received, my aunt clearly had a series of scavenging habits. When she would go to a coffee shop she would leave with twenty paper napkins, ten plastic forks, and fifteen plastic knives, but instead of being used they would simply pile up in the dining room or some other room and then be engulfed by the mess, never to be found again. When I would start to throw them away she would protest weakly, "But I might need them." And I would say, "Lally, two hundred plastic forks should be enough!" She would go into a Korean grocery that had these large rolls of plastic bags for you to put your fruit or vegetables in. She would walk home with a thick role of five hundred bags. After all, at the supermarket you could pay several dollars for plastic bags, she thought, and here they are giving them away for free!

At a certain point, to keep her from kibitzing over what I was throwing out, I gave her the task of going through a particular pile of trash and dividing it into things to keep and things to get rid of. Occasionally, I would look and see her dithering, picking up this or that object or piece of junk mail, inspecting it for several minutes, turning it over and looking at it again, and then putting it back where she had found it. I realized that she was totally paralyzed. She literally couldn't bring herself to throw away anything. Finally, I sent her out for coffee, to get her out of our hair, to give her something semi-useful to do, and to allow us to keep moving.

After she left, I broke out laughing when I found no fewer than two hundred programs from a Paul Klee exhibition at the Museum of Modern Art from, let's say, 1977. Not one, not five, not ten—two hundred. This explained exactly how she could accumulate so much junk over a lifetime. She obviously had gone to the show, liked the program with the Klee design on it, and walked home with a thick stack of them. After all, she probably thought, they were free and maybe she would give them to friends. Naturally, they simply ended up under another pile with the plastic bags, the plastic forks, the lottery tickets, the ancient utility bills, and the extension cords.

With her out of the room, we began to inspect the rest of the apartment a bit more. The two bedrooms in the back were totally uninhabitable. Beds, after all, were great flat surfaces for putting stuff on, and soon the piles had grown and taken over the room, leaving just enough for passageways around the edges for one to maneuver around in. Lally slept instead on a filthy cot in the living room without sheets, on top of a blackened, unwashed bedcover, no blankets. And even the cot was not free of stuff. Part of the cot was strewn with books, clothes, and even a couple of warped vinyl LP records that evidently spent the night there as she slept nearby.

The cot was in one corner of the living room, the great bulk of which was taken up by an enormous mountain of wool. This was perhaps my aunt's masterpiece, an entire room, the largest room in the house, filled with spool upon spool of knitting yarn stacked ten by fifteen feet across and several feet high. My aunt liked to knit, and it would not be an exaggeration to say that she had accumulated hundreds if not thousands of balls of yarn. I can imagine that whenever she saw wool on sale for cheap at some street fair she could not resist the temptation to add to her collection. The mountain of wool was not just a random pile. It involved a certain amount of construction work. It had foundation walls made up, appropriately, of an Italian knitting magazine, which was a supplement to the Italian women's magazine *Amica* (Friend), which was published by the same company as my father's paper and which my aunt insisted he get for her along with his usual packet of Italian papers and magazines. (Although normally mild-mannered, my aunt was surprisingly adamant and fierce in defending what she considered her prerogatives. Once she had fixated on something, she would never let it slide: "Do you have my *Amica*?" she would telephone my father to ask. "I'm coming over to get it." And so she would wait for a crosstown bus in all kinds of weather to fetch a knitting magazine to add to a huge pile of knitting magazines for knitting projects that were almost never finished. Instead of throwing them out, as wisdom would have counseled, my father put them aside as my aunt requested, even though he of all people could have suspected that we would find them, every last issue, in her apartment one day. Similarly, when he became the editor in chief of the *Corriere della Sera*, he had imprudently given in to Lally's pleas that she receive a subscription to the paper sent each day to her door via airmail (something that would normally cost thousands of dollars a year). Two years later, here were several hundred of them, almost all still in their cellophane bags, stacked up like sandbags in a World War I trench, together with the *Amica* knitting magazines, to fortify the walls of my aunt's mad fort.

Much of the yarn was still in the plastic bags in which she had probably bought it. The mountain of wool was for me the symbol of my aunt's folly, a kind of monument to her special brand of insanity. Within it were some abandoned knitting projects, a sleeve here, a sleeve there, long separated from the balls of wool needed to finish them, like fragments of a ruined statue. You could see that some of them had been partially devoured by mice that had many lunches and dinners there. My aunt was

deeply resistant to throwing away any yarn, but I put my foot down and
told her she could go through and keep exactly twenty bags of wool of
her choice, no more. She naturally was unable to make a choice, and so
this method was abandoned as I began throwing it all out en masse. After
hours of throwing away bags of wool, I began to spot the outlines of a
bicycle handlebar. And, bag by bag, the bicycle emerged. "Oh, that's my
bicycle," Lally said quite matter-of-factly, as if it was only natural that
there should be a bicycle under a mountain of wool. Then other treasures
emerged: a chair, a table, a sofa—the remains of a living room. Eventually, it became clear that my grandparents' entire living room set, including many things they had dragged from Russia to Italy and from Italy to
New York, was all there waiting to be liberated.

In the yarn, of course, we saw many signs that my aunt had not been
living alone, but was sharing the apartment with many families of mice.
There were chewed-up balls of wool, gnawed-away sleeves of unfinished
sweaters. Everywhere there was a light sprinkling of dead insects, cock-
roach corpses, and mouse droppings. Lally seemed to notice this for the
first time and to express great surprise that she had so much company in
her midst. She remained skeptical about the presence of mice even after
I showed her the mouse excrement, but finally conceded the point when I
found a partially decomposed mouse cadaver.

In some ways, the most disturbing revelation, however, was the bathroom, which was filthy with broken tiles on the floor and walls, chipped
paint, a stopped-up sink, and a bathtub that had turned almost black.

Seeing the bathroom, I thought of an incident that had occurred a
couple of years earlier, after Sarah had moved into my apartment. She
began taking Italian lessons with my aunt and became quite fond of her.
"We should have your aunt over more often. I don't know why you keep
saying that she's crazy. She's charming!" "Okay, fine, you'll see," I said.
So, one evening when we had my aunt over for dinner, Sarah suddenly
stopped and said, "I smell something funny," sniffing audibly. "I wonder
what it could be; it smells kind of like an overripe, stinky French cheese,"
she said, twitching her nose like a bunny. We were sitting around our
dinner table. "Actually, it smells a little worse than an overripe cheese—do
you think we could have a dead mouse in the apartment?" she said to me,
getting up from the table to check in the kitchen. And then after she sat
back down and continued her efforts to identify the source of the noxious
smell, I saw a look of recognition cross her face as she realized that the

"overripe French cheese" was none other than my aunt. She stopped sniffing, fell silent for a moment, and then changed the subject. My aunt sat there throughout, entirely and happily oblivious as far as I could tell, chatting amiably about her usual set of favorite topics.

After we had been in the apartment for a few hours, my aunt seemed to get used to our presence and was even happy to have us there. The taboo—the strict prohibition on letting anyone into the apartment and sharing her shameful secret—had been broken and nothing terrible had happened. Her situation, the strict ban against anyone crossing her threshold, reminded me of the wonderful Buñuel movie *The Exterminating Angel*, in which the guests at a fancy Madrid party are, for some mysterious reason, simply unable to leave; even though there is nothing and no one blocking the doors, some invisible force, a kind of inner paralysis, prevents them from passing through the living room doorway. Something—I forget what—eventually happens to break the spell, and they all file home. The spell worked in reverse in my aunt's case, but it had now been broken and nothing had happened. In fact, by mid-afternoon, my aunt, incredibly, relented and allowed my mother to come over. We had spoken to her several times by phone; she had been following the proceedings of the day with consuming interest and was champing at the bit to join us.

This was a job that my mother had been waiting her whole life to tackle. She was, after all, Mrs. Clean, the woman who loved order and created beautiful spaces and who could not tolerate clutter and would not rest until things were set straight. This represented the opportunity for a stunning and unexpected victory to turn the tide in a war she had been waging with immense difficulty for most of her life. She had been fighting against the Kamenetzki disease in my father for her entire marriage but had been held in check by my father's ferocity and greater power. My father would go berserk when she started trimming away at the edge of his piles of newspapers, and she would never have dared to try a wholesale cleaning. To be free to attack the Kamenetzki mess, with no holds barred, to throw out piles of stuff en masse, filling dozens, scores of garbage bags with useless objects, to scrub things clean to the very floor, with no angry Misha to step in and intercede, must have been like a kind of liberation after forty years of pent-up frustration. The Bauhaus finally got to take over the Kamenetzki *haus*. And this was not just any mess, or any Kamenetzki mess, it was *the* original Kamenetzki, the ur mess, the ancestral

Kamenetzki mess from which were descended all others against which she had been battling hopelessly. My mother now stood ready to do battle, her bright, clean holy sword raised at the ready, like the warrior Archangel Michael, who is often depicted as crushing Satan by standing on the neck of his prostrate body. My aunt understood instinctively that my mother was the most powerful enemy of her current lifestyle and thus had given strict orders that she should not be allowed to accompany us on our cleaning mission. But now that the gates of the citadel had been breached, there was no keeping the Archangel Michael out. With no fuss, my aunt agreed to let my mother come over. Perhaps she, too, was experiencing a sense of relief and liberation. She had given up her dark secret and the world hadn't ended and perhaps we might actually free her from what must have been a long, long nightmare, in which she was at risk quite literally of being crushed and evicted from her apartment because of the accumulation of a lifetime of stuff. Perhaps we could free her of this heavy, heavy burden and give her back her apartment. She knew that my mother was the person to complete the job.

I don't think that my aunt suspected the powerful passion that animated my mother's desire to take over the cleanup. My aunt's apartment was the physical manifestation of everything my mother could not stand about my father and his family: she came from and aspired to a world of light, order, and progress—the New Deal. This mess was the expression of a world of darkness, despair, and irrational pain, the fearful holding on to everything as a bulwark against everything that was lost. It was decidedly Old Deal, the detritus of a family, the first wave of stateless citizens who had crossed the major tragedies of twentieth-century Europe: the Bolshevik Revolution, the Fascist revolution, the racial laws, World War II. This apartment was its terminus, the storage depot at the end of the line. To my mother it was literally incomprehensible that my aunt could look at a faded old travel brochure for a place she had never been or a moth-eaten article of clothing that was not even fit for the Salvation Army and yet still not be sure whether to keep it or throw it out. As my mother surveyed the disaster of my aunt's apartment, she turned to Sarah, who shared my mother's neat and orderly habits (as well as her Wasp background), and said, "I wouldn't blame you if you decided to opt out of this gene pool."

While also being horrified by my aunt's habits, I understood them, having the Kamenetzki disease inside me—albeit to a much lesser degree. This mess, while beyond my imagining, was yet oddly and entirely familiar. My father was cut from the same cloth as my aunt and might very well have ended up in an apartment like this, had he not been successful and prosperous enough to afford a cleaning lady and sane enough to have married someone who would keep his worst tendencies in check. I was much better, but the instincts were the same. I felt the same twinge of regret and loss when getting rid of some object or paper, no matter how useless, to which memory clung. Papers would pile up on my desk until I could no longer see its surface. Mail piled up until I realized that I had lost an important check, and then I would engage in a furious search and purge. Books piled up on my bedside table and filled up my shelves until they were squeezed in sideways and looked as if they might all come tumbling down into the middle of the room. Art filled my walls, leaving almost none of the open, blank spaces that most people find restful. I realized that I had my father's same *horror vacui*—the fear of clear and empty space—and somehow felt comforted to be quite literally surrounded and embraced by familiar stuff.

For all its madness, the Kamenetzki mess was still an intensely human expression, what Yeats called "the foul rag and bone shop of the heart." I suspected that in that chaos, among the expired lottery tickets, the old bills, the yellowing letters, the scraps of old clothing, the grime-stained souvenirs, in the nature of the disorder itself, the neglect and clinging nostalgia, were the secrets and the essence of a world of pain: the terror of revolution and war; the heartbreak and loss of exile; the persistent memories of faces and houses and landscapes never seen again; the insecurity of a marginal, guest people always fitting in and yet always on the brink of expulsion; the cunning and self-hatred of dissimulation; the small triumphs and fatigue of remaking a life and the fear of losing everything; fleeting joys against a background of oblivion and annihilation; the shame of being branded as a despised, hunted race. Perhaps in that maelstrom lay the sources of much in my father's difficult character: his fits of rage, his fear of change, his driving ambition and neurotic paralysis, his fear and suspicions, his deep reluctance to speak of himself or the past; the variables in the complex equation—a long string of gains and losses—of a man who reinvented himself, who left behind this mess and this household and its world of pain, denying his parents and his origins, only to create a new and more successful life but with its own mess and his own pain.

That first day, we concentrated primarily on the dining room, and after working for several hours and filling no fewer than sixty large plastic garbage bags (the kind you use to collect leaves in the fall), we had cleared the floor of one-third of one room. As I lugged the sixty garbage bags down to the street and saw that we had barely scratched the surface, we realized that the magnitude of the job was beyond our physical resources. For starters, the New York sanitation department simply refused to take away sixty garbage bags a day, and so we were forced to actually rent a private hauling company and a Dumpster, a huge receptacle almost the size of a railroad car that sat in my aunt's street for nearly a month as stuff was carted from her apartment. My aunt was in the hospital for only a day or two, but my mother made the command decision that Lally should be sent to recuperate in a hotel in Midtown Manhattan, the San Carlos, paid for by my parents, while the cleanup continued. And so my aunt sat in this hotel watching TV and reading while my mother and her work crew set about taking apart and putting back together the apartment.

Although my mother had been spoiling for this fight for forty years, the monumental nature of the Kamenetzki mess nearly undid her. The project brought out both the best and the worst in her. On the one hand, it was an act of extraordinary generosity in which she was almost literally saving my aunt's life and performing the most thankless of tasks. (My aunt's toilet had to be cleaned at least ten times because the dirt and stains were so deep and encrusted that they simply would not come off.) At the same time, a tidal wave of anger and resentment, built up over nearly forty years of cleaning up my father's messes, came spilling out in fits of invective and rage. After the first couple of days, I returned to my work and left my mother in charge, stopping by only occasionally in the coming days and weeks. Mom had turned into a kind of Jekyll and Hyde: by day she was performing her saintly task cleaning the apartment, and by night, fueled by three or four vodkas, she was ranting and raving about my aunt, saying she wanted to put her in a nursing home and throw out all her belongings. Unfortunately, I wasn't seeing Mom's good works during the day but would get the phone calls in the evening with long, rambling, vindictive monologues, alternately asking for sympathy and threatening some drastic solution to the Lally problem. "We can't clean that apartment. All the stuff is ruined. I'm just going to have them take it all away." At one point, my mother even wanted to arrange with Lally's landlady to have Lally moved into a smaller apartment.

She had every reason to be angry, particularly at my father, who had dumped this project on her by refusing to deal with it over the past twenty years while it got worse and worse. But she was taking it out on Lally, who was, if nothing else, a pathetic and disturbed creature. "I find that entire family disgusting. Their whole way of life." Every morning my phone would wake me, my father on the line from Italy. "You've got to keep *la mama* from doing something drastic. She's furious. I don't blame her. But I'm counting on you to reason with her."

Eventually my mother agreed to hire some professional help with the cleanup. Even though she was often justified, her surprising mean-spiritedness in the whole business offended me and I began to chew her out. "Mom, your problem is that you're not content with being right; you insist on telling everyone you're right and demanding that they acknowledge that you're right. You are doing something very nice for Lally, but you also want to somehow triumph over her, liquidate her and force her to acknowledge your absolute superiority and her own unworthiness." Unable to get satisfaction from me and my father, Mom, in her tipsy, soggy dinners, eating baked potatoes and drinking vodka on lonely evenings after exhausting days of cleaning Lally's mouse-infested apartment, would phone anyone who would listen to her—my sister in California, my aunt and uncle in Chicago, my aunt in Wisconsin.

Gradually, the Kamenetzki cleanup became a national issue. "Aunt Lyndy has offered to come to New York and help me with the apartment," my mother proudly announced, referring to her brother's wife in Chicago. "Mom, I don't think Aunt Lyndy is going to appreciate the refugee aesthetic." Nonetheless, Aunt Lyndy did come and was soon followed by Aunt Ginny (my mother's sister) from Wisconsin. They no doubt wanted to help my mother in a moment of need, although they were also curious to see for themselves whether the Rabelaisian chaos on Seventy-Fourth Street was really as wild as in my mother's descriptions. This apartment had begun to take on mythic proportions, acquiring fame across the clean Formica kitchens of the Midwest. My mother and my aunts worked like Trojans, getting down on their knees and scrubbing the kitchen cabinets, unspeakably filthy with twenty years of accumulated grime that seemed to have eaten into the very metal.

Toward the end, Lucy, too, and her husband came from Los Angeles to give my mother some moral support. (But because the filth of the apartment represented a health hazard to their newborn son, they had to keep their distance from the cleanup site.)

As the cleanup project evolved into a heroic collective effort, which involved about a dozen different people at one point or another, it began to seem possible that the apartment might be restored to a condition of decent livability, and my mother began to thrive on the project. She loved the camaraderie with her sister and sister-in-law, as well as getting to know the members of her work crew, which included an out-of-work actor and a British would-be punk rocker. The rescue team from the Midwest must have also provided a kind of vindication of her basic worldview— the triumph of the good, decent people with whom she grew up over the folly and chaos of the Kamenetzkis.

When it was done, the transformation of the apartment was nothing short of miraculous. It looked like a normal apartment, a quite large, generously proportioned apartment with clean white walls and some reasonably attractive furniture. Despite her threats to throw everything away, my mother managed to preserve and refurbish most of Lally's and my grandparents' furniture. Now that they were cleaned off and placed in a light, clean apartment, one could finally see that my grandparents actually had some rather nice things. So as not to disorient Lally too much, my mother managed to surround her with a number of familiar objects: pictures, photographs, wall hangings that had been buried and covered with dirt for years. Rather than feeling that someone had simply come in and thrown out all her stuff, she would suddenly see a number of long-lost old friends.

The day we took Lally to see the apartment for the first time, we brought coffee and fresh croissants, orange juice and fruit, and we had brunch in the "new" apartment.

We were worried about how Lally would react. I was worried that Lally was going to complain about something that she couldn't find, and my mother was going to let her have it. But fortunately both were on good behavior. Lally seemed stunned and pleasantly surprised to rediscover the pieces of a former life, some of which had accompanied the Kamenetzkis from Italy and even Russia.

We asked Lally about many of the pieces of furniture and their origins. Occasionally, she expressed alarm over things she could not find—a wooden bowl that her mother had brought from Moscow. "Every Russian home has one of these wooden bowls. It's a tradition. And when

Mother and Father left Russia she carried this bowl on her lap instead of Misha. Father wanted her to try to bring jewels and other valuables, but all she cared about was this bowl." Luckily the bowl turned up.

Now, in the cleaned-up apartment with her family around, Lally enjoyed a moment of celebrity, queen for a day. She was the center of attention and regaled us with some of her favorite stories of her youth.

And when we left I had a suitcase full of papers that my aunt Ginny from Wisconsin had come upon in the course of the massive cleanup. There I found the mysterious D'Annunzio letter, as well as a thick trove of Kamenetzki family documents, which I then xeroxed and returned.

The Documents in the Suitcase

I. THE BEAU BRUMMELL OF BYELORUSSIA

Inside the Kamenetzkis' battered brown suitcase there was an old black-and-white photograph of a dapper young man wearing a fine tailored suit, a tall, stiff collar reaching up almost to his chin, held perfectly in place with an elegant tie pin. He wears a handsome vest and a sumptuous-looking tie, and a patterned handkerchief points up from his breast pocket. He has a pince-nez and holds a gentleman's walking stick in one hand and a fashionable hat in the other. At the bottom is the name of a photographic studio in Cyrillic script and the name of the city of Vilna, the capital of Lithuania, a major center of Jewish life in Eastern Europe. It is, improbably enough, my grandfather, the future dentist, Ilya Kamenetzki, of West End Avenue, as the picture of elegance, a Jewish dandy, a Byelorussian Beau Brummell.

The origins of my father's family are shrouded in mist and family legend. Unlike my mother's family genealogy, which can be traced back to the first settlers of America in the seventeenth century, most Jewish family stories don't go back much further than the first relative to leave Europe and come to the United States. (Elderly grandparents, having left lives of hardship and persecution, are often evasive about places and dates, referring to the "old country, "over there," or saying "You don't want to know.") Before that, they rely on unreliable family lore. In the case of the Kamenetzkis, I have only the family stories passed on through my aunt. In these tales, our ancestors sound more like characters from the Yiddish literature of Sholem Aleichem or Isaac Bashevis Singer than like historical figures.

According to my aunt, my grandfather's father was an orphan but was an extremely pious and learned man, the most brilliant Torah scholar in the town of Mir, on the border between Russia and Poland in what is now Belarus. In the Jewish tradition, it is a great honor to be connected to a scholar of the Torah even if he is poor, and so the richest man of the town married his daughter to him. As a result my grandfather grew up in a position of considerable wealth, albeit as part of a threatened and barely tolerated minority living in the "Pale of Settlement," the area in western Russia where Jews were authorized to live by the czar, but which were also frequent targets of pogroms. My father said that his father had witnessed pogroms as a young man.

My grandfather, the young Beau Brummell with the pince-nez and walking stick, was something of the black sheep of his otherwise respectable and well-to-do family. His older brothers had distinguished careers, one of them growing up to be a well-known economist who taught in Paris. Although his father, Israel Kamenetzki, was a religious and scholarly man—according to my aunt, the animating spirit of the Mir Yeshiva—my grandfather, the spoiled youngest child of a doting mother, neglected his studies. When he graduated from high school, his parents gave him a trip to Amsterdam as a reward. He quickly ran through the money he had been given after taking up with a dancer. He wired his family for more money, saying he needed it to come home. Instead, he followed the dancer to America—a bold and long voyage for a boy of eighteen from a small town in Byelorussia. After that money also ran out—and he and the dancer had parted company—this highly impractical ne'er-do-well did something eminently practical: he got a job as a dental technician and set about training to become a dentist. At a time in which the United States enjoyed a huge technological edge over Europe in dentistry, as in many other fields, my grandfather acquired a highly valuable set of skills.

After a couple of years in America, at about the age of twenty he returned to Russia to perform his obligatory year of military service. He went to dental school in Warsaw in 1909 and 1910. But after getting his degree, according to my aunt, he didn't practice dentistry for several years. "He traveled all around Europe and never seemed to lack for money—he must have gotten it from his parents," my aunt says. The photograph of him as a young dandy must date from this period in which he was a wealthy young man without fixed occupation.

At the time my grandparents met, my grandfather had worked himself into a position of some importance, heading up the department of dentistry and oral plastic surgery at a hospital in Moscow, repairing the jaws of Russian soldiers whose faces had been blown up by shrapnel in the trenches of World War I. The war was going badly, the czar had stepped down, and the Bolsheviks were preparing to take over.

2. THE KING OF MOLASSES

My grandparents could not have been more different. While my grandfather was from a shtetl, where he grew up speaking more Yiddish than Russian, my grandmother was part of the small cosmopolitan Jewish elite that was allowed to live in Moscow. Officially, Jews were forbidden to live in either Moscow or Saint Petersburg, but some, by special dispensation of the czar, were exempted. My grandmother's father supposedly ran the molasses industry of czarist Russia and was known as the King of Molasses. He had several factories for refining molasses, which in the early twentieth century was the principal sweetener for foods, as well as a key ingredient for making rum and other alcoholic beverages.

Of course, before coming to Moscow, the family had originally lived in the Ukraine, in the Pale of Settlement. According to my aunt, my great-great-grandfather was a poor itinerant peddler who was extremely shrewd; in his travels, he starting buying up land. Family lore has it that while he could not read or write, he was a whiz with an abacus, which accompanied him everywhere. One day, he saw a very pretty girl tending a goat and decided to marry her. He kept selling and buying land until he became enormously wealthy. His son, Moses Altschuler, went to university and studied law but, to his great disappointment, was not able to practice because of the restrictions in Russia barring Jews from the professions. He went into business instead, and it was he who started or bought up all the molasses refineries, making himself into the King of Molasses. He also moved the family from the Ukraine to Moscow, somehow getting around the law banning Jews from the capital. "With enough money, anything was possible," my aunt said.

My grandmother grew up in a large town house full of servants. She and her sisters and brother were raised speaking French and German as fluently as Russian. And, although only a couple of generations removed from the shtetl, they spoke no Yiddish and did not engage in traditional religious practices. They skied in the Ural Mountains and took the mineral baths at Karlsbad, Austro-Hungary. My aunt tells a story about how her grandmother (my grandmother's mother) had gone to a Karlsbad spa with her eldest daughter; when the daughter lost a ball in the gardens of the bath complex, a kindly older man with a large white handlebar mustache retrieved it and brought it back to her. He struck up a conversation with my great-grandmother and complimented her on her excellent German. For a week, they saw each other every day in the afternoons at the gardens. (It sounds a bit like Chekhov's "The Lady and the Lapdog.") When the old man failed to show up one day, another guest explained to my great-grandmother that the man with the large mustache was none other than Emperor Franz Josef of Austria. To be a Russian Jewish woman whose excellent German and good looks had impressed the emperor of Austria must have been a great satisfaction—since the story had obviously been told over and over and repeated many times to my aunt, who, in turn, repeated it to me.

My grandmother was highly cultivated, loved Pushkin, Turgenev, Gogol, and Tolstoy, and was a passionate fan of Stanislavski's theater, where she saw the original productions of Chekhov's plays. She loved classical music, and my aunt tells a story about my grandmother as a young girl being so moved by a concert that she rushed out to buy a huge bouquet of roses for the pianist, Ferruccio Busoni, at intermission and brought it to him backstage, where he pinched her shy, blushing cheek.

"But her real passion was literature," my aunt, who adored and idolized her mother, went on. She attended performances of the two great actresses of the early twentieth century, Sarah Bernhardt and Eleonora Duse, at a time when the theatergoers of Europe were ferociously divided between proponents of the French Bernhardt and supporters of the Italian Duse. My grandmother had the rare privilege of seeing the two rivals perform the same role in the same play (*La Dame aux Camélias*, recalled my aunt, who remembered everything: "by Dumas, performed in French"). "Mumi preferred La Duse [as she was known] but she later saw Bernhardt in another role in *L'Aiglon* by Rostand and said she was excellent," my aunt repeated. Her tone was full of obvious approval for her mother's fine, discriminating taste, preferring the slightly less famous Duse over the slightly more famous Bernhardt—"*troppo artificiale, la scuola francese*" (too artificial, the French school of acting), my aunt said with a hint of Italian chauvinism—as well as her sense of fairness in acknowledging Bernhardt's brilliance in another play. At the time, the followers of one diva almost always felt the obligation to denigrate the acting style of the other.

The Molasses King must have been fairly progressive, since he sent most of his six daughters to university at a time when educating women was almost universally considered a waste of money. In fact, Russian universities were closed to women at the turn of the twentieth century. Nonetheless, Moses Altschuler sent his eldest daughter, Rosa (my grandmother's sister), to Geneva, Switzerland, where she trained as a doctor. "Mama was in the first class of women to attend the University of Moscow," my aunt claimed. Although I don't have verification of this, the timing is about right. My grandmother was born in 1886 and would have been nineteen in 1905, when the universities finally opened up to women— one of many reforms that were granted in response to a series of strikes and protests, the so-called Revolution of 1905. Despite her love of art and literature, my grandmother majored in economics in order to help her father with his business, my aunt said.

Her favorite professor was Pavel Milyukov, who taught political science and was a leading light of liberal democratic thinking in prerevolutionary Russia. He was a brilliant linguist who spoke and read some fourteen different languages, facilitated by the fact that he was banned from Russia early in his career for his liberal political views and wandered about Europe and even the United States studying, publishing, and giving lectures in different languages. Milyukov was pushing for the idea of a constitutional democracy, in which the monarchy would be subordinate to parliament, the Duma. He founded what became known as the Kadet party, whose letters in Russian, "KDT," stood for the term "constitutional democracy." Milyukov was about a hundred years ahead of his time.

When her father died in 1914, my grandmother took over the molasses business and kept the factories going through World War I. But when the Bolsheviks came they expropriated the factories, and the family was ruined.

In the midst of this chaos, my highly cultivated grandmother met my shrewd and streetwise grandfather. "Under normal circumstances, they would never have married; they were too different," my aunt says. "They were thrown together by crisis." My grandfather by all accounts was extremely helpful to my grandmother as she tried to save the family from total ruin. He had access to food ration cards, knew how to get things on the black market, and understood which levers to pull to get a bureaucratic favor. "Father was at his best in a crisis," said my aunt. "He was bored by everyday life and created problems."

Apparently my grandmother's family distrusted and looked down on my grandfather, and questioned his motives. What could this dandy from the shtetl want with their serious-minded and cultivated Sara? Before the revolution, they might have suspected him of being a fortune hunter, courting a rather plain-looking heiress in her thirties sitting on a great fortune. But now that they were ruined economically, they suspected him of merely toying with her while having no intention of marrying. But they did marry. While my aunt maintains that they would never have married without the crisis of the revolution, she also insists there was another factor to their surprising union: *"Attrazione fisica."* Physical attraction. "My father fell in love with my mother."

From the few photographs to survive from their Russian days, they seem a rather unlikely couple. My grandmother, though in her early thirties, already looked plump and matronly. My grandfather, who, though no Adonis, considered himself quite a Don Juan, appears younger and more slender.

Along with having their factories expropriated, the Altschulers narrowly escaped being put on trial by the Bolsheviks for being capitalist exploiters of the proletariat. (According to my aunt, my grandmother's former servants came to her defense and insisted that she had always been kind and fair to them.) They were reduced to living in a room or two of their former town house, and my grandmother was the only member of the family able to get out before the years of Stalinist terror. My father was born in late 1919, and when my grandparents left Moscow in 1920, the White Army fighting the Bolsheviks was collapsing.

Getting out of Russia, now the Soviet Union—which was in pieces after World War I, and in the grip of a bloody civil war—was no simple matter. Luckily, my grandfather, unlike most Russians, had the right to leave by virtue of having suddenly become a citizen of Poland. The Treaty of Brest-Litovsk, which the Bolsheviks negotiated to extract Russia from World War I, made substantial territorial concessions that transferred

Byelorussia, where my grandfather had grown up, to Poland. But even so, it took about two years for them to physically make their way from Moscow to Wiesbaden, Germany, where my grandfather had a brother. Their trip was an epic voyage with constant stops and breakdowns through the snowy Russian countryside, with a thousand practical difficulties: scavenging for food; hiding jewels and money from police and customs officials. In 1921 a bad drought, combined with years of war, revolution, and the Bolsheviks' attempt to collectivize agriculture, led to a massive famine in which five million died. In the middle of the famine, my grandmother was pregnant for the second time. The family stopped in Riga in 1921 when my aunt Lally was born; although full-term, she was the size of a severely premature baby, weighing just a few pounds. The doctors thought she would not live but she pulled through, requiring a lot of special care. At his best in a crisis, my grandfather apparently worked wonders on the black market finding milk for the children and food for his family.

They were among the great wave of refugees fleeing Russia after the revolution, a humanitarian crisis that provoked an unprecedented international response. My grandmother Sara Altschuler became, from a bureaucratic point of view, one of the world's first displaced people. Rather than traveling with a Russian, Polish, Italian, or Latvian passport, she acquired something called a Nansen passport, a special kind of international passport for "stateless persons" that was created by the League of Nations, itself a fiction that was created in 1918. The Norwegian diplomat Fridtjof Nansen came up with the idea as a response to the mass exodus from the Soviet Union right after the Russian Revolution. Some 1.4 million Russians escaped the country after the Bolsheviks took power. Approximately 450,000 of these, among them my grandmother, received a Nansen passport, which was recognized as a valid legal document by fifty-two countries. The sudden concern for displaced people and refugees was part of the quixotic dream of the League of Nations, which, after the end of the War to End All Wars, was supposed to usher in an era of permanent peace. It all came apart with Fascism and World War II. Nansen and his office at the League of Nations were awarded the Nobel Peace Prize in 1938. Hitler invaded Poland the following year, and the Nansen passport is now a quaint memory of a handful of aged refugees.

3. THE REAL AND FICTIONAL LIFE OF JILIA KAMENETZKY, ELIA KAMENETSKY, ELIA KAMIENIECKI (ELJASZOWI KAMIENICKIEMU), ETC.

The family first settled in Naples, then moved to Formia (a town along the coast between Rome and Naples) because doctors told my grandfather that my aunt, who was somewhat sickly, would benefit from the sea air. And then they moved to Rome when my father was about twelve years old.

My grandfather was strangely and almost immediately at home in Italy. He quickly attained a kind of crude fluency in Italian, which (according to my aunt) never showed any signs of improvement over the next twenty years. The *hondling* (Yiddish for bargaining) of the market shtetl where he grew up seems to have prepared him well for the rough and tumble of life in Naples, known for its *arte dell'arrangiarsi*, the art of getting by. Having navigated through the Russian black market and the bureaucracies of both the czar and Lenin, he was very comfortable with the informal legal arrangements that tended to prevail in Italy. Because his Russian dental certificates were not immediately accepted in Italy, he practiced illegally through what the Italians call a *prestanome*, in this case another dentist who let my grandfather practice under his name in exchange for some financial consideration. My grandfather—litigious and strangely confident for a refugee working illegally in a country where he was not a citizen—broke at a certain point with the *prestanome*, who then promptly denounced my grandfather to the police. When a policeman arrived at my grandfather's office in Formia, he found sitting in the dentist's chair the daughter of one of Formia's leading Fascists, Pietro Fedele, who had been Mussolini's minister of education and was then a member of the Italian Senate. The policeman apologized profusely for his intrusion and left submissively.

From a series of documents it is evident that my grandfather quickly set about reinventing himself, manufacturing a new history in order to reinforce his fragile position in his new home country.

His papers testify to the constant bureaucratic hurdle-jumping that his life must have been and the considerable creativity he demonstrated in dealing with it. There is the documentation—in both Polish and Italian—of the dentistry school in Warsaw where he completed his formal training. There is the voluminous paperwork he amassed in order to obtain Italian citizenship, one of the great bureaucratic coups of his life. Italian law gave much fuller privileges to foreigners who had arrived on Italian soil before the year 1919. My grandfather came up with a brilliant device for getting around the fact that there was no record of his being in Italy before 1922. He began laying the groundwork by getting a dentist in Naples to state that my grandfather had worked for him as a dental technician in 1908 and 1909. The notarized statement ends with a beautiful phrase, *mansioni delicate* (delicate duties): "He always gave evidence of great ability in the application of his delicate duties."

Another document signed by the former Italian consul general of Fiume states that my grandfather had been living in Fiume between the years 1912 and 1914. Because this document dates from the 1930s, it seems likely that he was helping my grandfather backdate his history in order to build his case for citizenry by showing that he had been a de facto resident of Italy long before moving there in 1922. If he could show that he had been in Fiume, which was not part of Italy then but had been annexed by Fascism, thanks to D'Annunzio and Mussolini, it would strengthen his Italian pedigree and make his rather fanciful-sounding claim that he had been the dentist to D'Annunzio's legionnaires all the more convincing.

There is, of course, always the possibility that these documents or some portion of them are telling the truth. After all, there were these four or five years when he floated around Europe right before World War I; perhaps he had spent part of the time in Italy. Why, after all, did my grandfather choose to immigrate to Italy instead of America, where he had already lived and which was the preferred destination of most Russian immigrants?

According to my aunt and father, my grandfather had looked at the map of Europe and decided that Italy was the best country on the continent for Jews. But perhaps he had been to Naples (and even Fiume) before returning to Russia? However, the only solid evidence—a piece of paper in the yellowing files of the Italian police on which the Ministry of Interior in Naples marks the entry of "Kamenetzky, Jlya—Russian subject" on May 26, 1922—would indicate that the rest of his Italian biography was probably fictional.

The apotheosis of my grandfather's efforts to re-create his personal history was certainly the D'Annunzio letter, written in the large, gorgeous swirling handwriting of D'Annunzio, as excessive and colorful in its orthography as in its prose.

The letter read:

> As the extremely meritorious Doctor Elia Kamenetzky in this year of grace, 1933, eleventh of the new Era, with a decree of May 3 has been conferred with Italian citizenship, I am particularly happy and proud to be able to give him my personal testimony and renew to him my gratitude and that of my Fiume Legionnaires. Doctor Kamenetzky had already practiced the profession of dental technician in Italian Fiume in the years 1913 and 1914, as the Consul General of the Russian Empire Alessandro Salviati has testified. From the time of my entrance in Fiume, he continued to exercise his dental art in service of the citizens of Fiume and of my Legionnaires with a dedication and readiness that amounted to virtual self-abnegation.
>
> To the new Italian citizen, resident in Rome, confirming with a sense of human duty my personal witness, I wish him all the good fortune he merits for his soul and his knowledge.
>
> From il Vittoriale, October of Cattaro, January 29, 1933
>
> Gabriele D'Annunzio, (prince) of Montenevoso.

Thus my grandfather, a Jew from Byelorussia, not only became an Italian citizen but, along with Gabriele D'Annunzio and his legionnaires, joined the ranks of the patriots who had ushered in the new Fascist era through the exercise of "his dental art," which he had practiced "with a dedication and readiness that amounted to virtual self-abnegation."

My aunt for most of her life was convinced that my grandfather really had been in Fiume with D'Annunzio, largely because he spoke about it with seemingly genuine conviction. "He said he had been with D'Annunzio even before the taking of Fiume, when he flew over the city and dropped leaflets down on it," my aunt said. But, since my father was conceived and born in 1919, the year that D'Annunzio and his men took Fiume, and my aunt was born in Riga in August 1921, it is hard to see how my grandfather could have been physically present during the occupation of Fiume given the difficulties of getting in and out of the USSR at the time. And so D'Annunzio's testimony was almost certainly fraudulent. And yet it appears that my grandfather was something of a fabulist; although he may have come up with the D'Annunzio story for bureaucratic reasons, he enjoyed telling of his experiences with D'Annunzio as if they had really happened and may have gradually come to believe his own tall tales.

Because dentistry was taught at the university level in Italy but not in Poland, my grandfather was technically unqualified to teach it, but despite an official document rejecting his Polish qualifications, he somehow managed to get around the rules and land a position at the University of Rome.

Wily and creative, my grandfather managed to convince the Eastman Institute for Oral Health in Rochester, New York (a center for dental technology created by George Eastman, the founder of the Eastman Kodak company), to allow him to set up and serve as director of a Roman Eastman Institute.

Sometimes my grandfather's brash confidence got the better of him. At one point, he invented a new kind of artificial tooth that a big American company wanted to market. But Ilya drew out the negotiations too long, holding out for much more money, and ended up getting nothing. The company got fed up, decided to wait for the patent to expire, and then used his invention for free. "It was a terrible mistake," my aunt Lally explained, "because if he had a relationship with an American company it might have made it much easier to emigrate to the States when things got bad in Italy."

Nonetheless, he had a highly successful practice that included aristocrats, Fascist bigwigs, Soviet diplomats, and White Russians.

In Rome, my grandparents set themselves up in Via in Arcione, an attractive street just off Via del Tritone in a rather prosperous part of town near Piazza Barberini, with Bernini's Fountain of Triton in its middle. They had an apartment on a high floor, with a large terrace.

The move to Italy was much less easy for my grandmother. "Mumi had a kind of nervous breakdown after she got to Naples," Lally said. After marrying my grandfather in Russia, she had spent about a year and a half alone with two very small children in Germany, waiting for my grandfather to send for them. And when they got to Naples, she felt even more alone. Her husband had established his own life in Naples and was quite content living without family responsibilities. Once, in the middle of the night, my grandmother was awoken by my aunt, who had developed a high fever and needed to go to the hospital. My grandmother discovered that her husband had still not come home. He was out playing poker with his friends (or so he said). Who would look after my father while she rushed my aunt to the hospital? "She realized," my aunt explained, "that she had left everything in her life—her family, her country, her language—for a man she really didn't know very well and on whom she couldn't count. She had a kind of breakdown and spent about a year in bed. I think, although she didn't say this directly, that she felt she had made a big mistake in her marriage."

My grandmother's closest friend in Italy was, interestingly, not an Italian but a German, Caterina Zunke, the widow of an Italian husband and a neighbor of the Kamenetzkis in Naples. When the family moved to Naples and then to Rome, Zunke, who was known in the family as Zia Keti, moved with them, a permanent part of the household.

My grandparents had an active social life in Italy but led quite separate lives. "Father immediately felt at home in Italy," my aunt said. "It was the perfect country for him. He got to know people right away and was very interested in meeting the right people and entering high society in Rome, counts and countesses, senators and diplomats. Mumi never really liked Italy. She found all of that rather superficial and she remained very Russian. She became friendly with a lot of Russian artists who had ended up in Rome, many of them penniless. She would have an open house all day on Sunday with the samovar always hot, and serve food to whoever came. And all these poor Russian artists would come. It was probably one of their better meals for the week. Mumi would hold concerts and dance performances at the house and these performances became famous. They were written up in *Il Messaggero*, the Rome newspaper. They would use the dining room as the stage with the audience out on the terrace. People from nearby buildings and the street would try to watch."

If physical attraction had brought my grandparents together, as my aunt claims, it did not keep them together. My grandfather had a wandering eye and took up with various other women along the way. "Mumi said to him, 'You can do what you want, but you won't share my bed anymore,'" my aunt told me with a tone of admiration and approval. At a certain point, my grandfather had an affair with a Russian opera singer, whom my father and aunt used to mockingly call "Mazurka," because she would come bounding and pounding up the stairs to their apartment like someone doing the Polish dance. Her name was Paolina Novikova. She was, according to my aunt, the illegitimate daughter of a Jewish woman and a Russian nobleman. She adopted the aristocratic pretension of calling herself "Donna Paola." "This created confusion when she later moved to the U.S., where Donna is a woman's name," my aunt explained. "She was a quite brilliant and charming woman," my aunt grudgingly admitted. "And although she was far from pretty she had a success with men you wouldn't believe." Everyone in the household seemed to understand the situation between my grandfather and Mazurka, generating a lot of tension and conflict. Mazurka would generally bring her daughter, Sofia (known as Sofula), whom my grandfather would treat with special regard, something his children deeply resented. "Father used to always hold her up to us as a kind of paragon of virtue, while we knew she was a liar of the first order. Father used to favor her over us. When she wanted a tennis racket he bought her one but wouldn't buy them for Misha and me."

In a strange twist, my aunt ended up with a ring that my grandfather evidently gave Mazurka, commemorating a weekend of love they'd shared together in Florence. Perhaps Novikova had given it back when their affair ended. In any event, it remained among my grandfather's possessions at his death and my aunt, apparently unaware of the Oedipal implications, seemed quite happy to wear it as a kind of triumph over her detested rival. "In the end Father and Mazurka hated each other and she wanted to be Mumi's friend."

My grandmother had created a rather rich Russian life for herself in Rome, populated mainly by exiles of the Soviet revolution. She subscribed to the White Russian newspaper *Poslednye novosti* (Latest News), edited by her old teacher Milyukov, who had settled in Paris. My father recalled very fondly some of the Russian exiles who congregated in their house in Rome during his childhood.

"Rome was a much smaller town then, much poorer and with a very simple life," my father recalled. "There was only one nightclub, called Florida, it was on Via Francesco Crispi, rather near our house, just up from the Tritone toward the Hotel Hassler. People were standing outside to catch a glimpse of the ballerinas. People went to dance in some of the big hotels. In fact, these two good friends of ours, Pomerantz and Fabrickant, Jews from Eastern Europe, were the piano player and violinist in the orchestra at the Ambasciatori Hotel. They were very attached to our family, especially to my mother. There was also a group of furriers who knew my father and became friends of mine. They were very cultivated people, first-rate intellectuals, but to live they were in business as furriers."

During the 1930s, Milyukov's *Poslednye novosti* had extremely accurate reporting on the show trials that Stalin used to get rid of his rivals as he established absolute control over the Soviet Union. My grandmother lost all contact with her family back in Moscow. Once she sent a set of gifts and letters back to them with the wife of the Soviet ambassador in Rome, who had become a family friend, but when the woman appeared at my grandmother's family's door, she was told in no uncertain terms that they did not want any gifts or letters from relatives abroad, who were seen by Stalin as potential spies. At the time, Stalin was executing or sending to the Gulag millions of people for far less.

My grandmother's studies with Milyukov, who had been a Russian liberal and had fought for parliamentary democracy in Russia, first against the czar and then against the Bolsheviks, gave her much more of a political consciousness than my grandfather. Having suffered at the hands of the Bolsheviks, they were all anti-Communist, but my grandfather looked quite favorably on Mussolini and the Fascists. "He liked the idea of the strong man, a society based on order," my aunt said. The lack of political freedom didn't trouble him much. After all, he had other freedoms. He had arrived in Italy and had managed in a relatively few years to remake his life, setting up a successful dentistry practice, rubbing elbows with important people, and making a nice living. My grandfather liked gambling and sometimes was off playing poker while his waiting room was filled with patients needing their teeth fixed. "He loved lawsuits," my aunt said; "my mother hated them." My grandfather liked grand gestures and showing off. My grandmother was modest and unpretentious in her manners. "She treated everyone equally, from the wealthiest people to the illiterate peasant girl," Lally said.

My father grew up identifying strongly with his mother, the more sophisticated and intellectual of his parents. "Whenever we moved," he told me, "the first thing my mother did would be to find a lending library." Lending libraries are rare in Italy, and this must have taken some work on her part. At the same time, my father had a rather conflict-filled relationship with his father—perhaps because of his father's infidelities, his social ambitions, and his pro-Fascist sentiments.

My father was a natural student with an extraordinary memory who immediately rose to the top of the class in every school he went to. Italian schools had strict academic rankings at the time, and my father was almost always first in his class. He became well known for being able to recite backward and forward the names and dates of all the popes and the kings of France going back hundreds of years. When he was hospitalized for more than a month with typhoid fever in Rome at age nine, he wrote three little books. One was a history of the popes; another was about the War of the Roses and a third about the kings of France. At some of the parties his parents gave, my grandfather would trot my father out to perform for his guests, something he resented. "It was a lot of crap," my father said, "just memorization, but people were impressed."

In this small world, my father attended one of the top *licei classici* of Rome, the Liceo Tasso, a highly selective public high school where many of the Roman elite sent their children. He was in school with Il Duce's two oldest sons, Vittorio and Bruno Mussolini, and with the future prime minister Giulio Andreotti.

4 · EASTER CARDS

For all the apparent solidity of the Italian life my grandparents had made for themselves, there must have been an underlying insecurity and anxiety, evident in what may be the strangest documents in the Kamenetzki suitcase: a series of Christian holiday greeting cards signed by my father and my aunt. There is an Easter card with a little Baby Jesus floating on a cloud, benevolently blessing the world below with the following message:

Dearest Parents,

In these days of celebration every heart is elevated to a more beautiful joy, because it lives the blessing of Christ Reborn and is illuminated with the holiest and happiest peace.

There is a similar letter from my aunt and a few others like them from other holidays. My aunt said she and my father were encouraged or required to write these letters in school. Even if that is true, it is also true that my grandparents could have easily prevented this by telling the school that they were Jewish. During Fascism, Catholicism became the official recognized national religion, with priests and nuns allowed to teach in public schools, but Jewish children had the right to absent themselves during the "hour of religion." Obviously, my grandparents did nothing to inform the school authorities that their children were Jewish and should not be schooled in Christianity. Instead, there are traces of a regular correspondence between my grandparents and a group of nuns, who were exchanging warm Christmas greetings.

As it happens, my grandfather hired a nun, Sister Raffaella, to work as his dental assistant and did nothing to discourage her from believing that the Kamenetzkis were good Christians like everyone else. When my father came down with typhoid fever and my grandparents rushed him to a hospital in Rome, Lally was taken to stay at Suor Raffaella's convent in the city, where she lived for some weeks among the nuns. Because of the outbreak of typhoid, Formia was placed under quarantine and my grandparents remained in Rome for several weeks while my father was in the hospital. "I lived with the nuns and they spoiled me rotten," my aunt Lally said. "I think they thought we were Russian Orthodox . . . Suor Raffaella became so close to me that she decided she had to quit her job at Father's studio, because her religious vows required that she not be attached to anything or anyone in the world."

Indeed, it appears my grandparents went much further than that: according to both my father and his sister, they didn't tell their own children that they were Jewish until well after they had left Formia and moved to Rome. "Our parents didn't tell us we were Jewish until we were about eleven or twelve," my aunt explained.

In other words, in the first nine or ten years in Italy, my grandparents lived essentially as *maranos*, secret Jews who hid the fact that they were Jewish, both from the outside world and from their own children. In a small provincial town like Formia, with few if any Jews around, they obviously felt exposed and vulnerable. It was easier to be Jewish in a large city like Rome, with a small but visible Jewish community and a social circle that included other Russian Jewish exiles like themselves. Even so, according to my aunt, it was not until the approach of my father's thirteenth birthday that my grandparents explained that they were Jewish. At that point, my grandfather, from a highly religious family, found someone to give my father Hebrew lessons in preparation for a Bar Mitzvah.

"I never knew I was Jewish until I was about twelve—it was an incredibly funny thing," my father said when I asked him about it. "Because when we were in Formia and there were no Jews to be seen, my mother and my father agreed that it was better for us not to get into that. After we had moved to Rome, when my father told me, I was very upset.

Later, I felt guilty because I was upset, and then I started to be interested in the condition of the Jews and Israel. My father wanted me to do a Bar Mitzvah and so I went to take Hebrew lessons from a famous Italian Jewish scholar, Dante Lattes, who lived on the same street, but after four lessons, I refused to go, I quit even though I was very proficient at languages. So I didn't have any Bar Mitzvah."

My grandfather was certainly a protean figure who adapted easily to changing circumstances—Russian, Polish, Latvian, Italian, Jewish, Christian as necessity dictated. He had no trouble using a *prestanome* or re-creating his biography. Yet the attempt to camouflage the family's Jewish identity for several years suggests that despite my grandfather's seeming self-assurance and braggadocio, breaking off with his *prestanome* and engaging in lawsuits, there must have been a reservoir of fear and anxiety.

My father had no memories before coming to Italy, even though he spoke both Russian and German when he arrived, having learned the German from a nanny. But he was determined to be an Italian child and, despite having two Russian parents, apparently refused to speak Russian. Thus my father by the time he was three had shed his skin a few times; he had already lived in and forgotten three countries, learned and forgotten two languages. He had shed his religious skin, too. He had been born Jewish, become Christian for several years, and then learned he was actually Jewish after he was twelve.

A "Certain Silence," or the Other Ugo Stille

I. *DOPPIO DIARIO*

We met for the first time in the garden of the University of Rome under the cold rain of December entrusted to the usual disorder of our paramilitary training sessions. Shortly after me, they called a small boy with glasses whose name stood out because of the clash of Slavic consonants—Kamenetsky. I recalled that this was the name of a schoolmate of my cousin at liceo who was famous for his erudition and knowledge of history and I went over to speak with him. It was, in fact, him: a somewhat closed and indecisive boy, worried about the situation. Kamenetsky, whom I would soon simply call Mischa, would then become my best friend, who would—with a singular sensibility and splendid resources of intelligence—share almost all the experiences of our youth, and, finally, become inseparable from me.

It is fitting that the first trace of my father's existence in the historical record is a diary entry of his best friend, Giaime Pintor, whose papers were donated to the state almost fifty years after they were written.

Pintor's diary records the day on which he and my father first met, in December 1937, when they were both eighteen and were in their first year at the University of Rome.

Although still a teenager, Pintor traces an incisive portrait of my father as a young man at a very particular moment in time. He captures a number of things about my father, his "somewhat closed and indecisive" character as well as his "singular sensibility and splendid resources of intelligence," and, perhaps most important, the powerful bond that joined them. In December 1937, my father was certainly "worried about the situation," in particular the war clouds gathering overhead. Earlier that year, Mussolini and Hitler signed the "Pact of Steel," which codified a military alliance between the two Fascist regimes. The Mussolini government was celebrating its own contribution to the Fascist victory in the Spanish Civil War and was preparing for a larger war, for which the paramilitary exercises my father and Pintor were engaged in were a part.

Pintor and my father were members of a small world. Rome, Italy's capital, was a city of just one million people, as opposed to its three to four million today. Italy's educated elite, its leadership class, was far, far smaller. The entire university population in all of Italy in 1937 was only about sixty thousand. In the 1930s, Italy was still a predominantly rural country with a population in which a majority was either illiterate or barely literate. Compulsory schooling ended at eighth grade and had recently been raised from the sixth grade. A small fraction of the population finished high school, and of those just a tiny percentage attended university. When Fascism came to power, the Education Ministry, under the tutelage of the philosopher Giovanni Gentile, quite deliberately decided to limit rather than expand access to both high school and university. The children of working people—and only those with the ambition and desire to study past grade school—were steered into vocational schools, while highly selective exams limited access to the two types of *liceo*, the *liceo scientifico* and the *liceo classico*. Only graduates of the *licei* were eligible to attend university. Under the philosopher Gentile, the humanities came first and received most of the prestige and attention. The *liceo classico* was upgraded to provide a first-rate education, but it was meant to prepare a small but highly qualified elite, requiring students to learn both Latin and ancient Greek and study philosophy. Gentile, to his credit, kept Fascist ideology to a reasonable minimum and emphasized educational excellence. The irony is that the Fascist schools produced an extraordinarily well-educated elite that became the backbone of anti-Fascist culture in post–World War II Italy. The top students in the top schools in the country numbered in the thousands, and many of them knew one another. There were a handful of *licei classici* in Rome, and my father and Giaime were members of the same small world where the reputation of the best students preceded them.

Giaime was an extremely precocious child who excelled at school from an early age and lobbied his father to allow him to leave his parents in Sardinia to attend high school in Rome, where he had an aunt and uncle with whom he could live.

My father, too—as Giaime's diary entry indicates—was a precocious star in school, "famous for his erudition and knowledge of history." He had gone on from the lists of popes and kings to other impressive feats of memory and historical knowledge.

It is certainly ironic to think that the first time they met, my father and Giaime were almost certainly wearing Fascist black shirts. The paramilitary exercises that Giaime describes in his diary were those of the militia of the Gioventù Universitaria Fascista (GUF), the Fascist University Group, which was supposed to train the Fascist leadership of tomorrow. Membership was technically voluntary but in reality close to universal, as it was nearly impossible otherwise to participate in university social and cultural life; access to free movies, to student literary magazines, and to theatrical productions was limited to GUF members. Giaime makes a note in his diary that he went to the Cine-GUF to see two films of the French director René Clair, including *À Nous la Liberté*, the kind of foreign film that was becoming increasingly difficult to see as Mussolini fanned the flames of xenophobia and war. They joined the university militia for entirely practical reasons: by agreeing to spend their Saturdays and two summers doing military training, they could meet their obligation of a year's military service without losing a year of school. (They also got an eight-lira stipend for every day they participated.)

"Initially our anti-Fascism was really more cultural and aesthetic than political," my father explained. "We hated the rhetoric of Fascism, the stupidity of the propaganda, the absurdity of these endless parades, with these middle-aged men trying to stuff themselves into their old Fascist uniforms, which were now too small for them. I remember this one fat guy struggling to get his boots on." My father told me about the visit of a Fascist minister who addressed the students at the University of Rome, holding up his fist and saying, "This fist is worth more than any book."

My father and Giaime disliked the writers who were the favorites of the regime—D'Annunzio, Marinetti, and Papini—with their exaggerated nationalism, extravagant language, and glorification of war. Instead they preferred the "hermetic" writers, like the poet Eugenio Montale and the novelist Elio Vittorini, whose work was anti-rhetorical, and whose at times obscure style was scorned by some Fascist critics and appeared to contain a kind of implicit criticism of the culture of the day. A favorite

verse of my father's was the final stanza of the Montale poem *"Non chiederci la parola,"* which reads:

> *Non domandarci la formula che mondi possa aprirti,*
> *sì qualche storta sillaba e secca come un ramo.*
> *Codesto solo oggi possiamo dirti,*
> *ciò che* non *siamo, ciò che* non *vogliamo.*

> Don't ask us for the formula that can open worlds,
> Just a few broken syllables, dry like a branch.
> This is all we can tell you, now,
> What we are *not*, what we do *not* want.

At the time my father was starting university, in the fall of 1937 and
the winter and spring of 1938, Mussolini was beginning to prepare the
country for war. The pressures to defend oneself against "what we are
not, what we do *not* want" were increasing every day. The secretary of
the Fascist Party, Achille Starace—whom Mussolini himself labeled "a
cretin, but loyal"—was attempting to re-form the customs of the Italians
into those of a warrior people, and the military exercises that my father
and Giaime were taking part in at the university were part of the effort.
People were ordered to stop shaking hands, which was seen as a soft,
excessively friendly bourgeois habit; now Italians were supposed to use
the "Fascist salute," which the regime claimed was actually a Roman
custom rather than an imitation of the German *heil Hitler.* Starace abol-
ished the use of the pronoun *Lei*—the polite form for "you" in Italian—
and insisted on the use of *voi,* the second-person plural. *Lei* (which is also
used for the third-person "she") was derived from the courtly custom of
saying "His Excellency" and was condemned as an effeminate Spanish
importation. *Voi,* in contrast, was considered proper Latin usage and
would return Italy to the hard, martial valor of ancient Rome. Italian soldiers would now learn the goose step, an obvious aping of the Nazis, although it was being presented as the *passo romano.*
    In fact, the military exercises my father and Giaime were called on to
participate in during late 1937 and early 1938 were meant to train them in
the German goose step in preparation for Hitler's visit to Rome a few
months later. A third student, Jader Jacobelli, joined Giaime and my father in their military drills, and the three of them stuck closely together

during the months of training that followed. "So, we formed a trio to defend our integrity and our own judgment amidst the confused and violent movement of . . . [the text breaks off]," Giaime wrote. (Giaime's diary has frequent blank spaces, where he had been unable to find the right word and left it to be filled in, presumably, at some later time.) And so my father, a Russian Jew from Moscow, on the eve of the Italian racial laws, was spending his Saturdays dressed up in a Fascist uniform, learning the goose step in order to welcome Hitler to Rome.

How did one defend one's integrity while parading around in black shirts? For Giaime, my father, and their friend Jader Jacobelli, it meant talking—talking constantly during the military drills so that their minds roamed freely from topic to topic, from philosophy to the small change of daily life, amid jokes and laughter, even as the state took control over their bodies and had them marching up and down, lifting and lowering their rifles, goose-stepping in time. Among other things, they kept up an ongoing debate on the ideas of Benedetto Croce, the chief philosopher of Italian liberalism and the principal author of the "Manifesto of the Anti-Fascist Intellectuals." Talking helped them remain free individuals precisely at the moment in which the Fascist regime greatly accelerated its efforts to turn them into an obedient mass that moved as one to the command of their superiors.

Giaime wrote:

We talked continuously, provoking the scorn of our superiors and the diffidence of our comrades. Initially, this habit of always talking seemed to me a defect . . . In reality, I realized later that the austere silence of our fellow soldiers was a form of torpor; the patience that some of them showed when faced with the most exhausting duties was the result not of firmness of character but an inability to react. What exactly we talked about, I cannot recall: we touched on problems of culture and personal matters with equal curiosity: the philosophy of Croce was a common topic. Kamenetsky was a rigid Crocean, I had ideas that were rather heterodox, and Jacobelli was an eclectic.

Another form of freedom was writing. Giaime exercised his freedom by translating the work of the Austrian poet Rainer Maria Rilke, whose complex, mysterious, and beautiful poetry in German represented a kind of counterpoint to the crude thud of the jackboot during the Nazi goose step, an irony Giaime remarked on in a letter to his parents: "But I find myself always in the role of intermediary between German and Italian culture, now translating Rilke, the next introducing the goose step." His letters and diary entries were another realm of freedom. Giaime dedicated several letters and pages of his diary to the military exercises of early 1938 that he took part in with my father. He does not come out and denounce them. On the contrary, he appears to have enjoyed them, particularly for the camaraderie that he experienced with my father and their friend Jader. Writing about the military drills and the preparations for Hitler's visit in a light and subtly mocking tone was a form of self-defense, while also recording the flavor of the banter that went on between the friends.

A few months later, the endless drilling is wearing thin.

I don't know if I can survive this third week of military life or whether an ill-advised move on my part will cause me to end up in Gaeta [prison] for many years. No pilgrim returning from the Holy Land had sorer feet than I do; no warrior chieftain from the Etruscans to the Vikings wore a helmet as heavy as mine. In this state, soaking wet, body contorted, unshaven and with a depressed spirit, I march back and forth in front of the great leaders of "the platoon of iron" and the "company of iron" (it would seem that all of our units are made of iron).

Friday, a major rehearsal lasted from four in the morning until noon. Since it rained the whole time, when a friend of mine was asked by the inspector general, "How are you?" instead of giving the expected "Excellent!" he timidly answered: "Wet."

. . .

Military service imposes unexpected changes in program and limits more and more our freedom of movement. Now the "events of March" have been announced, which are the arrival of the Fuhrer and his Italian visit. All the armed forces of Rome have been mobilized and among the most insignificant components is me, university black shirt . . . In the evening we had to listen to useless lessons in military matters; the large number of listeners allowed each of us to go about our own business as long as we didn't make too much noise. Saturday afternoon, in militia uniform, we did drills in the university gardens. The greatest annoyance during the year were the mobilizations in order to teach us the *"passo romano"* (it was the period when, under Starace, the regime was trying to change our customs in preparation for Hitler's arrival). For entire days we were kidnapped from civilian life and led out to the outskirts of Rome for drilling. Endless waiting, orders, counterorders, all the inertia and fatigue of organizations . . . All these lost hours were a subject for complaint. Nonetheless they were not entirely a waste: they were a first lesson in collective life and they served to forge new friendships. Those departures at dawn, a cold clearness over Villa Glori, and the afternoons in the working-class neighborhoods with nothing to do but joke around with the servant girls and eat ice cream were a picturesque form of education. But above all we penetrated intimately into the theatrics of totalitarian regimes: we learned to disappear among the tens of thousands of men who took part in the drills, to immerse ourselves in the military music and enjoy the impersonality that a uniform gives you . . . During Hitler's stay in Rome we never missed a parade.

I remember my father telling me about himself and Giaime being among the troops who marched in parade before Hitler and Mussolini (he never mentioned anything about being in black shirts and doing the goose step, although he may have taken that as a given). I remember him telling me that he and Giaime had talked about the possibility of shooting Hitler, but he and Giaime, in all of their drilling, did not actually learn to shoot a gun—and, as a security precaution, were never issued live ammunition. They were toy soldiers on parade.

2.

In getting to know Giaime, my father was introduced into his family circle. When Giaime insisted on moving to Rome, he went to live with his aunt and uncle, the unmarried brother and sister of his father, known as Zio Fortunato and Zia Cecita, a bachelor uncle and spinster aunt who lived together and who were like a second pair of parents to Giaime. He had lived with them for a while when he was a little boy, before his parents were settled enough to support their own kids. "Giaime's uncle, Zio Fortunato, was a very decent, old-fashioned Italian liberal intellectual," my father said with obvious admiration. "He had been the chief librarian at the Italian Senate, but he quit rather than take the Fascist loyalty oath. He was not a very political man, but he didn't think a librarian should have to take a loyalty oath. When you went to his house you could find people across the political spectrum, usually the Fascists at one end of the room and the anti-Fascists at the other."

Italy's most important philosopher, Benedetto Croce, would visit when he came to Rome from his home in Naples. (Because of his international fame, Croce was allowed to live in relative freedom during Fascism long after most anti-Fascist intellectuals had been beaten up, killed, sent to prison, or forced into exile.) And yet Zio Fortunato was even closer friends (for reasons having nothing to do with politics) with the main author of the "Manifesto of the Fascist Intellectuals," Giovanni Gentile, the semi-official philosopher of Fascism. Fortunato Pintor had known Gentile twenty years before the advent of Fascism, when they were both at the Scuola Normale Superiore di Pisa. Gentile was an older, advanced student and acted as a kind of mentor to the young Fortunato. Gentile once described Fortunato Pintor as "a person of such ingenuous goodness, whose soul was of such simple candor, that we regarded him rather than as a little brother almost as a son." In fact, Gentile named one of his sons Fortunato.

Gentile was perhaps the most powerful figure in Italian culture during Fascism, occupying numerous positions, many of them simultaneously: minister of education, senator, director of the *Italian Encyclopedia* and of the *Italian Biographical Dictionary*, professor of philosophy at the University of Rome, rector of the Scuola Normale Superiore di Pisa, perhaps Italy's most prestigious university. Although he had not been an early Fascist, Gentile became a convinced supporter of the regime, which he imagined would complete the process of national unity and growth started by the Risorgimento. But because Gentile was already a man of middle age at the advent of Fascism, he had strong ties to many scholars who were not Fascists and, to his credit, ran the various institutions he headed up with more of an eye to scholarly merit than ideological purity. Faced with some brilliant but penniless scholar, Gentile's wife, Erminia, was known to call over to him, *"Giovà', dagli una cattedra!"* ("Giovanni, give him a professorship!") "Gentile, in fact, gave a lot of jobs to anti-Fascist scholars at the *Italian Encyclopedia*, people who couldn't work in the university system," my father said.

When Fortunato Pintor resigned his position as chief librarian of the Italian Senate in dissent against the "Fascistization" of the institution, Gentile rescued him by asking him to head up the *Dizionario Biografico degli Italiani*, Italy's *Biographical Dictionary*. With extraordinary modesty, Fortunato Pintor declined the offer, insisting there were younger and better qualified scholars. Gentile ignored Pintor's advice, and Fortunato Pintor was a greatly valued pillar of the *Dizionario Biografico* for the next thirty years.

"That's the funny thing about Italy under Fascism—he loses his job because he wouldn't take a loyalty oath and then he's saved by Giovanni Gentile," my father said. "There was a saying back then: 'We get our spiritual food from Croce, but we get our material food from Gentile.'"

Through Fortunato Pintor, my father was able to gain access to books that had been banned by Fascism but were still available in the Italian Senate. "I recall walking around with books like Piero Gobetti's *Rivoluzione Liberale* (Liberal Revolution) wrapped in newspaper as if I were walking around with a bomb," my father told me. Gobetti had been a forceful and brilliant young advocate of liberal democracy who died after having been ferociously beaten by Fascists in 1926, at the age of twenty-four.

3.

Giaime's diary and letters are often cryptic when it comes to politics. In committing pen to paper during the Fascist period, one used considerable caution. It was reasonable to suppose that police might open your letters—police files are full of private letters—and wise to use caution even in writing in a diary, which could be seized in a police raid. After all, Giaime knew that some of his close friends were involved in underground political activity and might well be under police surveillance—indeed, they all eventually wound up in prison. And, despite his caution, there is a clear indication in Giaime's writings of a shift in 1938 toward a greater politicization as the prospect of war, a war to be fought alongside

Hitler, became imminent and as my father and Giaime became increasingly close to a group of young men who were busy creating one of the principal Communist cells in Rome. The group included Lucio Lombardo Radice, Antonello Trombadori, Paolo Bufalini, Antonio Giolitti, Aldo and Ugo Natoli, Pietro Ingrao, Mario Alicata, and Manlio Mazziotti. All of them were either students or recent graduates of the University of Rome, and all would go on to play major roles in the cultural and political life of Italy after World War II. Giaime wrote:

> We talked a great deal about aesthetics; even after Michele [Kamenetzki] entered into our intimate circle of friends, we continued to talk about those problems; the sign of a new era was the gradual abandonment of abstract speculation for other more concrete issues with the passing months. In fact, during that year Lucio [Lombardo Radice] was moving toward increasingly radical positions and proposed that we read together political philosophy. So, we would get together in [Manlio] Mazziotti's house or at the university, Lucio, Mischia, me, and Manlio to read classic political texts. We began a systematic discussion of Rousseau. We read some Engels. We didn't get too far but the project served to form new tastes.

My father and Giaime were particularly close to Lucio Lombardo Radice, a brilliant young mathematician who was three years older than they were. Through him they were drawn into the orbit of the Rome Communist group, but they remained on the outside—in part because neither Giaime nor my father was a Communist and in part because neither felt prepared to make the commitment to underground activity, a commitment that was total and would lead, almost certainly, to prison.

"Giaime made it clear, even though he was aware of our conspiratorial activity, that he didn't want to be involved directly," Lombardo Radice said in a television interview in 1983, forty years after Giaime's death. "He said to us: 'I will start to conspire only for two reasons, if they beat up Benedetto Croce or if they start an anti-Semitic campaign.' He was very much a part of our Roman anti-Fascist group even though he did not want to take part in conspiratorial activity because he considered his cultural activity more important, he had more of that temperament. And this I think helps us grasp his freshness and lightheartedness."

Hitler's annexation of Austria in 1938, the so-called *Anschluss*, sparked one of the first demonstrations of anti-Fascism at the University of Rome, organized by Lucio and other friends of my father and of Giaime. The students, playing on the fact that Mussolini had bitterly opposed Hitler's designs on Austria just a few years earlier, protested against Hitler's invasion of Austria using Mussolini's own rhetoric, although it was perfectly obvious that the real object of the protest was Mussolini's new pro-Hitler policy.

That summer Giaime traveled to Besançon, France, to work on his French—it is clear that contact with a wide range of foreign students opened up new worlds to him. He listened to the news of Hitler's taking over the Sudetenland from Czechoslovakia with two young Czech students. And in response to his parents' letter urging him to return to Rome to take his exams in September at the height of the Czechoslovakia crisis, Giaime writes: "Central Europe is in flames and millions of Jews are in a state of anguish and you talk to me about exams?"

The Czech crisis was temporarily resolved with the meeting at Munich in which Britain's Neville Chamberlain agreed to Hitler's demands that the Sudetenland should be German, in order to avoid a full-fledged invasion of Czechoslovakia. Giaime makes it clear in his diary that the latest example of Nazi aggression has had a radicalizing effect on him. "It removed every illusion of peace," he writes. "Munich could not be the end of anything and several months later we heard the news of Hitler's tanks entering Prague, bringing distress to our souls."

A few weeks later, when Giaime was visiting his family in Sardinia, news came of Mussolini's new racial campaign, which suddenly reduced Italy's Jews to the status of second-class citizens. For my father's family, the news was crushing. "It was terrible, terrible," my father said. My father recalled the psychological devastation of some of the Italian Jews who were fiercely patriotic or even pro-Fascist. A Jewish colonel in the Italian Army called his troops together and then blew his brains out in front of them. The publisher Angelo Formiggini, who had created, among other things, a most entertaining collection of humor books that my father and his sister used to enjoy, committed suicide by jumping from one of the medieval towers in his hometown of Modena. With characteristic crudity, Achille Starace, the secretary of the Fascist Party who had my father doing the goose step, proclaimed that Formiggini had died like a Jew, jumping from the tower in order to save himself the cost of a bullet. "On a psychological level it did not shake me the way it shook some of the Jews who were pro-Fascist," my father said. "I was already anti-Fascist. But the practical element was terrible, the idea that we had to leave everything."

Giaime made a note in his diary: "News arrived of the new racial laws and I decided [blank space]. I wrote to Michele reminding him that I had posed that as the limit of my resistance."

Obviously, the letter from Giaime at that dark moment meant a great deal to my father.

> Dear Giaime,
>
> I received your letter with real pleasure, both because it gave me news of you, and because in such a moment it represented a genuine act of friendship: and for that I am grateful. As for me, although things do not look particularly rosy, I have not lost my calm or serenity.
>
> With this ends the serious part of my letter. The serious part prevented me from writing to you as I promised in a special idiom for Italians who have spent at least five days in France (a day in Paris counts for two) . . .

He proceeds to write in a kind of Italo-French pidgin for a couple of sentences and then gives Giaime a light chronicle of the doings of their various friends. ("Carlo Laurenzi made a noisy return . . . He claims to have been assaulted and bitten by a viper: so far all that has been ascertained is that the viper survived.")

My father's jocularity, making jokes after the heavy blow of the racial laws, sounds a bit forced.

The month after the promulgation of the racial laws in November 1938, Giaime returned to Rome and their friendship took up where it had left off.

> Toward the beginning of December I returned to take up my university life. I say "university" purely because that was where my life took place but not because it had much to do with school. The university was the gathering place for several hours a day; between the library and the gardens nearby all the people I wanted to see passed by, and without attending a single lecture, I would pass entire mornings talking and studying in those halls.

Giaime was enrolled in the law school, which was dominated by dull and militantly pro-Fascist professors. While he managed to pass all his exams and graduate in the normal four years, the bulk of his energy went elsewhere. He was busy translating various German authors, writing literary essays and criticism, and, perhaps most important, reading and discussing books, ideas, and politics with his friends.

In this period, my father and Giaime saw each other virtually every day, maintaining a kind of rolling conversation that continued more or less uninterrupted until my father left Italy in 1941. Sometimes they were so reluctant to break off their conversation that one would walk the other home and then they would walk back to the other's house, going back and forth through the quiet streets of Rome at night.

Giaime wrote in his diary:

> Each of our meetings deepened the intensity of our friendship. Timid and distracted as he was, Michele always left a certain margin of uncertainty in our initial greetings, then our conversation thawed naturally and we reached an understanding on all the most difficult points . . . I would see lots and lots of people; but on the return home, either in a carriage on the quiet nights of Rome or in long walks by foot, Michele was at my side and our ongoing commentary on everything and on all our friends continued uninterrupted up to the doorway and was prolonged by complicated goodbyes. That continuous and lively exchange about everything from culture to simple human experience became our principal support.

The events of 1938—the visit of Hitler, Munich, the racial laws, the invasion of Czechoslovakia—pushed Giaime and my father toward a greater political commitment. They engaged in increasingly intense discussions with their Communist friends, who, with war a near certainty, were stepping up their underground activity. But Giaime and my father pulled back from that ultimate step. "My ideological indifference regained the upper hand together with a certain suspicion," Giaime confided to his diary. "I regained a real sense of certainty only in the judgment of men."

4. DRÔLE DE GUERRE

Although war was the dominant reality looming over everything, it sneaked up slowly on my father. His life, eerily, changed less than that of any of his friends. While they were forced to complete their military service, my father's routine was undisturbed. He spent his time studying at the university library with occasional afternoons at the beach at Ostia. The main difference in his life was the sudden absence of Giaime and other friends who had been sent off to Salerno to officers' school. Twenty years old, he was in a strange position of privilege and discrimination: on the one hand, he was spared drilling in the hot summer sun and sleeping in barracks, and yet he must have felt the sting and humiliation of exclusion as well as the loss of the camaraderie that characterized life in a close group of friends.

Indeed, some of this comes through in a letter my father wrote to Giaime at Salerno.

> From what I have heard from Jader [the third friend from the university militia] your life seems slightly better than that of black plantation hands. You do some swimming and healthy physical activity, you have a kind of literary club, you write letters during the instructional lectures, you lie down in the woods during the reconnaissance exercises: in short, I don't think you have too much to complain about . . .

Later in the letter, clearly referring to his own family's precarious situation in Italy, my father writes: "Our situation is at the same point as before: nothing new and the same uncertainty."

Throughout that summer, even during his military service, Giaime wrote a humorous column for the magazine *Oggi* under the pseudonym "Mercutio," the name of Romeo's acerbic friend in Shakespeare's *Romeo and Juliet*. But in early September, when Hitler's troops invaded Poland, and France and Great Britain declared war, Mercutio bid his readers good-bye. In a column that made fun of the inanities of the British and French press at this time of war, Pintor ends by suggesting that the same charge could be made of his own column: "With every day's passing news the warning of Romeo comes to mind: 'Peace, peace, Mercutio, thou talkst of nothing.'" Making his thought clearer in a letter to his mother, Giaime writes: "It does not seem honest to be witty when France and England are fighting."

During the period between the summer of 1939, when Germany invaded Poland, and May 1940, Europe was in a state of suspended animation. The British and French had declared war but hadn't tried to invade Germany; the adversaries were engaged in what was called a *drôle de guerre* (phony war), which meant that they were technically at war but did no actual fighting.

That fall my father and Giaime returned to the University of Rome as usual. One day in December Giaime went to play tennis with his friend, but his partner, Lucio Lombardo Radice, didn't show up. "About an hour later, Giaime, very worried, called us and asked what had happened," Lucio's sister Laura said. "We replied vaguely, given the danger of the situation, 'Lucio couldn't make it. Come here.' Since Giaime was aware of Lucio's activities, he understood and rushed right over." Lucio and two other friends, also members of the Communist underground, Aldo Natoli and Pietro Amendola, had been arrested. Giaime helped Lucio's family find and destroy some books and papers that he had. "It must have made his heart weep to destroy those beautiful clandestine books we had at home," Lucio later recalled.

The *drôle de guerre* ended very suddenly on May 10, 1940, when Germany invaded Belgium and France, and in a matter of about two weeks, France was on its knees and the British were evacuating their troops from Dunkirk. With the invasion of France, Neville Chamberlain, who had hoped to appease Hitler at Munich, resigned. Winston Churchill was then made prime minister, telling the British Parliament: "I have nothing to offer but blood, toil, tears, and sweat."

The imminent defeat of France drastically increased the pressure on Mussolini to enter the fray. Italy could hardly demand French territory at the peace talks if it hadn't taken part in the war; and so, in rather cowardly fashion, Mussolini declared war about a week before France capitulated.

On the afternoon of June 10, a mass rally was planned in Rome's Piazza Venezia underneath Il Duce's office window. My father, Giaime, and their friend Valentino Gerratana decided to go, as Giaime describes in his diary:

In the city, posters were everywhere that showed a soldier in the act of breaking his chains: Italy breaks the chains that keep it from moving freely in its own sea. There was a certain ferment on the street when at one o'clock the radio began to play heroic music and programs. Then there was the news of the big gathering: I made an appointment with Michele [Kamenetzki] and Valentino [Gerratana]. So we joined the river of humanity that moved toward Piazza Venezia. An enormous crowd occupied the piazza; we were crushed in a corner in the middle of that curious Roman people that fights and laughs under the most serious circumstances. After much clamor and invocations, the shutters of the palace windows solemnly opened and Mussolini appeared. We couldn't hear much of the speech: we were in a deaf part of the piazza. "What did he say?" our neighbors asked when a shout of enthusiasm interrupted Il Duce. Then the words "ambassadors of France and of England," "submitted," . . . and we three knew that it was war. Up until that moment, we weren't sure. The speech was brief and then the whole noisy and happy crowd went up to the Quirinal to salute the king. Perplexed, we followed the movement of the crowd, watching the excited faces of the women and everyone enjoying the splendid sunset of June. So this long-awaited and feared moment entered our lives, and in all likelihood we would soon feel its consequences. Unaware of this, the public was sitting in the cafés and bars of the city and calmly spent that festive late afternoon. The orchestras played national and German anthems accompanied by benevolent applause. We three said almost nothing. We said goodbye with sadness at the train station: Valentino was leaving for Sicily that evening and we had no idea when we would all be together again. Each of the three of us took a different direction and I returned home late. I found my aunt, who had wrapped the lights in blue and wept desperately. It was a sad evening with little light and the windows closed. That evening there was the first air raid, which provoked great emotion. I naturally remained in bed.

The war, which had been in the offing since the day they met doing military drills on that Saturday morning in December 1937 at the university, had come.

Death by Bureaucracy

I.

My grandfather was clearly getting nervous. In the spring of 1938, Hitler had come to Rome, and the regime had begun to discuss the need for a new racial policy but no laws had yet been passed. Nonetheless, he wrote to the Fascist Union of Doctors of Rome to make sure he was still a member in good standing and able to practice in Italy. He received a reassuring reply: "This is to certify at the request of the interested party that the dentist KAMENETZKI ELIA (son of Israele) is enrolled in this union of dentists allowed to practice in the province of Rome." The racial laws were passed a month later. He wrote again and received an almost identical reply in early 1939.

So, in a strange Kafkaesque paradox, the racial laws had established that my grandfather was no longer an Italian citizen and lumped into a dangerous, inferior category of persons. Nonetheless, for the moment, he was still a member of the various Fascist professional organizations.

Starting in 1938, the number of official documents that my grandfather kept suddenly went from a trickle to a steady stream as he tried to contend with the impact of the racial laws and navigate the complications of leaving the country. The documents are written in the cold, stiff, and dull prose of bureaucracy, but, laid out together and placed into order, they tell a rather chilling story—of increasing desperation, the gradual stripping away of rights and privileges, the closing off of escape routes as Hitler's armies conquered more and more of Europe, the obtuse cunning of bureaucracies setting up hurdle after hurdle, and the dogged determination and resourcefulness of my grandfather in jumping over them. While I always took as a given that my father's family would have reached the United States—since that's what happened—reading over the papers, it is very clear that it almost didn't happen. It took three years of endless paper pushing and connection pulling. Even so, they got out just three months before it would have been too late.

The effect of the racial laws on my father's family was gradual, its course sometimes contradictory. The sense of the closing down of possibilities happened bit by bit—allowing them each time to reach a new level of normality. The three long years between the fall of 1938, when the laws were passed, and late September 1941, when they boarded a steamer in Lisbon, were a contradictory mixture of light and dark. They had in one stroke lost the Italian citizenship my grandfather had worked so hard to obtain with all his bureaucratic savvy; they had suddenly become stateless refugees and pariahs in a country they had come to love. Bureaucratically, they were in a terrible Catch-22 situation: the racial laws required that they leave the country, but the Fascist regime would not let them leave. Specifically, the government wouldn't give my father a passport, since he was of military age and they didn't want young men going to some other potentially hostile nation and joining its army. My grandparents made the decision that either the entire family would leave or the entire family would stay. At the same time, there were a thousand other difficulties, including getting through the highly restrictive American quota system, which set up strict limits for each country.

"We were getting more and more worried, but somehow we adjusted to all this and life went on," my father said. "I had my own life, which was very happy."

In fact, my father and my aunt Lally hardly felt any compulsion to leave Italy. Despite the objective deterioration of their situation—my aunt couldn't attend university—and the humiliation of losing their Italian citizenship and having the words "*razza ebraica*" ("Jewish race") stamped on their identity cards, they felt surrounded by solidarity and support.

My father recalled and spoke to me several times about what to him was one of the most meaningful episodes that occurred after the passage of the racial laws. One Sunday afternoon, a family they knew from Formia—poor, uneducated working people—turned up on their doorstep. The daughter, Concettina, had worked as a maid for the family when they lived in Formia. Her father was blind and repaired shoes, and they lived crammed into a tiny apartment. They may never even have been to Rome before—certainly they had never been to visit the Kamenetzkis in Rome—but on reading the news of the racial laws, they got on a train and appeared at the door as if they were simply passing through and stopped by for an impromptu visit, bringing my father's family some fresh fish from the seaside. "They handled themselves with a subtle delicacy of soul that was worthy of the most refined aristocracy," my father said. "They sat and talked of anything else. They never made mention of the racial laws, so as not to make us feel bad, but, then, toward the end, with great subtlety, indicated that if we should ever need them, they were always there. And then they went away." This episode moved my father so much that, despite rarely talking about his past, he told me several times about it, a rare emotion catching in his voice each time.

"If it had been up to me, I wouldn't have left Italy," my aunt said. "We were surrounded by friends and felt, being young and naive, that no possible harm could come to us." Although my aunt was forced to leave her Italian *liceo*, the Jewish community in Rome quickly formed a Jewish high school, which my aunt attended. The quality of the faculty was extremely high, since it included some Jewish university professors who could no longer teach in state universities. My aunt made new friends and felt at home. So, on a practical, material level, very little (at first) in the family's life changed. My grandfather continued his dentistry practice. My father continued his university career, studying philosophy in the midst of the racial campaign with Giovanni Gentile. My aunt changed schools but was very happy.

2. THE WRITING ON THE WALL

My grandfather—virtually alone in the family—was adamant, however, that the family had to leave Europe as soon as possible. Perhaps because he had grown up in a shtetl in the Pale of Settlement that had seen pogroms in his lifetime, he had a much clearer perception that things, even in beautiful Italy, could quickly get much, much worse.

My grandfather began the work of trying to emigrate almost immediately after the racial laws were passed in 1938. Their first choice, given the increasing likelihood of war in Europe, was the United States. But in order to get from Italy to the United States, they had to find someone in America to "sponsor" them, an enormous restriction designed specifically to limit immigration. It meant that the sponsor had to sign an affidavit stating that he or she was prepared to take full financial responsibility for the immigrating family, in case they were unable to support themselves.

My grandfather began frantically writing to anyone in the United States who he thought might be able to help him. He sent my father to the American embassy in Rome to pore through New York City phone books looking for possible friends and acquaintances. "I remember looking through the Bronx phone book," he said. "The name 'Bronx' sounded very romantic to me." My father wrote dozens of letters in schoolboy English on the family's behalf. They wrote to people with names like Kamen who might, possibly, be distant, distant relations. Most of these letters were like tossing messages in a bottle onto the open seas, hoping they might possibly wash up on some friendly shore. "I remember I wrote to someone named Wiener, which was the name of a childhood friend of my father's who had settled in New York. This very sweet old lady in the Bronx answered us, saying that her name was Wiener and she would like to help us but that she was very poor," my father said. They eventually found the correct address of my grandfather's friend Wiener—and they later learned he had received the letter—but he never replied.

At the same time, my grandfather was working on another bureaucratic front to get around the formidable quota system the United States had erected to limit immigration. Each country was assigned a certain number of immigrants that could be admitted each year. You could apply only under the quota of the country in which you had been born. My father and grandmother, who had both been born in Moscow, were able to get in on the Russian quota, largely because Stalin had made it virtually impossible to leave the Soviet Union. My aunt qualified under the Latvian quota, since she had been born in Riga, but since my grandfather's hometown of Mir had been handed over to Poland at the end of World War I, he was in trouble. The Polish quota, given the millions of Polish Jews desperately trying to leave Europe, was massively oversubscribed and offered no hope. My grandfather managed to contact some people he knew in Riga, where the family had stopped on its way out of Russia and where my aunt Lally was born, and convinced them to sign affidavits stating that he, my grandfather, had been born in Kreutzberg, Latvia.

One day, in early 1939, my grandfather received a reply to one of the dozens of letters he and my father had sent out. My grandfather had learned that a young man from his town of Mir, a certain S. L. Hoffman, who had left a life of desperate poverty in Byelorussia, had done extremely well in New York—become rich, in fact, running a factory that manufactured work uniforms in Brooklyn. Hoffman had received a scholarship to attend the local yeshiva, of which my grandfather's father had been a benefactor. Hoffman remembered the name Kamenetzki with gratitude, and even though he was on a winter vacation in Miami Springs, Florida, he fired off the following telegram to my grandfather as soon as he learned about my grandfather's letter:

I WILL SEND YOU THE NECESSARY DOCUMENTS LETTER WITH EX-
PLANATIONS MAILED TO YOU
SL HOFFMAN

My father and his family were stunned. The people they knew had refused to help. But a perfect stranger had just agreed to take on the onus of sponsoring them to the United States. The generosity of Hoffman's commitment is difficult to overstate. It was not enough to claim that you were ready to care for the immigrating family; you had to prove to the U.S. government that you were in a position to actually do so, which meant providing highly detailed financial disclosures, which by itself scared away many potential sponsors.

"That telegram was the most joyful thing," my father said. "But that turned out to be the beginning of a very long story."

3.

After the euphoria of receiving the telegram and letter from their American sponsor, S. L. Hoffman, my grandfather and father began contending with the sticky American immigration bureaucracy. Both in America and in Naples, where these matters were handled in Italy, the U.S. government threw up obstacle after obstacle.

My father recalled making trips down to the American consulate in Naples. "You could feel the anti-Semitism among these State Department officials. You could just tell they didn't want to let us in," he said. My father was a big American patriot, downplayed his Jewishness, and was not one to cry anti-Semitism readily; so when he said you could feel the anti-Semitism, I believe it.

Patient Mr. Hoffman had to provide document after document—despite being the sole owner of a highly successful business of more than five hundred employees—to convince the American government that he was, in fact, capable of sponsoring the Kamenetzki family.

The American consul general of Naples kept introducing a new roadblock at every turn, making it nearly impossible for them to emigrate.

By 1940, more than a year after he had initiated the affidavit process, S. L. Hoffman seemed to be becoming frustrated and exasperated and to be getting cold feet about having my father's family come to the United States. In a letter in March 1940, he advises my grandfather—unless his situation in Italy is intolerable—to stay put.

March 29, 1940

Dear Mr. Kamenetski:

I am enclosing a copy of affidavit which I forwarded to the Consul in Naples as per his request in his letter to you of February 1st. Let us hope that his affidavit will prove satisfactory.

In the last six months or so, you have not written to me regarding your present problems in Italy. I know you must realize quite well that when a family comes to the United States, they have to first struggle along before they establish themselves.

If your economic position is satisfactory and if you have no religious problem, my suggestion is that you should not come to the States. However, if your troubles are the same as they were when you first wrote to me, naturally there is nothing left to do but come to this country. I will do the best I can for you when you arrive.

Very truly yours,
S. L. Hoffman

4. WAR

With the war, everything suddenly got worse. Jews were suddenly excluded from a series of professions, including medicine and dentistry, and so my grandfather suddenly received, in February 1940, official notice that he was no longer a member of the Fascist Doctors' Union and could no longer practice dentistry in Italy.

His bureaucratic status had changed. Suddenly he was being referred to as a "stateless person, resident in Italy, and member of the Jewish race" (*"apolida residente in Italia . . . appartenente alla razza ebraica"*). And as such he received a notification that he had been expelled from the Fascist Doctors' Union: "The Rome Union of Doctors, with a notarized act of February 29, 1940, has communicated to the plaintiff that he has been ejected from the guild on the sole grounds that he belongs to the Jewish Race, taking effect from March 1, 1940." My father decided to seek the help of his old classmate from the Liceo Tasso, Bruno Mussolini, Il Duce's son. He eventually found him at the racetrack outside Rome where he spent a lot of his time. My father came up to him and asked him if he could help. Bruno stood there, looking down at the ground, a bit embarrassed, with his hands in his pockets and said simply: *"Non ci posso fare niente, non ci posso fare niente"* ("I can't do anything"). The next year, in August 1941, Bruno Mussolini, a pilot, would die in a plane crash.

With the war, Rome turned dark at night, lights being turned off in order not to provide targets for British bombers. Rome was largely spared air raids, because of its artistic treasures and the presence of the Vatican, but the curfew gave the city a dark and somber feeling. Every week the bread seemed to get darker as white flour became more scarce. Coffee and sugar disappeared from the markets, and fruit and meat were in extremely short supply.

The places from which you could leave Europe were gradually diminishing. With the German offensive during the summer of 1940, most of the capitals of Western Europe—Paris, Amsterdam, Brussels, Copenhagen—fell to Hitler, and the ports of Northern Europe were out. With Italy in the war, you could no longer leave from Genoa or Naples. Spain had agreed not to allow anyone of military age to pass through its territory to reach a hostile nation. Lisbon was one of the last open ports in Europe, but how could you reach Portugal without going through Spain?

Jews were suddenly seen as potential spies and were banned from frequenting seaside resorts, for fear they might be sending signals to enemy ships offshore or noting the movements of the Italian Navy.

For similar reasons, Jews were not allowed to own radios, and so one day the Italian police came and confiscated the Kamenetzki family radio. But my father's family was fortunate in having their German friend Zia Keti living with them. When the radio was confiscated, Zia Keti marched into the police station, insisted that the radio was hers, and demanded it back. "But, Signora," said the police officer, "why are you living with a family of Jews?" "I will live with whomever I choose—now give me my radio back!" she replied. She did far more than rescue their radio. Zia Keti trained herself as a dental technician and began to work for my grandfather, so that, if necessary, she might serve as a kind of *prestanome* should it prove necessary for his studio to be registered in the name of a member of the Aryan race. At the same time, my father recalled, Zia Keti, although obviously not a Nazi, was a German nationalist and remained serenely convinced, with a hint of pride, that the Germans would triumph in their war of conquest. That a German nationalist would be living with a Russian Jewish family in Italy, helping them in every possible way while also taking some pride in the victories of the Wehrmacht, was surprising to me but did not seem the least bit odd to my father. "Italy at the time was full of these kinds of contradictions," he said with a characteristic shrug.*

---

*Another curious example: on the eve of Italy's entrance into the war, Giaime Pintor's uncle Fortunato, who had resisted pressure to join the Fascist Party, suddenly applied—of his own free will—for membership. He explained his peculiar reasoning to his good friend the Fascist Giovanni Gentile:

> You should be the first to know that I asked to enroll in the Party. So, finally, this will remove a shadow that has been cast over our friendship for so many years. Certainly the decision has cost me a lot, forcing me to separate myself from ideals of men to whom I have been very close and who have had a profound effect on my spirit. But even these men, if they were alive today, would, I think, understand the new reality posed by events that makes necessary a unity of spirit of all citizens. Now it is to be hoped that the adhesion of hundreds of thousands of former soldiers—many of whom have held dissident views—will persuade Il Duce to temper his policies and stop some of the extreme and harsh tendencies like the racial policy which is certainly not worthy of a nation of high civilization.

The contradictions of Fortunato Pintor are fascinating to contemplate. Pintor refused to join the party when it was personally convenient for him to do so, but was willing to join at a mo-

5. POISON PEN

One of the nastier by-products of the racial laws—and the ban on Jewish professionals—was a proliferation of anonymous letters, written mostly by other, non-Jewish professionals, clearly aimed at driving their Jewish competitors out of business.

At some point during the ban, the Italian ministry received an anonymous letter written in an elegant cursive script that said the following:

> A certain Elia Kamenetzky (or Cameniechi) living in Rome in Via in Arcione n. 71—a dentist I believe—also has another studio in Segni where he goes once a week. Kamenetzky it appears is either a Russian or Polish subject, possesses considerable financial means, is a gambler, has numerous love affairs and, one hears, engages in espionage.

This particular snitch appears to have known my grandfather rather well—despite pretending not to know for sure whether he was a dentist—since he even knew the alternate spelling my grandfather sometimes used for Kamenetzky: Cameniechi.

6. OGGI

Paradoxically, the racial laws indirectly led to my father's first big break in the world of journalism. Giaime had enjoyed extraordinary early success writing for the magazine *Oggi,* and they wanted to give him a weekly column, but now that he was in uniform, Giaime could not do everything the magazine wanted and suggested my father, unable to serve because of the racial campaign, to stand in for him.

" 'This is Miscia, he will continue the column,' " Giaime told Arrigo

---

ment that he felt called for national unity. But he did so not out of ideological sympathy for Fascism, but as an extension of his old liberal values and out of a desire to raise a note of dissent in order to dissuade Mussolini from his racial policies and, presumably, the alliance with Nazi Germany. (These stunning contradictions make a mockery out of simplistic ideas of Fascism and anti-Fascism.) However, Pintor's request was denied, perhaps because he had explained his reasons.

Benedetti, the coeditor of *Oggi*. "When he returned with his young friend, we immediately noticed his extremely lively light blue eyes, the slight smile on his face, his face attentive to everything we were saying, not out of diffidence, but out of disposition of his intellect that was anxious to understand, to make sense of facts and remarks. From this point forward he would write the foreign policy column for us and with success."

Oggi was one of the few relatively free magazines in Fascist Italy. It was not an anti-Fascist magazine—no such thing was possible then—but it managed, for the most part, to be something rather close to it: a non-Fascist magazine. Its pages were full of work by anti-Fascist writers, remarkably lively pieces of criticism, news, commentary, and fiction that all but ignored Fascism. In the editorial pieces of political comment, the magazine supported the overall government line but without any rhetorical emphasis or use of Fascist slogans or language, and without demonizing or dehumanizing Italy's wartime enemies. The studious lack of rhetoric was itself a statement in a culture closely attuned to linguistic nuances.

Looking through the back issues of *Oggi*, which existed only between 1939 and 1941, when it, too, was suppressed by the Fascist regime, it is striking how lively and intelligent a magazine it was, given the constraints it was operating under. The two editors, Benedetti and Mario Pannunzio, put together an extremely impressive galaxy of great young and not-so-young writers. *Oggi* featured the fiction of the young Alberto Moravia and Elsa Morante (who would emerge as two of Italy's most important mid-century novelists). Vitaliano Brancati, a brilliant novelist and humorist, had a regular column. Ennio Flaiano, who later cowrote most of Federico Fellini's films, was the theater critic, while Alberto Savinio, brother of the artist Giorgio de Chirico and a writer not well liked by the regime, had somehow been smuggled into *Oggi* to write about music.

My father began writing under the pseudonym Ugo Stille, which Giaime had used but whose creation had been a collective invention of their close circle of friends. When Giaime had been teaching himself German and beginning to translate the poetry of Rilke, he made a mistake in translating the word "*Stille*." Because common nouns in German are capitalized, unless you understand the context well it is easy to mistake a noun for a proper name, and so Giaime had translated the phrase meaning "a certain silence" as "a certain Mr. Stille." His friends kidded him about the error and when he was trying to select a pseudonym, one of them, Ugo

Natoli, volunteered that the name, of course, should be that of the mysterious Mr. Stille, whom Giaime had already invented. Everyone liked this idea so much that Giaime took Natoli's first name, Ugo, and made the pseudonym "Ugo Stille." Although the idea was for Giaime and my father to share the column and write pieces on alternate weeks using the same name, the reality is that—partly because Giaime was busy serving in the army and partly because he was writing other things—my father ended up writing all but two of the roughly forty pieces signed by Ugo Stille that appeared in the pages of *Oggi* between November 1940 and shortly before my father's departure for the United States in September 1941.

"Pannunzio and Benedetti were both people of anti-Fascist feelings and so were most of the people who wrote for *Oggi*, but in order to cover up for this they had one regular column each issue which was completely conformist," my father explained. "The interesting thing was that *Oggi* was a kind of *salotto*, so that I would go there almost every afternoon, whether or not my column was due. The magazine had collected an extraordinary group of people, Moravia, Brancati, Vittorio Gorresio, Adriano Tilgher, a philosopher who had written a ferocious pamphlet against Gentile but *Oggi* was able to publish from time to time. We called him simply Maestro. There was Ennio Flaiano, who was brilliant and witty and spoke in epigrams the same way he wrote. I was at that time very timid and I would sit there listening to all these big names. They were incredibly friendly and immediately expressed great admiration for my work, since I was very young." My father recalled one incident when he had written about the same subject on a particular week as a very famous, established writer from Naples, who graciously conceded when the two pieces appeared. *"Ha fatto meglio u guaglione"* ("The kid did better"), he said, using a Neapolitan expression for kid, *"guaglione."*

It was in this period that my father began to establish a reputation for being brilliant and lazy. The editors of *Oggi* used to complain that they would send over a messenger to pick up the typescript of my father's piece and he would find my father lying on the couch eating bread and marmalade, asking the messenger to return in another hour or two.

My father often expressed a lot of pride over these early pieces he had written for *Oggi*, but, remembering that he was only about twenty when he started writing there and knowing that memory can play tricks on us (usually in our own favor), I approached the old collections of *Oggi* in the National Central Library of Rome with some trepidation, fearing I might be disappointed. Instead I was pleasantly surprised both by the liveliness and appeal of the magazine as a whole and by the quality of my father's pieces in particular. His column was called *"XX Secolo"* ("Twentieth Century") and dealt with virtually anything under the sun having to do with foreign policy. One week my father was an expert on Greek politics, the next on French foreign policy in Syria; one week on the relationship between the United States and Canada, the next on the relationship with Mexico. He wrote on India, Tunisia, and Iraq. Although a young man with limited access to foreign news—the already tight restrictions on information under Fascism were aggravated by the disruption of war—he managed incredibly to adopt, quite convincingly, a style that was omniscient, authoritative, erudite, full of witty and learned quotes, and enlivened with funny and telling anecdotes.

7.

Although my father wrote under a pseudonym, his newfound prominence among journalists also attracted some resentment. One day the phone rang and an anonymous caller said, "Get out! We don't need you here!" As it happened, my father recognized his voice. It was a fellow journalist who wrote for one of the newspapers of Telesio Interlandi, the leading anti-Semite of Italian journalism under Fascism (who published both a newspaper called *Il Tevere* and a magazine dedicated exclusively to promoting the racial laws called *La Difesa della Razza*). "I don't know why, but I was sure who he was. Later he came to America trying to get a job." It was the only episode of outright hostility during the period of the racial campaign my father could recall.

My father's life during his final year in Rome was a strange combination of normal and profoundly abnormal. He continued his university studies and wrote a thesis on the British philosopher Alfred North Whitehead, whose work was uncontaminated by the spirit of Fascism. He wrote virtually every week for *Oggi*, earning both a considerable journalistic reputation as well as something close to a full-time salary. In fact, although Jews were not supposed to publish in Italian newspapers, my father was earning two hundred lire a week writing for *Oggi*, the equivalent of a worker's salary. A thousand lire a month was a kind of standard of middle-class life in Fascist Italy, a salary on which a man could maintain a family in reasonable comfort. That my father came close to this on his own with his journalistic work while continuing to be a full-time student at the university is a sign that, despite the racial laws, the family's life continued in comparative ease.

Italy was at war, but the café life on the Via Veneto continued as before. My father and his new friends from *Oggi*—many of them the preeminent writers and journalists of the day—would sit and chat in one of the cafés after the end of the workday, sometimes joined by journalists from *Il Messaggero*, whose offices were just down the street on Via del Tritone, near my father's family apartment. Industrial cities of the north such as Milan, Turin, and Genoa were the objects of frequent air raids and large parts of their city centers were reduced to rubble, but life in Rome continued much as before. Jews had been officially banned from attending seaside resorts, in case they might provide information about Italy's coastal defenses. But in the summer, my father went almost daily out to the beach at Ostia.

During the first summer of the war, in July 1940, my father wrote Giaime, whose regiment was stationed in Perugia.

Carissimo,

Brief and hurried, this first letter. Sorry. I am writing you with a red nose, burnt shoulders, and the prospect of returning to Ostia tomorrow.

The most important thing to say is that your departure has left a great void: all the more so when I think that it will be a long absence. But we talked about that already in Rome as well as about reasons for consolation: memories of the past, the ties of the present. Better, then, to pass to the small change of everyday life. Carla's address is via Volturno 58. You must behave yourself and not artfully encourage hopes that the girl may still harbor in her heart. I see her frequently in Ostia and behave like a brother. And your poetry? At the beach, one wastes a lot of time, but I assure you I am not neglecting my studies! Soon you will have my first pieces [for *Oggi*] . . .

Be well, and write. I will soon write you something longer.

In August 1940, my father took the train from Rome to Perugia to visit his best friend, expecting to find him suffering through the rigors of barracks life, and found instead Giaime enjoying an intense intellectual, social, and personal life.

> Carissimo,
>
> The days in Perugia were truly a happy parenthesis, for which I thank you. Here I have fallen back into the heat and the worries: both of which are mounting.

A few weeks later, my father wrote again:

> I went to Perugia in the spirit of the "consoler" and I found you wonderfully situated. And so, as Bor'gognoni said, "you have villas, hotels, and women," and I will not be moved thinking of your military drills . . . and your letter home spoke of "unforgettable girls on bicycles." Who are they? You asked about my worries. They are produced by my Latin exam and from certain paternal professional problems. Now, school life is starting up again, many friends have returned, the libraries are open again. Time passes between books and conversations.

8.

Although my father (for fear of his letter being read by police and out of his characteristic desire not to dramatize) does not explain his "mounting" worries, or the nature of his father's "professional problems," in April 1940, my grandfather's dentistry office was raided by Italian police and my grandfather was put on trial with more than a dozen other Jewish doctors and dentists for violating the ban on Jewish professionals. Ilya Kamenetzki, who, after all, needed to live and was not allowed to leave the country, continued practicing with even greater caution, but one day one of his patients, running into a policeman as he left the office, panicked and immediately confessed to being treated by my grandfather. The policeman, who was there by chance, then turned my grandfather in.

Some months later (either in late 1940 or early 1941), my grandfather and the other Jewish doctors and dentists were convicted.

As the war proceeded and foreign Jews were unable to book passage out of Italy, the Fascist government began arresting foreign Jews and placing them in a handful of detention camps that were built quickly in southern Italy. As Mussolini's war went badly—in Greece, in Albania, in Russia—the regime raised the level of rhetoric against foreign Jews. "These undesirable elements," one government circular went, "drunk with hatred against totalitarian regimes, capable of any action that is harmful for the defense of the State and the public order, must be taken out of circulation . . . Hungarian and Romanian Jews must be removed from the Realm."

The idea of ending up in one of these camps, where they might be trapped or perhaps turned over to the Germans, became a source of daily terror to the Kamenetzkis. "Every evening when I came home I would look out for signs of the police," my father told me. "I never went straight to our door. I would wait at the corner to see whether there was anything suspicious. If I had seen police, I would have fled. I thought in my mind, 'Where would I go?' I thought I would go to Giaime's house, to his uncle and aunt's. And I remember that every time the doorbell rang after six o'clock we thought it might be the police. We had a big terrace in our apartment and I thought to myself, if they come to arrest us, I would go out on the terrace and then move to the roofs of the other building and escape that way. But, you know, people get adjusted to the most horrible things."

9. BRIEF PHOTOGRAPHIC INTERLUDE

Among the handful of photographs from my father's childhood in Italy are some pictures taken during the winter of 1940–1941. It snowed— something almost unheard of in Rome, city of a Mediterranean climate, palm trees, bougainvillea, and honey-colored light. The photos show my father and his sister and several friends playing in the snow up on the gardens of the Pincio Hill. The snow was so unusual that the event had to be recorded. They look totally carefree.

And yet on New Year's Eve 1940, my father wrote to Giaime:

Carissimo,

The end of the year has come, the period of traditional holidays and important memories, and I don't want it to pass without writing to you. If I had to be precise like our friend Valentino I would say that in this moment, I am rather sad. It is a state of mind that the falling of the last leaves can give to one who believes in the empirical value of the calendar. And then, it is an unusually foggy afternoon, a certain fatigue, thought of my thesis . . .

10.

Delays with visas, affidavits, passports, plane and boat tickets continued and multiplied. After the family had fulfilled all the various requirements posed by the American consul general, some new requirement would be demanded. At one point, the consul general's office insisted that they could not grant a visa until my grandparents had actually purchased boat tickets. They could not get boat tickets in Lisbon until they obtained a transit visa through Spain.

Along with working with S. L. Hoffman and the U.S. government, my grandfather was busy in Italy trying to get a transit visa through Spain, without which they could not reach Lisbon. He called on the help of his former client Senator Pietro Fedele, the former Fascist minister of education. Although Fedele may have introduced the Fascist salute into Italian schools, to his credit, he never abandoned my grandfather, even in the throes of the racial laws when foreign Jews were being rounded up and sent to Calabria.

Fedele, in turn, used his connections at the Vatican to intercede with the government of Spain, writing personally to both the Apostolic Nuncio in Rome as well as the Vatican's secretary of state, Giovanni Battista Montini, the future Pope Paul VI (whose letter we still have).

My father recalled taking some documentation to Montini's office to facilitate obtaining the transit visa. But all this took time—and by the spring of 1941, it was getting late, very late. The war had been going on for two years. Virtually all of continental Europe was under Nazi or Fascist domination. In March 1941, President Roosevelt had started the Lend-Lease program, designed to help Great Britain against Hitler, bringing the United States decisively closer to war. The moment the United States entered the war—as it would before the end of the year—virtually all passenger ships between Europe and America, at risk of being attacked, would stop.

"My father had a crazy idea about our going to Madagascar," my father recalled.

And yet with the solving of each problem, a new one would arise. My grandparents got the Spanish transit visa and the boat tickets in Lisbon. And they still didn't have a Portuguese visa, which meant another set of hurdles to be jumped.

I I.

The date for my father's departure kept changing so often, being set and then postponed, that it became a kind of standing joke among himself and his friends. "I remember running into a friend from *Oggi*," my father recalled, "who said to me. 'By God, are you still here?' "

The life of the University of Rome continued—despite the war—much as before. But there was a subtle change in the political atmosphere. The conduct of the war, which Mussolini had promised would be swift and glorious, had hurt morale in Italy. The Italian Army had difficulty conquering tiny Albania and had to be bailed out by the Germans when it invaded Greece; the difference between rhetoric and reality along with reports from their friends at the front led to a revival of anti-Fascist feeling among university students.

In May, some of my father's and Giaime's good friends at the university organized an ingenious anti-Fascist protest. The Fascist university group GUF planned a demonstration of solidarity with the regime, and several GUF members who were closet anti-Fascists decided to sabotage it and turn it into an anti-Fascist protest. They prepared hundreds of little pieces of paper twisted into the shapes of stars and wrote anti-Fascist slogans—Death to dictatorship! Long live liberty! Down with Hitler and Mussolini, long live Italy!—inside them. These pieces of paper just looked like festive confetti to be thrown into the air during the demonstration; it was only when you opened them that you saw the messages inside and their subversive content became evident. And so the saboteurs handed them out to the organizers of the pro-Fascist demonstration, who enthusiastically threw them in the air. It wasn't until after they were all over the courtyard of the university that a few people began to notice the anti-Fascist messages inside. In order to clear up the situation, the pro-Fascist students decided to march down to express their support in front of Mussolini's office window in Piazza Venezia. One of the organizers of the anti-Fascist protest had the bright idea of calling the police and telling them that the students at the university had lost their heads and distributed anti-Fascist messages, and were now heading to Mussolini's office to continue their protest. When the column of pro-Fascist students headed downtown, they suddenly found themselves facing a squadron of riot police. In order to increase the impression of spontaneity, it was not uncommon for demonstrators to have to push through police cordons, which offered little resistance. So the students pushed forward but were suddenly attacked, beaten, and arrested by the riot police. The university was closed down for a few days to deal with the crisis, and, in the initial confusion, some thirty of the demonstrators (all enthusiastic pro-Fascists) were expelled. Only later did the authorities realize that the incident had been orchestrated by a group of anti-Fascist subversives, whom they set out to identify.

The next month, my father defended his thesis before a committee headed by Giovanni Gentile. Just three days before the defense, Hitler invaded Russia. Despite a lively debate with one of the readers and the fact that my father was technically a "stateless citizen of the Jewish race," he was given the highest possible honors. Immediately afterward, writing with a "bad pen and bad paper"—the quality of paper had deteriorated markedly during the war—my father wrote to Giaime to share his good news.

June 25, 1941

Carissimo,

I defended my thesis today. A brilliant result: 110 with honors along with a fight with Carabilese. So ends a definite period of life. But this appears to be only the prelude to a much larger end: our departure, which for various reasons we are trying to hurry up, seems set for July 7. Try, therefore, to make it down here toward the beginning of July. I am totally disoriented and I really need to see you . . .

Try to come, *ti abbraccio*.

Michele

For those in my father and Giaime's circle of friends, his graduation—and imminent departure—represented a kind of painful milestone, the end of a period of youth. Even though some members of their group, like Lucio Lombardo Radice, had gone to prison and others were in uniform, this seemed the beginning of something worse, the permanent breakup of their childhood group.

Laura Lombardo Radice, the younger sister of Lucio (who would later marry the Communist leader Pietro Ingrao), wrote to this effect to Giaime the day after my father's thesis defense.

Rome, June 26, 1941
Dear Giaime,

Now it is becoming reality, a present reality, a concrete fact that we can no longer avoid with a kind of incredulity of which we are fond: the departure of Michele and his family, which we have so often glimpsed and then put out of our minds. It is fixed for July 7 and only some very improbable external impediment could annul a decision that has now been worked out in all its details: nor—all things considered—would we want such an impediment.

I must confess that I am unable to accept with peaceful resignation Michele and his family's departure: along with definitive departure, in which return is so uncertain, are the harshest ruptures of our existence.

Giaime, every time that some new laceration occurs I feel less able to stand it: truthfully, it is too difficult to live just waiting . . .

Laura

12.

After the latest bureaucratic snafu, the Kamenetzkis' departure was fixed for July 7; but then there was another delay and the date was pushed back to early August. When my grandfather appeared at the U.S. consulate in early August to pick up their visas, he received a brutal shock. The consular officials told him that because nearly two years had passed since the time that S. L. Hoffman had first provided his affidavit and the documentation of his ability to sponsor them, he would have to provide new documentation to make clear that he was still in a position to do so—never mind that the U.S. government was almost uniquely responsible for the two-year delay.

With the United States edging closer to war, this delay might have been the final blow to their plans to leave Italy and go there. They waited.

Meanwhile, every week, my father continued batting out more pieces for *Oggi*. They continued to be lively, funny, and interesting.

With Hitler's invasion of the Soviet Union in the summer of 1941, the Russians suddenly entered the war and became the de facto allies of the British, who up until that point had soldiered on alone. It is not hard to detect a certain enthusiasm in the article my father wrote for *Oggi* about the latest developments.

> "Now for the first time since 1917 I can drink a vodka in good conscience," a columnist of *The Guardian* reports. The term "alliance" initially seemed to frighten the most rigid conservatives, the so-called diehards. For a day in London people spoke of a special juridical relationship (everything having to do with Russia is special), of a relationship of "co-belligerency," a neologism that expresses the profound differences between comrades in arms . . . Winston Churchill, not a man to be afraid of words, prefers the clear and heavy meaning of the old term "alliance" rather than the philological elegance of "co-belligerence." "Now we are the Russians' allies." The House of Commons applauded. The columnist from *The Guardian* can drink his vodka.

On July 31, my father wrote Giaime about another obstacle. "As for us, nothing new except for a delay in the boat, and so our departure is delayed for another ten days."

Giaime came down to Rome to see my father before he left, but yet another problem presented itself.

> Saw Michele, who brought me up-to-date about things: he has the Spanish transit visa but there is trouble with the tickets. Then we separated . . . At dinner with K[amenetzki] at the Lombardo Radice's house. Very much a family atmosphere. We talked until late with great vivacity: we talked about France. They are certainly extraordinarily vital people. We returned home slowly, crossing the Villa Borghese.

Leaving Rome and my father for the last time on August 9, 1941, Giaime had the impression of having—despite the war and the curfew that darkened the city at night—a last taste of the sweet life of his boyhood.

> Later an appointment with K . . . Walked toward the Trinità dei Monti. The impression of leaving Rome with its friends: the "*douceur de vivre*" ["sweetness of living"]. The streets are dark but the air is warm and they are full of people talking. How long can it last? This enjoyment of everything, of the girls on the street and the seasons?

There was another delay with the American visa, and their departure was pushed back from the end of August to the beginning of September, but at last the American visas came and they were ready to leave. In the final days, my father told me, they stopped answering the phone, afraid that one of the several bureaucracies on which they depended might raise a new problem and try to put off their trip. They held their breath and waited. Nonetheless my father wrote stories for *Oggi* throughout August and into September, up until the day of his departure.

On the day they finally left, September 4, 1941, Laura Lombardo Radice wrote to Giaime, describing the event.

> Giaime carissimo,
>
> An hour ago in Piazza dell'Esedra, lit by a tenuous dawn, we left our Michele and his family, with a farewell characterized by stubborn but indeterminate hopes of seeing one another again.

But we said goodbye to one of the many expressions of our youth, which separates itself from us, leaving us more alone and full of thoughts.

The evening before leaving Italy, my father, unable to see Giaime, went over to his home and visited Zio Fortunato Pintor, who in turn wrote to Giaime about the final visit:

> Michele left yesterday morning after overcoming new difficulties, which cropped up at the last minute. The evening before, we went over to say goodbye to his parents: then he came over to our house, and stayed around until midnight, with his "questions" and "notes." In truth he was unable to leave this room behind, or rather leave you behind, his youth, with all its cares, and his homeland. [Giovanni] Gentile, hugging him, left him with rather uncommon words, and gave him a letter for a colleague of his. I am sure, we are all certain, that he will go far. He was extremely moved by your letter.

(It is interesting that Gentile, the official philosopher of Fascism, would have come to say goodbye to one of his Jewish students forced to leave the country because of Fascism's racial laws.)

The day after my father's departure from Rome, September 5, Giaime wrote:

> Today Ugo Stille should be arriving by plane in Lisbon: this, too, is a funny thought after all the telephone calls and meetings in the years when we were always together.

By now, Giaime had begun referring to my father by his (and their) pseudonym. On the day my father left, he thought a lot about their friendship, later recording those thoughts in his diary.

> In those days I thought about the essence of our friendship . . . For four years we were always together and not only without there ever being a disagreement between us but almost in the belief that any difference between us that was not resolved by a brief ironic comment would be simply absurd and ridiculous. When we lost

ourselves with our friends in the long and memorable discussions of our youth, one of us would talk and the other would simply nod his head. With Lucio, with Valentino, or with Manlio, [very close] friends, there were times when I couldn't understand them and we reached points of genuine disagreement; with Mischa it was impossible because it was immediately recognized as a question of how the problem was presented and considered thus eliminated. The daily commentary that we made together had almost the character of a monologue.

13. LISBON

On the family's arrival in Lisbon they had to pass through passport control—a moment of terror. Even though my father's family had been able to assemble all the necessary papers, they also knew that some of them were not 100 percent kosher. Their Portuguese visa, for example, had been made out by sympathetic diplomatic officials in Rome who had acted on their own initiative without having cleared everything with the central office back home. So the family waited with considerable anxiety, wondering how closely the police official on duty would inspect their papers. "I will never forget," my father told me, "this Hungarian Jew who was in front of us in line—an intelligent-looking, cultivated man—the look on his face when they turned him away, sending him back to Hungary." The look that crossed his face was the knowledge of almost certain death: a vast majority of Hungarian Jews were rounded up and killed. A year earlier, the great German Jewish writer Walter Benjamin committed suicide after being turned away from the Franco-Spanish border, which then reopened the next day. My father and his family watched with trepidation as the same officials scrutinized their less-than-perfect papers—and then waved them through.

Lisbon was a pleasant revelation, especially after a year and a half of war in Italy. They had gradually gotten used to life during wartime, in which the city went dark at night because of possible air raids and many of the pleasures of life had become increasingly scarce. "When we were in Lisbon, it was wonderful to be in a city that was lit up in the evening and where we could eat white bread again," my aunt said.

Uncertainty carried them all the way to the final departure at the Port of Lisbon. Although they made it through the border patrol, most of their baggage, which was being sent in a separate shipment through American Express, had been lost, and I have a couple of telegrams my grandfather sent from Lisbon to American Express in Rome trying to track down their possessions. Luckily, the bags turned up in time to make the boat.

My grandfather had been able to take advantage of the fact that there were four members of the family to convert a fair amount of Italian lire into dollars, and the family carried the money around in a brown paper bag to make it look as inconspicuous as possible. One day when my father and grandfather were walking around, my father suddenly realized that his father had put down and forgotten the bagful of dollars in a store. My father ran back; it was still there, the dollars inside.

I learned this story many, many years later under rather funny circumstances. I was over at my father's apartment in New York and was getting ready to go across town to my own apartment. At the time, New York buses cost a dollar and you needed exact change. I asked my father if he had a dollar in quarters. He did and gave them to me. A week or so later I saw him, and he said to me, "What about that dollar you owe me?" I started laughing and made fun of him, a highly successful man in his sixties, hounding his son for a dollar. He then told me the story of almost losing the family's money in Lisbon. "After an experience like that, I can never look at a dollar quite the same way."

On arriving in Lisbon, my grandfather rather incautiously gave an interview to a journalist of the Associated Press who wanted to know about conditions in Italy, where the American press was no longer allowed to report. My grandfather let loose with a diatribe against Italy and told the journalist that the Italians had no stomach for war and if the British would step up their bombing, the Italians would surrender in no time. The story was picked up by *Il Messaggero* in Rome and caused a bit of a stir; in theory, the Italian government might have tried to have my grandfather stopped and sent back to Italy, which luckily did not happen.

On September 9, before getting on the boat, my father wrote a final letter to Giaime back in Italy.

Lisbon, September 9

Carissimo,

Many times during this trip I have missed everything I have left
behind and now that we are getting ready to board ship I begin
to fully grasp the heavy weight of this decision. A period of life is
closed: it is a past to which I want to remain attached. In it are all
the elements with which to build a new life. Of this period of life
our friendship is the most important element of all, the certain
central reference point for all other experiences. We traveled
together down an important road: now the essential thing, as you
wrote once, is not to lose each other. We must make sure that
when we see each other again our different experiences serve to
enrich each other, as has always been the case in these last years.
We must write to each other often, and this new correspondence
will try to reproduce our old ongoing conversation and will unite
me to this, our world.

Thanks for your last letter: it was the best farewell. Mine,
unfortunately, as usual, is written in a hurry. But perhaps this is
not bad: it is a sign of "continuity," and shows that I am always
the same.

Un arrivederci ed un abbraccio
Michele

Sergeant Michael Kamenetzki

I. THE BOAT

On the boat trip from Lisbon to New York my father and aunt had a grand time. They immediately made friends with a German family with three children, two the same ages as them. Their new friends were from a formerly wealthy family with friends in first class, and my father and aunt left their crowded, uncomfortable quarters down below and spent the entire trip up in first class, talking, dancing, eating lovely meals, drinking, and having a wonderful time. "We practically never slept in those nineteen days," my aunt remembered. "Occasionally, we would sit down in these comfortable armchairs in the first-class lounge and take a little nap and only returned to our room to change our clothes."

There was a tense moment when a British destroyer approached, stopped their ship, and insisted on examining the passenger list, looking for people who might be enemies of Britain. My father and aunt's new friends the Kleppers were terrified, since they were German but not Jewish; proving their anti-Nazi bona fides might be difficult. Their father (who was not on the boat) had been a close associate of Walter Rathenau, the German Jewish economist and government minister who was assassinated by German nationalists. The father had left Germany earlier, set them up on the island of Majorca, and abandoned them to their fate. The wife, when her money ran out after she got to New York, had to go to work as a maid. Unable to maintain a family on her modest wages, she was forced to farm out her children. Otto, my aunt's friend on the boat, was sent to boarding school, and the two daughters were sent to live with families in New Jersey and California. "The whole family was destroyed," said my aunt. "I've never seen anything so tragic." But when they all met on the boat, they had no idea what fate awaited them. The British destroyer let the Kleppers continue their voyage; they returned to first class and, for the rest of the Atlantic passage, at least, continued to have a grand time with my father and aunt.

2. NEW YORK

Arriving in New York, my father and his family finally met their great benefactor, S. L. Hoffman. He had arranged, very kindly, to meet their boat and had rented a little apartment for them in Brooklyn. That evening they went to dinner at the Hotel St. George in Brooklyn Heights. My grandmother, still feeling sick and exhausted from the ocean crossing, stayed home. My father couldn't remember much specific about Hoffman but paid him what, for my father, was a very high compliment: "I never once heard him say anything stupid."

The apartment Hoffman rented for them was a bit cramped and dark, and not long after moving in, the Kamenetzkis, somewhat to Hoffman's surprise, announced they were moving out. Hoffman may have found this a sign of ingratitude, but they were not used to being wards of charity; they were used to making their own life, and they soon made their way up to the Upper West Side of Manhattan, where they were still living when I was a child. My aunt, however, continued working for a couple of years as a messenger and office assistant for Hoffman's uniform-manufacturing company.

My father loved New York, loved New York from the start, the big buildings, the intensity, the freedom, the funny quirks, and the humor and gritty power of American slang. Back in Italy, he had watched American movies, movies like *It Happened One Night*, with Claudette Colbert and Clark Gable, and what impressed him most was the body language and the dialogue. "The people moved like they were free. No one in Italy moved that way," my father said. At the same time, he found a congenial group of Italian refugees and intellectuals, anti-Fascists and/or Jews who ranged from the architect and historian of architecture (and my father's schoolmate from the University of Rome) Bruno Zevi to the writer Niccolò Tucci to Max Ascoli, a Ferrarese Jew who had also been an early anti-Fascist and was now a professor at the New School for Social Research, where he managed to get my father a small scholarship to continue his studies. At the New School, he met, among others, Franco Modigliani, a future Nobel Prize winner in economics and an Italian Jewish refugee like himself. My father attended political meetings at the Mazzini Society, a gathering place for Italian anti-Fascist exiles in New York founded by the great Italian historian and anti-Fascist Gaetano Salvemini. There my father, having grown up under Fascism, was exposed to free and open political debate for the first time in his life. He attended public political speeches in Union Square with large crowds. The reading room of the New York Public Library was a kind of haven for the large number of stateless, homeless intellectuals who descended on New York and needed a place to read books and foreign newspapers, congregate, talk, or just keep warm.

Sometimes they would go eat lunch nearby at the Horn & Hardart automat—a futuristic concept in dining that seemed like a glimpse into the world of tomorrow. You waited in line with a tray, as at any cafeteria, but the food was served from behind little glass doors; you put coins into a slot at the side and the window would magically pop open. Although there was a staff of human beings behind the little glass doors making the sandwiches and salads and pieces of pie and putting them into the little glass windows, the gleaming wall of chrome, aluminum, and glass, the coins, and the little doors swinging open automatically made it seem like a gigantic machine out of which food materialized through some purely mechanical process. It looked like a stage set from Fritz Lang's *Metropolis*. It's not clear that all this mechanized apparatus actually saved any human labor, but the idea and look of it—the gleaming metal and glass, the illusion that food was somehow popping miraculously out of a great machine—satisfied a desire for a perfectly efficient futuristic world. My father had seen the future—and it worked!

About ten weeks after the family landed in New York, the Japanese bombed Pearl Harbor and destroyed almost the entire American fleet. My father was devastated—it seemed a crippling blow that might take years to recover from. To him, as a European, it represented the latest in a long string of catastrophic defeats: Spain, Czechoslovakia, Poland, Belgium, France, Denmark, Holland, Greece, etcetera. He was surprised and enormously impressed by the American response, by Roosevelt's magisterial calm in his speech before Congress the following day.

My father was equally impressed by the ordinary Americans he spoke with, all of whom, rather than being in despair over the devastation and loss of life at Pearl Harbor, radiated a sense of total certainty: that America, reluctant to enter the conflict, would now prosecute the war with an implacable determination that could lead only to victory. My father was in love—in love with America. He almost always referred to it as America and not the United States. America was much more than a name; it was an idea.

On New Year's Eve, my father and aunt and their friends from the ship went to Times Square to witness and participate in the long-standing tradition of watching the ball drop from the top of the old New York Times Building. The little group of refugees watched with excitement as the ball—a huge four-hundred-pound metal sphere festooned with lights—made its way down the flagpole. After years in the war-darkened cities of Europe, they had come to a world of light. My father and aunt had the number 1942—the coming year—written in ink on their foreheads, looking forward to a better year in the new land.

3 . SCARLET PIMPERNEL

Several weeks after he left Rome, the Italian government issued a warrant for my father's arrest. The episode at the University of Rome in which some of his good friends had thrown confetti with anti-Fascist slogans in the air during a pro-government rally had provoked a big investigation, and many of my father's school friends were rounded up and arrested.

A few of them who were able to confer with one another in prison decided that, as a defensive strategy, they should attribute to my father—since he was safely outside of Italy—some of the facts that they could not deny. As a result, when they got in a tight spot, they would say: "It was Kamenetzki. Kamenetzki did it." And so my father began to loom large in the minds of the police inspectors investigating the Rome Communist underground as a dangerous figure who had somehow slipped through their fingers. At a certain point, one of the interrogators supposedly said to Antonello Trombadori, one of the real members of the group, *"Ma 'sto Kamenetzki, dove sta?!"* ("This Kamenetzki, where is he?!")

And so my father enjoyed a brief, albeit fictional, life as a kind of Scarlet Pimpernel of the Italian Communist underground when he was in fact already in New York.

4. LETTERS FROM G.I. MIKE

After Pearl Harbor, my father was drafted by the U.S. Army. Although not an American citizen, he was of military age, twenty-two, and the army needed men. In fact, being drafted into the army put my father on the fast track toward citizenship, and so, from a purely bureaucratic point of view, it was a boon. Almost overnight, my father had a new name and a new identity, Michael Kamenetzki, American citizen.

A private in the U.S. Army, my father now found himself shipped off to basic training in Fort Dix, New Jersey, and then to Fort McClellan, Alabama. It would be hard to imagine a place farther from Rome—the cradle of the Roman Empire, center of European civilization—than the middle of rural Alabama. "I thought to myself," he told me, "what in the world am I doing here, and how am I going to get out?" Still, my father was impressed by the democratic nature of the U.S. Army; he loved the bizarre mix of people from all over the vast country, people from different backgrounds, socioeconomic groups, religions, and ethnicities (except blacks) who were thrown together in the barracks.

My father told me that he managed to befriend the officers in his company by giving them advice about their love lives, helping them interpret their dreams, and giving them a little free psychological counseling. My father had read some Freud and was able to put his more sophisticated culture to some sound practical use in making friends and avoiding being picked on as a short, scrawny foreigner with thick glasses and a thicker Italian accent. The part about the dream interpretation reminds me of the position of little Joseph, the Jewish boy who finds himself in Egypt and ends up interpreting the dreams of the pharaoh.

My father loved the camaraderie of the army and later enjoyed singing old G.I. songs he had learned there.

The coffee that they serve us, they say it's mighty fine:
It looks like muddy water and it tastes like iodine.
Oh, Ma, I wanna go home!

The biscuits that they serve us, they say they're mighty fine.
One rolled off the table and killed a pal of mine.
Oh, Ma, I wanna go home!

Still, he was enormously relieved when they were shipped overseas to North Africa, the beachhead from which the Allied armies were preparing their invasion of Europe.

Because of his knowledge of Italian and of Italy, my father requested to join the Psychological Warfare Branch (PWB), a section of U.S. intelligence partly concerned with journalism. In North Africa, he and his colleagues—generally immigrants from Nazi-occupied parts of Europe—listened to and reported on enemy radio broadcasts to try to suss out what was going on in their native countries. And when the Americans arrived in Italy, the PWB's job was to take over Italian media and de-Fascistize them.

One of the friends he had made while in New York was Nicola Chiaromonte, a brilliant Italian anti-Fascist of a slightly earlier generation than my father. He was born in 1905 (fourteen years before my father), and his early, immediate, intransigent anti-Fascism had forced him to leave Italy in 1934. Chiaromonte moved to Paris, where he became good friends with leading anti-Fascist intellectuals such as André Malraux and Albert Camus. When my father was headed to North Africa, he was given a message to carry from Camus to his wife, Francine, who was living with her sister in the Algerian city of Oran. My father's recollection of the visit: "They were both extraordinarily beautiful women."

In North Africa the American troops were together with the British troops. I recall my father telling me about meeting one British soldier who sat in a tent in the desert heat drinking steadily for hours, his uniform perfectly pressed and showing no signs of drink, until suddenly, after one last shot of whiskey, he simply fell backward and passed out. Another officer told him about his initiation into the Royal Navy. "On his first day, he was raped by the other men in his unit," my father said.

In the spring of 1943, my father began writing his letters home in English. He says that he was doing so in order to make the censor's job easier, but I suspect it was also a sign of how happy and integrated he felt in the American army. "I have many good friends in our outfit and we have a swell time . . . What's new in dear old New York?" he wrote in good, colloquial American English.

After Algeria came the invasion of Sicily. But my father was not one of the soldiers who emerged from the amphibian vehicles charging the

shore into a rain of enemy fire. He had a very comfortable war. He did
not see any action, fire any guns, or dodge any bullets. As a member of
the PWB, his first big job was to run the news division of Radio Palermo. Because all the Italian radio stations and newspapers had been in
Fascist hands, the Allies needed to take them and remake them. William
Paley, the founder of CBS, was ostensibly the head of this operation, but
because Paley and other high-level officials at PWB didn't speak Italian,
it was left to my father, a lowly private of twenty-three (he would eventually rise to sergeant), to actually put together the Italian-language news
broadcasts of Radio Palermo.

The Palermo that my father found when they arrived in July 1943
was a city in ruins. The bombing had been heavy and had destroyed
many of the most beautiful palaces and churches of the old city center.
Even so, with its large number of aristocratic parks and villas and palaces,
Norman churches and former Arab mosques, surrounded everywhere by
palm and orange trees, Palermo was one of the most beautiful cities in
the world. It is almost unrecognizable today, more because of the brutal
reconstruction that followed the war—a mass of cheap concrete construc-
tions built in coordination with the mafia—than because of the wartime
bombing. The Palermo my father found was a strange mixture of haunt-
ing beauty and the remains of recent destruction; among the people
there was hope and exhilaration at war's end along with real hunger and
desperation.

In the parts of southern Italy that the Allied Army occupied, they
found people who were so badly reduced by hunger that they were prepared to do almost anything for money, for a tin of rations or a package
of cigarettes—or something else that could be sold easily on the black
market. Norman Lewis, in his beautiful memoir *Naples '44*, describes
walking through the square of an Italian town where many women of the
town, dressed in black like almost all southern Italian women, were simply sitting there waiting, saying nothing, with empty ration tins next to
them. When a soldier finally climbed on top of one of the women, Lewis
realized that they were prepared to have sex with any G.I., right then and
there, in exchange for a ration tin. They didn't solicit business—they
were ordinary housewives and mothers, not prostitutes—but they were
simply desperately hungry and needed to find a way, any way, to eat. At
a certain point, the Allied military government estimated that roughly

one in three women of marriage age in Naples was engaged in prostitution during the war.

My father found a similar situation in Palermo. On the evening of his seventy-fifth birthday—his last, as it turned out—feeling rather happy and expansive, he gave way to some bawdy memories of his youth.

"On the second day after our arrival in Palermo, some soldiers from my company asked me if I could find some girls and arrange a party. We went to this apartment that was being used as some kind of Fascist headquarters and we said, 'We are requisitioning this apartment for the U.S. Army.' Then I found this girl—not exactly of the highest type—and she brought seven or eight of her friends. Then, in the middle of the whole thing, I heard this big noise out in the hall, banging on the door. It was the military police. These people we had kicked out had called the military police. I told them there had been a misunderstanding, but we broke the whole thing up . . ."

"Was the party going on?" I asked.

"We were screwing!"

"So you had acted as a procurer for these soldiers?"

"I was screwing, too!" he said.

Along with meeting their sexual needs on reaching Palermo, they set up their radio station, Radio Palermo, in Piazza Bellini (named for the composer of the opera *Norma*), right in the middle of the old city, a few blocks from Palermo's city hall, with its enormous and very beautiful Renaissance fountain that miraculously avoided damage. The station's building, located just off Via Maqueda, on what had been one of the city's most elegant streets since the seventeenth century, had a hole in its roof from a bomb.

Because most of the more established journalists in Sicily were compromised by their relations with Fascism, my father hired a group of young Sicilians to work on the Radio Palermo broadcasts. "Your father gave us some beautiful lessons in democracy," said Salvatore Riotta, one of the young men who started their journalistic careers at Radio Palermo. "I remember the way your father just sat there with his feet on his desk when the colonel who was the head of the PWB came in. You would never know who was the superior from the way they acted. They talked as equals. In the Italian Army, everyone would have jumped up to attention and treated him with a lot of bows and scraping. Instead there was great cordiality among the Americans and between them and us. There was no sense of them as the conquerors and us as the conquered." Riotta remembered a small episode that meant a lot to him. At a certain point, the American officials went out to lunch and Riotta and another Italian colleague had to remain behind to work. The Italians had no money and no food but said nothing. My father returned with a set of American army rations and gave them to them. "As he was returning from the restaurant, the idea occurred to him, the charitable idea, I would say, given my religious formation, the Christian idea of bringing us something to eat. These were our 'conquerors' who worried about our having enough to eat. It was a great lesson in humanity." (This particular detail is rather touching to me, since, generally speaking, consideration for others was not among my father's strong suits.)

At the same time, my father gave them important lessons in journalism that ranged from mere technique to deeper principles: "In radio, keep your sentences clear and simple. Repeat the subject. Repetition is annoying in print, but radio listeners don't mind repetition and it can easily keep them from losing their place in a story." Riotta remembered a more important lesson my father taught him at a point when the Allies were winning on all fronts. They were preparing the evening broadcast, and my father told him that they needed to redo the news. "Find me some bad news!" my father said; they needed to lead the broadcast with some bad news. "But," Riotta replied, "everything is going well." The Allies had landed at Normandy. They had taken Rome and broken through the Gothic Line in Italy. The Russians were advancing rapidly, and the Americans had taken several islands from the Japanese in the Pacific. "Why do we need to start the broadcast with some bad news?" My father replied, "The Italians have been living with propaganda for twenty years in which they have been told every day that everything was going great. And so if we tell them that we are winning on every front, they won't believe a word of it. If we start off with some bad news, they might believe some of what follows." And so, Riotta said, he managed to find a news dispatch about an American submarine being sunk somewhere in the Pacific.

5. THE LAST LETTER

In October 1943, a few months after he had been at Palermo, my father, miraculously, received a letter from Giaime, who had managed to make his way to Naples, which had just been liberated by Allied troops. Through Allied intelligence there, he had been able to track down my father.

Giaime had spent most of the war, quite unhappily, in Italy, far from the theaters of action. He had been preparing to go to the front in late 1940 when his uncle, Pietro Pintor, one of the highest-ranking generals in the Italian Army, was killed in a plane crash.

The war was going badly for Italy. In the wake of his uncle's death, Giaime was assigned to Italy's Armistice Commission with France, which his uncle had headed up. It was based in Turin, just over the Alps from France.

When Giaime's father died of tuberculosis a few months later, his fate was decided: as the eldest son in a family without father or uncle, he would not be sent to fight. As a result, Giaime would spend the war in a strange state of suspended animation: feeling utterly useless in a military bureaucracy he came to despise. Paradoxically, Giaime requested several times that he be sent to a fighting unit, even though he clearly did not support the Fascist regime or the war. He felt extremely guilty that he had a cushy desk job while friends of his were dying at the front. For better or worse, the war was the dominant fate of his generation, which he felt a need to be part of. At the same time, the war seemed the stupid negation of every value he held dear.

> If I have hated this war so much it is because there were too
> many other things that were worth living for . . . I had managed
> to build a free and intelligent life in which everything that
> attracted me was within reach and, for a brief period, happiness
> was within my own hands. Hence the bitterness I have felt with
> the impossibly large obstacle of the war. Some of my friends
> didn't feel this same bitterness because they were fully formed:
> revolution, a life of scholarship, or the love of a woman absorbed
> all of their energies. For me, travel and friendship, new books
> and new passions represented too rich a world to give up. The
> pain of losing these riches turned later into a hatred for the world

in which I was forced to live, that of the military . . . in which I
came to know the worst part of human society.

Despite his frustration, despite the restrictions of a military life for which
he had no taste, Giaime was nonetheless astonishingly active during the
two years between my father's departure and his return in mid-1943.
While keeping him pinned down in a city he didn't care for and in a job
he despised, Giaime's dull desk job seemed to leave him plenty of time for
his own work. He churned out numerous essays and translations and
took advantage of being in Turin to work extensively for the nascent
Einaudi publishing house, which was attempting the difficult task of
maintaining a free and independent culture in Fascist Italy.

But still, Giaime felt ground down by the war, and in the spring of
1943, as my father was in North Africa and the U.S. Army was preparing
the invasion of Sicily, he wrote to his friend Filomena D'Amico:

> Sometimes in moments of well-being or depression, I think of
> the nervous words of praise you once used about me which
> struck me particularly, because they penetrated right to the heart
> of what I consider my least apparent and most serious virtue: my
> constant pleasure in living. Rarely has it been put to the test as in
> these last years, which I would have wished to be very different.
> In these years of hard military slavery, those energies have been
> held in suspension: I feel like a mill with great capacity to work
> but with no water to move.

During the spring and summer of 1943, particularly after the Allied invasion of Sicily, as it became increasingly clear that Italy would lose the
war, Giaime's long period of suspended animation began to come to an
end, bringing water for his mill. Acting against Fascism had simply not
been possible when the regime was at the height of its powers; now, as
dissatisfaction spread among the military and even high up in the Fascist
regime, there was suddenly room for action. Giaime used his close ties to
the Italian high command to try to help organize opposition to Mussolini, and acted as a point of contact (one of many) between the military
and anti-Fascist groups. He was on his way to Rome on July 25 when in
fact Mussolini was unexpectedly voted out of power by the Grand Council of Fascism, a little-used body that had, up until that point, acted as a

rubber stamp for Mussolini's decisions. The Italian king, Victor Emman-
uel III, had Mussolini arrested the next day when he appeared to tender
his resignation. Although the king appointed Marshal Pietro Badoglio as
prime minister and held Mussolini prisoner, the new government did
very little to prepare the country to withdraw from the war and protect it
against Nazi Germany, which was still technically its ally. They dragged
their feet in negotiating an armistice with the United States and Britain
and made almost no military preparations to defend Rome and keep part
of the country out of German hands. The Americans hoped to land in
central Italy, cutting the German Army in two, occupying the south of
Italy, and trapping a number of German troops. But, realizing that they
could not count on the indecisive and fearful Badoglio for serious help,
they decided to land much farther south and, so as not to delay the landing any further, announced the armistice on their own on September 8,
1943. Despite having had two months to prepare for this day, the Italian
government seemed to have no plan of any kind. The king and Badoglio
fled south, giving no clear instructions to the Italian Army. Before leaving, Badoglio gave a hasty and confusing speech in which he urged his
countrymen to defend the country against enemy attack "from whatever
direction it should come." Italian soldiers had no idea whether they were
supposed to fight against the Germans or the Americans. While Italian
troops greatly outnumbered German ones within Italy, without orders
from their superiors, many soldiers stripped off their uniforms and fled
or threw down their arms as the Germans rapidly moved in to seize control of Italy. Some tried, desperately, to organize a popular resistance
to the German troops heading rapidly toward Rome. One woman saw
Giaime "headed toward a barracks in search of arms, inciting the people,
frightened and hidden behind half-closed front doors, to do battle against
the Germans." Another observer who recalled the tragic days following
the armistice said, "Not everyone was for moderation, for giving up.
Giaime Pintor . . . waving a big Italian flag, passed by yelling: 'To the
San Paolo Gate.' Groups of fighters climbed onto trucks, others tried any
way they could to reach the ancient walls, where the last fires of the battles were being consumed. They didn't give up, they were looking to
make a gesture, to struggle, perhaps for death."

Rather than stay behind in occupied Rome, Giaime managed to find
his way—despite the presence of German troops streaming into Italy—to
the southern tip of Italy at Brindisi, the place where the king and Badoglio

were trying to set up a kind of government in exile. At the end of September, the people of Naples staged a series of riots in the streets to protest the German occupation of the city, and with the Allies approaching, the Germans retreated, leaving a liberated Naples. Giaime, disgusted by the inaction, disorganization, and cowardice of the Italian high command, fled a second time and reached Naples. There he entered into contact with both British and American intelligence in an attempt to set up new Italian resistance groups. Among others, he met people at the Psychological Warfare Bureau, the part of the American army that my father was working for. Through them, he was able to reach my father in Palermo and send him a letter. In it, my father recalled, Giaime laid out his plans to recross enemy lines, which the Germans had now fortified heavily, in order to join scattered resistance groups outside of Rome.

Although we don't have the letter sent to my father, Giaime sent another letter to his brother, Luigi, at about the same time, explaining both his plans and his thoughts on the eve of this dangerous mission.

The letter began:

> I am getting ready to leave on an undertaking of uncertain outcome: to reach scattered partisans near Rome, bring them weapons and instructions. I send you this letter in the event I should not return in order to explain the state of mind in which I have accepted this mission.
>
> The details that led up to it have a certain biographical interest, but they are too complicated to explain now; some of the friends here can tell you about my flight from Rome, how I arrived in the territory controlled by Badoglio, how I spent ten terrible days in Brindisi with the Italian High Command, and how after becoming fully convinced that nothing had changed among our military leaders, I managed to make a new escape and reached Naples.
>
> Here, it was easy to find a congenial group among the political refugees and friends who fled here, and I have helped to create an Italian Propaganda center that could have a useful purpose and which allowed me to return temporarily to my usual activities and a quiet rhythm of life. But in all this period the need to participate in a more active way remained in suspended animation and I no longer felt that under the current circumstances I could justify the

comfortable life of psychological warfare; the growing impasse
of the military situation, and the prospect that the misery in
which the majority of Italians find themselves appears destined to
grow much worse made the decision more urgent. So . . . I
accepted to organize this expedition with a group of friends. It is
the natural conclusion of this last adventure, but above all the
point of arrival of the whole arc of the experience of our youth.

He went on to explain why a young intellectual with no combat experience, safe in Allied territory, who would have been well justified in doing
political or intelligence work on behalf of the anti-Fascist cause, felt the
need to participate directly in a difficult and risky military action.

In reality, the war, the last phase of triumphant Fascism, has
acted on us in deeper ways than appeared at first glance . . .
Without the war, I would have been an intellectual with
predominantly literary interests: I would have discussed political
problems and issues, but I would have regarded the story of
mankind as, above all, a matter of profound curiosity; an
encounter with a girl or a flight of imagination would have
mattered more to me than any political party or doctrine . . .
     I can assure you that the idea of going off to be a partisan in
this period holds little appeal to me; I have never appreciated as
much as now the advantages of civilian life. I am well aware that
I have been an excellent translator and a good diplomat but will,
in all likelihood, be a mediocre partisan. Nonetheless, this is the
only possibility open to me and I am taking it.

The ending of the letter is of particular interest to me, because it contains
a reference to my father.

If I should not return, do not be inconsolable. One of the few
certainties I have gained in my experience is that there are no
irreplaceable individuals and no irreparable losses. A man alive
always finds sufficient reasons for joy among other men alive,
and you who are young and full of life have the duty to let the
dead bury the dead . . . It would have been difficult to write this
exhortation to our mother or to our aunt and uncle, and the

thought of their anguish is my greatest worry at this moment. I can't linger on such a difficult emotional subject, but I want them to know my gratitude: their affection and their presence have been one of the principal positive forces in my life. Another great reason for happiness has been friendship, the possibility of overcoming solitude by establishing sincere relations with others.

The friends who have been closest to me, Kamenetzki, Balbo, a few of the girls I have loved, share these serene thoughts with you and assure me that I have not spent uselessly these years of youth.

The letter Giaime sent to my father spoke about the same extremely risky plan of crossing German lines, and my father, alarmed, managed to convince his superiors to send him to Naples, ostensibly to interview the philosopher Benedetto Croce for Radio Palermo, but principally to talk Giaime out of his mission. "When I got there I learned that he had left the day before—and been killed," my father said. He had been blown up by a German mine near the town of Castel Volturno, north of Naples. On his shattered body, they found an identification card made out for "Ugo Stille." Giaime had chosen, in what would prove the last act of his life, to take up again the pseudonym he and my father had used three years earlier when writing together.

Giaime's "last letter," with its uncanny and yet serene tone of someone writing as if from beyond the grave, became almost immediately one of the most famous documents of the Italian resistance. Published immediately in the clandestine anti-Fascist press, it became a kind of anthem of the partisan struggle, and after the war it was widely republished, becoming a manifesto for the figure of the politically committed intellectual, or *intellettuale impegnato*, as the Italians put it. It was touching to think that my father—the Kamenetzki in the final sentence—was one of the very last people Giaime thought of before undertaking the dangerous mission in which he was about to die.

But it was also maddening to think, given the beauty and historical importance of Giaime's last letter, there was another last letter, the one to my father, which may have contained other details, other thoughts, perhaps specifically directed to my father.

What became of the letter? I asked. "I don't know. I must have lost it," my father said with a shrug when I asked him. How could you lose it?! "I'm an idiot," he said casually.

I was hoping, perhaps, for a better reason: that Giaime's letter had been destroyed in a bombardment, that my father had been forced to destroy his personal papers in order to maintain military security. It was much more banal. He simply hadn't taken the trouble to save it, as he hadn't taken the trouble to save any of Giaime's earlier letters. Giaime, as the papers deposited in the state archives make clear, saved everything: thousands of pages of diary entries and correspondence with scores of people, including several letters from my father. It is not, I don't think, that my father didn't care. Quite the contrary. My father's letters to Giaime make numerous references to Giaime's wonderful letters, mentioning how much they meant to him. A letter sent after the passage of the Italian racial laws was "an act of real friendship for which I am truly grateful." On the eve of his departure, my father wrote that Giaime's letter to him was the "best goodbye," and their correspondence constituted his lifeline to the world of Italy that he was preparing to leave. But while Giaime kept all my father's half of the correspondence, my father had kept none of Giaime's.

6. "MA NON ERA L'AMORE"
("BUT IT WASN'T LOVE")

My father had a Sicilian girlfriend during the war, who, unlike the women he picked up after they first arrived in Palermo, was a nice girl from a "good" family. As a boss in the occupying army who was also an Italian, he must have cut an impressive figure. He seems to have had a fairly easy time winning her over. "Basically, I was kind of a scoundrel," my father said.

"Well," he said, "after the first few dates, in which we had only been kissing, I told her I wanted to go to bed with her. She said no. But then one day she came to my apartment. I had this apartment in Palermo over a restaurant. She took off her dress and she had a bathing suit underneath, and then . . . We spent the day there and had dinner brought up from the restaurant."

"Did you tell her you intended to marry her?" I said.

"Well, not exactly, but sort of."

A few months later, my father moved on to run Radio Naples and on up the boot of Italy along with the American troops, leaving this Sicilian girl, Enrica, behind. He appears to have led her to continue hoping that they would marry while in fact having no serious intention of doing so.

One of the documents in the Kamenetzki suitcase is a letter from Enrica, in which she finally breaks things off with my father more than three years after they met.

Genoa, January 3, 1947

Michele

At various points I have started to write this letter without being able to because I haven't had the courage, but now that I have gathered all my strength I feel I can write you, if not with serenity, with enough calm as is needed. The reason for the letter will be apparent quickly enough, but I do not want to end without first telling you what I think of you. You have taken from me, drop by drop, all the faith I once had in you. You have dangled me on a string without having any serious intention toward me. You took my affection at your own convenience and with a cynicism without bounds, leaving me with a little hope each time you would see me on your travels, just enough for me to live off for another year. So each time you would renew my hopes and you would then keep me at bay for as long as it was convenient for you.

Ingenious without a doubt, but ruthless as a system . . .

There is an epilogue to the story of Enrica. One day in the mid-1980s—about forty years after the Allied invasion of Sicily—my father got a phone call at home in New York. *"Ciao, sono Enrica."* "Hi, it's Enrica, I'm in the United States, on a vacation tour with a group of friends from Genoa, and we're passing through New York. Could we get together?" My father invited her to come for a coffee or a drink to my parents' apartment on Sixty-First Street in the afternoon, when he finished his daily story. When she sat down in my parents' living room my father quickly began to have a rather strange and negative sensation: that Enrica, despite the passage of forty years, was still carrying a torch for him, as if no time had passed at all. "You look exactly the same," she said, something that could not be further from the truth. He had been a very skinny kid when he was young and then, through a mixture of terrible eating habits and a resolutely negative attitude toward exercise, had put several inches onto his waistline and probably gained about forty or fifty pounds. His hair had gone gray and was getting thin. He had taken rather poor care of his physical person—overweight, out of shape, with brownish nicotine-and-coffee-stained teeth. The same, or worse, was true of her, according to my father. "She looked terrible," he said. "She had been a very pretty girl, but now she was an old bag." And yet as she talked, it became increasingly clear that she was flirting with my father. "I married, and my husband was a very nice man, *ma non era amore.*" (But it wasn't love!) She said the word "*amore*" with emphasis, as if to contrast it with the wild, mad passion she and my father had enjoyed in Palermo in 1943. She told my father a bit about her life, but the point of every story seemed to be her irresistible appeal to people of the opposite sex. "I tried to work for a while, but the men in the office wouldn't leave me alone, so I stopped," she said. She told him a story about a man who had desperately wanted to marry whom she had refused. Years later, the man, who now had a family with another woman, told her: "After what you put me through, you owe me, at the very least, *una notte di amore*" (a night of love). Was she implying that my father, having put her through something similar, owed her *una notte di amore?* She told my father that she followed his career closely, cutting out his stories from the newspaper, and she always looked out for whenever he appeared on Italian television. In fact, she had a network of female friends who were all on the lookout for him and would immediately telephone Enrica to let her know: "Turn to channel two! Misha is on!" And so she rarely missed an appearance of his. Gradually it became clear that she had maintained the idea of their affair in Palermo in 1943 and elevated it in her mind and in her life with her friends into the great love of her life, a fantasy, which increasingly parted company with reality. When my father, who was more and more disturbed by what she was telling him, reacted rather gruffly to something, she said, "You're the same, as irascible as ever," interpreting a rebuff as a charming character trait. My father, in fact, was so alarmed by Enrica that he got up and telephoned my mother, who was in the office working. "Come home immediately," my father said. "What is it? It's only four in the afternoon. I'm working." "Just come home right away!" "What's the big mystery?" my mother said. "I can't explain, but I need you to come home right away!" And so my mother was sent for in order to reassert her territorial rights to my father and their apartment and send Enrica back to Genoa.

"She gave me the shivers!" my father said, retelling the story a couple of days later, seeming to shiver visibly at the thought of this woman spending forty years tracking his every move and keeping alive the flame of what, for my father, had been the wartime fling of a caddish G.I.

7.

From Palermo my father went to Naples, where he witnessed one of the extraordinary spectacles of World War II: Naples during wartime. "Naples is a city of three million people," my father told me, "half of whom would wake up without knowing how they were going to eat that day." The millions of forms of human creativity with which they solved the problem of how they were going to eat was an astonishing thing to watch. The novelist Curzio Malaparte described a scene in his novel *La Pelle* in which a gang of Neapolitans picked apart an American tank piece by piece, as if they were a pack of starving dogs picking apart a carcass, so that in a matter of hours it had literally disappeared. "That was the way Naples was," my father recalled. My father's unit, the PWB, estimated that commerce in stolen Allied food, cigarettes, and supplies accounted for two-thirds of the GDP of occupied Naples, and Norman Lewis noted that at the opening of the San Carlo opera house "*every* middle-class and upper-middle-class housewife arrived dressed in a coat made of a stolen army blanket."

In setting up Radio Naples, my father hired a series of other smart young men to help him, including Francesco Rosi, the future director of such great films as *Salvatore Giuliano* and *Le mani sulla città*.

Like Radio Naples, many major institutions were suddenly opening up under the pressure of events. Since everything had been run by people chosen by the Fascist regime, there was a frantic search for younger people not heavily compromised by Fascism. Suddenly all the people whom my father had known before the war—his friends at university, his friends and colleagues at *Oggi*, the people he knew through Giaime in his military service in Salerno, Perugia, and Turin—had gone from being marginal, barely tolerated dissidents to becoming the new leadership class of the nation. Some had gone from Fascist prisons into the assembly that was writing the new Italian constitution, serving in the Italian parliament, starting and or editing newspapers, and running publishing houses.

In Milan, my father met the novelist Elio Vittorini, who had become a close friend of Giaime's and who was starting a new magazine, *Il Politecnico*, which he wanted my father to write for. Mario Borsa, who had been put in prison twice during Fascism, was made the editor of the *Corriere della Sera*. Since my father was planning on returning to New York, the *Corriere*, Italy's largest and most authoritative newspaper, asked my father to be a freelance correspondent for them from New York. Since my father was a U.S. citizen, he did not, unlike other Italian journalists, have to wait for a visa from the U.S. government, which was just reestablishing relations with Italy after years of war. The arrangement was considered temporary, until the *Corriere* was able to send a more experienced, permanent correspondent.

In Rome, my father saw many of his old friends again. Many of them had fought in the resistance and some had had highly adventurous experiences. His university friend Antonello Trombadori (a member of the Communist group at the University of Rome) had nearly died in one of the infamous German massacres in Italy, in which the Germans had killed 320 Italians in retaliation for the ambush of a German military convoy on Via Rasella in downtown Rome in which thirty soldiers had been killed. The Germans rounded up mostly Jews and partisans who happened to be in their custody at that moment. Trombadori was in the Gestapo headquarters on Via Tasso in Rome, but because of a high fever he happened to be in the infirmary when they were looking for people to send out to be shot at the Ardeatine Caves on the periphery of the city. After having narrowly escaped death at the caves, Trombadori worked with the director Roberto Rossellini, who shot the classic film *Roma, Città Aperta* (*Rome, Open City*), which described life under the German occupation—and retold the story of the ambush on Via Rasella and the Ardeatine Caves massacre.

Giaime's younger brother, Luigi, had nearly been killed as well. He was arrested in mid-May 1944, was tortured by a sadistic neo-Fascist band operating in Rome, and was scheduled to be executed. A last-minute intervention by the Vatican, organized by Zio Fortunato, resulted in a stay of execution, and he was saved when Allied troops entered the city several days later.

My father never mentioned anything to me about going to visit Giaime's family, Zio Fortunato and Zia Cecita, as he almost certainly must have—or about the emotion of seeing friends from childhood again who had each passed through adventurous travails, endured hardships, escaped dangers, and, in some cases, lost close friends and relatives. Or about returning to his home to visit Zia Keti, the German woman who had lived with them throughout his childhood and who had taken care of their house during the war. Instead, I remember him telling me of an episode when he and his men took over the radio station in Milan, the Rai headquarters on Corso Sempione. Because of the war and the draft, most of the people working at the station were women. The station manager was giving my father a tour of the offices and showed him into a news-room full of (in my father's possibly exaggerated account) overweight middle-aged women, girls with harelips and mustaches. At a certain point, my father asks his tour guide, "What is behind this curtain?" He opens it and finds a roomful of pretty young girls, whom the station manager had been hiding from the Americans, as if they were a conquering army intent on rape and pillage. "We'll hire these!" my father said.

He told funny stories about meeting Carlo Levi, the painter and novel-ist, who had been hiding out in Florence during the German occupation. As a Jew with a recognizably Jewish name and a conviction for anti-Fascist activity, Levi was in grave danger of deportation or the firing squad. But my father described his walking serenely out into the streets of Florence, without a care. " 'I don't look Jewish,' Levi said," my father continued. "He was the most Jewish-looking man you can imagine, like the portraits of Moses you see!"

8.

It is interesting that almost all my father's stories about the war were light and even frivolous in nature—whoring around in Palermo, behaving like a scoundrel with Enrica, the chaos of Naples, the girls hidden behind the curtain at the Milan radio station. And he said almost nothing about the tragic or painful things that he must have always witnessed, the hunger in Palermo and Naples, the bombed-out houses, the broken lives, the stories of friends who had died or lost relatives in the war— instead the emphasis was lighthearted. Perhaps it was because my father didn't see combat; perhaps because he was on the winning side, because he was young and the collapse of Fascism and the end of the war represented an entirely new beginning full of possibilities for him. Or perhaps it was the passage of time that filtered out the dark and made everything else appear light and funny. But there may be another explanation. In the memoirs of William Barrett, a professor of philosophy who knew my father and his circle of friends right after World War II, there is a curious passage that describes this exact phenomenon of my father and his friends Nicola Chiaromonte, Saul Steinberg, and Niccolò Tucci telling funny stories about the war:

> The conversation I walked into was anecdotal and rollicking. The whole War seemed to collapse into a swarm of amusing stories about Americans and Italians confronting each other in comic and pathetic misunderstanding. Each of us there, in his own personal way, was aware of the desolation and misery that the War had visited upon the Italian peninsula; but in the mood of the moment we could let these things be forgotten. The War was behind us, and we could even dare to look at in amusement.
>
> Not so long ago I happened to run into Steinberg . . . When I recalled this earlier conversation to him, the memory of it came slowly back. I told him that I remembered the liveliness of the conversation that afternoon rather poignantly now because it seemed typical of that whole period in its exuberant confidence that a great new world lay before us. Then, as his memory focused, he gave that sharp and reflective look at us, like a jeweler squinting sidewise at a questionable gem. "No," he said, "there was something else there too. Something simpler beneath our big ideas. It was the simple feeling that we had survived."

In confirmation of this theory, I recalled another story my father told about the end of the war. "After the fighting had ended we were sent for some days to Salzburg, Austria. We lived in a castle, this beautiful Austrian Schloss. The war was basically over and there was nothing to do. And there was this pilot with a plane and I asked him if he would teach me to fly. He said sure. So we went up and had a first lesson. A few days later, we had a second lesson. When it came time for the third lesson, I asked someone, 'Where is he?' He said, 'He's dead. His plane crashed.'"

The story seemed to sum up a certain absurdity in my father's experience of war: he could have died in so many ways, deported to a concentration camp if the family had not been able to get out of Italy, or killed in North Africa or in southern Italy, where fighting was going on; instead he almost died for no reason at all in a fluke plane crash after the fighting had ended.

That my father favored the light over the dark stories about the war is hardly surprising. Perhaps the most important passages of my father's life are composed of absences and of silences. His losing all of Giaime's letters, his decision not to return to Italy after the war, his decision to change his name, his reticence or outright refusal to talk about his early life, and his never taking us to Italy or teaching us Italian seem all of a piece; were part of a concerted, if entirely unconscious, effort to bury the past and put it behind him.

This attitude of apparently ignoring his past does not negate its importance for him. Quite the opposite, I suspect. When he finally began to talk about his early life with me, in his last years, he said quite plainly that the years of his late adolescence in Rome were probably the happiest and most important of his life—despite the fact that Europe was rapidly falling under the domination of Hitler, that his own family's position was becoming increasingly precarious and dangerous, and that Italy was plunging into the abyss of war. They were also the years of intellectual discovery and political awakening, in which he studied philosophy and graduated from university with top honors, years in which at a very young age, together with Giaime, he established himself as a young prodigy—*enfant prodige*—of Italian journalism and met a host of people who would go on to play an important role in his life professionally and personally. They were the years in which, in many ways, he put together the main elements of his future life; his friendship with Giaime was very much at the center of it, like the hub of a wheel.

It was not until 1993, at a ceremony for the fiftieth anniversary of Giaime's death—less than two years before his own, when he was already very sick—that my father agreed for the first time to speak publicly about Giaime:

I have often asked myself, and I think others have asked themselves, why I have never written about Giaime Pintor, who was my best friend in the years of my youth and the person who most

deeply influenced my development and my life. The explanation
lies in the reluctance I have always had to talk about myself, and
to write about Giaime meant inevitably to write about myself, so
deeply entwined our lives were between 1938, when we met, and
1941, when I left for America. We were, as he himself wrote in
Doppio Diario [his posthumously published diary], "inseparable":
we talked and saw one another every day, we exchanged not just
ideas and opinions, but impressions, judgments, comments on
everything that happened around us, on the important things as
well as the smallest ones. In other words, we observed the world
together every day. Friendships have a different quality in the different phases of life, and ours meant, then, "growing together."

It was a bond that made each of us a part of the other and which
we both recognized as such. The choice of a common name, Ugo
Stille, for the column that we wrote together, on alternate weeks,
for the magazine *Oggi* was the outward symbol of a state of mind
that we considered essential. When, after the Liberation, I met
Elio Vittoroni, I had no need to introduce myself: he knew everything about me from Giaime and our meeting was like the reunion
of two old friends who are seeing one another after a long time.
The same immediate rapport tied me, through Giaime, to the Tu-
rinese intellectuals at the Einaudi publishing house. "I am glad to
finally meet the other half of Ugo Stille," was the phrase with
which Massimo Mila greeted me.

Although it was refreshing to hear my father speak about himself and his
most important friends, this moment of apparent self-revelation hides
more than it reveals. By saying that he was reluctant to talk about Giaime
because it meant talking about himself, he evades the real question: Why
was he so reluctant to talk about himself?

My father's extreme reticence—greater than that of his fellow Italian
anti-Fascists—is tied up, I expect, in his condition of double exile. "Italy
was our paradise lost," the cartoonist Saul Steinberg told me, speaking of
his own and my father's experience as Eastern European refugees who
had found a home in Italy, only to lose it again with the racial laws and
the war. Steinberg, like many refugees, shared my father's reticence. Perhaps being kicked out of paradise had made it too painful to talk about.

PART III

BOGERTS

Letters Home: Money, Clothes, and Boys

I. LEAPS AND BOUNDS, OR CUTTING IN

One evening in May 1948, my mother went to a party in New York with her first husband and left it with her second, my father.

It was a party for Truman Capote, flush with the instant success of his first novel, *Other Voices, Other Rooms.*

My father, who always had an eye for beautiful women, engaged my mother in animated conversation. He wasn't very good-looking, but he was a hell of a talker and was doing his best to talk her off her feet. At a certain point, her husband, Bob Wolff, came over and announced, "Okay, we're leaving." "But I'm in the middle of a conversation," my mother said. "Then I'm leaving," Bob said, and stalked off. Later that evening— much later, in fact—my father walked her home. She left her husband three days afterward.

Six months after the party, my mother took a plane to the U.S. Virgin Islands in order to get a quickie divorce.

My mother was rebellious and impulsive and romantic—it is easy to understand why her parents were always worried about her. She began smoking and wearing lipstick at the age of fourteen, driving around in cars as a teenager before there were age restrictions on driver's licenses. My grandparents, although financially comfortable, spent money very carefully, especially during the Depression; my mother was free-spending, generous, and slightly extravagant and, as a result, often short of cash and in debt. Her earnest, serious-minded parents had a purely utilitarian attitude toward clothing, while my mother loved nice clothes, had excellent taste, and always fought to get her parents either to buy her clothes or to wear something better. When she was arranging a first meeting between her parents and the parents of one of her boyfriends, my mother wrote her mother a note of warning: "But, Mother, wear lipstick and no lisle stockings—for me."

Part of my mother's apparent frivolity was a rebellion against the somewhat dour atmosphere of the Bogert household. At one point, she was delighted because her mother wrote about an unusually jolly time the family had over Thanksgiving.

> I'm so glad you had such a lovely time over vacation. It all
> sounds very gay and exciting—just the way everything should
> be . . . I got a lot of vicarious pleasure in reading about your
> lovely Thanksgiving. Didn't I always tell you it was fun to go
> places and be merry? You should try it more often. (Ask your
> daughter—she'll bring you up properly.)

My grandfather had been a star student who had won highly competitive scholarships and worked his way through college and law school. My mother was often on the brink of flunking out, refusing to work in courses she didn't like and constantly in and out of trouble at both boarding school and college for various infractions, particularly missing curfew and staying out too late. She had a plainly irreverent attitude toward most of her formal education.

> School is just as dull as ever. There's nothing doing but lectures
> and things . . . For gosh sakes, Mom, don't make George and
> I come here next year. I don't think he'll like it any better than I
> do . . . I've decided that I don't want to go to school so far from
> home. If possible—in Chicago.

There are references now and again to things my mother is learning. She mentions attending a lecture given by the father of a student about the prison system, but my mother, very unpretentiously, interrupts her account of the lecture to let her mother know about a song she's listening to: "The radio's playing 'Night and Day.' I requested that at all the dances during vacation." My mother seems to have been routinely in trouble, especially for getting back late on weekends.

In one letter, rather incredibly, she writes: "Enclosed is a discredit slip of which I am very proud. Only 2 in one week is pretty good." With a certain brazen insouciance, my mother suggests that a possible solution to her discipline problems would be having her own car, so that she wouldn't get caught out late on weekends coming back from Philadelphia!

But for all her battles with her parents, my mother's letters are perhaps most surprising for their openness, especially her candor and volubility about her love life. One might have thought that she would have wanted to downplay her romances to her rather puritanical mother, who had no real love life before her marriage—I remember hearing my grandmother make a sternly disapproving remark about increasingly rampant premarital sex in the late 1960s. "I'm certainly glad I am not a girl today!" My grandmother had reason to worry that her rather giddy teenage daughter was neglecting her studies. This did not prevent my mother from impulsively scrawling things like "I got another letter from Phil" on the envelope of a letter addressed to her mother, after the letter had been sealed. My grandparents—or at least one of them—may have been more sympathetic than one might think.

At the end of another letter, written when she was sixteen, she writes:

P.S. *for Mom only*
Phil is trying to get a job in Chicago next summer and if he does he'll get a car, too, and so he can come and see me, can't he, for a week-end now and then? It would be swell. Now all he has to do is get the job.

A string of excerpts from her letters reveals a decided pattern:

Dean still wants a date with me and we're going to a Memorial Day dance. [Mouse-eaten part] I'll wear my new dress if I go—hey, hey—wish me luck with Jimmy! . . .

Mom was clearly the object of a great deal of male attention, something that she clearly enjoyed but that occasionally caused problems with her female friends.

Mrs. Klevan met us at Pottstown and we had a lovely dinner at their house. Oscar was simply swell—the only objection being that Ruthie and Blanche think so, too. I kind of got myself into

trouble because Blanche had thought I'd just be a pal to Oscar
but then I'm used to that. I still think he's the best bet since Phil.
Life ain't so bad . . .

Sometimes there is a wonderfully fresh and unpretentious exuberance
in these letters. At the end of one, she writes simply, "Isn't spring
wonderful?"

In September 1936, when she was seventeen, she interrupts one passage and exclaims, "Honestly, it's so much fun to be me. I'm enjoying
everything so much . . ."

Along with all the partying and joie de vivre, she was clearly, at the
same time, a dutiful and loving daughter. She is often visiting sick relatives in the hospital and bringing them books and flowers, having lunch
with her dim-witted aunt from Scarsdale, and asking her mother for
people's addresses to whom she owes thank-you notes. In one letter, she
returns a dollar she owes her mother, promising she will send a second one
soon, to settle a debt. But her own exuberant and flirtatious sexuality
comes out again and again.

> I had a grand time over the week-end. Saturday I bought my
> dress (which is just precious) and went to a one-horse (literally)
> circus. Saturday night Ruthie, Ellie, Ellie's room-mate (Kay) and
> I had a delicious dinner at Ellie's with our dates and went up to
> Sunnybrook afterwards to hear Hal Kemp. It was a perfect evening
> plus Hal Kemp plus an open car with a radio in it plus Tommy
> plus me made everything wonderful. We went double date with
> Dick and Ellie and didn't get in till about 4:00 am.

But at times, there is something a little frantic, even compulsive, about
the constant references to boys. After a while the cavalcade of young
men—Phil, Oscar, Ted, Bob, Mal, Tommy, Jimmy, Dean, Herb—
becomes a blur. While there is probably nothing unusual in a teenage girl
palling around with six or seven boys in a two- or three-year period, the
need to tell her mother about every twist and turn seems unusual and a
bit obsessive.

The fact that most of these letters are addressed specifically to her
mother and occasionally contain warnings like "for Mom *only*" makes
clear that something about all this romancing—or at least my mother's

need to relate all the details of her romances—has to do with the particular dynamic of her family: her strained relationship with her father and her especially close relationship to her mother. Despite my grandmother's being a prudish and high-minded woman, she had made my mother her private confidante about the difficulties and unhappiness of her own marriage and had even confided in her (surprisingly) about her unrequited passion for another man. My mother seems to have responded in kind. The caution that one might expect a rebellious daughter to show toward a somewhat censorious and disapproving mother clearly did not exist.

My mother seems to have passed these years in a kind of frenzy, so focused on boys and her social life that there was room for very little else.

> I'm now waiting (on pins and needles) for Tommy to come. He'll be here any minute I guess. He called me up when I was at Ithaca and he sounded exactly the same, only better. I'll write you when we get up to Ithaca—it's going to be swell.—I went down to White Plains this morning early and had my hair fixed and it looks nicer than I've ever seen it I think. I hope Tommy thinks so, too.
>
> Well, I guess I'll close now—I'm really too excited to know what's going on, anyway. Write soon.
>
> Love to all,
> Betty

In a postscript to the same letter, she tells her mother of another romantic conquest she made on a train into New York.

> P.S. I road [*sic*] down here on the train with a Cornell senior (male) (aged 25) and he took me to Grand Central in a cab and got me some magazines. He told me to call him up (at the Waldorf, s'il vous plait) if I came in, but I thought I'd better not. His name is Bob Lokmeyer (not Jewish) and he's much too sophisticated for me. He wanted to buy me a Dobbs hat because he thought it would become me. Crazy?

This reference to Jews is especially interesting to me in light of her eventually marrying my father. Clearly, she grew up with a certain amount of superficial, casual anti-Semitism. This was a time in America, after all, when the Ivy League universities, of which Cornell was one, had quotas to limit the number of Jewish students, and my grandparents may have communicated the fact that it was bad form to date Jewish boys.

She applied to Cornell (the only Ivy League school that was coeducational at the time), where her father had gone to college and later taught, and was admitted even though she was a rather indifferent student. "I got in with the greatest of ease," she told me much later. "If you could pay, you could go, and it didn't cost much." At a certain point, my grandfather had three children in college at the same time on a salary of $10,500, and it was not an economic strain on the family.

Rather than cooling off her social life, being in remote Ithaca as one of the relatively few girls on a mostly male campus had quite the opposite effect. "I was overwhelmed. It was incredibly glamorous and there were all these boys," she told me when we did our long set of interviews at her sickbed. "It was predominantly a boys' school, so if you were a pretty girl, you were just rushed off your feet. I had a lot of boyfriends immediately and I was taken immediately by the best sorority, Alpha Phi." The social life at Cornell was intense and it centered around the fraternities and sororities, with girls being bused in from places like Vassar and Smith. "First-rate bands played, people like Benny Goodman, Tommy Dorsey, and Jimmie Lunceford. You could get a really big band for about a thousand dollars. We stayed up all night and didn't go to sleep at all and had punch with milk and brandy for breakfast. Prohibition was over, and there was lots of drinking. Beer parties in the afternoon, drinking around the clock. All the boys had cars. It was still the Depression, but the kids who were there were kids whose families had somehow escaped the consequences of the Depression."

We get a pretty good idea of how heady this social-romantic life was from my mother's letters home, full of beaux and complicated stories involving multiple dates.

At the bottom of one early letter, one finds:

P.P.S. Every where I look I see a handsome young Cornellian driving around in a handsome convertible coupe. Whee! Lots of them stop by to pick us up but Frances and I have remained virtuous.

At the end of her first semester, she is both trying to persuade her mother to let her go spend a weekend with her Westtown boyfriend, Tommy, and his family in Philadelphia on her way back to Chicago for Christmas and letting her mother know that she intends to see a lot of a boy from Cornell named Mal when she returns home for the vacation.

Her mother nixes the Philadelphia scheme, but it hardly slows my mother down:

> I'm awfully sorry you decided against my going down to Phillie. I didn't really imagine you'd let me, anyway, so I wasn't horribly surprised or disappointed. I understand your reasons perfectly. But, anyway, I'd have loved to have gone. Tommy will be very disappointed but he can see me some other more convenient time—oh-dear!
>
> I had a perfectly wonderful weekend. Friday night was the Alpha Phi pledge dance—a great occasion indeed. I went with Mal. I revamped my black velvet into a sophisticated-looking jobbie with a plain low-cut neck. Mal sent me four luscious gardenias and I put them across the pout. They looked swell but the pins pricked me—especially with some of these bear-hug dancers. It was a smooth dance—loads of stags and just as much cutting in. Saturday night I went to a fraternity dance—Phi Kappa Sigma—or something. I had a lot of luu and felt very gay. Went with Dick Kinscherf—a very screwy person—but good looking and a good dancer.

In reality, the scene of my mother arriving at the party with her first husband and leaving with her second was something of a pattern that repeated itself more than a few times during her time at Cornell. In fact, in one instance, my mother went to a fraternity party with one boy and then, tiring of her dull date, jumped out of the second-story window in order to run off with another. Because of the small number of girls and the preponderance of single boys ("stags," as they were called), the students institutionalized the practice of "cutting in," whereby a boy without a dancing partner could tap the shoulder of another boy partway through a dance, and the original partner was expected to step aside.

My mother seems to have had a reputation among her sorority mates, who made up a humorous song about her.

Betty Bogert, dark and fair,
Has a flame most debonair,
When he phones
He moans and moans
Because she's never there!

Although the great majority of my mother's letters were addressed specifically to her mother, this particular one—with its references to Tommy and Mal, and her "sophisticated" dress with its low-cut front and "bear-hug dancers," and the poem about "Betty Bogert, dark and fair"— was addressed to both parents. At least some of Mother's advertising her busy social whirl, various flames, and juggling of two jealous suitors must have been for her father's benefit as well as her mother's. It seems strange that she would mention young men pressing her close on the dance floor, since her father had himself "bear-hugged" her on the dance floor. Could it be that appearing as an attractive sexual creature was the one way she had—for better or worse—of successfully getting her father's attention?

In her second year, my mother got involved with a rich boy from Kentucky named Bobby Y., whose family was in the oil business and had a big horse farm back home. Bobby came to Cornell with a string of polo ponies. "He had a lot of money. He lived in a way that I'd never been around before. He wouldn't bother to have his shirts washed; he just went out and bought new ones. He had a charge account and his father just paid it. He had a car and he treated me to a kind of swanky life. Bobby Y. was a hard-drinking, horsey man. He wasn't especially good-looking, but he had an intensity that I liked."

I have a distinct memory (and it would be hard for a child to forget something like this) of my mother telling me that she had her first sexual experience with Bobby Y. I remember her telling me something about having sex on the cold marble floor of a classroom building at night. (It is strange that a mother would tell her own children about her first sexual experience, but it is of a piece with my mother's experience, marked by a surprising lack of boundaries between parents and children: her mother using her as her own romantic confidante, her father's slow dancing and pressing her close to him, my mother sharing the twists and turns of her adolescent love life with her parents and then with Lucy and me.)

Her relationship with Bobby Y. didn't last the year, in part because she began to find him dull and also because there were so many other interesting young men around who kept "cutting in" at dances.

> We had our spring formal before I came down with poison ivy. I wore my satin print and Bob sent me 3 gardenias and a pale yellow orchid which looked very nice. I was cut in on all the time much to Bob's jealousy. We had a smooth time.

In a later letter:

> I gave Bob's pin back—much to his hurt and disappointment. I really didn't see much point in wearing it, though, because it wouldn't have meant much as far as I was concerned. I mean—I still think as much of Bob as I always have but as long as I like to go out with other people I won't wear it. Bob was willing to let me go out with others and wear it too—but I couldn't see that . . . He wants me to take it afterwards . . . and have it mean that we're engaged.
>
> Last night I was in charge of an informal dance we had here at the house. It was a great success—no credit to me—just that people made their own fun and plenty of it.

One of the men who kept cutting in at dances and the one who cut Bobby Y. out of the picture of my mother's life was Clinton Rossiter, who was to become her most serious college beau. "There was an Alpha Phi party and I went with Bobby Y. and there were always a lot of stags. There were always a lot more boys than girls. And Clinton Rossiter said, 'I'm going to take that girl away from that no-good guy.' So he would cut in, kept cutting in. And he made a play for me. He had been a very serious student and hadn't paid any attention to girls at all. Bobby Y. was kind of a rounder. And so Clinton made a big play for me. I was fed up with Bobby Y., because he was very jealous and possessive and demanding and he didn't like anyone very much. Anyway, I fled. I became Clinton's girl."

With Clinton Rossiter my mother discovered a different world. Rossiter was a dedicated student who spent his evenings in the library and was determined to make his mark in the world. He would in fact go on to get his PhD in history, return to Cornell as a history professor, and in his mid-thirties author a major book that won the famous Bancroft Prize for the best work of history that year. "She was fascinated by Rossiter because he was bright and clever," my uncle George said. "Rossiter and his friend Erston Keasby—I'll always remember the name—who was a real cut-up, always had something funny and interesting to say. They were full of laughs and jokes and fun."

Rossiter went to Germany to study during the summer of my mother's sophomore year, and it seemed for a time that they were drifting apart. "By the time he came back, he seemed to have cooled, but I was still crazy about him. I took up with a couple of other people. There was one of Clinton's fraternity mates who was in love with me. He was much more handsome than Clinton but didn't have Clinton's intensity and brilliance. Anyway, this guy was crazy about me and trying to get me away from Clinton. He told me that Clinton was in love with someone else, someone he had met on the boat to Germany. I was heartbroken but I carried on. One weekend, I went to a house party with another guy named Lyford Cobb, who was in the same fraternity, Psi U, where my brother lived, and it was right next door to the fraternity where Clinton lived, Kappa Alpha. So I went to the Psi U house party and Clinton kept sending me notes and messages. Lyford Cobb was very boring. And I just jumped out the window and ran off with Clinton. And we went to a dance at which Jimmie Lunceford played, who was very good in those days. And my brother came and got me. He said, 'You've got to come back. It's a disgrace that you agreed to go to that dance with one of my fraternity brothers and then deserted him.' After that, it began to get very hot and heavy with Clinton. I seduced him."

A study I read about sexual abuse among young women found that they were much more likely to be sexually precocious and sexually aggressive if they had had any of the following three experiences: been the object of sexual abuse, been the victim of parental violence, or witnessed a lot of fighting and contention between their parents. Although we have only her side of things, my mother arguably fit into all three of these categories. And it might help explain her powerful, nearly constant need for male sexual attention and approval and her relatively early sexual initiation, somewhat unusual for my mother's time and social milieu.

Thinking of my mother in her breathless state waiting on pins and needles for her date to arrive, being swung back and forth by young men "cutting in" during dances, going to a party with one boy and then jumping from the second story of a fraternity to run off with another, I find myself thinking of one of the more moving cantos of Dante's *Divine Comedy*, in which the tragic but damned lovers are portrayed as leaves being blown helter-skelter in the wind for eternity together but entirely in the grip of a force much more powerful than themselves.

2. LIVING THROUGH MEN . . .

My mother, like many women of her generation, channeled her ideals, ambitions, hopes, and dreams into the men in her life. It never really occurred to her that she might accomplish something important on her own. "Behind every great man, there is a great woman," went one of the favorite expressions of the day. Véra Nabokov (wife of Vladimir) gave up her own career as a writer to type manuscripts and do secretarial work to help support the author of *Pale Fire* and *Lolita*. Of course my grandmother, Lolita Bogert, had done the same thing as well—at least initially. Their life was set up, as was the norm at the time, so that the wife would take care of all practical details—the running of the household, cooking, and cleaning (or hiring someone to cook and clean), the raising, feeding, and schooling of the children—so that my grandfather could concentrate on his work during the day and be left in peace in the evenings. A good friend of my mother's explained to me once how she made sure to bathe and feed the children and have them ready for bed before her husband, who had an important job at the United Nations, came home. "I have to contend with the Arabs and Israelis all day long, I don't want to have to deal with the children squabbling with one another," he would say. My mother's friend Jane Gunther did much of the research for many of the books of her husband, John Gunther—*Inside Russia*, *Inside Europe*, *Inside Asia*—allowing him to turn out close to a book a year from the 1930s to the 1950s.

Of course, living through someone else's career is a dubious bargain, often fraught with resentment and disappointment. After all, the husband may have different ideas and goals than the wife. This was certainly the case with my grandmother, who was much more of a liberal and champion of social causes—women's rights, civil rights—than her more scholarly, cautious, and skeptical law professor husband.

Virtually all of my mother's close friends fell into this category: women who had married smart, ambitious, interesting men and who either didn't work or worked on an occasional basis at jobs that were meant to supplement the family income or to keep them happily occupied, as long as it didn't interfere with the husband's more important commitments. And all the important men in my mother's life fit into this category: Clinton Rossiter; her first husband, Robert Wolff; my father; and of course her own father.

Several letters from Rossiter to my mother, which survived several decades in the attic of my grandparents' farm, offer something of a picture of Rossiter and of their relationship, as well as his plans for their future:

> You must understand, that no matter whether I am a teacher (even at Westminster), business man, writer, or bum I mean to live in an intellectual home through all my days. Art, good music, religion, philosophy, current events—these are the subjects I like to discuss at the table, plus athletics and dirty stories to keep things well-rounded. I am damned if I will ever be a pedant, but I'm also damned if I will be a Philistine. Do you see what I mean? We will cross the best features of our two families, and the result will be ideal. Are you with me?

In one very revealing letter, he puts pressure on my mother to type his papers.

> Darling, when are you going to learn to take short hand and type? You know perfectly well that that would be a tremendous help to me in my career (whatever that is), and would make us practically collaborators in my work. Did I tell you that this woman at Sarah Lawrence who is nuts about me wants to type my report (30 pages) on the S.E.C. (for Professor Corwin) for nothing? That's devotion. I'll admit it was back around Christmas, and she was full of that old cheer, but I'm sure I could hold her to it. I'm working on the thing now, as you probably know, and will be to eternity.

. . . Well, sweet, be good, and remember that I love you. I'm working for you just as much as for me—don't forget that.

All my love,
Clinton

My mother did in fact type some of his papers, unpaid, although she, too, was in school.

I found a memoir of Clinton Rossiter written by his son Caleb and published online. At a certain point, Caleb Rossiter wonders how his father, who had considerable responsibilities at Cornell, lectured widely, and enjoyed an active social life, was able to be so productive. The answer, the younger Rossiter says, was that he had a full-time unpaid research assistant and secretary in his wife, who was a very smart, college-educated woman with experience as a journalist. This was a very typical husband-wife arrangement in academic couples at that time. Caleb Rossiter writes:

> How could the professors of the 1950s both write and teach so fully? The truth is that they couldn't—at least not alone. In my parents' circle, husbands and wives were teams. The wives not only maintained an environment at home that made their husbands' professional life unencumbered, but they also assisted with research, editing, and the thinking through of concepts. Born just one or two generations away from taking the lead and not the supporting role, they could only explore their own intellectual interests with their friends, their books and, in a combination of the two, their weekly "reading group," where the discussion was of as high a caliber as any taking place on the campus between their husbands. When my mother and her friends started the reading group, each of the husbands told his wife that he would be glad to come and lead the discussion on a particular book. The women demurred: they heard what their husbands thought about things all the time.

Along with his placing my mother in a position of subservience, there are some hints of cruelty in Rossiter's conduct, and his love for my mother is expressed in the rather aggressive language of ownership. He signed some letters to her "Your possessor."

My darling,

This is just a short line before I go to bed to tell you how much I love you and miss you. I really feel terrible, and I need you so badly. I honestly can't understand how I could have been at all mean to you last night, because now I love you so much I just would be afraid to be that way. Anyway, that all came out alright, didn't it? I hope so.

  . . . Good night, my love. I love you awfully, and I need you awfuller. Think of me often, and remember that I possess you. See? And will do the same.

All my love, darling,
Your Clinton

Although my mother finally began to apply herself more seriously during her third year at Cornell, during the summer of 1939, after my mother returned home to Chicago, her mother, Lolita Bogert, decided to do something radical: to take my mother out of Cornell and send her to a brand-new school that had just been started in Chicago, the New Bauhaus. She concluded, not without some reason, that my mother was wasting her time at Cornell among all those proms and fraternity and sorority parties and that perhaps what she needed was an education that was closer to my mother's particular gifts. "My mother thought I was brilliant and artistically talented," my mother said.

Lolita Bogert had read about this new school being set up in Chicago out of the ashes of the old Bauhaus school that had been hounded out of Hitler's Germany. The Bauhaus, founded by Walter Gropius in 1918, had been set up in Weimar and closed down by Hitler after the Nazis took power in 1933, a leading symbol of the decadent modern art that Hitler abhorred. The school, which attracted such modern masters as the architects Gropius and Ludwig Mies van der Rohe, the painters Wassily Kandinsky, Paul Klee, Josef Albers, and Lyonel Feininger, and the designer and architect Marcel Breuer, was perhaps the most powerful center of modernist artistic thinking in continental Europe.

The Bauhaus wanted to bring technology and industrial materials into art, architecture, and design for everyday living. Despite the aesthetic achievements of modern art—cubism, surrealism, futurism, expressionism, abstraction—art remained the individual creation of unique, hand-crafted objects and hadn't really come to terms with the world of industry and technology. Didn't new industrially produced materials such as steel, aluminum, and plastic offer the possibility of creating things of beauty that were mass-produced, inexpensive, and available to everyone that also bore the geometrical, abstract beauty of modern art? Hence Mies and Breuer designed beautiful sleek chairs out of shining steel tubes.

"Form follows function," "less is more" were some of the watchwords of the Bauhaus: a love of simplicity and abhorrence of useless ornament and artistic bombast. The Bauhaus sought to bring together the various arts—painting, architecture, theater, photography, weaving, printing, and poster design—in which the distinctions between fine and applied arts were dissolved. Klee, although known now mostly through his painting, taught workshops in bookbinding and weaving, among other things. Herbert Bayer, also an architect, taught printing and advertising. Breuer was first a student at the Bauhaus and then taught the furniture workshop. "It is harder to design a first-rate chair than a second-rate painting—and much more useful," wrote Alfred Barr of New York's Museum of Modern Art, introducing the Bauhaus spirit in 1938 to American audiences. Although the Bauhaus was not explicitly political, it was supported by the Weimar Republic and tried, among other things, to build attractive, low-cost housing for workers and their families. One of its members, Hannes Meyer, was a Communist and designed a modernist trade union school outside Berlin. Moreover, it was an international, highly cosmopolitan movement, bringing together artists who were German, Hungarian, Swiss, American, and Russian, some of them Jewish.

This international spirit, its openness to new currents of art, abstraction, Russian constructivism, and German expressionism and its love of simplicity, of clean, unadorned modern geometries, could not have been further from the insanely grandiose plans that Hitler and Albert Speer drew up for a neoclassical Berlin whose massive scale would put the grandeur of ancient Rome in the shade. And so the Bauhaus was shut down and many of its leading lights—Gropius, Mies, Breuer, Feininger, Bayer—ended up in the United States after 1933. Gropius and the artist László Moholy-Nagy explored the idea of remaking the Bauhaus in England but couldn't find the necessary funding. But in 1937, a group of Chicago industrialists asked Gropius to form a New Bauhaus in their city. Gropius, who had just accepted a position at the Harvard architecture school, declined. But he recommended Moholy-Nagy, a charismatic Hungarian Jew who was best known for his beautiful and extremely innovative photography, but was also a brilliant commercial designer and had taught the metal workshop at the old Bauhaus.

The New Bauhaus, known from 1939 to 1944 as the School of Design, was an untried experiment. And it went broke and briefly closed after several months, generating a series of lawsuits and countersuits when it turned out the industrialists hadn't put aside enough money for a full year's operations. And so it was to this rather improbable educational gamble—a bunch of wild European avant-gardists operating on the brink of bankruptcy—that my grandmother, a member of that high-minded, idealistic Chicago upper crust, decided to entrust her beloved elder daughter.

When my mother and grandmother arrived for an interview at the School of Design, Marcel Breuer flipped quickly through my mother's thin and amateurish art portfolio and said to my grandmother, "I will accept your daughter because of her beautiful forehead."

It was a rather daring move for my grandmother, who was unconventional in her thinking but hardly bohemian. But my grandmother was impressed by the idealism and seriousness of purpose of the Bauhaus—which aimed at nothing less than reforming art education in America—and felt it would bring out the talent and potential of my mother, who had distinguished herself at Cornell as a rather dizzy prom-trotting coed.

In fact, my mother, through her relationship with Rossiter and her own reading, was already searching for something more substantive. She was ready for this encounter with the Bauhaus world, and it suddenly gave a direction and purpose to her life. This extremely intense group of European intellectuals and artists, refugees and political dissidents, introduced her both to the great political conflicts of the twentieth century and to a host of big ideas and "isms"—constructivism, functionalism, formalism, expressionism, surrealism, socialism, anarchism, communism, and fascism. My mother was hit by it at a receptive moment, having tired of the proms and fraternity parties of Cornell, and it suddenly gave her new energy and a set of all-consuming interests. She expressed her new enthusiasm for the doctrines of modernism to Rossiter, and this was clearly threatening to her would-be "possessor."

He responded very defensively by attacking the Bauhaus approach. In one letter:

My sweet,

I am so glad to hear that you are going on a campaign to write me more often. I am behind it 100 percent. Also I am delighted that you want me interested in what you are doing, since it reflects the thoughts I wrote you in my last letter. You know perfectly well that I consider your work worthwhile, and I am terribly pleased that you have a real interest at last, one that you can take through life. I just don't want you to succumb to this modern idea, in no way peculiar to the realm of Art, that what is old is worthless at best, and probably harmful. I understand your theory of functionalism in Art, but remember that true Art is an end in itself, a "per se," and it needs no practical use to justify its place in our world of beauty. The more functionalism the better, I say, because it may bring Art to people who otherwise would never know it—but don't carry the thing too far. Think about these things; don't accept the tenets of your so-called "new school" as the awful truth. Ars gratia Artis! I think!

Rossiter was rather conservative in his artistic taste—he loved Beethoven and Wagner—and was highly skeptical of the avant-garde. No doubt she was writing him with the naive idealism of a twenty-year-old who has discovered something new and exciting. He does his best to crush it and put her back in her place. He apparently held out to her a vision of life in a white farmhouse in somewhere like Connecticut with a station wagon and a houseful of kids, and she evidently criticized this as conventional and conformist, to which he responded with fury and sarcasm.

Darling,

Don't you think I'm wonderful writing you so many letters? I do. Of course, I think I'm wonderful anyway.

I practically split a gut over your last letter. Dearest, you are trying so hard to be an artiste, but you are failing miserably with me. If I ever thought you were about to become a long-hair, I'd come out there, put you over my knee, and pound the hell out of you. I don't know just what kind of life you really want to lead, but it's got me worried. The things I do and the way I want to live are not the result of any desire on my part to conform to anybody's idea of what's right. I happen to like white farmhouses, Connecticut, tradition, station wagons, etc, per se—and not because they are the thing to do. As a matter of fact, I think it's too bad that people like you have the idea that <u>everybody</u> who likes that sort of thing is just a lousy conformist. That's where you're wrong. If I were a conformist I would now be working in some advertising company and be looking forward to a grey-stone house in Westchester—with lots of bratty suburban children, etc. Really, you misunderstand (and ridicule) me without any factual basis. After all, baby, you're no eagle. Just why is it you wear sweaters and skirts? You're just another damned conformist. There, see, you're mad. Why, because I understand your philosophy completely. Isn't that what you are saying? This is rich. I'd better stop it before I get you mad at me. And by the way, baby, I have a new woman absolutely nuts about me, absolutely nuts. I am doing nothing to encourage her; have done nothing. What is there about me? Damned if I know.

All hooey aside, I miss you very much. I think of you a lot, darling. I used to dream about our future, but that is becoming harmful—because it brings dissatisfaction in its wake. Now I think about our past. (woo! woo!)

. . . I trust you, darling. I love you, too. You need a little going-over, but I love you anyway. You're [r—ble?] I'll bet you'd love love to have a black coat with a mink collar. I'll buy you one someday. We'll live six months in the city and six in the country. We'll have piles of brats. Yours can be long-hairs and bring Jew friends from college. Mine will be harmless snobs like their father and bring other harmless snobs from college. I love you. That's all that counts. I hate cocker-spaniels. I'll stick to T.B. and Hooty.

All love,
CL

Another bone of contention in their correspondence was a ring. Rossiter had given my mother a special Tiffany ring that belonged to his family. Although it was not officially an engagement ring, it clearly had a similar symbolic value to him. Unfortunately, the ring didn't fit my mother very well, and she lost it in either a sink or a toilet bowl. Rossiter was furious but even more so determined to have my mother pay to buy a new ring.

> I hardly slept last night thinking about it, both because it was a great loss to me, and because I don't want you to feel badly about it. I know how $51 looms up to you, and you know how the ring and its meaning looms up to me. What are we to do?
>
> Get this straight: I want to know exactly how your family regards my part in this fiasco. I think they secretly are very mad at me and think I'm making an impossible demand that you get me a new ring or else. I hope I'm wrong. There's your situation, darling, and I feel awful about it: the ring is lost, a new one is $51.00. I don't know what to do, and whatever happens—one or the other of us will be in debt to the other, and your family will be sore at both of us. Maybe I can go forever without my family noticing it. What's the answer?

My grandmother coughed up the $51 for the Rossiter ring, but my mother felt that the affair of the ring was characteristic of a certain stingy, shabby mean-spiritedness in Rossiter that she didn't like, and it helped bring their romance to an end.

But perhaps even more decisive in their final break was that she had embraced the world of the New Bauhaus, having traded one set of ideals for another. She had been attracted by Rossiter's intelligence and seriousness. But in the end she had found the world of Ivy League scholarship and the prospect of living in a house with a white picket fence and typing his articles and books less appealing than the more bohemian world she had discovered in the Bauhaus. It was inevitable that my mother would meet a man who embodied those ideals. This came about in the form of her painting teacher, a dashing young artist named Robert Jay Wolff, who cut in and took my mother away from Rossiter.

From Bauhaus to Our House,
or the Detective Report

I. THE DETECTIVE REPORT

When my grandfather George Gleason Bogert learned that my mother had taken up with her painting teacher, Bob Wolff, he became apoplectic and hired a private detective.

The detective agency's report moldered for decades in the attic of my grandparents' farm in Michigan. The farmer who bought their place seemed to have a greater interest in my grandparents' personal papers than they did, and he found it. But it was lost when the farm was sold again.

It would be fascinating (to me) to know what it said, but I doubt it contained any major facts that were not common knowledge. My grandfather had several reasons to consider Wolff an unsuitable match for his daughter. He was a married man with a seven-year-old daughter; he was my mother's teacher; he was an impecunious artist; and, last but probably not least, he was Jewish.

"When we met, I was twenty and he was thirty-four," my mother told me. "He was beautiful. He was a gorgeous, beautiful man and women were wild about him. He was a big fish in the world I had just entered. He was the head of the Illinois art project; he was a sculptor and a painter. He had been to Yale and had lived in Paris."

That her father objected to their union only pushed my mother further toward Wolff. Rebellion against her industrious and stern father had always figured heavily in my mother's behavior—smoking, wearing lipstick, and staying out late. But if attending parties and running around with boys in open cars was a fairly empty form of rebellion, in taking up with Bob Wolff, my mother was embracing an entire world and a world-view, an alternative set of values—the world of art and literature, as well as a freer, less conventional, more bohemian life. Bob Wolff was not a hard-drinking fraternity boy but a man who carried some weight and was respected in the world my mother had chosen to inhabit, in the school where her mother had sent her to study.

2. SANITY IN ART

Through the School of Design, my mother formed relationships with people who represented a different world from the one in which she grew up. She formed a series of lifelong friendships with some of the women she met there.

Perhaps the closest friend to come out of her Bauhaus days was Katharine Kuh, who ran the first (and, at the time, the only) gallery of modern art in Chicago. Katharine was an extraordinary woman who had overcome extraordinary odds in her life: she had had a crippling case of polio that kept her in a body cast for most of her childhood and left her severely hunchbacked for the rest of her life. Although she had been married for a time, she had rebelled against the role of suburban housewife, gotten divorced, and decided, improbably, to start a contemporary art gallery. She had studied art history at Vassar College and had been infected by the enthusiasm of Alfred Barr of the Museum of Modern Art with a love for the experimental, modernist art emerging from Europe at the time. In the late 1930s, operating with almost no capital, she was often the gallery's only employee and practically lived in its offices, doing everything from hanging pictures to writing up invitations and brochures and giving art appreciation classes in the evenings to help pay the bills.

Contemporary abstract art was so little known in Chicago at the time that Katharine was able to buy a beautiful expressionist landscape of Kandinsky's for twenty dollars when a major local collection was put up for auction. "What am I bid for this Timpansky?" the auctioneer said. "Only a blithe neophyte would have been brash enough to start a contemporary art gallery in the Middle West, at that time the home of entrenched conservatism," Katharine later said.

The Katharine Kuh Gallery did the first shows in Chicago of such acknowledged twentieth-century masters as Wassily Kandinsky, Paul Klee, Josef Albers, Joan Miró, Fernand Léger, Alexander Calder, Isamu Noguchi, Ansel Adams, Le Corbusier, and László Moholy-Nagy. While it provided my mother and many others their first serious exposure to contemporary art, the gallery also became the object of fierce opposition and attack. A movement sprang up called the Society for Sanity in Art, whose purpose was to keep all abstract art (especially foreign abstract art) out of Chicago's museums and art galleries, while promoting the healthier values of representational and preferably American art. "I have been called an iconoclast, and indeed I am one, in that I am trying to destroy false gods that have been forced upon us," the movement's founder, Josephine Logan, the wife of a prominent Chicago businessman, wrote. Sanity in Art found ready support from the city's most powerful newspaper, the *Chicago Tribune*, owned by archconservative Colonel Robert McCormick, and the Hearst newspaper the *Herald and Examiner*. Paul Gilbert of the *Herald and Examiner* wrote a story called "Moderns Are Weird" and called the drawings of Léger "nightmares."

The *Tribune*'s chief art critic, Eleanor Jewett, who had no background in art but happened to be the grand-niece of the paper's owner, waged an ongoing campaign against Kuh's gallery. She dismissed Josef Albers's abstractions as nothing more than "nursery school efforts." About Le Corbusier, she wrote, "One hopes he does not build like he paints."

"She became a terrible enemy of the gallery," Katharine said. "Here we were living in a marvelous period when the great artists from Europe were developing a new visual language, really a new philosophy, and she was hell-bent on destroying them. The *Tribune* had an enormous circulation and most people in the city really took it as the word of God." Women from Sanity in Art, generally dowdy-looking matrons with large hats, would come and try to disrupt the openings and harass potential customers.

When Katharine put up a show of the Mexican abstract artist Carlos Mérida, three women from Sanity in Art came to the gallery and, seeing Mérida sitting and reading a newspaper, began berating him for putting such "meaningless garbage" up on the wall. Almost totally deaf, Mérida couldn't understand a thing they were saying and thought, seeing their excited visages, that they were enthusiastic admirers of his work. "He was beaming, and the more he smiled the more heated they became," Katharine recalled. "The next thing I knew, he picked up the head lady's hand and kissed it fervently. She didn't know what was happening. The women were overwhelmed with confusion, and they departed in total befuddlement."

During the Joan Miró show, someone smashed the gallery's plate glass window. Gilbert of the *Herald and Examiner* wrote an article implying that the vandalism was comprehensible, as Kuh was "the leader of the leftists."

As the women from Sanity in Art kept coming and chasing away her clients, Kuh finally called the police, who made the women leave for disrupting the legitimate conduct of business.

Moholy-Nagy's New Bauhaus/School of Design became a natural ally to the Katharine Kuh Gallery. Katharine put on a show of Moholy-Nagy's work as well as one of the work of my mother's new love interest, Bob Wolff. She collaborated with Moholy-Nagy and the Hungarian artist György Kepes to create a highly innovative show on the art of modern advertising and design. She got so caught up in the excitement of the show's material and ideas that it wasn't until it was ready to open that she realized that she had forgotten she was running an art gallery—there was nothing in the show for sale.

Given these various connections, my mother and Katharine were naturally drawn together.

"When I met [Elizabeth] she was just a girl, but she was absolutely adorable," Katharine said when I interviewed her many years later. "She was very serious about her work and I think she learned a lot at the Moholy school. Juliet [Kepes] was as beautiful as Grace Kelly, and Ann [Binkley, future wife of Paul Rand,] was extremely beautiful as well, but Elizabeth was more attractive. By attractive I don't just mean pretty; I mean that people were literally drawn to her like a magnet. If the three of them were in a room, I can promise you the men gravitated to Elizabeth. She had an extraordinary magnetism, a freshness, and a kind of unselfconscious charm that men found irresistible. She flirted like the devil, and I mean men were *crazy* about her."

One day, according to my mother, her teacher Bob Wolff announced to her that he was madly in love with her and was leaving his wife. My mother found this extremely romantic—she loved intensity—and threw herself into this new affair.

"He was a smart and cultured man and he had great enthusiasm and he read all kinds of things I had never heard of. I knew the classics,

Shakespeare and that sort of thing, but I didn't know a lot of the newer stuff, writers like Sherwood Anderson and Richard Wright, he introduced me to all that. And he knew modern art and he taught me a lot about that. I admired him. He was the father that I had never had."

"I think she was attracted by Bob, but he was always insane about her," Katharine Kuh said. "Till he died she was his favorite person."

Because of my mother's close friendship with Katharine, my grandfather came to see her in an attempt to convince her to help him break up my mother's relationship with Bob Wolff. "One day I was sitting in my gallery and your grandfather came in and introduced himself as Professor Bogert, and he said, 'My daughter admires you very much and everyone says that you know her fiancé quite well, so I thought I ought to talk to you—I disapprove highly of this marriage. I particularly object to the fact that this man is a Jew, am I right?' I was enraged, just enraged. I was a Jew. And he kept saying, 'I wish you'd try to persuade him to find someone else.' And I said, 'I'm going to persuade you to walk out of that door!' I was furious. I said, 'I happen to be a Jew myself, but I would have asked you to get out anyway.' And he left. I was amazed at an educated university professor talking this way."

Anti-Semitism was a widespread and simply accepted attitude in the world my mother grew up in. It was not a virulent ideology of racism so much as an automatic, unreflective posture of distrust and disapproval toward the "wrong kind of people." But clearly it was strong enough that it had been communicated in some measure to my mother growing up. In one of her letters from college, my mother felt it necessary to write "(not Jewish)" when describing her encounter with a young man with a strange and suspicious-sounding name, Lokmeyer. Clinton Rossiter seemed to share the prejudice: in expressing his disapproval for my mother's new circle at the School of Design, he refers half jokingly to "Jews and longhairs," and refers to himself as a "harmless snob." It was anti-Semitism as a form of "harmless snobbery," but it appears to have been a strong part of my grandfather's vehement disapproval of Bob Wolff.

But her father's violent opposition to Wolff caused my mother to dig in her heels. "If they hadn't made such a big deal of it, I probably wouldn't have married him," my mother said. Much of my mother's early life can be seen as a form of rebellion against her powerful, stern, and disapproving father.

Despite her parents' opposition, my mother's wedding was held at my grandparents' house on Greenwood Street in Hyde Park, and Katharine Kuh, despite her blowup with my grandfather, was among the guests.

Even though my mother claimed to have married Bob Wolff in part to spite her father, it is hard not to see that she was seeking someone rather similar to him. They were both professors. Wolff was fourteen years older than my mother—the exact same age gap as between my grandfather and grandmother. And yet, unlike my grandfather, Wolff was attentive and affectionate. "He was the father I never had," as my mother said.

They were married in 1941, when my mother was twenty-two. Later that year, the United States entered World War II, and Wolff was drafted and sent to Maryland to work in a division making maps.

3. LOVE, BETTY

When my mother begins writing home as a married woman after her marriage to Bob Wolff, she seems almost like a different person compared with the dizzy sorority girl at Cornell. It may simply be the passage of time—there is a four-year gap in my mother's letters home, between her last spring at Cornell, 1938, and the summer of 1942, when she writes her parents from Baltimore, where she and Wolff lived at the beginning of the war. Whatever the reason, her voice is much more mature and her letters much more descriptive and interesting, with broader political and literary interests.

[July 13, 1942]

We are getting more and more fond of Baltimore for no special reason at all. I guess the answer is that we are very happy, and so we think it's a wonderful place we live in. . . .

You'd be amazed and delighted at the way Bup and I have been converted to country life. We spend our Sundays roaming the woods in back of these apartments. The trees are lovely and Robert has fallen in love with leaves, which he has arranged in every available vessel throughout the apartment. Robert is quite ignorant about plants, so I teach him the names of flowers and trees, which I learned from 22 years in the bosom of the Bogert family. We hate being dragged into the city over the weekends for any kind of party. We like to be free to stay here and work on our apartment, walk in the woods, and go to the country movie early. Liquor would be a minuscule item on our budget if we had a budget.—Is minuscule a real word—or did I make it up?

While in the past, almost all of her letters home were addressed exclusively to her mother, now they are almost all addressed to both parents. Being a married woman seems to have partly reconciled my mother to her father. There are even some flattering references to my grandfather.

> Tell Daddy that I've met several prominent (I think they are) lawyers here and when they discovered whose daughter I was they were most impressed and kept asking me questions such as "How long does your father think the war will last?", "Does your father think Roosevelt will run again?" etc. etc.

In fact, in some letters she addresses her parents as one entity: "Woozan-pop," "Wooz" being her nickname for my grandmother. Her letters are extremely affectionate to her parents, sometimes beginning with salutations like "Dear Folkies" and closing with expressions like "Much love, Babies," "Much love, darlings," and so forth.

After her twenty-sixth birthday (January 13, 1945), she writes:

> Dearest Wooz and Daddy—
>
> Thank you so much for your generous birthday presents. You are so good to me and now that I'm getting on in years, I appreciate my parents more and more. And it isn't just blind filial devotion—but the more I see the rest of the world, the more I know what a fine family I have. Perhaps that's a funny sort of thank you for a birthday present.

My mother got a job with the cartography division of the navy while Bob was doing design work for army intelligence that ranged from creating posters and maps to camouflage. "I start work tomorrow . . . I don't even know the difference between longitude and latitude, but they don't expect that apparently. My Bauhaus training is bearing some fairly decent fruit."

There are some funny observations about wartime Washington. My mother gives her mother stamps as a birthday present, both because she doesn't know what else to get her and because it's patriotic, giving the government money for the war effort. My grandmother cooks up the idea of going to work on the assembly line of a munitions plant. My mother tries to dissuade her, encouraging her in an alternative scheme of growing lima beans to help increase agricultural production. "It's just as patriotic, too—maybe more so, with all the farm youths getting drafted," my mother writes.

In contrast, the atmosphere she finds in the American war machine is considerably less inspiring.

> Certainly in Washington, there's an incredible waste of manpower and time, not only in the Army but in non-war govt. agencies like the one I'm in. You never saw a more un-hurried atmosphere. Everyone says "You're working for the government now—take your time." And all the deferred draftsmen sit around for hours on end making bets on the World Series. It seems to me they've got three people for every job that could be filled by one man—or woman. At any rate—I'm not very happy about my job. It's dull as dishwater and all you have to do is master the intricacies of red tape—which forms to fill out, which rubber stamp to use, what color ink to use under what circumstances.

There is also a decidedly new political consciousness in my mother's letters, the sense of her being connected to a wider world. Being in the South of the United States for the first time made her more aware of the issue of race than ever before.

> I was, of course, very interested in Daddy's activity in helping the imprisoned colored boy. Let me know how the case comes along. I don't want to get started on a diatribe—but I certainly believe that for anyone not actively in war work or fighting—

working for a decent break for the negroes is the most important activity. Baltimore could certainly use it—it's heartbreaking to see how cruelly they are treated.

In another letter, she mentions reading the black novelist Richard Wright and sending the books on to her mother.

> Will mail you "Black Boy" tomorrow. It is even more powerful, I think, than "Native Son" because it is so objective, just facts.

My mother is outraged by the efforts of the Daughters of the American Revolution (DAR) to keep the black opera singer Marian Anderson from singing to an integrated audience at Constitution Hall in Washington.

> P.S. In front of all his men, Major Smith said the other day that the DAR should ban Marion [*sic*] Anderson permanently. "How can she sing, anyhow?" he said. "She's just a nigger and she'll always be a nigger." He's a fine leader and I think it must be illegal for him as a commanding officer to say such a thing to his men.

Eventually, with the support of President Roosevelt and Eleanor Roosevelt, Anderson gave an open-air concert on the steps of the Lincoln Memorial.

My mother writes frequently about the newspaper *PM*, which for a period of time was the United States's only widely circulated left-of-center daily newspaper.

> I can't tell you how we love *PM*. This is a pretty conservative town and there are plenty of slums and social evils, so it is a constant reminder that somewhere people are still fighting for democracy in all the small corners of America.
>
> Maybe [George]'d get the lift we do from *PM*. Believe me, you need the realization that liberals are still fighting. I've tried having lunch with some of the girls in my building and they are so stupid and unaware of anything important and so smug in their false superiority. I just get fighting mad and try to argue with them. They don't understand at all or care to understand . . .

If I weren't tied down, and I'm delighted that I am, I'd
hot-foot it to New York and get myself a job on that paper by any
fair or foul means I could.

Good night for now from your loquacious but loving daughter,

Betty

In fact, partway through the war, Bob Wolff managed to get transferred
to New York. One of the first things my mother did was walk into the
offices of *PM* and ask for a job. Given the wartime labor shortage, they
told her to start the following morning.

PM had adopted the novel strategy of not taking any advertising in
order not to have its editorial policies influenced by commercial interests.
But to generate readership, they developed what was considered to be the
best coverage of consumer news, on prices of merchandise and stores'
sales. And it was for this section that my mother went to work.

My mother clearly enjoyed the move to New York.

May 19, 1943

After all those nights in Baltimore and Washington we sat
around, it is amazing there are so many interesting people in
New York—people you like immediately and vice versa.

They found a nice one-bedroom apartment on Sutton Place, near the
East River. My mother writes:

It occurred to me after we moved in here that we are located in
an extremely bomb-worthy area, being right next to the
Queensboro bridge and the river which has an enormous traffic
of vital shipping. It's almost worth being bombed to hear the
boats. I always feel on the verge of a long voyage when I hear
their noise.

Interestingly, despite their small income, my mother hired a full-time
maid ("a colored girl") to cook and clean up, paying her $17 a week,
nearly all of my mother's $25 or $30 weekly salary.

For a time, she appears to have liked her job at *PM*. But like someone who loves sausages but has never been inside a sausage factory, my mother changed her view of *PM* somewhat once she began working there.

[August 18, 1943]

Our editor is a nice harmless dope who lets himself be bullied by <u>his</u> editor and tries in vain to defend his spineless actions to a bunch of female sharpies like me and the rest. It's too complicated to go into here but the poor man just doesn't know what he's doing and nobody respects him and he's awfully unhappy. As a result, the Shopping News is just running itself and we're all working like dogs and wondering why. It can't last long—at least, the editor can't. I don't care much—as long as I get enough experience to get a job on a better-organized page. This is no reflection on the rest of the paper—or even Shopping News— just our set-up at the moment.

[September 21, 1943]

My job is beginning to get under my skin. I seem to be as fickle with jobs as I used to be with men. Enclosed is my latest masterpiece. Don't you wish I were as thorough about my own moving as I sound in that article! I am now considering getting a job on *Time* magazine in their map department. I hear they want someone and will pay $45 for a five day week. Their offices are in Rockefeller Center, which would be far pleasanter than 42nd and Broadway.

The war news has been so wonderful lately and I'm beginning to be one of those stupid optimists the commentators denounce. It's beginning to feel as though the end were dimly in sight. It was a great thing to hear today that Congress passed the Fullbright [*sic*] resolution. Not such a bad old world after all, when it gets going.

We are beginning to discuss having a baby in the not-too-distant future. What do you think of the idea? It's going to be a boy, of course—Bob insists on that!

My mother was clearly keen to get pregnant, but for some reason it didn't happen.

[Postmarked April 1944]

Dearest family—

Golly, I am sorry to have taken so long to answer your letters. Things have been popping around here recently and for a change I've really been busy. The American abstract artists had a show which opened last Saturday, for one thing, and I volunteered to help them get out invitations, etc., etc. Also we've been having quite a bustle of social activity, plus the usual housewife routine. So!

Two weeks ago I was sure I was pregnant and we were both grinning from ear to ear, but my hopes have been shattered again. It was surprising to me that Bob was so pleased. I thought he'd immediately start worrying about how he was going to send the child through college. He says he doesn't really want me to get pregnant for the present but if I do he will only think of the bright side. Meanwhile, we are doing nothing to prevent it.

Back in New York, they reentered the artistic world that my mother and Wolff had been a part of in Chicago and stayed in regular touch with Moholy-Nagy, who was continuing to try to put his School of Design on a sound footing and bring them back to Chicago.

And back in New York Bob Wolff's artistic and teaching career appeared to be taking off.

[October 3, 1944]

Things are starting to pop for Bob, too—and . . . the thing that set it off was the museum job. This morning—as soon as he got in—he got a call from [Serge] Chermayeff at Brooklyn College saying that he was so anxious to see Bob's things at the Museum and wanted Bob to come out to look things over at Brooklyn and discuss "plans for the future." Since he once made Bob a tentative offer, it could mean only one thing. He was also alarmed to hear

that Bob had been in Chicago and wanted to know why. Since
Chermayeff, despite his name, is a very frosty Englishman—it's
all very funny. Also a trustee of Bennington is recommending
him for a job at Bennington. Also the editor of a new art
magazine soon to be published by the publishers of <u>Look</u> came
here to look at his stuff while he was in Chicago and was very
impressed and wants to publish some of his things. And Moholy
made him the magnificent offer, for Moholy, of $4,000. All in all,
we decided we needn't starve in a garret for the rest of our lives. I
have a feeling that this is only the beginning since the Museum
job has not even been seen by anyone, much less circulated, and
is still only in the layout stage. It's funny how you can work for
years and one little thing on top of all the others will just tip the
scale.

Things seemed to be falling into place for Bob Wolff. Moholy-Nagy's
School of Design was going to be incorporated into a new, larger school—
what became known as the Illinois Institute of Technology, with a new
campus designed by Walter Gropius, who would head up its architecture
school. But Moholy-Nagy was diagnosed with leukemia and died in
1946, and the return to Chicago and the School of Design never materialized.

After the war, with the transition back to civilian life and a renewed
focus on building careers and making money, my mother's marriage
with Wolff appears to have foundered. Bob Wolff's painting career didn't
take off as he had hoped, and he took a job teaching at Brooklyn College,
where he remained for most of his career. He and my mother seem to
have always had money problems and were always paying off small debts
to her parents.

But the problems ran deeper. While my mother may have thought she
was marrying the father she never had, Bob Wolff seems to have wanted
the mother he never had—a bad combination.

"I discovered almost immediately and I should have acted on it, but I
was a very young woman, that this successful, respected older man was
very insecure, very needy, very indecisive," she told me. "Even though I
was much younger, he really needed a mother. His mother had died when
he was a baby and his father, who was a dashing businessman, had left
him and his older sister in the care of a very strict German governess,

living in a hotel somewhere in Chicago. He was basically a motherless child and very needy and dependent on me. It didn't matter so much during the war because he was working for the government—we had a pretty good time. But after the war, the problems were very evident. He couldn't make up his mind about anything. He quarreled with people. He started out with wonderful relationships with lots of people in the art world, but then he'd make little fusses—'You didn't hang the pictures right'—and he made things much harder for himself."

A little bit of this comes through in my mother's letters home. Already, in 1944, she writes:

> Bob was at home sick most of last week . . . Bless his heart, he is a very demanding patient. Maybe never having had a mother, he has stored up a reservoir of need for a mama's care. At any rate, he is very good at saying "Tootsie, I'm hungry" in the most pathetic little voice two seconds after he has finished saying "Tootsie, I'm thirsty."

It is obvious that by 1946, their marriage was in serious trouble. There is mention of my mother's wanting to see a psychiatrist, and my mother is reassuring her parents that she and Bob are not splitting up, a clear sign that they had been considering it. On the day of her twenty-eighth birthday, January 6, 1947, my mother writes that things are going better, in part because she is trying to dedicate herself more (at her mother's urging) to traditional wifely tasks such as making her husband breakfast.

Jan. 6, 1947

> Everything is going well here. Bob and I are getting on beautifully for the first time in many months. I don't know exactly why but I think Wooz was right and it had its small beginnings in a little thing like getting breakfast. Then several other things have happened which have been very pleasant for both of us. 1) Bob got nearly $500 from a piece of his father's property in Chicago 2) He sold a picture 3) He got invited into Who's Who 4) He is working on a picture which is really the best he's ever done. The holiday helped a lot, too, since it made him feel less hemmed in by his work at Brooklyn. Also he finally

bought himself a new suit—the only one since he first got out of the Navy—and it has done something, too. All these things plus my improved behavior have cheered him up 1000% which in turn has its effects on me. Let's hope this non-vicious circle keeps going.

A marriage being held together by breakfast would not appear to be in particularly good shape. A few weeks later, Bob Wolff sent a rather sad letter to my grandparents in which he alludes to this reconciliation in their marriage, but in which his attempts at optimism are so unconvincing that they convey a sense of foreboding.

1/27/47

Dear Folks -

Eliz. seems to be settling down again. She's begun work on re-editing a novel which she's no doubt told you about and is looking for other work. It is difficult to look upon these things objectively and analytically especially when one is not quite grown up in such matters oneself. But I believe we will work things out. I am not used to the role of the wise old bird or to the fact that my other attractions are less than they used to be. Yet the problem is lessened in my case by the increasing tempo of my work. Work, too, is one solution for Elizabeth though I feel a little sad that the correction does not lie in the relationship itself but in distraction from it. Of course such a problem is more or less universal and not exclusive with us. And I suppose we will solve it better than most.

In many ways, this is an exceedingly strange letter for a man to write to his parents-in-law. There is a fairly explicit reference to my mother having lost much of her sexual interest in him: "I am not used to . . . the fact that my other attractions are less than they used to be." And it is a devastating admission for him to say that focusing on work may help distract them from the problems in their marriage.

Unfortunately, my mother seems to have reproduced one of the worst aspects of her parents' relationship with each other as well as of her relationship with her father: namely, endless fighting over money. "Bob was even more penurious than your father used to be," Katharine Kuh told me. "She was adorable and he whined at her all the time, and he was terribly jealous. Every time she spent five cents—and you know that your mother was extravagant—he would start whining. If she ordered a champagne cocktail when we went out to dinner, he would make a scene and she would then order two or three!"

Whining would not appear to be a winning strategy for keeping his hold on a young woman looking for a strong, authoritative father figure. Clearly, at a certain point, my mother lost respect for Wolff and began treating him with a measure of contempt (ordering extra champagne cocktails over his whining objections). Contempt is a clear sign of the death of passion.

And yet, in a letter written in late 1946, my mother sounds an optimistic note.

> PS To Mother: I'll surprise you yet with a little Wolff. I've always had complications with simple things, you know—like growing up . . .

PART IV

WORLDS COLLIDE

Worlds Collide
("Don't worry about me")

I.

It was supposed to be my father's big break—an exclusive interview with Italy's prime minister, Alcide De Gasperi. It was the first time an Italian head of government had visited the United States and a crucial turning point for postwar Italy. It was 1947—the beginning of the Cold War. President Harry Truman was laying out the Marshall Plan that was meant to lift war-battered Europe back on its feet and keep it from going Communist. De Gasperi went to Washington to work out the terms of American aid to Italy and agreed, on his return, to kick out of his ruling coalition the Italian Communist Party, which had been cooperating with a government of national emergency. After visiting Washington, De Gasperi was passing through New York, from which he would leave for Rome.

In Italy right after World War II, news from the United States was highly limited. Because the two countries had been at war, all relations between them had broken off. Correspondents from Italy had returned home and needed a visa to revisit the United States. My father, already an American citizen living in New York (thanks to his time in the U.S. Army), had a decided advantage over his competitors. But he was working only on a freelance basis for the *Corriere della Sera* until they could get organized and send a big gun to occupy one of the paper's prime foreign postings. An exclusive interview with De Gasperi was just what my father needed. But when he showed up at the Italian consulate on Park Avenue, he was greeted by the consul general, who informed him that, unfortunately, the prime minister was feeling a bit tired, had gone to take a nap after lunch, and would not be able to do the interview. "I suspected that De Gasperi probably wanted to give his first interview about his trip to America to *Il Messaggero* when he got back to Rome," my father said.

The consul general said goodbye to my father and sent him away. As he headed toward the front door, my father suddenly thought to himself, What would an American journalist do? Scenes from American movies such as *The Front Page*, *Foreign Correspondent*, and *Deadline, U.S.A.*, with daredevil reporters ready to do anything—lie, cheat, or risk their lives—to get their story, raced through his head. On a wild impulse, my father decided to do something crazy: he hid behind a thick red velvet curtain near the consulate's front door, and he waited there, trying not to make a noise, until he heard the consul general's footsteps die out as he returned to his office. Then, when it was quiet, my father crept up the stairs to the residential part of the consulate and began to look for the napping De Gasperi. He found him in a bedroom, stretched out on a bed asleep but with the vest of his three-piece suit on. My father tapped him on the shoulder: *"Allora, Signor Presidente, facciamo 'sta intervista?"* ("So, Mr. President, are we going to do that interview?") At that moment, the consul general, hearing something upstairs, came bursting into the room and began yelling, "You! What are you doing here! How dare you?" But De Gasperi, a great gentleman, said, "I'm awake, and besides, I did promise to do the interview." So they did the interview. It was a big scoop, and the *Corriere* decided to make my father their full-time correspondent.

2.

The dearth of correspondents in the United States and the drastically reduced number of other news sources available at that time, together with the great importance of the United States after World War II, gave my father's work—as the sole U.S. correspondent for Italy's largest paper—an importance that no Italian correspondent in America had had before or is likely to have in the future. Most Italian newspapers, given the severe poverty in Italy at the time, couldn't afford full-time correspondents. At a certain point, through some complicated technical quirk, the Rome newspaper *Il Messaggero* figured out a way of intercepting my father's daily dispatches, which were sent via teletype machines from New York, and reprinting them almost verbatim. The editor of the *Corriere* at the time called up the editor of *Il Messaggero*, Mario Missiroli, and protested. Missiroli, with a mixture of humor and gallantry, replied, "All right, if you really must have Stille, we will lend him to you." ("*Se lei proprio deve avere Stille, velo prestiamo!*")

My father was rapidly making a name for himself. Italian diplomats complained to their people at the embassy in Washington: "Why do we need you when we can simply read Stille?"

My father's stories ranged from sober pieces of political analysis—of the kind that made the diplomats look bad—to lighter, more colorful pieces about American customs and society.

There is a nice piece from 1946 on the success of Adam Smith in the United States, using the mind-set of the local butcher to show how deeply ingrained the ideas of supply and demand were in the American mentality, in order to explain why already, in 1946, the United States was the only major country to abandon the wartime system of price controls. The decision was sparked by the so-called meat crisis.

> The disappearance of meat, attributed to price controls, had become one of the most potent weapons used by the Republicans on the eve of the elections. In Brooklyn the Republicans organized a procession led by a horse carrying a sign saying: "Truman wants me to end up in your frying pan. Save my life and vote Republican." And so the president decided to eliminate price controls on meat.
>
> And now the trouble starts because while the law of supply and demand is spoken about like rain in a time of drought, it's quite another thing when it starts to work. It was said that increasing production would lower prices, but prices are going up. Meat went up by fifty percent in just a few days and the cost of living in general jumped by another seven percent. The dollar of 1941 is now worth sixty-nine cents.

The other common type of piece is one of serious, careful political analysis, which became his bread and butter.

Here he describes the debate within the American State Department about whether the new security arrangements in Europe should include or exclude the Soviet Union, a debate that would lead to the formation of NATO and shape the workings of the Marshall Plan and the structure of the Cold War.

A series of important meetings at the State Department on certain aspects of the three-party conference in Paris has confirmed without doubt that we have reached a decisive moment in the history of relations between the United States and Europe. Naturally, the functionaries of the State Department refused to comment on the results of Paris, but it is no secret that the conference seems to have brought about the victory of the anti-Russian faction within the State Department over that of the more moderate faction. The moderates argued that one must at all costs include Russia in the program if one wants to truly resolve the problems of Europe. The more conservative elements did not hide their opinion that the only way to effectively carry out the Marshall Plan was the creation of a Western bloc without Russia, if not, in fact, with a specifically anti-Russian basis. These elements, which represent the right wing within the State Department, noted that it would be extremely difficult to get Congress to vote the funds for a plan that included Russia among the countries to be helped and that the only way to win the approval of Congress of aid for Europe was to play the anti-Communism card. Now the results of Paris have strengthened that faction given Molotov's refusal to accept the premises of the Marshall Plan, meaning that the only road open to American diplomacy is the creation of a European system without Russia.

3 .

At around the same time, in early 1947, my mother attended a memorial show dedicated to her former teacher László Moholy-Nagy, organized by the Baroness Hilla Rebay, who was the curator of the Museum of Non-Objective Painting, which became the Guggenheim Museum in New York, of which my mother gave a memorable description:

The Moholy memorial show opened yesterday and Sybil [Moholy-Nagy] of course came here for the opening. She insisted on our going with her after it to have dinner with the Baroness Rebay who runs the Guggenheim foundation and who put on the exhibition. What a crazy woman! She believes that the spirit of

Van Gogh entered her body when she was 3 months old. As we were having dinner she said "Moholy is with us now" and she beamed in his supposed direction. At any rate, she has gotten together an amazing collection of pictures for old Solomon Guggenheim, the copper king—some are priceless and some are ghastly. She is the one for whom Frank Lloyd Wright is building a new museum next to the Metropolitan. I think she wants to buy some of Bob's pictures. I hope so.

Bob's troubles are over at Brooklyn [College] now. He won every fight and has emerged as G—'s[?] fair-haired boy. The enrollment has increased so much, he is allowed 2 new professors. He has a wonderful faculty. Everything is lovely.

4.

Naturally, it took my father a while to fully acclimate to the United States and grasp the nuances of its customs and language. Once he saw a huge headline on one of the New York tabloid newspapers: INDIANS MASSA-CRE SENATORS! He was convinced that angry Native Americans had slaughtered various members of the U.S. Senate. But when he picked up the paper he realized it was just a hyperbolic headline about two baseball teams.

Through his work and his Italian connections, my father had a rich social life. His friend Nicola Chiaromonte introduced him to the crowd around the magazine *Partisan Review*, people like Mary McCarthy, Dwight Macdonald, and Robert Lowell. Through the Italian critic Paolo Milano he met Saul Bellow (who dedicated his novel *Herzog* to Milano).

My father was enormously impressed by the caliber and integrity of the Americans he met when he began covering American politics. Although the United States was a deeply democratic country, its government was run to a good extent by a highly educated elite, mostly from the Northeast, with a deeply ingrained sense of public service. Europeans wrongly looked down on American politicians as provincial, while in my father's view, men such as Dean Acheson were people of genuine vision with a rich culture and notions of the public good that were difficult to find in Europe and virtually impossible to locate in Fascist Italy.

He was amazed by the openness of the American system. A man like the South Carolina politician James Byrnes, the son of an Irish-American dressmaker who had lost his father soon after birth, could become secretary of state under Roosevelt. Byrnes was a shrewd politician, but when asked to perform the job of secretary of state he acted like a statesman.

My father loved the earthiness of ethnic politicians like Al Smith, the governor of New York who became the first Catholic candidate for president. He liked to repeat a phrase of Smith's: when people referred to him as the "king" of New York politics, Smith responded with indignation, "Yes, I am the king, the King of Oliver Street," referring to the street on the Lower East Side of Manhattan where he had grown up in a poor immigrant family.

My father loved the old bosses who, while often corrupt, frequently had the shrewdness to put forward first-rate candidates who actually governed in the public interest. In New York, Al Smith came up through the Tammany Hall system, run by the boss "Silent Charlie" Murphy, but went on to become a major promoter of progressive legislation. (He loved the little book called *Plunkitt of Tammany Hall*, in which an Irish-American ward leader in the old Tammany system expounded his political philosophy—"I seen my opportunities and I took 'em"—made clear the distinction between "honest and dishonest graft," and explained why Tammany bosses continued to win out over do-good reformers.)

The Missouri boss Tom Pendergast ran a corrupt system and eventually ended up in federal prison for tax evasion, but he had the good sense to back Harry Truman, who was a person of complete personal integrity. My father used to repeat how much he admired Truman for the loyalty and courage he showed by going back to Missouri to attend Pendergast's funeral, even though the president had little to gain and potentially much to lose by attending the funeral of a disgraced man. Although thousands of politicians had benefited from Pendergast's patronage and help, Truman was virtually the only elected official at the funeral. To those who asked him why he had come, Truman answered with a disarming and unimpeachable simplicity: "He was always my friend and I have always been his."

My father loved Fiorello La Guardia, who read the comics out loud over the radio during a newspaper strike in 1945 and had a high, squeaky voice but had taken a number of courageous positions throughout his career, denouncing Hitler and taking on organized crime in New York— physically destroying the slot machines of Frank Costello and demanding that his police chief arrest Lucky Luciano on any charges whatsoever: "Let's drive the bums out of town!"

He found the earthy concreteness of the American politicians—who knew how to fix potholes and make cities work—refreshing after the highly rhetorical nature of Italian politicians.

My father had found his way in life—a job he loved and would keep more or less for the next fifty years—by the time he met my mother in May 1948.

5.

In the spring of 1947, my mother wrote an apologetic letter to her mother.

> Don't be upset about the money business with Bob and me. I didn't realize when I wrote you before that in order to 1) rent the summer cottage and 2) buy the jeep (without which the cottage would be useless) Bob had to use my money as well as his. As he says, it's my summer, too.

My mother, apparently, had earned what at the time was a substantial sum, five hundred dollars, and had hoped to use it to repay a loan from her parents. My mother and Bob Wolff always seemed to be on the edge, in and out of small amounts of debt. It was somewhat comprehensible during wartime, when Wolff was forced to serve in the navy and was unable to hold down a real job, but it appeared to continue after the war as well. It was frustrating to my mother that her husband simply appropriated the money she had earned. She made a couple of halfhearted attempts to leave him in this period, going home for a few weeks but always coming back. My mother makes another reference to wanting to see a psychiatrist—a clear symptom of serious marital trouble with Bob Wolff—but she seems to have abandoned the idea.

> I didn't go to a psychiatrist and there is certainly no reason why you should contribute to anything else. We'll have to get it back to you slowly over the summer unless we get an unexpected windfall between now and June 15 (which isn't impossible). This is not our old irresponsibility—it's the Jeep.

The need for the jeep came from Wolff and my mother's desire to spend the summer in an especially beautiful and inaccessible part of Cape Cod, with sandy dirt roads near the beach. None of the roads were paved.

In their last summer together, Wolff and my mother discovered the artistic and intellectual community in Wellfleet, Cape Cod, where a number of the Bauhaus crowd had settled. György Kepes, their good friend from the New Bauhaus, had bought some land on a beautiful lake (with an unlovely name, Horseleech Pond), for which his friend and neighbor Marcel Breuer had designed him a house. My mother became extremely close and lifelong friends with Breuer's wife, Connie. And the Breuers had a house on another pond nearby. These artists and intellectuals had discovered an extraordinary series of freshwater ponds, which had remained totally undeveloped because the area was infested with mosquitoes. There was a brief period right at the end of World War II—after the government eradicated the mosquito problem and before it stopped all building in the area to protect its natural beauty—when a small number of houses went up in the woods among the ponds. Generally, poor artists put up inexpensive bungalows and converted chicken coops into houses. Once the area became protected they were not allowed to even add a bathroom to these simple structures. While they remained places of great simplicity, they were in one of the most beautiful possible spots in the entire United States, houses on dirt roads, placed right next to ponds large enough to sail on but clean enough to drink from, all within easy walking distance of beautiful white sand ocean beaches with high dunes. The Wellfleet woods attracted an extraordinary collection of writers and artists, from the painter Edward Hopper to the writers Edmund Wilson, Mary McCarthy, and Edwin O'Connor, to the historian Arthur Schlesinger, as well as my parents' friends Serge Chermayeff, the Kepeses, and the Breuers.

Clearly, my mother found much in the simple, bohemian life in Wellfleet highly appealing, as she later wrote to her mother:

> We are having a big party Saturday night for Bob's birthday and also to pay back all the people who have been so nice to us here. I have never known such a pleasant social atmosphere and I think one reason for it is that the children are an integral part of it. And somehow the people here, some of whom have made messes of their own lives, have done a wonderful job with their children.

Tonight we are having dinner with the Mattsons. He is quite a successful popular writer and she is the beautiful daughter of an apparently famous socialist, woman's suffrage, etc. family named Walling. Until quite recently he was an alcoholic—they lived up here all year round and though they are extremely intelligent their lives were definitely mixed up. But their kids are the nicest, most grown-up, poised and attractive children I've ever met. Somehow the mixture of eccentric parents, happy children and beautiful surroundings and complete freedom is extremely pleasant.

On July 31, 1947, she writes to her parents:

Late again but it has been such a series of perfect days that to sit still and write letters is torture.

. . .

Bob is getting a lot of painting done in spite of a somewhat full social life and the temptation presented by the ocean and beach. He went deep-sea fishing the other day with a group of men . . .

I have been doing a little work but seem to spend a lot of time with Juliet Kepes, Connie Breuer and others in the daytime and going to parties at night. The trouble is there's no real excuse up here for refusing invitations and then, of course, once you've accepted you have to reciprocate. But anyway it's a wonderful place and we are happy as larks. The only real spot on the horizon is that for the first time since I've been married there are a couple of men around who are rather stuck on me and Bob gets terribly annoyed by it.

And so the stage was set for my father's arrival on the scene.

6.

They met at the house of Ira and Edita Morris. He was an American journalist from a wealthy family, and she was a Swedish writer who had published a novel and a collection of stories. They had lived around the world and had a large, handsome apartment in New York, where they decided to host a party for Truman Capote, who had suddenly become the toast of the town with *Other Voices, Other Rooms*. Their apartment was decorated with pieces of Japanese art—their son, Ivan Morris, was a Japan scholar who had worked for U.S. intelligence during the war. He had visited Hiroshima not long after the bombing, and the family had become passionate advocates of nuclear disarmament.

My mother was working at the time for the Dodd, Mead publishing house. "It was a rather swinging party," she recalled. Capote was twenty-three at the time and, according to my mother, looked like a boy of about seventeen. The book, which became a bestseller, caused some controversy because of the photograph of the author on the dust jacket, showing Capote as an effeminate young man stretched out on a couch, gazing languidly at the camera. One reviewer wrote that Capote looked "as if he were dreamily contemplating some outrage against conventional morality."

The party was on East Fifty-Seventh Street, not far from where my mother and Bob Wolff lived. "Meanwhile, this very intense, rather peculiar-looking guy came up to me and started talking to me in the most fascinating way," my mother said. The very intense, peculiar-looking guy was my father. "He just zeroed in on me. In those days, if you were young, if you went to a party and you were pretty, I wasn't treated like a married woman. Misha, I don't think he ever stopped talking to me. He just talked and talked. Bob was extremely bored at this party, because it was a literary party, and he wanted to go home and wanted me to go home. I refused to leave. I said, 'I will come when I'm finished with my conversation, thanks.' He was disgusted with me. He said, 'Okay, you stay.'"

Wolff stormed off and my mother and father stayed. "We talked and talked. It got later and later, two or three in the morning, something like that. And he said he would walk me back. Bob had left hours ago. Well, anyway, Misha and I walked from Lexington Avenue and stopped to have a drink somewhere on Second or Third Avenue and when we left it was almost light. Do I have to tell this?" she asked, but didn't wait for an answer. On cortisone, my mother had no brakes. "All of a sudden in the middle of Sutton Place he began to kiss me passionately and make this very big scene, and Bob Wolff was waiting up for me—no, he didn't see it, but he was furious.

"That was the end of it. That's how it all began."

My mother had provoked a rupture in her marriage, but she had no way of getting in touch with the new man in her life. He didn't even have her phone number. "I went to work maybe two days or so and I didn't hear a word from Misha and I didn't have the foggiest idea where he lived. Then he called me at work, sounding very passionate, romantic, and I believe we had dinner. It started getting very intense then." And within a week of the party for Truman Capote, my mother moved out of the apartment she had shared with Bob Wolff.

7.

"I had a feeling that something was going to happen to me that year," my father said, reflecting on that initial meeting with my mother. "Then I met your mother and she left her husband almost immediately and I had to rise to the occasion. She was a dream, a dream. I can't tell you how beautiful and how charming she was—a dream."

He fell in love with my mother in part because she was very much a product of the America that he had come to love. She had the freedom, naturalness, irreverent wit, and beauty of some of the women he admired in the movies of the 1930s—Rosalind Russell in *His Girl Friday*, Jean Arthur in *Mr. Smith Goes to Washington*. She was natural and unstudied. She had none of the layers of convention and centuries of breeding that many European women had; she was genuine and direct and yet had impeccable manners and delicacy.

While my mother's conduct toward Wolff was certainly questionable, she was unquestionably honest. She was reckless but was acting on what she saw as her own moral code, a kind of romantic monogamy—in which you acted on your feelings but with one man at a time. She did not want to deceive Wolff and would have considered it immoral to conduct a clandestine affair behind his back. As soon as she met my father and decided that she was through with Wolff, she left him on the spot.

She had grown up in a household with two unhappily married parents who desired other people but who, for a variety of reasons (at least in my grandmother's case), didn't act on their desires. My mother had entered into a bohemian world where people followed their passions rather than worry about disrupting the tranquil surface of things or about what others might think—sometimes at considerable cost to themselves and others. She had traded the world of her family for this new world.

My mother had what my father saw as an extremely American sense of fair play and honesty. If my mother realized that a cashier had inadvertently given her too much change, she'd walk several blocks to return the money. "They'll deduct it from her paycheck!" she would say. "They might fire him for stealing!" My father would laugh and make fun of her for this. He would probably have pocketed the money ("They usually give you too little change, so it evens out") but secretly admired her for doing otherwise.

And of course there was the not insignificant fact that she was beautiful, in an interesting, unconventional way. She was not your usual corn-fed kind of midwestern beauty; she had dark hair, a larger-than-normal nose, a shapely figure, and a very individual sense of style that didn't come from Marshall Field's. There was something slightly exotic about her. She had a very American kind of freshness, openness, and innocence together with something knowing and sexy—a powerful combination. Once, when my mother was waiting for a bus, a somewhat tipsy older black man said to her, "Honey, if you was a minute, you'd be an hour!"

And what did my mother see in my father? He was not handsome. He was short, about five-foot-seven, pale with black-rimmed glasses with thick myopic lenses and a look of great seriousness and intelligence. When I first saw photographs of Jean-Paul Sartre, I was struck by the resemblance to my father, thinking to myself, there must be a factory somewhere in Europe where they turn out these small, dark, serious, intellectual types who are born with glasses on. He had a fierce intensity that somehow made him attractive, and he was an extraordinary talker who, when he was well disposed, could charm the cherries off the trees. He had lived through some of the crucial events of the twentieth century— revolution, civil war, Italian Fascism, World War II—about which he spoke with the authority and feeling of one who had lived history directly on his own flesh. He had seen far more of the world than my mother and spoke English, Italian, French, German, and a little Russian, and also knew Latin and ancient Greek. At the same time, his conversation had a wonderful lightness and humor to it, moving from frivolous and funny topics to world affairs and serious observations about life with great agility. At twenty-nine he had already made himself into a highly respected journalist and intellectual in Italy. He had incredible energy and burning ambition and could work twelve-hour days and stay out at parties till two in the morning—and do the same several days running. He had much greater force of will than Bob Wolff, who was something of a hypochondriac, already developing the role of the underappreciated artist, as if resigning himself to a life of disappointment. And as soon as my father met my mother, all of his intensity and charm were fixed, like a laser, on her. He wanted her with all his being and my mother liked being wanted.

My mother moved briefly into a fleabag hotel. "It had a fancy name but in fact it was a whorehouse, but I didn't know it. Everybody else received men, but I didn't. I stayed there a week or two."

Bob Wolff moved out of Sutton Place to a little apartment in Greenwich Village. He desperately wanted my mother back. Almost immediately after my mother left him, he made the unusual decision of writing to my mother's parents and telling them that my mother had betrayed him with another man and asking for their help in convincing her to return—not an especially strong move for a man trying to win back a woman. My mother wrote to her parents:

May 14, 1948

Dearest Wooz and Daddy,

Forgive me for not writing sooner. I've been busy and tired and upset and still am. Bob is better, more reasonable and controlled. I feel rotten to be the cause of so much suffering but I know that it was the only thing to do. We will be able to face our mistakes and either remedy them together or separately. He has found a wonderful studio in Greenwich Village—a really perfect place with a garden, etc. I am to move into Jeanne Reynal's house this week-end—or rather on the top floor of her house . . . The address is 240 West 11th Street.

I'm worried stiff about the financial end of this move. I hate to have to go to you for help and as soon as I am settled I'm going to look around for some small outside job that will pay the rent at least. It is going to be tough since I'm expected to look like an executive on a slave's pay. But I know there is a future for me here and that it won't be too long a haul. If it is, at least I'll have the publishing experience to get a better salary elsewhere.

Don't worry about me. I am amazed at my own good sense, calmness, etc. And much love and get a good rest in the country. Perhaps I can come out this summer to see you before you take off for California.

B.

My mother moved into a room in the brownstone of a woman named Jeanne Reynal, who was a highly accomplished mosaicist but was also a major collector and patroness of other artists such as Arshile Gorky, whose career she championed and whom she tried to help in various ways.

Reynal, a woman of means in a circle of starving artists, held a kind of ongoing salon at her house attended by the artists she collected—Gorky, Rothko, Noguchi, and de Kooning, as well as many others. "Jeanne Reynal gave the most superb parties," Elaine de Kooning recalled. "She'd have perhaps eighteen people and have drinks before dinner—wonderful, luxurious drinks—and wine with dinner and drinks after dinner. And the walls were covered with Gorkys and then she had a superb painting by Mark Rothko. And later she bought some paintings of Bill's [Willem de Kooning's]." Alcohol evidently played an important role in the festivities, and Jeanne Reynal made frequent use of a nearby liquor store, which delivered to her house. In fact, around the time my mother entered the picture, Jeanne began an affair with the young "Negro" man (as he would have been called then) who delivered the liquor, Tommy Sills, who was eleven years younger than her. Jeanne and Tommy ended up marrying, and he, under the influence of Jeanne and the many artists that came through her house, became a respected painter in his own right. (I remember meeting them much, much later in life. They had stayed together through the years and seemed a happy couple.)

Filling out the unusual and rather lively household my mother moved into was Mougouch Gorky, who had just left her artist husband, taking with her their two young children. An American woman originally named Agnes Magruder, to whom Gorky had given the exotic-sounding name "Mougouch," she had fallen in love with the Chilean surrealist painter Roberto Matta. She decided to leave Gorky, although she kept the unusual name he had given her. Arshile Gorky was a tortured, ominous presence skulking around the house when my mother moved in. In the space of a few months, his entire life had fallen apart. Much of his work had been burned up in a fire in his studio; he was suffering from cancer; his wife had left him, taking away his children; he had nearly been killed in a car accident in which he had broken his neck and lost the use of his right hand; he was nearly broke and couldn't paint. Gorky was forced to wear a heavy leather collar around his neck in the heat of the New York summer, walked with a cane, and was in constant pain. He seemed to have gone mad and at one point attacked Matta with his cane in the middle of Central Park. The Chilean artist ran away because he was afraid that if they started fighting, Gorky's head would fall off. Jeanne Reynal tried to convince my parents to buy a Gorky painting for five hundred dollars—one that would now probably be worth tens of millions. But my parents begged off. They didn't have the money—five hundred dollars in 1948 was a lot of money for an impecunious young couple.

As my mother and father began their relationship, my father frequently spent the night down at Jeanne Reynal's house. My father kept later hours than my mother, who went off to her job at Dodd, Mead every morning. When she came home at the end of the day, she was surprised to find the bed wet with urine. "Gee, he seems like a terrific guy, but evidently he's a bed-wetter," my mother thought. After this happened several times, my mother finally realized that it was Jeanne Reynal's dog, who had free run of the house, who would come upstairs at some point in the afternoon and pee on the bed my father left unmade.

At one point, Mougouch Gorky asked my mother to move out for a week so that her lover, Matta, could stay with them. Mougouch agreed to pay for most of my mother's hotel bill and Matta gave her one of his pictures. The first few days she stayed "in a pretty nasty place called the San Jacinto—dingy, dirty and apparently a house of ill repute since they treat all females of a reasonable age as if they were prostitutes," she wrote her mother.

My father was away for a good part of that first summer, covering the 1948 presidential election campaign. The Republicans had their convention in June, the Democrats in July. Both were in Philadelphia.

He was again amazed and impressed by the openness of American politics. You could walk right up and interview Robert Taft, Mr. Republican, or Dickie Russell and Lyndon Johnson, the Democratic power brokers of the Congress. There was considerable drama at the Democratic

Convention. The party bosses were secretly working to dump Truman, who was hugely unpopular at the time, and replace him with General Dwight Eisenhower. Eisenhower wouldn't cooperate and they reluctantly stuck with Truman. The young Democratic mayor of Minneapolis, Hubert Humphrey, had made a powerful speech in favor of civil rights, urging his party, which was the party of segregation in the South, to "get out of the shadow of states' rights and walk forthrightly into the bright sunshine of human rights." More than thirty Southern Democratic delegates walked out of the convention. They formed their own Dixiecrat Party, with Governor Strom Thurmond of South Carolina, a staunch segregationist, as their candidate.

A week after the Democratic Convention, Gorky hanged himself.

My mother spent much of the summer in a state of emotional crisis, trying to sort out the end of her own marriage. She went out to see her parents at their farm in Michigan to think things over, and when she got back in August she wrote to her parents:

Sunday—

Dearest Wooz—

Thanks ever so much for your sweet note. I was worried by the phone call but you should never take my silence as lack of affection or interest. I think of you so much and I'm so glad that I had those few days with you in Michigan. I remember with special pleasure, for some reason, our visit to the International Garden.

As [her brother] George [Bogert] has probably told you, things have been somewhat out of hand. I have handled things with Bob in a bad way. In my moments of weakness and fear—and there are plenty of them—my impulse is to go back. Translated into action, this makes for bad times for Bob and me and Michael. Especially Bob. But maybe after all things simply can't be done always with strength and wisdom. At any rate, Bob is much better. He is now able to face the idea of permanent separation and before he really couldn't. I am not seeing him and have promised not to try unless I am ready to go back.

It has been terrifically hot here, as I guess it's been in the mid-west, too. I am trying to gird my loins to do outside work again. I've just got to augment my income now instead of waiting around for the change at Dodd Mead—which will come all right but it will come sooner if I don't wait for it too desperately. I've had dinner with Tommy Dodd a couple of times and he is very positive about my future there.

I enjoyed seeing George so much, even though his visit was brief and under rather disorganized circumstances. He is certainly a sweet person and what a male beauty! I suppose now all of us will see increasingly less of each other. It makes me sad.

When are you coming to New York? Michael can't wait—he thinks you are so wonderful. Whenever he talks about America he always says "but it's the people like your mother who are the hope for this country." I hope you will like him. George was rather unimpressed, I'm afraid, but I don't think you will be.

. . .

I love your letters so do write when you can and try to be tolerant of my silences. Things will be quieter from now on, I promise.

Much love to you, darling, and thanks again for my trip to Michigan.

B.

My father spent part of that fall following his first presidential election. When he wanted to follow Truman's famous "whistle-stop" campaign, the White House press office simply told him where Truman's train would be stopping during the next few days. My father, armed with nothing more than press credentials, hopped on the train when it stopped somewhere in upstate New York and found himself in a single train car with Truman and a crew of a couple dozen journalists. The presidential campaign was not the media circus it later became; there was not the kind of "gotcha" journalism that later made politicians extremely careful about anything they said in the company of the press. The time on the train was assumed to be informal, off-the-record conversation where a candidate could speak freely, joke around, and inform the press about his way of thinking, without fear of finding his words in the next day's paper. My father loved the simple informality of it all and was enormously impressed by Truman's plainspoken intelligence, toughness, and sense of humor. His campaign seemed doomed to go down in defeat. His approval ratings were at rock bottom; his party was split in three, with former Democratic vice president Henry Wallace running to the left of Truman and Strom Thurmond running to the right of Truman, threatening to take several Southern Democratic states. Much of the country, after twenty-six uninterrupted years of Democratic government, appeared ready for a change. But at stop after stop Truman showed no signs of resignation or defeatism. He gave fiery speech after fiery speech, lambasting the "do-nothing Republican Congress" in a campaign that earned him the nickname "Giv'em Hell" Harry. My father loved the simplicity of Truman's habits. He supposedly washed his own socks in the White House, and he treated his wife, Bess, and daughter, Margaret, with charming, old-fashioned deference.

My father was back in New York the night of the November elections. The polls, still in an early, primitive state, predicted a landslide victory for Thomas Dewey over Truman. My father and mother listened to the radio in the dark of her room at Jeanne Reynal's house, and as the night went on, Truman won a series of early states. The newscasters dismissed these early victories as irrelevant to the final outcome, but as my parents sat up listening to the radio past midnight, Truman kept winning state after state; they grew more and more excited. By morning he had won.

My father would often refer fondly to that night as a moment of particular closeness and harmony between them.

8.

By that time, my mother had decided, after a period of uncertainty and doubt, to move forward with a divorce. Bob Wolff, after trying desperately to win her back, had then reacted angrily when his attempts failed, his anger fueled by my mother's vacillations. Now, he was pushing harder than she was for immediate divorce.

She wrote to her parents:

> About the divorce. Maybe it's harder to get one than I think but
> I'm sure it's not as difficult as you think. Consider the statistics—
> one out of every three marriages ends in divorce. Moreover, the

more I have heard about the Virgin Islands, the better I have liked the idea of going there for a divorce. I have heard now from several people (including 3 or 4 who've been there) that it is easy, cheap and quick (4 weeks) to get a divorce there, and, that, moreover it's a delightful place and an inexpensive one to live. There is a Virgin Islands travel bureau near Dodd, Mead and I will go up there next week to get full information—Reno, from what I've heard, is terribly expensive—a real gyp joint.

　. . .

As for my wanting the divorce—I <u>do</u>. Perhaps that was not quite plain in my confusion and nostalgia when Mother was here. But I am convinced now that I am better off without Bob, no matter what may happen in the future.

I'll get more information about the Virgin Islands and write you what I learn.

　. . .

Michael is writing Mother. He was so delighted with the letter. He's been so wonderfully steady in the middle of all the confusion—he is certainly far from being the devil-may-care seducer.

This is enough about my problems—I'm sorry to burden you with them, but I think from now on they'll be on the down-grade. Whatever you do, don't worry about me. I'm in good spirits. And thank you both for being so understanding and so helpful.

Four days after Truman's election, Bob Wolff wrote to my grand-mother:

Nov 6 - 48

Dear Lolita -

I discussed with my lawyer the matter of retaining a lawyer in the Virgin Islands as suggested in your letter and it is entirely agreeable to me.

I am just beginning to realize the damage I have done to myself by clinging to the thought of her all these months, seeing her and continuing to hope while she was building a new life beyond me. I only made the path back to normalcy more difficult by not striking out sooner and realizing earlier in this nightmare that she would never want me as a husband again. She only needed the moral support of my suffering—no doubt it hurt her, but she needed it—needed to have periodic evidence that I was still desperately in love with her and waiting for her—she needed this to help her through the uncertainties and fears of the new life that in her heart she was permanently committed to from the beginning. I cannot see it as anything else. I have made a terrible tangle of myself—but as Elizabeth would say and has said, nobody asked me to so I have no one to blame but myself.

But I will untangle and my hope is that both of us will be settled soon again each in a new life that rests not on the pain and irritation that you give or take from others but on something good and deep and decent. We are both so capable of this. The great regret for me is that somehow we did not have this or try again to build it with each other. But I know now it is over—without hope of renewal at least that is something.

The divorce I know will go smoothly. I spoke to Elizabeth by telephone and she is informed. I too am sorry all this had to be but I am glad that you and I are still good friends.

Fondly—Bob

Love Letters ("The hawk is biting")

I.

Inside my mother's bedroom nightstand was a little blue woolen pouch pulled closed by a string. It contained the love letters between my mother and father—about eighteen telegrams and seven letters. Most of the letters are written by my mother and the telegrams by my father. As he often admitted, my father was a lazy letter writer but was bombarding my mother with almost daily telegrams with expressions of passionate, undying love:

Jan 25, 4:48 am

NEW YORK LOOKS FINE BUT NEEDS YOUR LOVE

MICHAEL

Jan 29, 3:29 pm

I AM COUNTING THE DAYS AND LOVE YOU MORE AND MORE

MICHAEL

Feb. 3, 1949 (3:13 pm)

I LOVE YOU I LOVE YOU I LOVE YOU

MICHAEL

An hour and twelve minutes later:

Feb. 3, 1949 (4:25)

DONT   WORRY   FUTURE   IS   OURS   STOP   THINK   YOU   ARE   MOST
WONDERFUL PERSON IN THE WORLD I LOVE YOU

Since I saw few signs of cordiality, let alone passion, between them, it was
good to know that once, for a time, things had been different. The correspondence is even, at times, rather steamy. Because they made frequent
use of telegrams, which were semi-public documents, my parents developed a kind of code language for their sex life. "The hawk is biting" is
the phrase they used (my father's coinage, I believe) to describe intense
sexual desire.

On December 27, 1948, my father wrote:

TRYING TO GET THROUGH TO YOU ALL DAY CALL ME TOMORROW 9 AM
YOUR TIME THE HAWK IS BITING HARD

The correspondence takes place during a six-week period between
Christmastime of 1948—December 23—and sometime in early February 1949, when my mother was in the Virgin Islands getting her quickie
divorce. Divorce in most states at the time, including New York, was a
long, cumbersome, and expensive process. "You couldn't get a divorce in
New York without proving adultery, and you had to hire a detective and
be caught in bed and blah blah," my mother said. If you wanted to avoid
this unpleasantness and speed things up, you needed to go to Reno,
Nevada, which specialized in a kind of divorce tourism, offering rapid
no-fault divorces to people who qualified for residency in Nevada by
spending six weeks there. (Las Vegas had not taken off yet, and how else
was Nevada going to get people to come to a desert?) For a brief period,
between 1944 and 1949, the American Virgin Islands decided to compete
with Reno in the divorce tourism market. The islands now known as
the U.S. Virgin Islands had been a Danish colony for a couple of centuries before the United States literally bought them from Denmark in 1917.
But the nation didn't do much with its new territory; the islands took a
few days to reach by boat from the United States and remained little
developed. That changed right at the end of World War II, with two big

changes: the first commercial airline flights to the area started, and the Virgin Islands' assembly passed a law that allowed people to obtain divorce easily after establishing residence. The law was shot down by the U.S. Supreme Court in 1949, but there was a four- or five-year window during which the Virgin Islands were a little divorce haven in the Caribbean. During that time, a cluster of hotels on the main island of St. Thomas and in its capital, Charlotte Amalie, filled with young women (and men) cooling their heels waiting for their divorces to come through. Oddly enough, even though the quickie divorce business was a patently mercenary scheme meant to drum up tourist dollars, it also contained moralistic elements that served as fig leaves covering over its real purpose. Although most of the people seeking a rapid divorce had someone else they were anxious to marry or be with, the divorce seekers were not supposed to be seen with their new lovers. Along with spending six weeks establishing themselves as legitimate residents of the U.S. Virgin Islands, they were also supposed to establish their moral reputation, living in a kind of sexual quarantine, out of sight, at least, of any paramour, in order to qualify (morally) for divorce. This made for a very peculiar brand of tourism: people from all over ripped out of the normal context of their lives, in an extremely particular state of mind, suffering perhaps over the painful dissolution of a marriage, at the same time infatuated with someone else, in a perfect spot for a romantic vacation but all by themselves or, rather, with others stuck in the same predicament and all with a lot of time on their hands. "There was a whole gang of people, men and women, getting divorces down there," my mother told me. "And some of them were having a wonderful time. They were free and easy. They had to wait and all these people were footloose and fancy free, so I had plenty of pals."

There were all the elements for having a grand time but the visitors were in a state of suspended animation, waiting for their real lives to resume. "Everyone down here recognizes that everyone else has his own real life elsewhere—so it's very easy to be friendly without complications setting in," my mother wrote to my father. "We're all feeling rather sad—and I'm the saddest of the lot." Of course, some of this may reflect my mother's desire to reassure my father that she wasn't having *too* good of a time there.

My mother's letters to my father from Charlotte Amalie are lively and descriptive and provide a glimpse into a strange, now vanished world and a time when the U.S. Virgin Islands were perhaps the only piece of

American territory where blacks were on an equal—or even superior—footing with whites. The Jim Crow segregation laws that applied in places like Florida, or in other parts of the Caribbean, did not apply to the Virgin Islands. Blacks, in fact, were the dominant group economically as well as politically there, which made the islands an attractive tourist destination for successful American blacks who were eager to live, perhaps for the first time, without racial discrimination, as the people who ran the show.

St. Thomas is everything it's cracked up to be—and more. It's not only beautiful and interesting—it's quite exciting. It operates on several layers—as every place does—but here somehow the real life of the place permeates everything on the surface. There is absolute racial equality. But in actuality there is a light-skinned Negro aristocracy which doesn't consider itself Negro at all. The big shots here are Negro—the big property owners—government officials—and of course it's a favorite place with the Negro uppercrust in the States—Duke Ellington, etc. But it seems to me these people would much rather drink in the rather swank bars on ostentatiously equal terms with whites than bother about the poor blacks all around them. They are so delighted with being on top of the heap—especially the ones from the States—that they forget why they're there. The Governor, I understand, is absolutely hated by the blacks for just this reason—you <u>have</u> to come down.

Everyone is incredibly friendly and I have many acquaintances after only three days. I even have a would-be boyfriend who has taken me out twice—the designer of a new hotel which is going up soon. He is exceedingly gentlemanly and I am exceedingly ladylike and he bores me stiff, even though he's quite sweet and not unintelligent. I keep thinking of you all the time.

Every time I come back to the hotel I hope I will find a cable from you—just any sort of word. Please, please let me hear from you soon—I'm getting sadder and sadder. It's my misfortune—and yours—that I don't seem able to show my feelings—or even be fully aware of them—until I'm off by myself. But I knew from the minute I got here—actually the minute the plane left LaGuardia—that you were the center of my little universe.

Goodnight my sweet pussycat—I love you and I hope to God you write me something soon—

Liz

Much of their early correspondence reflects the difficulty of communications at the time. The only way to receive an international phone call was to be physically present at the cable office in downtown Charlotte Amalie, and circuits were open for only a few hours at a time.

For the first ten days after my mother's arrival, the post office in the Virgin Islands failed to deliver my father's letters, making her feel that he had abandoned her.

Darling—

I have so much to tell you but most important is that I miss you so terribly much. I sort of ache all the time from wanting to hear from you and to know that you miss me, too. I hope you do but I'm beginning to be afraid after all these days without word that perhaps you've decided now's the time to extricate yourself from a difficult situation. If you <u>have</u> you'll learn in a hurry just how tough and persistent I can be.

He sent a barrage of telegrams (which did get through) to go along with the letters.

Darling—Another day. I got your cable and answered it. Sweetie, I haven't had a single letter. Can it possibly be that you were so idiotic as not to send your letters airmail? It takes 10 days or more for regular mail to get here. If I have to wait 10 days, I don't know what will happen. I'm nearly crazy now. My whole life is conditioned by going to the post office. Every morning I wake up under my mosquito netting and have breakfast in bed in luxurious anticipation. Today, I think, I'll certainly get a letter. By sundown when there's no more hope, I'm drooping and sad, but glad at least that one more day has passed. Darling, for Christ's sake write me and send your letters airmail. Addressed to me at the Center Hotel. In desperation, I've gone to the travel bureau and every where else, but they don't have anything. Cables don't make me happy at all—they're so impersonal.

Tonight I'm going to see "Gone with the Wind" which at least has the virtue of being extremely long. It's a great problem to kill time and I'm so restless without word from you, I can't read. Yesterday, I stayed so long at the beach that I got quite burned and couldn't go today.

When I write you this way I feel as if I were talking to myself. You can't imagine what a change will occur when I get a letter. I amaze myself by missing you so terribly and in such a complete way.

Goodnight my sweet darling.

Liz

My father, although he had in fact been sending letters (by airmail), sent more cables to reassure my mother. Two on New Year's Eve, one just after midnight.

Dec. 31, 1949

MAILING TODAY LETTER WITH FUTURE PLANS STOP DO NOT TAKE ANY TRIPS BEFORE RECEIVING IT LOVE

MICHAEL

Jan. 1, 1949

MIDNIGHT AND THINKING ONLY OF YOU

MICHAEL

There were a lot of New Year's Eve parties in Charlotte Amalie, and my mother wrote my father about her plans while trying to play down the gaiety of the occasion in order to reassure him.

My plans for tonight are quite simple. I've gotten friendly with a
girl named Joyce Marston who lives here—I think I wrote you
about her—and another girl, Mary Myers from New York.
We're all more or less in the same spot and it's a good thing to
have their companionship. Anyhow—the three of us are having
dinner with three very decent guys who've sort of taken us under
their wing. We'll probably go to a few of the many parties in
progress and come home early. Everyone down here recognizes
that everyone else has his own real life elsewhere—so it's very
easy to be friendly without complications setting in. We're all
feeling rather sad—and I'm the saddest of the lot.

   . . . Baby, I've got to get dressed now. I'll be thinking,
wishing every minute I could be with you. It won't be too long,
darling, and then we can have as much time as the atom bomb,
nature and our own inclinations will allow—and none of those
worry me much.

I love you—Liz.

Finally, after New Year's, some of the letters my father had been sending
arrived in a batch, which my mother discovered almost by chance; she
received a notice from the post office because a letter from Mougouche
Gorky had arrived with one penny of postage too little.

my darling,

three letters today! my system, which has been starved ever since
you left, is not accustomed to such a rich diet. i can't quite get
over it. all I want to do is to be left alone to read and re-read your
letters and then sit and dream about you—and this is almost
exactly all i've done the past two days . . .

   darling, how i loved your Sunday letter and what a difference
it would have made for me if I'd gotten it when it arrived last
Tuesday. the way you write to me is just the way you talk and
every time I read your letters (which is with extreme frequency)
I can hear that funny, wonderful voice of yours which is like no
one else's in the world. I still remember just the way you said to

me "this is the voice of italy" when you called after our first
meeting and how happy and excited and frightened I was.

. . .

at this time next week we will be together. it will, of course,
be Saturday night and we'll be able to sleep late the next day. the
idea of being with you and being completely free to do whatever
we please almost frightens me I feel so happy. i want to do
everything with you: work with you and travel with you and stay
in one place with you and have friends with you and be alone
with you and have children with you and, of course, make love
with you—but most of all just be with you.

darling, i love you very, very much

Elizabeth

Sadly (and strangely), we do not have the letters my mother is referring
to or any of the other letters she received from my father in the Virgin
Islands. Although my mother kept the packet of love letters safely in her
nightstand for the rest of her life, at some point she appears to have lost
my father's letters while keeping all the telegrams. My father, on the
other hand, appears to have done an uncharacteristically good job of
keeping my mother's letters. A strange role reversal, since she took the
trouble to collect all the letters from him and save them carefully in the
blue woolen pouch in her nightstand.

It was obviously a strain for my parents, who had known each other
only about seven months at this point, to be away for a substantial period
of time when their relationship was still undefined and uncertain. They
began plotting a way to sneak my father into the Virgin Islands without
attracting the attention of the officials handling her divorce—not an
entirely easy matter. My mother wrote:

The more I see of this place, the more I realize how difficult it
would be for us to live together if you come down . . . Anyhow,
we'll manage it somehow. You've got to come—I can't stay 7
weeks without you. Even my healthy mid-western appetite has
deserted me, and you know how serious that is. I love you and
miss you in the way you describe as "the hawk" and I think I

may die if I can't talk to you this afternoon. If I can't, I'll send
you a cable telling you when to call tomorrow.

So my mother began investigating the possibility of finding a remote island in the archipelago of St. Thomas where they might stay in secret.
She found out about a tiny island called Anegada, which at the time had
about a hundred people living on it. The only way to get to the island was
in the plane of a man who flew there about once a week to check on some
lobster traps he had there.

"He had a route where he would take two passengers with him and
leave with the plane full of lobsters," my mother said. "So he left us alone
on this island with these natives. There couldn't have been more than
about a hundred people on the island. They were incredibly poor and
most of them had syphilis—which had made many of them blind and
many of them crazy. The island was tiny and flat as a pancake. As a result, you couldn't see it from the sea and it had been the site of many
shipwrecks. And the wind blew constantly. There was this one tiny village and the rest of the island was empty. We had a little cottage with a
cook. She cooked everything on charcoal. We were the only white people in what looked like an African village. Almost as soon as we arrived,
the village elders came calling. The mayor—the most important person
of the village—was the only man with a radio on the island and owned a
little store where you could buy a few things. But it was so poor that you
bought cigarettes individually—they didn't sell them by the pack, because
no one could afford them, even though they were very cheap. He became
our mentor and told us that one of the only things to do on the island was
to go to church and persuaded us it would be a good thing if we went.

"Perhaps about a mile from this little village to the north there was an
absolutely gorgeous beach—the cleanest sand I've ever seen. Very pure,
marine blue water, like a swimming pool except that it was natural and
full of all kinds of fish and coral and things like that. And you would sort
of sit in the shade if you wanted—not be in the sun—but mostly it was
sunny. The natives didn't bother to go swimming; they were busy doing
other things. And so Misha and I went there with a little picnic lunch that
the cook had prepared for us. The beach was deserted and far from the
village, so we took off all our clothes. We had a bottle of brandy with us
and so we spent the day swimming, eating, drinking brandy, and making
love—since there was no one around."

But not everything was exactly as it seemed.

"At a certain point, we realized that some of the natives were hiding in the trees nearby, watching us screw!" my father said, telling me about the incident and clearly relishing the memory. For both my parents, their time in the Virgin Islands was a key moment and something both of them talked about quite willingly. Eventually, they realized that one of the reasons why the natives stayed away from the beach and didn't swim in its clear blue water was that the water was filled with barracudas and sharks. "The barracudas would dart at you—we were lucky they didn't attack us," my mother recalled.

It sounds like my parents' moment in *From Here to Eternity*, James Jones's World War II novel and the blockbuster film featuring Burt Lancaster and Deborah Kerr rolling around the waves and sand of Hawaii in what was, at the time, one of the sexiest love scenes in movie history. Except that with my father, bespectacled Jewish intellectual, the story has an ending more out of Woody Allen.

"As the afternoon went on, Misha was getting red, since he had very white skin that burns easily, and by the end of the afternoon we finally went in because he was getting terribly uncomfortable. We went back to our cabin, where the cook was preparing something to eat. By this time, he was starting to get a fever and was pretty sick from the sunburn. We didn't have anything to put on the sunburn and you certainly couldn't get it there. I put cold compresses on him, but as the night wore on, he was more and more in agony and his fever shot up. That went on for two or three days at least and I began to long to get off of Anegada and back to St. Thomas to search the skies for the plane. It wasn't due for a couple more days. We practically ran onto the plane when it came. After that, we decided to hell with the secrecy and Misha paraded himself around town and, in fact, there was no trouble in the end."

Obviously, in spite of the sunburn, the trip helped to solidify their relationship. Shortly after his return, my father sent my mother the following telegram:

DARLING HOPE YOU GOT MY LETTER MAILED THURSDAY BUT AM CABLING ALL THE SAME TO REPEAT HOW MUCH I LOVE YOU AND HOW CERTAIN I HAVE COME BACK OF THE FUTURE STOP DELAY LETTER CAUSED BY AIR TRIP WASHINGTON TUESDAY ON IMPORTANT STORY STOP GOT BACK WEDNESDAY NIGHT AND HAD TO WORK ALL NIGHT BUT

KEPT THINKING OF YOUR LOVELY FACE AND EVERYTHING WAS EASY STOP FEEL SO FULL OF ENERGY AND AM EVEN GOING TO GET MY TEETH CLEANED (AND ALL BECAUSE I FEEL THAT MY LIFE HAS DEFINITE DIRECTION) STOP EXPECTATION SOMEHOW RELIEVES BITING OF HAWK BUT STILL I MISS YOU TERRIBLY AND TODAY WITHOUT LETTERS FELT MISERABLE STOP BUT MY SWEET BABY I FEEL AT THE SAME TIME SO SURE THAT I CAN BUILD AROUND YOU AND WITH YOU A WONDERFUL LIFE STOP IT IS NOW COMPLETELY UP TO US AND I FEEL THAT WE WONT FAIL STOP BUT DARLING I NEED TO FEEL YOU CLOSE TO ME DURING THIS LAST PERIOD STOP DARLING I WANT YOU TO THINK ONLY OF ME ALL THIS TIME STOP I LOVE YOU

MICHAEL

It is difficult for me not to laugh in reading, in the midst of this romantic telegram, the phrase "am even going to get my teeth cleaned." For my father this was a radical, radical move.

My mother seems to have calmed down some after my father's visit.

Wednesday night (I don't know the hour)

My sweet darling—

I feel so close to you now and I feel you so much a part of my life that I no longer feel the need to tell you about it.

That is assured—not taken for granted, but as far I'm concerned, so solid and unmistakably inevitable that no more two-week separation can ruffle it. I tried to tell you this in my cable about the hawk (my own particular hawk), which I hope you got and I'm sure you understood. An indication of my peace of mind is the fact that I've been reading voraciously— something I've been incapable of for a long time. I've gotten way into "Roosevelt and Hopkins" and find it fascinating, though I think it jumps about in a rather disorganized manner. I've also read several chapters of "The Plague." What a thing to watch a superb mind really click . . .

Joyce just came in to tell me that Carl, after several tortured days, finally got a cable saying that his papers were signed and on the way. He had fully expected to have to return a month or so later and get his divorce by default. She and I are giving him a farewell party tomorrow night—buying food and cooking it at Jacobsons and inviting the charter members. We're going to get a lot of extra stuff and leave it—thereby making them a gift without embarrassing them, we hope.

I'm hoping I'll get a letter tomorrow to pore over, and leave with the wonderful anticipation of returning to it. You are never out of consciousness. I'm always aware of you and of belonging to you.—Today my lawyer's wife, of all people, told me how much better I looked since my "boyfriend" had been down! Fine thing.

Darling, I'm sleepy and I'm living for the day when I come back to you. I love all of you with all of me and I want so much to get so deep into you that you'll never get me out.

Goodnight, my sweet love,

Lizzie

When my father was down in St. Thomas, he met my mother's new-found friends there. Jokingly, they referred to themselves as "charter members" of a kind of divorce club. There was a lot of drinking and merriment, and while people were welcoming toward my father, he was clearly suspicious of my mother's active social life, the drinking and partying, which he found both frivolous and probably threatening.

darling, I loved your angry letter because even though I think you're wrong about my succumbing to it what you have to say about the environment, the "drinking through false gaiety into idiotic dullness and insensitivity" is so right and true.

darling, you are so intelligent but what you have is much more than intelligence. There are, after all, plenty of intelligent stinkers. I hesitate to use the word "good," though you are that, too, whatever it is, I love you and want to be with you always and to be everything to you that you want me to be. I was thinking again today of what seems now the miracle of our meeting and how wonderful it is that our instincts hadn't been dulled by cocktail party socializing so that we both really knew each other that first night. [Added by hand] I knew that you were right for me.

Be relaxed, darling, and don't worry about anything, I love you so and I am only waiting to be able to tell and show you directly.

Elizabeth

While it is nice to know that my parents enjoyed their moment in paradise—not something that everyone in life gets to experience—still, one can already see a snake or two in the garden. Both are prone to considerable insecurity; my mother worries after a few days of not hearing from my father "that perhaps you've decided now's the time to extricate yourself from a difficult situation." My father seems to have suffered from a serious case of jealousy, quick to suspect the worst and to accuse my mother of things she doesn't appear to have done. Still, it might have been natural for my father to worry about my mother being alone surrounded by potential suitors in the party atmosphere of the Caribbean. After all, she had left her first husband for him in the course of a single evening at a crowded party. From my mother's point of view, it had taken her about eight years of growing boredom and unhappiness with Bob Wolff to act on her feelings; she was intensely focused on my father, so why was he making a fuss about things of absolutely no importance? When she doesn't write him for a couple of days, he immediately assumes the worst.

in self-defense, I must tell you that when i don't write it doesn't mean that i'm being active socially. it's more likely to mean that I am sad and don't want to worry you by revealing it. so I wait until I can write a happy, confident and positive letter which will be an encouragement and not a discouragement to you; when I don't hear from you, I feel completely dead—and, as a matter of fact, quite incapable of being with others.

You are wrong about my being at a similar party. I have spent most of my evenings reading in bed and none of them getting, or attempting to get, drunk. What's more, even when I try hard I seem incapable of adjusting to the mediocrities down here,—but

I'm not going further in refuting your charges because I know you know that I am basically capable of seeing things as they are and acting on my convictions.

As my mother wrote, in a letter that was to prove prophetic:

> Green in italy is the color of hope, you say. In America, and I suspect a lot of other places, it is the color of jealousy. darling, i am proud that you are so possessive and I would die if you didn't love me so much and want every part of me to belong to you and "only to you." I feel exactly the same way about you. But I just hope you will always know when you are being unreasonable. because jealousy isn't always a passionate and positive thing; it can get mean and petty and suspicious and then there is nothing good about it.—i haven't had a single "date" since you've left and, if i had, i would never have forgotten for a second that i belong to you—or allowed the other person to forget it. how could i? i'm yours and that's that.

And yet my mother may not have been above provoking him now and then, with mentions of "would-be boyfriends" and "dates," perhaps out of insecurity when she didn't hear from him.

> I promise not to worry you again, either by not writing or by sending frightening cablegrams. It was selfish for me to scare you yesterday when I know how hard you are working. Mrs. Barbell was absolutely overcome by the quantity of your cabled responses and said that if she could be young again she'd want "mr. michael" to love her.—on the other hand, I was so desperate that I wanted you to know it and do something about it.

A certain amount of anxiety and doubt would have been natural—two lovers who are separated for seven weeks at the height of their passion in a situation of uncertainty—and yet this element of desperation my mother refers to is reminiscent of the frantic tone of her letters home about her busy social life, waiting on pins and needles, being so excited she can barely think.

There is a highly revealing moment in one of her letters from the Virgin Islands that partially diagnoses the problem:

> what our mutual misery boils down to is that we love each other
> very much and that we are still not solid enough in our
> relationship, after all these months of chaos, to be able to stand
> separation calmly and confidently. I'm sure that will come with
> time. When you left for new york, I felt so sure of the future that
> i thought I could take this period rather easily, but it seems
> not!—i feel like a puppet which only comes alive when you pull
> the strings.

The final phrase—"I feel like a puppet which only comes alive when you pull the strings"—is a remarkable admission. It fits with the impression that emerges from the letters she wrote her mother about her high school and college boyfriends, of a woman who lives through the men in her life and feels worthless without constant signs of male attention and approval. My father, for his own, quite different reasons, suffered from his own demons, and together they amounted to what my mother described as "mutual misery."

PLEASE DARLING HAVE CONFIDENCE IN MY LOVE AND OUR FUTURE

MICHAEL

2.

There is also an extremely interesting letter my mother wrote to her parents from Charlotte Amalie about her future with my father. My grandparents, worried about their impulsive, headstrong daughter, and knowing next to nothing about her future second husband, were trying to find out what they could about him. My grandfather evidently asked an Italian member of the University of Chicago faculty, Giuseppe Antonio Borgese, a literature scholar, to check out my father. Borgese apparently came back with a glowing report of my father as a brilliant young rising star of Italian journalism. Evidently, they made some reference to his "investigation" in a letter to my mother.

My mother wrote:

After I got your letter about Borgese's note, I wrote Michael
about it. I thought he might be upset at being "investigated"—
but he thought daddy was perfectly justified in wanting to know
"who is the swindler who is trying to swipe away his darling
daughter." He is planning to write you a long letter about himself
and his history when I return to new york. As to his family—I'm
not terribly concerned because he doesn't have awfully much to
do with them. He dislikes his father intensely for both political
and personal reasons and admires and loves his mother. His
father, apparently, was at one time a very successful dentist in
rome. They came here during the war and his father, unable to
work as a dentist because of the u.s. laws, worked as a technician
in a laboratory and gradually built up a business in exporting
dental equipment, particularly to italy. According to Michael, it
was a good idea and there was great demand for equipment in
italy but his father is quite unbusinesslike with this business—
his father wants to return to Italy; his mother wants to stay; his
sister works for some large chemical concern which has offices
both in new york and rome and plans to stay in the u.s. I am
naturally anxious to meet them—especially m.'s mother. she is,
according to Michael, a very intelligent, courageous and vital
person who has more or less sacrificed her own life to a
somewhat eccentric and irresponsible husband.—we shall see, at
any rate, I am sure they are nothing like Eileen mcquillan's
family! Maybe they're awful—but they'll be awful in quite a
different way.—incidentally, Michael is going to have his name
legally changed to STILLE which is the name he writes under.
He is better known under that name, likes it better and anyway
nobody can pronounce Cameneschi. His full pen name is Ugo
Stille, but he is going to keep "michael" because he likes it better
than "ugo." So do I!

In this period, my mother appears to have permanently abandoned
her childhood name, Betty, for Liz, Lizzie, or Elizabeth. And my father
is calling himself Michael Cameneschi, having tried to soften or perhaps
Italianize the Slavic-sounding "Kamenetzki," since Z's and K's are sel-

dom used in Italian. Extremely evident is that my father has told my mother almost nothing about himself. He has told her that his family came to the United States during the war, but he evidently did not explain why: that the family was forced to leave Italy because of the racial laws. It's also obvious that my father has explained nothing about his friend Giaime, saying simply that Stille is "the name he writes under." My mother clearly favors the name change. "He is better known under that name, likes it better and anyway nobody can pronounce Cameneschi." Cameneschi (or Kamenetzky) sounds much too foreign, too ethnic, and perhaps (to an ear tuned to such things) too Jewish.

After my mother got back from the Virgin Islands, my parents agreed to get married and move in together to an apartment on Leroy Street in the West Village, not far from Jeanne Reynal's house.

A month after she returned from St. Thomas and three months before they were married, my mother wrote her parents:

> Life goes along busily and happily for me . . . I've been working hard in my spare time getting the apartment furnished—making curtains, etc., preparatory to marriage. We still don't know when we'll take the leap. It's a question of time mainly, since Michael is on the go six days a week and sometimes seven. We went Friday night to the annual dinner of the Overseas Press Club—at which the principal speakers were Marshall and Acheson. They are certainly two opposites, at least in outward characteristics, though each is impressive in his own way. Also Michael took me last week to dinner at his friends the Max Ascoli's. So you see I have by now met highly reputable friends of Michael's who think very highly of him—including the Italian Ambassador!
>
> Shortly after your last visit last fall, Wooz, I asked Michael if he was Jewish and he told me he was. I was terribly hurt that he hadn't told me before, and he said he didn't think it made any difference to me so he hadn't bothered. This didn't sit so well with me either and I told him so. So he then divulged his life history which he'd kept pretty much to himself, and which is rather involved. I wanted him to write you himself—and I still do but, knowing how busy he is and what a capacity he has for putting off all but the most urgent projects, I'm sure it will be a while before he gets around to it. I'm sure all this sounds very

mysterious. Actually, it isn't particularly. It's just that Michael by nature doesn't like to talk about himself or to let people know much about his personal life. It is a curious and disconcerting trait—according to his mother largely natural, but probably accentuated by underground and intelligence activities during the war. At any rate, there's nothing in his life that isn't entirely to his credit—I'll let him tell you his story in his own way and his own time.

. . .

I've got to get up now, put myself together and fix some dinner for Michael who's coming in a little while.

Much, much love to you both, E

Obviously, my father's standing in the journalistic world was reassuring to both my mother and her parents. But the paragraph about my father finally admitting he was Jewish is interesting for many reasons. It indicates that my father was more or less hiding the fact of being Jewish at this time in his life—something my aunt, his sister, later confirmed to me. "Let's not get into that with people," my father apparently told her. While it seems bizarre by contemporary standards, it seemed less so at the time. Even in the America of World War II, there was a considerable amount of anti-Semitism. Travel agencies asked you before booking a hotel, "Gentile or Jew?" as matter-of-factly as they might ask, "Double or single room?" The major American universities had Jewish quotas; many New York law firms and athletic clubs routinely excluded Jews (as well as in some cases Irish), as did many of the buildings along Park and Fifth Avenue, bastions of Wasp privilege. And yet hiding it from the person you are about to marry is another thing. My mother was obviously hurt and angry. How could he possibly think it would matter to her? she wondered. After all, hadn't she been married to one Jewish man already?

This paragraph of my mother's letter is extremely curious: posing as a kind of revelation of truth, it is a masterpiece of evasion and self-deception on everyone's part: my mother's, my father's, and my grandmother's.

My mother insists that her negative reaction to learning that my father was Jewish was simply that she felt hurt and betrayed that he hadn't been straight with her. But pretty clearly it was a bit more complicated than that. My father had good reasons for being nervous about how my mother—and her family—would react to his family background. (After all—although he may not have known this at the time—my grandfather had objected violently to the fact that my mother's first husband was Jewish and had had him investigated by a private eye.) The letter makes quite clear that my grandmother had asked my mother about my father's being Jewish when she visited New York to check out her prospective son-in-law, prompting my mother to press my father about it. Clearly—while it may not have mattered too much to my grandmother (she liked Bob Wolff)—it was not an entirely neutral piece of information, like asking whether my father was left- or right-handed. The fact that it was something that had to be "admitted" makes quite clear that it still carried a stigma.

My father was, similarly, being equally disingenuous in saying that it hadn't occurred to him to mention it because he didn't think my mother cared. My father's entire presence in the United States—the sole reason for his losing his Italian citizenship, being forced to leave Italy—was uniquely owing to the fact of being Jewish. So, in order to explain anything about his recent life, he would have to omit (or paper over) many of the most pertinent, important events of his life in order to avoid revealing that he was Jewish. Clearly my father responded by telling my mother almost nothing about himself. "It's just that Michael by nature doesn't like to talk about himself or to let people know much about his personal life. It is a curious and disconcerting trait—according to his mother largely natural, but probably accentuated by underground and intelligence activities during the war."

Even my grandmother Mumi gets into the act in this comedy of deception and self-deception. My grandmother describes his reticence to talk about himself as "natural," when in fact it was clearly a learned habit, a habit he had learned directly from her and my grandfather. They had hidden the fact that the family was Jewish from him (and the world) throughout his childhood. He had learned directly from his parents the art of reticence and silence, the deep-seated fear that being Jewish was a dark secret that, if admitted, could have dangerous and unpredictable consequences.

My mother's speculation that it was "accentuated by underground and intelligence activities during the war" is equally off base. My father ran radio stations, not secret spy missions, but attributing my father's extreme reticence to "underground and intelligence activities" makes for a more compelling and romantic story than the messy and painful reality of a boy who spent his childhood unaware of his own Jewish origins and then experienced the trauma of being suddenly branded as a member of an inferior race, losing his Italian citizenship and identity all because of a mere accident of birth, experiences that left him closed and somewhat ashamed of his origins.

3.

At some point before they married, my father introduced my mother to his mother and sister. They met—not at his parents' apartment but at the Russian Tea Room, which during the lean years right after World War II was a very expensive place frequented by the very wealthy. And my father's father was conspicuously absent. For some time—I don't know whether this was the case at this point—my father's story was that while his father was Jewish, his mother, Sara Altschuler, was not. "Her name, Sara Altschuler, was not particularly Jewish, and she didn't have anything Jewish about her," my mother said. It was one of the many stories she told me on her deathbed.

"We had gotten a table. We were sitting and I was surely having a vodka or something. In comes this very dignified but shabby-looking, very fat lady, beaming from ear to ear. So I didn't know a thing about her, whether she was Jewish or not. She was bearing a bunch of flowers in my honor. She had no money but she had brought a gift. That's my memory. She spoke English, but extremely broken English. But she obviously was a person of some substance—she was a lady. I remember they had strolling musicians that went around and played. It was all fake, but trying to be Russian, and they played a couple of Russian songs . . . and I thought now why don't they go away? But Mumi brought out three dollars, which was a lot of money for her, and tipped them. Those things stay in my mind. She managed to create an aura around herself as an intelligent, kind, and dignified person."

My aunt Lally was there as well. "They said quite openly in front of me—they discussed me as if I were a horse that they were gonna buy—how much I looked like Greta Garbo and how much I looked like Marlene Dietrich. Misha had captured this fabulous beauty. What her character was like was beside the point. She was beautiful. Lally had brought me a present, too. A much more expensive present than Mumi's, but it was the most impractical thing imaginable. It was a bottle of perfume, in a bottle shaped kind of like a dagger that lay flat. But when you tried to pour some out it always spilled, and so I threw it out. But I liked Misha's mother from the start even though we could barely communicate. She gave off an aura of dignity and intelligence and I was just thrilled to have this rather odd woman as a prospective mother-in-law. At that time, we talked about getting married almost from the beginning until the day we married."

The Wedding License

While my mother had hoped to marry Michael Stille, in fact, she married Michael Kamenetzki instead—as a copy of their wedding license indicates.

While America was the country where you could be who and what you wanted to be, the past clung to my father (and my mother) with a certain stubbornness. "I was married as Elizabeth Kamenetzki," my mother said, not hiding her distaste for the name. "We intended to formally change it but we had to get a lawyer and so for three or four months, I was Elizabeth Kamenetzki."

They were married at New York's city hall at about ten in the morning on June 2, 1949. There was no thought of a large wedding. Neither of them had much money and my father hated ceremony, considering the fanfare of traditional weddings—proposals, rings, printed invitations, rehearsal dinners, and receptions—nothing more than silly bourgeois conventions. It was all quite bureaucratic—the blood tests, the number of documents needed to prove that my father really was who he said he was and an American citizen and that my mother was divorced. They received an appointment for 10:00 a.m. and were in and out in about fifteen minutes. The only witnesses were an Italian diplomat named Vittorio Ivella, one of the few Italian friends my mother had met, and my father's sister, Lally, both of whom my mother barely knew. That was it.

The wedding had to be in the morning and the wedding celebration immediately afterward, because my father had to file a story that afternoon.

After the wedding they took the subway all the way uptown to my grandparents' apartment on 106th Street and West End, at the time a somewhat run-down part of town with once-elegant prewar apartment buildings now filled with many Eastern European refugees. They were going to take a cab, but since the wedding was at ten and they were going for a midday meal, they were in no hurry. "There was plenty of time to kill, believe me," my mother said. In fact, when they got to the Kamenetzki apartment, she found things in a state of chaos, the wedding lunch nowhere near ready.

"Mumi was bustling around the kitchen trying to get lunch ready. Mumi was about four foot nine and so fat that she had a hard time getting through the door. But she somehow managed to be charming. But having had servants most of her life, she had very little idea of what she was doing in the kitchen."

When my mother entered the Kamenetzkis' living room, she saw for the first time her new father-in-law, Ilya Kamenetzki, whom my father had managed to keep under wraps until that time. "He was dressed in a totally inappropriate way for what was supposed to be a formal lunch. He had a clean shirt but it wasn't properly tucked in and he had no jacket on. He had a big potbelly and he could not—or didn't bother to try to— close the belt holding up his pants. He was sitting over by the window when I came in the room. Misha and Ivella were talking on in Italian. Mumi was in the kitchen, taking forever with this lunch. Lally was coming and going, trying, with maximum inefficiency, to help with lunch. I was stuck with Grandpa. He didn't stand up to greet us when we came but he sure took me in. He wouldn't take his eyes off me. He bragged about how handsome he had been, showed me pictures of himself, to show me how dashing he had been. He implied to me, with many winks and smiles, that he was a devil with the women. And he would be with me, too, if I hadn't been his son's wife. I thought he was the most repulsive man I'd ever met, but I tried not to show it. I thought to myself, Hitler killed six million Jews and he had to spare this guy!?

"If ever there was somebody that would make you automatically anti-Semitic it was that man," my mother said, lying on what we thought was her deathbed, almost forty-three years after her wedding day, remembering it all in minute detail. I was a bit shocked by the Hitler remark. She was in bed with six brain tumors and on massive doses of cortisone, so she expressed herself on all topics in an extreme fashion, without any diplomatic filters. Still, I expect the revulsion she expressed was real enough. My mother had grown up in a midwestern Wasp culture with a certain vein of reflexive, unthinking anti-Semitism. She had rejected it as part of a midwestern narrow-mindedness—and had married

Bob Wolff in defiance. "I was crazy about Jews," my mother said. But Wolff and the other Jews she had come across in the artistic and intellectual circles in which she had moved in Chicago and New York were highly assimilated, secular Jews. They were like everyone else but had different last names; and they were, in the main, better educated and more sophisticated than the average Chicagoan. In my grandfather, my mother found herself with a kind of Jew she was not used to: a real, unvarnished Eastern European Jew from the shtetl. My grandfather had a heavy Yiddish accent, and he would preface whatever he was about to say with *Nu*—a Yiddish word that means "well" or "now" or is sometimes used like "and so" to prompt someone to answer. ("Mumi didn't have a Yiddish accent, I was so grateful for that, the Yiddish accent creeps into everything," she said, in her cortisone rant about meeting my grandparents.) When my mother would give my grandfather a gift, instead of simply thanking her, he would ask her how much she had paid for it. My mother would find herself caught between two conflicting norms: her Wasp upbringing had taught her that it was polite to answer questions but, at the same time, that it was impolite to talk about money. Finally my grandfather would persist and badger the price out of her. "*Twenty dollahs! Twenty dollahs!* You overpaid! I have a friend, a shop on Second Avenue who give you the same sweater—the same exact sweater—ten dollars." When my parents had him over to dinner he would bend the spoons to find out what they were made of. "He wanted to find out if they were real silver. If they bent, they were real silver, but of course it ruined the spoons," my mother said.

The lunch was excruciatingly late and the conversation was almost all in Italian, with my father and his friend Ivella arguing about politics and my grandfather occasionally joining in. "His voice was booming but no one was listening to him," my mother said. Unable to follow, my mother watched with a sense of alienation and also of horror.

My mother had thought she was marrying an Italian intellectual and journalist, not the son of a Yiddish-speaking shtetl Jew who had the instincts and manners of an itinerant peddler. She had told herself that my father's family didn't matter to her because my father had little to do with them, but now she was closer than she ever imagined. And not only was she his daughter-in-law, she bore his name; she was now Elizabeth Kamenetzki.

"I kept thinking to myself, 'God, I have made mistakes in my life, but this one tops them all. I am crazy about Misha, but I should never have gotten married to somebody in this family.' I almost bolted, but I was already married. I thought, 'I've got to undo this. I've got to get out of this.' They were comparatively young, in their sixties, and I thought these people are going to be an important part of my life for a long time." After lunch, my mother, my father, and Vittorio Ivella all took the subway back downtown. The conversation continued in Italian and my mother sat, as if alone, sinking deeper and deeper into despondency with every passing minute. My father got off at Times Square to go to his office and write his story, and my mother continued home to her room on West Eleventh Street, where she was still living in the house of Jeanne Reynal. She was alone when she got to the house. Mougouch Gorky, who was sharing the floor with my mother, had cleared out that day in honor of my mother's wedding. "I cried, one of the few times," she said. "I was beside myself and I thought, 'I've got to get out of this marriage.' The bed was unmade and I took out the laundry. I had a lot of errands to run while Misha wrote his story. Depressed—that was me on my wedding day. Misha did the gallant thing and actually made a reservation for dinner at a fancy restaurant. It might have been in a hotel. It was along Fifth Avenue, around the corner. There was nobody else but me and Misha and I remember Misha saying, 'Thank God, we're married at last!' I tried hard not to cry during that dinner, but I had no appetite and I had to force myself to eat this fancy meal. I think we even had champagne. But my heart was heavy—that's all I can say. I knew I was paying a heavy price, a very heavy price for this decision. I was thinking, 'I should have stayed with Bob Wolff after all. I could easily get out of this.' We had no children, after all. I was just so depressed. You've seen a lot of depressed brides. Some of them for silly reasons. But I had good reasons to be.

"But just when I thought I couldn't stand things a minute more Misha would charm me. By the end of the evening perhaps he was beginning to charm me. I suppose we slept together. I suppose we managed that. He was a passionate but not very adept lover. And we used to talk—that was where we had our real talks." During that long wedding night my father began to win her back, talking, talking, and talking. He talked with much greater frankness about his family, his origins, and the fact of being Jewish, about which he had been so cagey. "I think by then I knew for sure his father was Jewish, he'd admitted that it was true. I learned a lot of things about things. He admitted—there was no denying his father was Jewish. His mother was really Jewish but she hadn't practiced. So he came out with the whole Jewish business. Slowly, slowly, slowly. By morning, it didn't matter whether they were—I didn't care. We talked all night, and by morning I thought, 'Oh well, maybe I'll make it after all.' "

Memory can play tricks on a person, and I have strong reasons to doubt that the day of my parents' wedding was the moment in which my father finally admitted that he was Jewish. There is the letter from March 1949—three months before their wedding—in which my mother writes with a very hurt tone that my father had hid the fact of being Jewish from her.

It would be easy to attribute my mother's error to the fuzziness of memory, but the field of oral history has taught us that the mistakes people make in their recollections are themselves "facts" that need to be examined carefully. When people began doing oral history, errors on the part of interview subjects were a source of embarrassment to be pointed out with an editor's note, "[*sic*]," and corrected. But gradually, oral historians realized that when a subject conflates two events or changes the date of an important event, those are moments of particular interest that may have great meaning. In this case, by remembering or misremembering that the revelation of my father's Jewishness happened on her wedding day, my mother was (unconsciously) giving it even greater importance.

No doubt my mother felt, as she described, a desire to bolt from the room and undo her marriage, and on meeting her father-in-law for the first time, it was as if she had suddenly realized, "Oh, my god, they are *really* Jewish."

Personal, Confidential—Destroy After Reading

I.

The letter could not have begun in a duller, more quotidian fashion:

Dearest Elizabeth,

We were interested to hear from your last letter what use you and Michael were planning to make of our birthday checks. Whip cord slacks sound fine, as does your plan for china or a scrubber waxer. Pop loves his long johns, wears them most every evening these cold nights. For the same reason I have not yet worn my pretty robe—but shall use it lots once it warms up again.

Most of my grandmother's letters are somewhat routine and chatty and fairly conventional in tone and content: lots of basic family news; her and her husband's health; how this year's garden is growing; the travails of the peach orchard; updates on the Wisconsin and Chicago branches of the family; the latest antics of our midwestern cousins. (Before the 1960s, when long-distance telephoning became relatively inexpensive, my mother's and her mother's letters served to communicate the small change of daily life, details of trip arrivals, money troubles, suggestions for possible birthday presents, and information about clothing sizes.)

But this particular letter, with its unremarkable account of my grandparents' winter in San Francisco, lulls you into boring normality and leaves you unprepared for what then feels like a shot to the solar plexus at the end, following the words: "P.S. for Elizabeth only":

Second thoughts. The conviction that your father and I share—
that Michael <u>must not strike you</u>—is unshaken; but on thinking
it over further I think the decision is wise to wait until May with
doing anything drastic (unless of course the provocation is
extreme)—Meantime I think it should be a matter of sober study
for you to try to work out ways and means of effectively and
permanently dissuading him from such conduct.

I witnessed a great deal of verbal cruelty between my parents—my father,
in particular, ridiculing my mother and reducing her to tears—but I never
witnessed any physical violence. But obviously it had happened and was
a serious-enough problem that my mother had raised it with her parents.
In fact, whatever happened was serious enough that my mother was already thinking of leaving my father after only a few years of marriage,
despite having a small child. My grandmother, while in no way condon-
ing my father's behavior, urges her to be cautious, to wait and see before
leaving my father. In fact, she makes a genuine effort to try to understand
my father's behavior and attributes some of it to a cultural difference
between the two of them:

> I think M. is a good man, basically, and that he is at heart
> devoted to you and Lucy. His European attitude toward women
> may give him something to learn in his dealings with an
> <u>American</u> woman—(though I feel certain no gentleman even in
> Europe would so lose control of himself, if he were in his right
> mind), and his mother has undoubtedly spoiled him by tolerating
> this abandonment of self-discipline.
>
> But he is your husband, and Lucy's father, and those facts
> compel a careful effort to conquer the difficulties.

My grandmother, in an interesting reflection on her own marital choices,
suggests that part of the problem lies with marrying an intellectual.

> I feel quite sure that nerves are at the root of the difficulty—
> Michael's is a tense calling, and he having the keen mind he has,
> multiplies its inherent tenseness to the 11th degree. As a
> psychiatrist told me in reference to Daddy, "There is no doubt a

woman takes on something when she marries an intellectual."
Ay, Ay! There are obviously compensations. <u>But there is no
reason on earth</u> why a man and wife should not work out
together ways of minimizing the trouble, instead of as at present
maximizing it. Michael should listen to reason and not play the
fool by risking, for good, everything that means anything to
him.

The letter, although undated, must be from the early to mid-1950s, since
it makes mention of my sister, Lucy, who was born in October 1951, and
none of me, born in January 1957.

2.

What had gone so wrong that my parents went from rolling in the sands
of Anegada (à la *From Here to Eternity*) to violence and the brink of divorce in a few short years?

Not long after they married, my father took my mother to Europe.
Her first impression was a contradictory mix of extreme beauty and extreme poverty. Europe in 1949 was still recovering from the destruction
and poverty of the war. Some of the cities were bombed out, and "it was
very poor, you'd see mothers carrying sick babies—and they were really
sick—begging," she said. "You would see people walking barefoot
through the streets. I had never seen people without shoes in a city before." At the same time, she came into contact with places of a beauty she
had never seen before. They stopped first in Paris. I remember my
mother telling me how moved she had been to see, on her first trip to Europe, the *Winged Victory*, also known as the *Nike of Samothrace*, an ancient Greek sculpture that shows the torso of a winged goddess. The
statue has no head, but the graceful and powerful bearing of its torso—
which was probably placed on the prow of a ship—seemed to conjure up
the sense of the beauty and divinity of the ancient Greek world.

But then, one of the first nights of the trip, something happened. "Timidly, I went out and bought some postcards and a bottle of perfume and I
got overcharged—I didn't know French currency and I lost maybe fifty
cents. He started hitting me in a restaurant. Over fifty cents. It was the

most horrible evening in my life—one of them. Why I didn't leave him right then and there I don't know. He really clobbered me on that trip. It was not fun."

I don't have my father's version of these events. I would never have dared to ask him. While I never witnessed him being physically violent with my mother, I certainly saw him fly off the handle and become enraged over tiny, unimportant matters hundreds and hundreds of times. So, unfortunately, I don't have a hard time believing my mother's story. When I asked her about the nature of the physical violence, she said, "He used to hit me a lot. He didn't beat me up, but if he got mad, he would hit me in a kind of childish way. He would try to terrorize me."

Aside from the frequent arguments, the trip (from my mother's point of view) was pretty much a disaster. When they got to Italy, relations between the sexes, even among my father's friends, were what my mother considered antiquated. The men would kiss her hand and then turn their backs on her. They were full of old-world gallantry, but nobody would talk to her. She eventually figured out that in this culture (at this time) paying attention to another man's wife was considered impolite, and so they ignored her. After dinner, the wives would be herded into a separate room—like the veiled women of a harem—while the men smoked and talked of world affairs. The fact that she spoke no Italian and few of them spoke any English didn't help. My father would frequently tell my mother that he was going out for an hour and then disappear for several hours, talking to his friends or visiting his journalist colleagues. If women were ignored at the private parties she attended, in public it was just the opposite. When she went out on the streets alone, fat old men made kissing sounds when she walked by, while younger men followed her for blocks and blocks trying to get her to stop. Italy, where women were concerned, seemed to her like a Middle Eastern country. She stayed in the hotel, uncertain about going off on her own, not knowing her way around, not knowing the language, waiting and getting angrier and angrier by the hour.

When she got back she went out to Michigan to attend her brother George's wedding. He had married much closer to home, a lovely girl from a prominent Chicago family, Adelyn "Lyndy" Russell, whose father was a banker and a trustee of the University of Chicago. They had a beautiful house right on Lake Michigan a few miles from my grandparents' farm. The wedding took place just next door at the house of Harold

Swift, the heir of the great meatpacking fortune, who in a gesture of extraordinary generosity had given Lyndy's father forty acres of beachfront property, on which they built their house. "They were the most handsome couple you can imagine," my mother said. "George looked superior to Gary Cooper, and I had this little fat man tormenting me about fifty cents.

"So I've had an interesting life to say the least."

3.

It is surprising that I should have been surprised by my grandmother's letter about my father's striking my mother. After all, I had already interviewed my mother about my father's hitting her in Paris on their honeymoon trip. I had sat there and listened to and recorded the story about his hitting her, but I had managed to forget it, so I was surprised all over again when I came upon it in the transcript of the interview many years later. Evidently this was a fact I simply didn't want to take in.

4.

It is one of the strange and difficult-to-resolve contradictions of this story that while I almost never heard my mother say anything positive about her marriage to my father, I almost never heard my father say anything bad about it.

In talking about the early years of their marriage, I remember him telling me about how much my mother wanted to get pregnant. "She was so sweet, so cute. She had a hard time getting pregnant and she wanted a child so badly. She saw doctors and took drugs and then starting checking her temperature to figure out the perfect time. I remember her telling me, 'Come here quickly, my temperature's up. The time is now!' I felt like a stud horse!" my father said, obviously liking that image of himself very much.

A letter my mother wrote to her parents when she was pregnant with Lucy reflects something similar:

I'm delighted to hear that you are thoroughly pleased by our good news, not that I thought for a moment you'd be anything

but—one of the nice things, though, about a pregnancy that
was so long in materializing is the pleasure and surprise it
gives you, your friends and family when it finally happens. I still
have to pinch myself now and then because I feel not only normal
but better than normal, and nothing in our lives (or my figure)
has altered as yet, except for minor carefulness in matters of
health.

After their idyll on the Virgin Islands, there is a trickle of other love
telegrams that would seem to demonstrate that the passion did not die
right out—at least for my father.

EVERYTHING FINE BUT MISS YOU TERRIBLY LOVE

MISHA

WESTERN UNION
FROM MILANO VIA PO
DEC. 22, 1950

IMPOSSIBLE TAKE PLANE BEFORE SUNDAY STOP WILL FLY CHICAGO
DIRECTLY STOP CANCEL MY TRAIN RESERVATION AND PROLONG
INSURANCE STOP AM TERRIBLY LONELY AND NEED ALL YOUR THOUGHTS
STOP I NEED YOU AND LOVE YOU ALL THE TIME

MISCHA

HOTEL CARYE
BOULEVARD RASPAIL

ELIZABETH MY BEAUTIFUL DARLING, JUST A NOTE FROM PARIS TO TELL
YOU HOW MUCH I LOVE AND MISS YOU—AND THAT GOES FOR LUCY AND
SANDRO TOO—NATURALLY—BUT I WANT TO SAY THAT IT IS NOT ONLY
THE CHILDREN—BUT ALSO AND ESPECIALLY YOU—I HAVE BEEN
THINKING A LOT ABOUT HOW MARVELOUS YOU ARE—HOW SWEET AND
PATIENT AND INTELLIGENT—ALL QUALITIES REFLECTED IN YOUR
LOVELY FACE AND THE BEAUTIFUL LINE OF YOUR BODY—YOU WILL
PROBABLY LAUGH AT THE MIXTURE OF ELEMENTS IN MY DESCRIPTION—

BUT THIS IS THE WAY IN WHICH YOU SPEAK TO MY THOUGHTS AND
FEELINGS—AND THIS IS LOVE—

MISHA

I HOPE YOUR MOTHER IS FULLY RECOVERED FROM HER OPERATION—
GIVE HER AND YOUR FATHER MY LOVE—AND TAKE CARE OF YOURSELF
AND THE CHILDREN—

LOVE,

M.

Strangely enough, I have no doubt that my father genuinely adored my
mother and that, unfortunately, he gave much less weight to his explo-
sions of anger than she did. It was almost as if a switch had been flipped
the moment my father got married: he now had permission to behave
badly, to show his dark and angry side. Family was a safe haven in which
he could blow off steam, give free rein to his free-floating anxiety, aggression, insecurity, and rage, be fully "himself."

Here, my grandmother may have been right that cultural differences
played a role. Screaming certainly—and perhaps even hitting—did not
have the sort of irrevocable quality of having crossed some metaphorical
Rubicon from which there was no turning back. I remember once in 1983,
when my mother was in the hospital following a cancer operation (about
ten years before her actual death), my father suddenly turned to me and
said, "I don't know if you remember, but when I was young I was given
to fits of rage. How foolish I was. I didn't treat your mother as well as I
should have." What was most incredible to me in this was the idea that I
might have trouble remembering his fits of rage. They were the background music of our childhood.

Lucy and I would hear our parents fighting and creep down the stairs
to try to perch on the stairway, listening. Was that laughing or crying?
Are they joking or screaming? We knew, of course, that it was screaming
and crying. Sometimes Lucy, who was five years older, would go down
and, like a little child lawyer, try to reason my father back upstairs. He
praised her for her logic and her cool, detached approach. Perhaps unsur-
prisingly, she ended up negotiating for a living, as a literary agent in the

film industry. I, younger and more emotional in my approach, would give way to tears and anger. "Look what you've done!" my father would say to my mother, "you've gotten this poor idiot all worked up!"

In many ways, from my father's point of view, his life worked very well. While my mother talked constantly about divorce, I never heard him say a word about it. In fact, once when my mother was on the brink of leaving him, he went to my sister and told her, "You've got to talk her out of it!" He had a rich and successful professional life. He was greatly respected and well liked in his work. For Italian politicians and big shots, seeing my father was an indispensable stop on any trip to New York. When Gianni Agnelli—the president of the Fiat car company, as close as Italy came to royalty after getting rid of the monarchy in 1946—came to New York, my father would be summoned for an audience. He was a desired dinner guest and invited to all the most interesting parties. At the same time, he had a beautiful wife who gave him two cute little children, whom he enjoyed bouncing on his knee now and again. She took care of all the practical aspects of their common life and kept a beautiful, well-maintained house. She was an excellent cook and helped him give great parties. Given the extreme turmoil of his early life, I don't think he could believe his good luck that his life had turned out so well.

Several times a year, someone comes up to me and says, "I don't know if you know, but I was a *great* friend of your father's. Didn't he tell you? He was one of the most wonderful people I have ever known. It wasn't just that he was brilliant and wonderful company. It was his human qualities. He was *simpatico*. He was wise. He had a wonderful sense of humor." All these things were true, as far as it goes.

My father led a bifurcated, schizophrenic life: his professional life entirely Italian, his personal life entirely American. He had a social life related to his work where he was charming and wonderful, and a family social life where he was alternately charming and totally impossible. I think my father managed an extremely complex operation in his psychic economy that resembles one of the strategies financiers adopt when rescuing troubled companies: they split the company in two, into a "bad" and a "good" company. They dump the toxic assets into the bad company and the valuable assets into the good company, which is then brought back into the market in a healthy condition. It seemed as if he dumped all of his deepest neuroses and anxieties, his fears and insecurities, his anger and self-hatred into the intimate sphere of his life, taking much of it out on my mother, the person whom he loved the most, perhaps because he felt more secure in that realm. In his professional social life (where relations were more superficial), with the scores and scores of people he met at parties and dinners, he was able to keep his demons away and could express the best parts of himself.

It is a strange form of tribute, but I suspect my father behaved badly around my mother because he felt safe with her and at home, whereas he knew he had to be on good behavior when out in the world.

My mother was an anchor for my father, an anchor in America helping ground him in his life as well as in his work. As much as he liked to mock—when the evil mood was on him—my mother's provincial midwestern background, he needed the sense of security her Americanness gave him. Europe, with all its intellectual sophistication, had stripped him of all his rights and his citizenship, and had left him a few steps from the gas chambers. America had given him protection, rights, and citizenship. My mother and her solid do-good midwestern family represented the kind of decency and respect for rule of law that my father believed would prevent anything like the Holocaust from happening here. (That it didn't prevent slavery, segregation, and the near elimination of Native Americans did not change his view.)

My mother's American roots, my father readily admitted, were an asset to him in his work. I remember him telling me how she had helped him interpret one of the great crises of the Korean War. General Douglas MacArthur exceeded his orders and crossed the 38th parallel, provoking the Chinese invasion of South Korea and drastically expanding the war. Truman responded by firing MacArthur and ordering him back to the United States. "MacArthur arrived in San Francisco and there was a huge crowd which greeted him as a hero," my father said. Instead of flying to Washington, he came back by train, and everywhere he stopped, there were the same huge, adoring crowds. To someone who had grown up under Fascism, which came to power with Mussolini riding by train from Milan to Rome on what was the March on Rome, this all felt eerily familiar. "Elizabeth told me, 'Don't worry, Truman will win this hands down,' and she was right." Similarly, when Senator Joe McCarthy started his "witch hunts" in the early 1950s, many European correspondents saw it through the lens of European Fascism and were convinced that the United States was heading down the Fascist road. "McCarthy won't last," my mother said. "This will blow over." She proved right, and my father's reportage benefited from her feel for American life, which most European journalists didn't have access to.

My father was a European realist who understood power politics and tried to remove his emotions as much as possible from his analytical judgments. My mother was passionate, idealistic, and openly emotional in her approach to politics, something my father alternately ridiculed and admired. I remember him telling me affectionately how she had wept the night that Eisenhower defeated Adlai Stevenson. My father liked Stevenson, too, but he also admired and liked Eisenhower, who was often wrongly underestimated by their intellectual friends who were infatuated with the more intellectual Stevenson.

"You could tell that Eisenhower was really very shrewd, even though he did his best to hide that under his good-natured air," my father said.

On the other hand, the cultural differences between them also, I suspect, aggravated their difficulties, acting as a kind of explosive and toxic element. My parents, I think, each succeeded in making the other feel bad about where they came from. When my father would get really angry, he would often say something like "Why don't you go back to Three Oaks, [Michigan,] where you belong?"

My father acknowledged as much in talking to me. "I used to be very hard on her parents. I thought they were narrow and provincial and uninteresting. And that wasn't true. I was wrong. They were both very intelligent." But my father's behavior was not so much a reflection of his actual opinion of his parents-in-law as much as a means of hurting or getting at my mother. "He would insult my mother all the time," my mother recalled.

My father in reality was jealous of almost anyone who was close to my mother. Because, in fact, my mother was his emotional center, he attacked, tried to tear down the people she was closest to. Part of it was a simple jealousy born of extreme insecurity. But there was something else, too. My father was drawn to my mother because of her rootedness, her Americanness, but at some level he must have also resented needing that. It must have burned him that he needed to be accepted and to seek the approval of people when he started his life over in the United States. He was, after all, one of the finest products of centuries of European civilization; he had a great classical education, spoke and read several languages, ancient and modern, had read reams of history and philosophy. He knew and was admired by the finest minds in Italy. But then suddenly he had been cast off as a member of an undesirable race, reduced to the role of refugee. He had to prove himself worthy to my mother's family, with all their smug certainties, submit to being "investigated" and approved by a bunch of what he considered midwestern Babbitts. It would be hard to imagine anyone appearing more unlikely and out of place than my father at the Chikaming Country Club, where my grandfather played golf in Michigan and where we attended square dances, or at the beach complex of my aunt Lyndy's family, a beautiful spread along Lake Michigan belonging to my aunt's family, a little like a smaller version of the Kennedy compound at Hyannis, a family property with several houses on the bluffs of Lake Michigan, its own perfect self-contained world that had all the earmarks of American privilege and establishment. They were rich, blond and handsome and athletic; they had their own tennis court and there were enough good players in the family that they could have their own tennis tournament. The Russell family patriarch had been a bank president and a trustee of the University of Chicago, and his sons and sons-in-law were the kind of people who were at home in the boardrooms and country clubs of America. My father would not have fit in there at all, and some members of the family probably regarded him with a mix of bewilderment, suspicion, amusement, and unease. There was also a strain of anti-Semitism in this Michigan milieu. The Chikaming Country Club, of which my grandfather was for a time president, did not admit its first Jewish member until the 1980s. My father, in turn, must have resented being condescended to and perhaps looked down on people he considered intellectual lightweights.

"I never much let snobs bother me at all," my father once told me, wandering around our apartment in his boxer shorts. "The way to get them is to out-snob them. I always had an advantage as a European, and as a man who has, through sheer necessity and circumstance, been through a lot of the hard experiences of Europe in the thirties and forties. And I played this card to my advantage. I always felt myself basically to be superior to everyone, that I had greater intelligence, that essentially my values were right." Despite this attitude of apparent superiority, no doubt the need to "out-snob the snobs" masked a certain deep insecurity as well.

I suspect that my mother must have aggravated my father's insecurity, by, in some ways, making him feel that she didn't think much of his family or where he came from. She certainly must have communicated the instant repulsion she felt for my father's father, tinged with a vein of anti-Semitism.

My mother's sense of disapproval may have been even more explosive because my father, in part, shared it. My father had reacted with anger when his parents first told him that he was Jewish, followed by a feeling of guilt. He also described the sense of revulsion he felt in suddenly finding himself surrounded by Jews when he was forced to visit the offices of refugee organizations that were set up in Italy for Jews looking to leave after the racial laws. "I remember I spent a few days going to these Jewish organizations to find where you can get a visa, and I was so sickened by the people I met, I couldn't stand actually all these Jews there. And then my father took over that."

Being Jewish was not something that my father felt to be part of himself, but was an identity that had been imposed on him from one day to the next, an identity with all sorts of negative consequences. He was part of a generation of highly assimilated Italian Jews who did not identify as Jewish. I remember that when I telephoned Alberto Moravia and Giorgio Bassani to interview them for my first book (about Italian Jews), they both responded in a very prickly fashion, telling me, "I am not Jewish, I am an intellectual." This surprised and annoyed me. What did it mean? Did they think that being an intellectual excluded being Jewish? But I came from a culture where having a hyphenated or a multiple identity— Italian-American, Jewish intellectual—was the norm. But my father and his Italian Jewish intellectual friends had grown up with the belief that they were totally assimilated and accepted, that they could be whatever they wanted to be. They defined themselves by what they did; they worked as artists, philosophers, writers. And all of a sudden a treacherous bureaucracy took it all away from them, telling them, in effect, "You cannot be a doctor or an economist, a writer or an Italian; you are a Jew and only a Jew." This had, I suspect, scarred my father quite badly, causing him to try to hide his Jewishness even after the war. At the same time, he felt guilty and angry at himself for hiding his Jewishness and denying his own father. My parents saw very little of my father's family even though they all lived in New York. I suspect it suited both of them. My mother was not keen to have too much to do with her in-laws, especially her father-in-law, and my father, in his heart of hearts, seemed to feel the same way.

But hating a part of yourself breeds anger. And being made to feel shame about his family must have been salt in my father's wounds and made him want to lash out at my mother. Of course, it didn't help that my father had grown up disliking his own father and with a model of married life that hardly predisposed him for conjugal bliss.

Still, I suspect that some other element, some nameless anxiety, perhaps the extreme insecurity of my father's early life, came into play. I can recall watching my father in his periodic fits of rage and—despite my childish fear—observing him with a strange, almost clinical detachment, thinking, "There is something very wrong with this man." Part of me listened with a kind of amazement, almost a degree of admiration, thinking, "Wow, I had no idea a human being could scream that loud!" At the same time, as I watched him screaming until the veins in his neck seemed to bulge out so that I thought he might have a heart attack, I thought, even though I was only a child, "This is like the wail of a small, injured child." Clearly, the immediate pretext of his rage—a missing issue of *U.S. News & World Report* or a larger-than-expected phone bill—was negligible, and it seemed obvious that his scream came from some deep, unhappy place inside of him—somewhere far away and long ago. In the late 1960s, someone came up with the idea of primal scream therapy, whereby the therapist encouraged patients to relive some childhood trauma and to let it out in the form of a primal scream. I thought to myself, this must be what my father was doing, although it didn't seem to have much therapeutic effect.

Whatever the case, their relationship for some years oscillated between two extremes: huge blowups and threats of divorce followed by passionate reconciliations and extravagant vows of love on my father's part.

What did they both get out of this? A family therapist my mother once took us to see said, "Fighting is your parents' way of making love." I am not sure that's true. Or rather it depends what you take this to mean. I have little doubt that constant wrangling and fighting killed off much of the passion between them. If anything, fighting gradually replaced lovemaking as one of my parents' principal modes of communication—perhaps this is what the therapist meant.

5.

My father's bad behavior, of course, did not occur in a vacuum. It takes two to tango, as they say.

While my mother claimed to loathe fighting, she was not above provoking it from time to time. My father was almost always the aggressor in their battles, but my mother had some of the qualities of what in boxing is known as a counter-puncher—a fighter who lets his opponent take the lead and then tries to land punches right after he has fired his punch and left himself vulnerable. Sometimes when my father wasn't doing anything particularly reprehensible, my mother might provoke him: "See what your buddy Nixon has done now?"

For most of my childhood, I accepted my mother's version of things, that she was essentially a passive victim and that, in other circumstances, with a more reasonable husband, she could have had a much happier life.

Maybe, but maybe not. The fact remains that all of her important relationships were remarkably similar, and all of them reproduced elements of her unhappy relationship with her own father. All of the men she became seriously involved with fit a definite pattern: they were highly intelligent, ambitious, but difficult men who didn't treat her particularly well.

Clinton Rossiter was a university professor like her father and a difficult, domineering man who tried to convince her to take typing and shorthand so she could help him with his work and ridiculed her when she went to art school, making clear that he expected total subservience in a wife.

Bob Wolff was also a university professor and was fourteen years older than my mother. Like my grandfather (as well as Rossiter and my father), he was tight with money and kept my mother on a short leash. He wasn't cruel to her, but perhaps that's why she got bored and left him.

My grandfather had treated my mother with cruelty and even a certain amount of physical violence. She had been led to believe that this was what she could expect—and perhaps what she deserved—from men.

Both my parents intensely disliked their own fathers (however much they may have also loved them), both married outside their tribe in order to make a very different life for themselves, and yet both managed to recreate some of the worst elements of their childhood in their own married life. They were both in the grip of the force of things.

6.

Even though it had an inner logic, my parents' marriage was not in a stable state of equilibrium. A few years later things reached another point of crisis, the traces of which we have in another, and in some ways more extraordinary, letter that my grandmother wrote to my mother.

The letter, written on pink stationery, is marked in uppercase letters at the top: <u>PERSONAL, CONFIDENTIAL</u>, DESTROY AFTER READING. The normally chatty, conventional tone of my grandmother's letters is nowhere to be found. This letter is radically different: straight, direct, and to the heart. She deals with the most difficult and sensitive things in hers and my mother's lives: a crisis in my mother's marriage with my father and the considerable difficulties of her own marriage.

Darling Elizabeth,

[This letter] is mainly to tell you how much I enjoyed being with you in Washington and New York, and Mischa too, tho I didn't see so much of him as I would have liked. The whole thing was a wonderful whirl for two staid oldsters and I regret only the one jarring incident toward the end, which upset both you and me next day for aunty's visit. I must share the responsibility for it. I should have handled it more tactfully, in everybody's interests. My apologies.

Several things deserve comment on this subject: 1) So far as Pop and I are concerned, while these things occur once in a while, it is still true that, by and large, we are more amicably adjusted since his retirement from teaching. Nothing basic is changed, but settled in Michigan, we are both more relaxed, and pursue our varied interests continually, sometimes jointly, sometimes separately. I know Pop's and my relationship has a bearing on your problems too; that is why I want to reiterate that things are generally smoother for us.

2) As to your own relationship with Daddy, whatever it may have been in your early years he has, I think a genuine affection and admiration for you now. This does not prevent him from saying and doing things at times that are awkward, and that

hurts. Sometimes he does them where he considers a principle is at stake. I.e., he considers you extravagant, not mature in money matters. Superficially this is true. But what he lacks the imagination and insight to see, is that this is not a thing of itself, apart, but aside from an inner tension; and such awkward situations as he brought into being Fri. evening (with my help, to be sure) only compound the inner turmoil and increase the disregard for a practical recognition of financial limits.

At other times, these awkward incidents seem to arise from pure human selfishness and lack of consideration for other people. This probably has neurotic sources and this late in life will not change. I recall Doctor Woodruff's advice to me when we were first married: "Give him his lead most of the time but sometimes pull him up short." It is good expedient advice, I think. I try to practice it, not always successfully. The pulling up short at times is necessary; whatever the deeply seated phenomenon is, else one would be a doormat and no one better off. "A man's world is not a good thing even for a man." Rachel Yarros.

But, within the limits of Daddy's ability to love anyone, he is fond of you, and thinks you very competent in most ways.

3) He, like M., is skeptical of the wisdom of your putting so much money into psychological help. As with M., I think part of this attitude is based on fear of being disgraced. I recall reading that that is the greatest fear of a neurotic person. He asked me about that visit to Dr. Weyl, as to how much longer he thought it would be required. I told him after arriving home what Dr. Weyl had told me about the areas still to be "unburied," as the nearest answer I could give to his question. He was disturbed and launched into the theme of the uselessness of going to a psychiatrist. I reminded him of Bob Hutchins.

I have a hunch we are all more or less neurotic, but in this respect at least I am not: I don't want your loyalty to me to keep you from acting on things as you see them, wherever the chips may fall. "The truth shall make you free," holds good here as elsewhere. And the sooner you and Dr. Weyl get at the truth the better we all will be.

. . .

> After all the above, I think you're coming on finely under
> Dr. Weyl's guidance, and so are the children, and I love you
> more than life itself. Your happiness is of the greatest importance
> to me, and however fallible my slant, I want you to consider it,
> whether to accept or reject.

The letter, although undated, dates, I believe, from either late 1957 or 1958, the year of or after my birth.

Obviously, my mother's life was in crisis again and she had decided to see a psychiatrist. Both my father and my grandfather opposed my mother's decision to see a shrink, and my grandfather contemptuously dismissed it as her latest form of irresponsibility and extravagance, although he did ultimately agree to pay for it. In the course of the discussion, my grandparents appear to have had a nasty fight of their own, and my grandmother is writing to apologize because she realizes that their marital problems are an important factor in my mother's own psychological and marital problems.

It is in many ways a shockingly frank and courageous letter, containing a devastating portrait of my grandfather and his relationship to my mother: "Within the limits of Daddy's ability to love anyone, he is fond of you, and thinks you very competent is most ways." I was very struck by the quote "A man's world is not a good thing even for a man" and wondered who this person Rachel Yarros was. It turns out she was a psychologist as well as a socialist and radical feminist who worked at Chicago's Hull House, one of Chicago's leading progressive institutions. It was interesting to think of my grandmother—the woman in plain frumpy dresses and orthopedic shoes—being conversant with the ideas of a radical feminist thinker and being able to quote her from memory. And the quote itself—"A man's world is not a good thing even for a man"—is a powerful and simple thought that reflects the position of women who lived in a world where men effectively held all the power. My grandmother, for example, at one time wanted to visit her mother back east, and my grandfather, who didn't much like his mother-in-law, would not give her the train fare. So my grandmother had to save her nickels over a period of months and take the bus instead. This was living in a man's world. My grandmother's formula—in order to avoid becoming a doormat—was to "give him his lead most of the time but sometimes pull him up short." My grandmother had survived—and to some extent thrived—by butting heads with her husband from time to time, threatening to leave him when he hit my mother too often, taking charge of my mother's education, sending her to boarding school and then to the Bauhaus, assuming the presidency of the Illinois League of Women Voters even though her husband preferred a stay-at-home wife.

My mother had always regretted that Lucy and I had not had a chance to get to know our grandmother before she was afflicted by Alzheimer's. The long correspondence between them—and this letter in particular, which my grandmother said she wanted my mother to destroy—gave me a glimpse into my grandmother as my mother knew her: a very strong, thoughtful, and deeply honest as well as loving person. It also gave me an idea of the network of solidarity that existed among women in coping with the difficulties of marriage in the age before feminism. These women confided a great deal in one another and gave one another a lot of support in dealing with the travails of married life, in which women were in a position of considerable vulnerability and subordination.

7.

The crisis that provoked my mother's decision to seek psychiatric help was an extramarital affair.

At some point, around 1956 or 1957, my mother fell in love with a close friend of my father's, Saul Steinberg, the illustrator and artist. Like my father, Steinberg was an Eastern European Jewish refugee who had settled in Italy and had, like my father, been cast out after the racial laws. Like my father, he had been drafted by U.S. Army intelligence and posted in North Africa and Italy during the war. Like my father, he was brilliant, charming, a wonderful talker, and ambitious, and he was even more professionally acclaimed. His obvious talents were immediately recognized in the United States, and *The New Yorker*, for which he would go on to do ninety cover illustrations and some twelve hundred drawings, sponsored his entrance into the United States. Already, in 1946, his work was featured in a show at the Museum of Modern Art.

Saul, however, was married to someone else, and his wife, the painter Hedda Sterne, became a close friend of my mother's. Saul and Hedda, in fact, had an intense, almost symbiotic bond that survived numerous affairs and lasted, despite separation, until the end of Saul's life. It seems that initially the relationship with my mother was romantic but not sexual and deeply tied up with Hedda and the fact that my mother had children. Hedda, an extremely talented artist in her own right, made two different portraits of my mother, which she gave to her. "Saul loved and respected his wife, whom he regarded as an equal but then would tumble into bed with someone else. I was going through a very rocky period with Misha, so he chose a vulnerable moment. He and Hedda couldn't have children, and I think sex had pretty much ended between them, and I think I was her choice. We became a little ménage à trois. And they both adored everything I did. And they were obsessed by you children."

Saul made a book of drawings with a series of poems in it for my sister, Lucy, and at one point Saul took Lucy up in a helicopter in order to look at Manhattan from the air. "Mom told me that she used me as a kind of 'beard' on her visits to Saul," Lucy said.

In the midst of this crazy situation, I was born in January 1957. "When you were born, they had a fit about this baby boy. They sent flowers. I am sure I have a picture of me nursing him casually and they were sitting there in awe. I sat there casually nursing and smoking, nursing and smoking, and they were—I mean, it was as if—that baby belonged to them, there was no doubt about it. Saul kept making drawings for you. He made a book for me, which he addressed to Lucy."

Given that the affair coincided with my own birth, I asked my mother, as she was on her deathbed telling me the story in detail, whether there was any possibility that my own father might not be my biological father. "No, it's a physical impossibility," she said. At a certain point, she explained, they tried sleeping together but it didn't work out. "I tried to go to bed with him [. . .] He was on top of me, he was doing all the right things. I was just lying there, and something put him off and he began shrinking. All of a sudden we were talking instead of making love. Well, he didn't have it for me. He had plenty of affairs with other women, but I think he couldn't with women he loved. Saul was one of these men who made a huge distinction between the women he loved and admired and the women he slept with. There was a whole syndrome in Europe when he grew up where it was okay, even expected, that a young man of a certain age would be taken to a whorehouse by his father, while in his home he behaved like a perfect gentleman. Saul, I think, had something of this tendency."

This did not prevent Saul from proposing to my mother that he; my mother; his wife, Hedda; my sister; and I all live together in a kind of *ménage à cinq*, a notion my mother found unappealing. "He was in love with me in some cuckoo mixed-up way where he couldn't do much about it."

But there are a few other versions of this story. Toward the end of her life, Hedda Sterne talked to our mutual friend Claire Nivola about what, for her, was a pivotal and still extremely painful moment in her life. She had indeed suffered through Saul's chronic infidelities. "He was like a butterfly collecting nectar here and there," she said. She became extremely close to my mother and had no idea (at least consciously) that there might be something romantic between Saul and Elizabeth. Things began as an intense friendship between the two couples. "They were both so entranced by the Stilles that it was almost as if they were competing over who could become closest to them," writes the author Deirdre Bair in her recent biography of Saul Steinberg. What began as a square then turned into what Hedda Sterne referred to as the "Elizabethan triangle," with both Hedda and Saul intensely focused on my mother. Oddly, one of the things that made Hedda suspicious was Saul's sudden intense interest in Lucy and me—he had previously found children a nuisance. Instead he appeared delighted by a story of how I flushed a twenty-dollar bill down the toilet when my mother was too weak with the flu to stop me. Saul prepared an alphabet book in which the letter *E* was a drawing of my mother as a swan. To her astonishment, he then proposed to Hedda that the two families live together on Long Island in the *ménage à cinq* configuration he had suggested to my mother. Saul spent a lengthy period in Europe trying to clear his head and figure out what to do. On his return, Hedda hoped that things had blown over. "The behavior of Saul and Elizabeth became too obvious for others to ignore," Bair writes. Ruth Nivola, the Steinberg-Sternes' neighbor on Long Island, decided to confront Saul and Hedda in order, she insisted, to save both marriages. Saul turned white and left for the city to see my father, since Ruth had apparently threatened to tell him if Saul didn't do it himself, according to Claire Nivola.

Their marriage had endured many such crises, but something about the intensity of this relationship with my mother—perhaps also the closeness between Hedda and my mother—seems to have had a shattering effect on the Steinbergs' marriage. Saul moved out in a major crisis over the end of both his marriage and his affair with my mother. Hedda never forgave Ruth Nivola for her meddling, and Saul asked my mother for the book he had made for Lucy back and crossed out the text that he had written to accompany the pictures.

For years, I believed that my mother—as she herself seemed to believe—could have easily led a better and happier life with a different husband. But in the one instance she actually reached out for someone else, she found someone who was almost a carbon copy of my father: Jewish, Eastern European, Italian-speaking, brilliant, a wonderful conversationalist and storyteller but equally neurotic and impossible. In trying to climb out of the mess with my father, she had placed herself in an even bigger mess with someone even less likely to make her happy. Even when she tried to change her life she had reproduced a new but similar form of misery. Perhaps the problem wasn't entirely my father but lay partly within herself.

My parents stayed married and my mother decided, finally, after talking about it for years, and following the debacle with Saul Steinberg, to see a psychiatrist.

8.

The discovery of the affair didn't end my parents' marriage, perhaps because my father had apparently had affairs of his own. While my mother mentioned her affair with Steinberg several times over the course of her life, she almost never mentioned anything about my father's infidelities. This was quite strange, as she rarely passed up an opportunity to point out my father's faults. The one time I can recall my mother mentioning the topic was to make light of it. "I never worried about Misha because he was much too disorganized to conduct an affair," she said, gesturing toward the chaotic piles of newspapers and magazines in my father's room. "One time he had something with a woman who worked in the old New York Times Building, where he had his office. But he ended up coming to me for help: the woman then claimed she had gotten pregnant and needed five hundred dollars for an abortion. He didn't know what to do and needed my advice. I think she was just conning him for the money!" my mother said with a laugh. The thrust of the story was that my father was a decidedly unthreatening adulterer, a dupe who needed his wife's help to get him out of a scrape. My aunt Ginny, my mother's sister, told me a somewhat different account of things: that my mother had told her that she was upset about my father's wanderings. Perhaps she didn't talk about them because they actually did bother her. Whatever the case, extramarital affairs were not the central problem in their marriage, and neither seems to have seriously considered leaving the other for someone specific.

9.

Of course, the truth (whatever that is in matters like these) did not set my mother free. My parents remained on the brink of divorce for years afterward, but my mother insisted that psychotherapy did help her to some degree. The one specific thing she said about it was that the psychiatrist had told her that she had three options: stay and be a doormat, leave, or fight back. "I fought back," my mother said. I didn't find this a particularly convincing answer at the time, since it seemed to me she was generally getting pummeled by my father. But perhaps I was underestimating her taste for the ring. Perhaps she honed her skills as a counterpuncher as a result of her therapy and she was landing more blows than I could see. At the very least, physical violence had been replaced by verbal violence—progress of a sort, a milestone in the march of civilization, as when human sacrifice was replaced by ritualized animal slaughter or when regulated dueling replaced indiscriminate killing.

The Beginning of Something

My darling Lucy,

Thank you very much for your letter. I am glad to hear that you are having a good time. Here the weather has been better than expected and I have been able to work without being bothered by the heat. Your monkey Pincer is fine; he spends most of his time eating peanuts and bananas, and writing short Japanese poems called "haiku." He hopes to have them published eventually in "Partisan Review," with the help of an influential editor he knows. Sometimes he sings also a little song about going to Freedomland, that he must have learned from you.

Our street is rather quiet these days, Andrew is still here and now the Haydon children are back. But without you and Sandro running up and down, our "block" does not seem to show much life. Give my love to Mummy and Sandro. I hope to see you all soon, and I am sure you will bring back some new jokes, of your inimitable variety.

Love and kisses

Daddy

This is the only letter that I have to either my sister or myself. My father was a lazy writer (and a lazy father), but he could be, as this letter shows, a sweet, affectionate, and playful one as well.

Although my father had an office in Times Square, he preferred to work at home and as a result was, for better or worse, present. Although he did not tend to any of the practical aspects of our upbringing—I doubt he ever changed a diaper, walked us to school, or attended a parent-teacher conference—he liked small children. Both Lucy and I recall playing a game with my father where he was a monster named Zeppo (some kind of Italian version of Godzilla or King Kong) and would chase us around the piles of papers in his office, a role he played so convincingly that we would then beg him to stop.

Things were not always bad at our house. We lived in a duplex apartment in the upper half of a beautiful brownstone on West Eleventh Street in Greenwich Village, one of the prettiest blocks in New York City. Before that area became prohibitively expensive—now only investment bankers, corporate lawyers, and cardiologists can afford to live there—it still had much of its bohemian charm, with a curious mix of artists, writers, and immigrants, along with more prosperous people who owned the brownstones that people like my parents rented. We lived in a spacious four-bedroom apartment overlooking green leafy gardens in back. My friends down the street lived in smaller, dingier apartments and lived lives that seemed much more chaotic: I was surprised and troubled to see unmade beds with stale, unchanged sheets in the middle of the day—something my mother would never have tolerated. My friend Andrew's mother screamed at him a lot in a loud, raspy voice and sometimes her boyfriend fell asleep, drunk, on the couch. (He was a cop and you could see his gun and holster underneath his jacket when he slumped over.) My parents did not have a lot of money back then, but my mother managed to make things look extremely attractive with rather makeshift furniture and paintings and drawings made by artist friends of hers. I remember pleasant Sunday mornings in spring with the windows open, overhearing someone playing opera or soulfully working their way through a Beethoven piano sonata, which mingled happily with the smell of my mother's Sunday dinner, spaghetti with tuna or pot roast. My father, when in a good mood, would sing one of his army songs or an old Italian song popular after World War I, when many soldiers came back with various missing body parts.

Aveva un occhio di vetro e una gamba di gesso
Ma mi piaceva lo stesso
Mi piaceva lo stesso

He had a glass eye and a wooden leg
But I liked him just the same
I liked him just the same

We lived upstairs from the owners of the building, Abe and Sylvia Ellstein, who were both in the entertainment business. Abe was a composer for the Yiddish theater, first in Europe and then on the Lower East Side, and was known for a time as the Irving Berlin of Second Avenue. He had written the music for the comic opera *The Bridegroom from Berditchev*, as well as another famous hit, "*Oy Mame, Bin Ikh Farlibt*" ("Oh, Mama, I Am in Love"). His wife, Sylvia, who was born in the United States, was a playwright, and the two of them wrote a couple of musicals together that were produced on Broadway as well as an opera about the Golem, which was shown at the New York City Opera when we were living on Eleventh Street. They were a funny mix of old-world Yiddish culture and glamorous showbiz people; they gave large parties on their parlor floor, which was dominated by a large grand piano and a wall of smoked mirrors. One of my father's favorite stories from my childhood was the day that I managed to get Abe Ellstein locked out of his house. I came home with my friend Andrew, and when I found no one at home, I rang the Ellsteins' bell, hoping that they would let me into our apartment. Abe, evidently a late riser, came out onto the landing that led up into our house and into the upper floor of his apartment in his boxer shorts. But he forgot the keys, and the door to his apartment closed suddenly behind him, meaning that he was stuck out in the foyer in his underwear with me and Andrew, getting more and more agitated as we all waited for my father to return home with another set of keys. "Calm down, Mr. Ellstein! Calm down!" my father recalled hearing me say as he opened the door to our house. "Calm down, Mr. Ellstein!" he enjoyed repeating.

2.

Besides my parents, there was a large supporting cast of friends, relatives, colleagues, and acquaintances. Although my father generally disapproved of my mother's family, they continued to be an important part of our lives.

My grandmother and her sister, Louise Metzger, whom we called Aunty, were both present, as it happened, at the time of my birth. Grammie had come east because her mother, Grandma Metzger, was dying and because she wanted to help my mother with the new baby. Grandma Metzger died just a few days before I was born. My father threw an absolute fit when Grammie and Aunty returned from the hospital carrying a suitcase of their mother's clothes. It was incredibly bad luck—practically like making an invitation to the evil eye—according to Russian custom to bring a dead person's belongings into a house where a child was about to be born. My father shouted and screamed, and continued shouting and screaming until he literally drove Aunty and Grammie, confused and grief-stricken, out of the house and back to White Plains with the offending suitcase in hand.

Aunty's semi-regular presence was a sign of a certain tolerance and generosity, despite my father's constant complaining, that characterized our household. There was no more annoying relative than Aunty, a rather sour, teetotaling woman who had carved out for herself the unfortunate role of family scold: she was always sending out newspaper clippings about the dangers of whatever it was we were interested in doing—stories of children electrocuting themselves playing dangerous games or poking their eyes out with toy swords. We dreaded her visits, during which she was principally preoccupied with telling us children what to do (always wear galoshes) but above all what *not* to do. She told us not to run, not to jump, not to make noise, not to go outside, not to watch television, not to take off our sweaters, not to leave our toys lying around, not to eat sweets, not to eat chocolate—all this on Christmas, a day we children looked forward to all year as the moment of maximum indulgence in which we could finally do all things we were not normally allowed to do. And instead we had this spooky-looking old lady—stick-thin, with witchy white hair and jagged teeth—scolding us every five minutes. Her favorite publication was *Prevention* magazine, which she cited like the Bible in dispensing advice on what things to eat or do or not to eat and not to do in order to avoid this or that ailment. *Prevention* seemed to sum up her life strategy, which seemed concentrated on preventing things from happening.

Already, back in 1943, when my aunt Ginny fell in love with and decided to marry her husband, Aunty, in typical fashion, wanted to prevent that, too, as my mother noted humorously in a letter to her mother:

Aunty called me a couple of days ago and I told her about the great event. Her first remark was "Don't you think they should wait until after the war?" Poor Aunty, I'm afraid it is the caution for caution's sake that has made her life so empty.

When my grandmother wrote her that she was looking forward to expanding the size of her farm in Michigan, Aunty wrote to discourage the idea: "Think of the CONS as well as the PROS of any such undertaking." Rather than looking on the bright side of life, Aunty always found the cloud in every silver lining, the reason not to do things. When my mother got an exciting job opportunity that involved flying out to meet an author who lived in another part of the country, Aunty was quick to point out the alarming increase in plane crashes.

Just days after being banished by my father with their dead mother's clothes, Aunty and Grammie were back in time for my birth. They were sleeping in my mother's room when, in the middle of the night, she started getting contractions and my mother tiptoed back into her room to gather clothes to take to the hospital. Aunty turned to her and said, as she might have to a client at Gimbels, where she worked, "Well, my dear, I hope everything will be satisfactory." To which my mother replied, "Don't worry. If not, I'll ask for my money back."

My mother—who told this story a number of times—found Aunty as annoying and unintentionally humorous as the rest of us. But family and family occasions were very important to my mother, and she invariably invited Aunty to stay at our house every Christmas and included her in other family gatherings, even inviting her a couple of times to visit us on Cape Cod during the summer.

I remember those early Christmases only vaguely. It is hard to imagine a more unlikely collection of people than Aunt Louise and my father's family, the Kamenetzkis, who were also fixtures at those Christmases—my aunt with her various health obsessions (sugar was roughly equivalent to the Antichrist in Carlton Fredericks's philosophy) and my overweight and indulgent Kamenetzki grandparents, who invariably showed up weighed down by boxes of chocolates and Italian Christmas cakes. The conversation between Aunty and my immigrant grandparents must have contained exhilarating moments of high comedy and mutual incomprehension. (And one can imagine, since the Kamenetzkis were, in the last, increasingly infirm, years of their lives, that there must have been long discussions of symptoms and ailments, with helpful health advice from Aunty.) And yet the Kamentezkis and their imperfect English somehow managed to coexist year after year with my mother's aunt from White Plains.

A quite detailed account of one of these holidays at our house survives in a letter Aunty wrote to her sister at Christmas in 1962. In some ways, it is a classic Aunty production, starting with her usual minute attention to detail—"I left White Plains on Monday 12/24 at about 2:45 and arrived at Betty's at about 5 P.M." And nearly half the letter—a dense page and a half of single-spaced type—consists of a long list of the presents that everyone gave everyone else.

Aunty worked, appropriately enough, in the complaint department at Gimbels, where she investigated alleged misconduct by the department-store staff. She was, in effect, a company snoop. Her Christmas letter has the same "just the facts, ma'am" prose style she perfected working for the Department of Adjustment. And yet, despite the stiff, brittle bureaucratic prose, a number of things come through in the letter, a certain appreciation of the abundance, warmth, and more-the-merrier spirit that my mother managed to give the occasion.

> Christmas was lovely at the Stilles . . . Betty prepared dinner
> herself—a very lovely dinner of roast beef, etc. for ELEVEN!
> Her table looked beautiful. The dessert was a delicious chestnut
> and whipped cream combination and coffee with raisins, assorted
> nuts, prunes, candied cherries and grapes. She had this little
> Italian maid, Igli, who was here in past summers at Cape Cod, to
> help her serve. Igli is half-maid, half friend of family, and joined
> in when Betty served cocktails, and after dinner joined at table
> for dessert & liquor.

Aunty is clearly both intrigued and mildly horrified that a maid/babysitter we had at the time, whom she identifies as Igli (I believe she was named Egle), was treated almost as another guest.

Author of innumerable reports for Gimbels's adjustment department, Aunty was, if nothing else, a careful observer and a dogged chronicler of things. Her account of Christmas at our house in 1962 contains quite a bit of information.

Many of the characters of our childhood pass through the letter. Our landlords, the Ellsteins, came for a drink, bringing for the children "a huge plastic cane filled with smaller candy canes—about 2 ft long and 2 inches in diameter" as well as "a chocolate Santa and a chocolate turkey both about 6 inches high." There was a visit to St. Luke's, the school Lucy and I attended as children. Although it was chosen for its proximity, it was (and is) an Episcopalian school. And Aunty, used to more spare Protestant services, remarks on the High Church, almost Catholic flavor of the midnight mass they attended in order to hear Lucy sing in the choir.

She notes, quite significantly but without editorial comment, that my father did not attend Lucy's choir performance and explains the sleeping arrangements in the house with exact detail:

> Michael went to a party somewhere. Igli stayed at home with Sandro and stayed overnight. She did not want to go home after midnight, so she slept in Lucy's room, Lucy and Sandro in Betty's room, I in Sandro's room, and Betty on the living room couch.

Even her tedious lists of all the foods served and the presents exchanged contains a certain mixture of disapproval and appreciation for the festive abundance of things:

> In the two days of Christmas, the children were surfeited with gifts. Memory completely fails me, sorry to say, but to give you some idea of it all, I'll try to recall as best I can . . .

And then, after a page and a half of listing gifts, she concludes:

> I'm sorry I do not recall any of the others—and there were many others—but in the confusion, it was like a 3 ring circus and I failed to register what was given and by whom. Sorry!

She notes that she gave both Lucy and me records by Harry Belafonte, which we actually loved as children. I remember those records and remember being mildly surprised that our killjoy, scolding great-aunt would give us these exuberant collections of calypso songs.

In her list of the presents, Aunty writes that my mother gave her her first camera, a "Brownie Fiesta"—the latest in consumer snapshot cameras. It came with a roll of film and several little flashbulbs for indoor pictures. Among the relatively few photographs that survive from my childhood—my parents were not sentimental family photo types—is one of me in an aluminum knight's outfit, including the visor with the long red ostrich feather. I am in the absurd "on guard" position, holding a sword. Evidently, it was Aunty who took the picture.

She was, in some ways, one of the only members of our family interested in documenting our life.

After she died, my mother and Aunt Ginny, who went to clean out her apartment in Florida, where she lived during her last years, made a rather startling discovery: Aunty had created one of the largest—perhaps the only—collections of randomly found and personally documented coins. Every time my great-aunt would spot a penny on the sidewalk or a nickel left on a shop floor, she would pick it up and note carefully the time and place of her discovery. All the coins were carefully wrapped in pieces of paper—generally the cheap brown paper torn from supermarket grocery bags—with the place and date where the coin had been found. "Corner of Laurel Street and Orange Grove Drive, June 6, 1974." "In front of Woolworth's, Bank Street, Winter Park, April 3, 1971," and so forth. There were hundreds and hundreds of these carefully documented coins. There was nothing remarkable or valuable in the coins themselves: she was not looking for buffalo head nickels or the old pennies with sheaths of wheat on the back or the special "steel pennies" they made in 1943 during the war when precious metals were scarce. No, these were just random pennies, nickels, dimes, and quarters. After my mother and aunt undid all the little paper wrappings, the huge pile of coins added up to something like $53.15. My aunt, who was extremely frugal, no doubt took very much to heart the old Benjamin Franklin adage "a penny saved is a penny earned" (written at a time when a penny was actually worth something). In late-twentieth-century currency, if you calculated the hours of labor, the many hours and days that my great-aunt dedicated to collecting and classifying and wrapping her pennies, her project was pure folly. Over the years, she must have spent dozens and dozens of hours, the equivalent, perhaps, of a few weeks of time, for her $53.15, which of course she never actually spent. It was passion and not profit that drove her—but a particularly pointless passion.

3.

My father never did any of the conventional things that American fathers did—play catch, teach me to ride a bicycle (how could he have, when he himself didn't know how to ride a bicycle?), take me to school, or attend my school athletic events. He had his own peculiar, bookish parenting style. Perhaps because they were few and far between, I have vivid memories of the things we did together. I remember him taking the French editions of Voltaire down from the shelf and relating to me some version of his novels, *Candide* and *Zadig*, although I am not sure I understood what he told me. I remember him telling me a story about the fourteenth-century painter Giotto, who, when asked by the pope's emissaries to provide an example of his work for an important commission, painted a circle with a single brushstroke. The circle was so perfect and beautiful that they granted him the commission. The notion that a circle might be the ultimate expression of beauty and perfection appealed to me, although it seemed like a dubious old wives' tale. I was happy, many years later, to find the story in Vasari's *Lives of the Artists*; since Vasari was writing two hundred years after the death of Giotto, it still may have been legend rather than fact, but I was pleased that my father had correctly passed on the story from Vasari to me.

When my mother was in the hospital after my birth, Lucy needed urgently to have her tonsils removed and the operation couldn't wait until my mother returned home. My father insisted he was too busy with work to take her, and so a friend and neighbor of ours took her instead. But years later, when Lucy moved from a neighborhood school in Greenwich Village to a fancy private school on the Upper East Side where they studied Latin, my father tutored my sister in Latin—something she always remembered fondly, a moment of closeness between them in an otherwise stormy, complicated relationship.

Neither Lucy nor I remember our parents reading much to us. They were very busy with their own lives. But we as children absorbed a love of literature and an almost boundless appreciation of writing, books, and erudition. There was a book in my father's library by Isaac Babel whose title, *You Must Know Everything*, seemed to sum up his worldview and served as a kind of imperative for the impossible, possible pursuit of knowledge.

While our parents didn't do many of the conventional things parents often do with children, they didn't exclude us from their lives, either. I remember sitting and listening to many dinner conversations that I only partly understood but that fascinated me. I recall hearing the critic and writer Alfred Kazin speaking passionately about the Spanish Civil War, one of the great causes of his youth, still shaking with anger as he described the complicity of the Stalinists in the killing of thousands of Spanish anarchists, aiding, thus, the final triumph of Franco and the Fascists. What was this evil Comintern about which Kazin spoke with such scorn? We saw and understood most of this through childish eyes. When my father was stung by a bee and his face became swollen, Lucy and I proclaimed, "Daddy looks just like Alfred Kazin!" (But something sunk in. Lucy ended up doing a college thesis on Clara Zetkin, a pivotal figure in the development of German socialism.)

My parents had a rich and interesting social life. It was a time, before television and video took over our culture, when writing was everything, and the people of my parents' generation generally believed that ideas, books, art, and architecture could change the world. People at smoky parties argued late into the night about art and social change, about the Vietnam War and the Black Power movement, or rehashed debates about Fascism, anarchism, Trotsky, Stalin, and the Moscow Show Trials, about the relationship between Marxism and Stalinism, about poverty, race, capitalism, freedom, and democracy. Now the lives of New York intellectuals are much tamer; they became much more sober, cautious, and upstanding members of the middle class, attending health clubs, minding their 401(k) accounts, watching their diet and alcohol intake, reading parenting manuals, spending most of their evenings at home with their families. My parents' friends lived much more wild and disorderly lives. In the 1950s and 1960s, New York writers and artists spent most of their evenings at parties, talking and drinking to excess, arguing loudly and experimenting with the 1960s counterculture, where a group at one party might drift to another and end up at Andy Warhol's Factory, or listening to the Velvet Underground at Max's Kansas City. My father was too much of an old-world intellectual for most of that, though he cautiously took a few puffs of marijuana to see what all the fuss was about. Still, he took in the scene out of curiosity and with the justification that it was important for him to understand the country he was covering.

In this floating circus of their social life you might find intellectual heavyweights like Hannah Arendt, Dwight McDonald, Mary McCarthy, Arthur Schlesinger, Jr., Irving Howe, Alfred Kazin, Norman Mailer, and Philip Roth, with a sprinkling of people from other fields—the fashion model Twiggy, Warhol protégée Edie Sedgwick, the actors Shirley MacLaine and Warren Beatty, Paul Newman, or some new emerging star of the antiwar movement like the Yippies Abbie Hoffman or Jerry Rubin, who had closed down the New York Stock Market by throwing dollar bills from the gallery onto the trading floor and had been arrested for trying to "levitate" the Pentagon. I remember taking coats at one of my parents' parties and hearing my sister say "That's the guy who stabbed his wife" as Norman Mailer appeared, some time after the incident in which he in fact stabbed his wife, Adele, during the hipster phase of his career, in which he was trying to be a White Negro. (Lucy recalls that Mailer was carrying a copy of Philip Roth's early novel *When She Was Good* and asked her if she had read it.)

I recall seeing my father at one of these innumerable parties, at which a crowd of people would form around him to listen to him talk like a flock of birds collecting around someone with his pockets full of crumbs. His conversation would move lightly and humorously from contemporary politics, to quotes from the letters of Madame de Sévigné or the memoirs of the Duc de Saint-Simon, to funny anecdotes from everyday life.

One little story I recall from one of these occasions: "And so Talleyrand found himself seated between Madame de Staël, who was of course one of the great intellects of the time, and Madame Récamier, one of the great beauties of the age. And Talleyrand said, 'What pleasure to be surrounded by such beauty and intelligence,' but as he said 'beauty' he nodded toward Madame de Staël, knowing that the plain-looking woman would like nothing more than to be praised for her looks, and as he said 'intelligence,' he looked toward Madame Récamier, whom everyone flattered for her beauty, while she craved to be admired for her intelligence."

My mother liked parties but participated much less in this life than my father. "Misha would go to any party, even if it was the introduction of a new lipstick by Elizabeth Arden," she would say. "Most of that stuff bored me stiff."

"You fool, you understand nothing! That's useful for my work!" my father would respond when she made the same point in his earshot.

Life in Greenwich Village during our childhood provided a kind of front-row seat to the 1960s. The changes in the world seemed to unfold in front of our naive, unknowing eyes. I recall when I was very small seeing a man with a shaved head, wearing sandals and an earring, playing bongo drums on the steps of one of the brownstones on our block and someone whispering, "Those are *beatniks*." Gradually, over the course of several years, the beatniks were replaced by earnest young people playing guitars aspiring to be the next Bob Dylan or Joan Baez. One of my sister's babysitters was John Sebastian, a Greenwich Village boy who went on to be a singer-songwriter and the head of a group called the Lovin' Spoonful, which had a number of hit songs. My mother came home one day with the Beatles' first American album, *Meet the Beatles!*, just out of curiosity. And my sister attended one of the Beatles' first concerts in the United States, at Carnegie Hall, just as Beatlemania was beginning to sweep the country at gale force. Girls were screaming so loudly and incessantly that she could barely hear the music. During one brief pause in the shrieking, a young girl called out "Ringo!" followed by an enormous collective sigh. After his enormous success in the movie *The Graduate*, the actor Dustin Hoffman moved into a brownstone on our block. One day, perhaps to show that he was just a regular guy, he offered to play catch with me and my neighborhood friends. I had seen and loved *The Graduate* but pretended not to know who he was in order to respect his privacy or to not seem uncool.

The folk singers were then followed by young people with longer hair, tie-dyed shirts, love beads, and peace buttons. In 1968, when I was eleven, I volunteered to work for the peace candidate, Eugene McCarthy, and sold McCarthy buttons and bumper stickers on the street corner. Just down the street, in a handsome building that is now a public library, there was a women's prison, which we sometimes passed on our walk to school. You could hear pimps down on the sidewalk yelling up to their girls inside: "Just wait a little more, baby, we gonna get you out!" At one point, the Black Panther leader Angela Davis was being held there. My mother proposed making her some food and taking it to the prison. Even to my childish mind, this seemed the height of absurdity. "Ma, Angela Davis would eat you for breakfast, and you want to take her lunch!"

I remember a boy named Eddie, four or five years older, who would come hang out on our block. He would carry around a chess set and beat everyone he played. Everyone said he was a brilliant student. Then I didn't see him any longer, and someone said he had overdosed on heroin. One day I came home from school and our entire block had been cordoned off by police. Members of a protest group called the Weather Underground had been trying to make bombs in the basement of one of the members' parents' elegant brownstones and accidentally blew it up. Rich kids playing at revolution. Three members of the group were killed and two others, both young women, escaped. Our next-door neighbor, thinking at first it was an accidental gas explosion, took in one of the women, offered her a bath and a fresh set of clothes; soon she had sneaked out of the house and disappeared. The brownstone that blew up was right next door to Dustin Hoffman's building, and suddenly there was an enormous hole in his living room wall, which now looked out at the street, and an empty lot where the blown-up building had been. We never saw Dustin again.

Amid these dangerous excesses, I was secretly happy to live in the protected confines of a rather orderly middle-class household where, despite the tumult between our parents, my sister and I were well fed, well cared for, well loved, and given a good education. I was happy, in many ways, to watch the sixties safely from the sidelines, too young to participate. Rather than attend the epic Woodstock music festival, I went to the movie about it with my best friend at the time—my mother in attendance. The movie was PG, and we had to be accompanied. To satisfy our need for independence we sat apart from my mother in the theater, but, as the movie required "parental guidance," we needed her to get in.

My mother worked during these years at *The Reporter*—a biweekly news magazine (edited by my father's old friend Max Ascoli) that in its day was extremely interesting and had its measure of importance—and for a period of time was perhaps the most influential newsmagazine after *Time* and *Newsweek*.

The famous gonzo journalist Hunter S. Thompson (future author of *Fear and Loathing in Las Vegas*) wrote some of his first pieces for *The Reporter*, as did the young Henry Kissinger. Meg Greenfield, who became the editor of the *Washington Post* editorial page, was one of its chief political writers. My mother was only a copyeditor but did extensive revisions to work by highly knowledgeable authors who wrote poorly. She was known by her colleagues as "the queen of the cutters." Every year, my parents hosted the *Reporter* Christmas party, and we have lots of pictures of these festive events featuring dozens of people inevitably holding a drink in one hand and a cigarette in the other. At one of these parties, apparently, someone approached my sister and told her, "You're so lucky that you have two such sexy parents!" A rather strange thing to say to a child of twelve or thirteen, but it was the sixties. The magazine came apart at the seams in 1968 over the question of the Vietnam War and support for President Lyndon Johnson. The editor, Max Ascoli, as fierce an anti-Communist as he had been an anti-Fascist, supported Johnson and the war in Vietnam even after most moderate anti-Communist Democrats, such as Arthur Schlesinger, Jr., had abandoned the cause. Ascoli was out of step with virtually the entire staff of the magazine and, perhaps more important, with its readership and advertisers. After a poor showing in the New Hampshire primaries, Johnson dropped out of the presidential race. Bobby Kennedy (the likely Democratic candidate for president) was assassinated, just a year after Martin Luther King, and there were riots at the Democratic Party convention when the party imposed Vice President Hubert Humphrey as the presidential candidate. The Democrats were violently split over Vietnam, and Ascoli closed down *The Reporter.*

The equilibrium between my father's realism and my mother's idealism broke down in this period over the question of Richard Nixon. For my mother, Nixon was an immoral, unscrupulous skunk who had made his career by helping to lead the Communist witch hunt and by destroying the career of Alger Hiss. He had lied about wanting to end the Vietnam War and conducted (with the help of my father's friend Henry Kissinger) the secret bombing of Cambodia; he hated Jews and blacks. Over a period of years, the stack of Nixon books on my mother's bedside table (*Nixon Agonistes*, *Nightmare: The Underside of the Nixon Years*, *What Nixon Is Doing to Us*) grew higher and higher, as if she was building a fortress to protect her from evil.

My father insisted that one should not let moral judgments cloud one's political judgments. Diplomacy without deception was simply impossible. Nixon was smart and, being more knowledgeable than most American presidents, had a complex understanding of foreign policy. The details of Vietnam and Cambodia were messy, but one should not lose sight of the big picture: détente with Russia and normalization with China. The United States could not afford to show weakness in Vietnam when it had to show strength in dealing with the Soviets and the Communist Chinese. They both had valid points. Nixon, as my father argued, was a much more complex figure than the liberal caricature of him ("Tricky Dick") would grant: some of his policies were intelligent and farsighted. But my father's ridiculing of my mother's emotional, moralistic take on Nixon meant that he failed to capture some of the qualities of deceit and paranoia that would eventually bring Nixon down in the Watergate scandal, which my mother had predicted for years.

4.

Although my mother's marriage with my father was never good or easy, she enjoyed a much greater degree of independence than did most of her close female friends. My mother worked and most of her friends did not. My parents' marriage, like those of almost all my mother's female friends, was originally founded on the Great Man model, in which the women sublimated their energies to the comfort and greater glory of their brilliant and ambitious husbands. But the level of conflict between my parents meant that this model broke down. My mother worked so as not to have to ask my father for money and to be able to do as she pleased without answering to him. Many of my mother's friends were extremely timid and deferential with their husbands. I recall my mother telling me in disapproving tones about one of her friends who was afraid to buy her own clothes without her husband present to approve both her taste and the expense. They were lovely and charming women, but some of them were also a bit stunted and childlike. My mother had far less serenity but considerably more power and autonomy than many of her friends.

My mother, in fact, was away from my father every summer for at least two months. One month we spent on Cape Cod and the other with my grandparents at their farm in Michigan, where my father almost never set foot. On the Cape we generally rented a house on one of the beautiful freshwater ponds in the Wellfleet-Truro woods. Here my mother reconnected with some of her oldest and closest friends, many of them from her Bauhaus days in Chicago or her life in New York before she met my father: Juliet and György Kepes, Katharine Kuh, Marcel Breuer and his wife, Connie. We frequently rented one of two houses owned by Serge Chermayeff, who had taken over the School of Design after Moholy-Nagy's death. We even saw a certain amount of Bob Wolff, my mother's first husband, who had remarried and had another family, with Connie Breuer's sister. Bob and my parents were on good terms, and I, who knew very well who he was, thought it quite civilized that people who had once been married could maintain friendly relations.

I remember those summers as the closest thing to paradise I had experienced. There were three or four generations of people, from elderly great-grandparents to troops of small children with whom Lucy and I could play. My father would usually come up for an occasional weekend, at most for a week, arriving by plane at Provincetown. He was usually foul-tempered for a day or two and then gave in to Cape Cod's relaxing, narcotic appeal. My mother had introduced him to Wellfleet and he loved it. But the Cape was essentially my mother's domain, the place where she maintained many of the close friendships of her Bauhaus days, and which no doubt served as ballast in dealing with life with my father during the rest of the year.

The other month we spent at my grandparents' farm in Michigan, which was idyllic for other reasons. So as to be able to host their grandchildren without disturbing our irascible grandfather, my grandparents built a little guesthouse, which became a kind of children's domain where we could run and scream and jump on beds to our hearts' content without fear of censure. We caught fireflies in glass jars and used them as lanterns. We ate wild raspberries and blackberries right off the bushes and made honey butter and peach and blackberry pies with our grandmother. Lucy and our cousin Phoebe, instead of playing Hide and Seek, would play "Hide Sandro," which involved hiding me, the youngest cousin at the time, in improbably small and hard-to-find corners, drawers, and crawl spaces. We played in a tree house and put on little skits, some of which made gentle fun of the family. I remember one in which my grandfather tells my grandmother to "can it, Lolita!" "I am! I am!" she says, and is shown furiously canning fruits and vegetables, which was one of her constant occupations. Our uncle George would generally be portrayed working away at an ironing board, illustrating a favorite joke of my grandfather, who enjoyed saying, when George was courting his future wife, our aunt Lyndy, that he was "pressing his suit." We enjoyed the company of our cousins, and most days we would ride over to the beach where Uncle George and his family stayed all summer, where we covered ourselves with sand rolling down the dunes and then washed ourselves off in Lake Michigan. We would ride over in my grandmother's big, old-fashioned Chevrolet station wagon, and as we crossed the railroad tracks she would sing to us the "train song."

Over the bridge, across the lake,
A mile a minute it has to make,
A terrible snake with gleaming eyes,
It wriggles and wraggles across the ties.
The cinders fall in a fiery rain,
The tunnel is waiting to swallow the train.
Goodbye, goodbye, get out of the way, go 'long!

Sometimes we went to the outdoor drive-in movie theater—seeing a movie from your car seemed like the greatest thing ever—and drank "black cows," a midwestern concoction of root beer and vanilla ice cream. In this family setting, my mother was in her element: adored daughter and admired older sister, at home but also standing out—the glamorous out-of-towner, the sophisticate from the great metropolis.

The End of Something

I.

Some time around 1967, when I was ten years old, my mother learned that she had breast cancer.

She told me that the doctors weren't certain whether she had cancer and were only going to do an exploratory operation to make sure. In all likelihood, she said, they were just going to remove some tissue from her breast and then she would be as good as new. Although I very much wanted to believe this benign account of things, somehow I suspected it wasn't true and that the world was ending. The night before she went into the hospital, I recall getting into her bed and placing my head protectively on her breasts and weeping. The next day I felt better and we all went out for lunch at a little restaurant in the West Village, La Crêpe. It was a beautiful day and I did my part in maintaining the fiction that everything was fine; but then, in the middle of lunch, Lucy suddenly burst out crying, shattering the appearance of normality. Strangely, I recall being relieved by her reaction: it was a note of truth and authentic emotion that expressed something I was trying to anesthetize.

The day after the operation, I remember getting a phone call from my mother in the hospital; with a calm, unwavering voice, she explained that unfortunately the growth they had found was, in fact, cancerous and that they had had to remove her left breast. My face suddenly got red, hot, and prickly with anxiety and I heard myself say, "Fine, if that's how it's going to be!" and slammed down the phone in anger. I reacted with the fury of a lover who had been lied to and jilted. Then, seconds afterward, I realized how selfish my reaction had been and was seized with terror about how my mother might have responded and what she might do. I wanted to call back but, in a panic, realized I didn't know the hospital phone number. Then the phone rang again and I was relieved that it was my mother, calm and cool as ice, calling to reassure me. She told me that other people we knew had had the same operation and were doing fine, that there was nothing to worry about. I always thought this was an act of some small grandeur on my mother's part: she was focused on re-assuring me rather than on her own fear and pain.

When my mother came home from the hospital, we prepared the house by putting a ring of chairs near the entry to the living room so that our dog, Ben, would not jump on my mother and hurt her.

At the time, breast cancer surgery was extremely primitive by today's standards: doctors performed radical mastectomies, removing the entire breast as well as a great deal of surrounding tissue, gouging out the lymph nodes underneath the armpit. My mother was left with a huge, scarred cavity where her breast had been and one arm swollen to almost twice its normal size. She wore a rubber breast pad inside her bra, but it didn't cover everything, and when she wore a bathing suit or a low-cut blouse you got a glimpse of the damage.

It didn't take much to imagine how devastating such mutilation would have been for the self-image of a woman in her late forties whose physical attractiveness had been such an important part of her identity, let alone one who was always considering the possibility of leaving her husband and starting over with someone else. Her beauty was my mother's trump card, a card she could hold in reserve, to be played when she needed it most. So she must have felt that she lost her freedom and her future as well as her looks to the surgeon's knife.

After my mother got home from the hospital, my sister and I were shipped out to the country to stay with family friends, the Nivolas, who lived in Amagansett, on Long Island. No one explained why, but I later learned (from my sister) that our parents felt that it was good for us to be away for a time while my mother regained her physical strength and ad-justed psychologically to her new condition. It was beautiful in Amagan-sett and the Nivolas were very kind. My main occupation was learning to ride a bicycle. In the urban jungle of New York City, riding a bicycle was more difficult—and dangerous. We didn't have bikes and my sister, for example, never learned. But I took advantage of the flat terrain of Long Island to learn and rode up and down past the potato fields of Old Stone Highway, where the Nivolas lived. Their neighbor right across the road was Saul Steinberg, my father's old friend and my mother's former flame.

I don't remember meeting him during the visit, but I recall being vaguely aware of his presence. I am pretty sure that my mother had already told us about her affair with Saul, which somehow seemed normal to me. (I had, after all, no other parents than my parents, no other mother than my mother.) And then one day I was presented with a "bicycle license" that Steinberg had made for me, one of those beautiful and whimsical fake official documents he became famous for—a figure on a bicycle, decorated with the elaborate, flowing arabesques of a cursive script, in illegible and incomprehensible bureaucratic language. Evidently, he had been watching me riding back and forth, remaining in the shadows, like Boo Radley in *To Kill a Mockingbird*, out of sight but watching with a protective, interested eye. Lucy recalls that we went over to his house one day and he made masks for all of us by drawing faces on plain brown paper bags and cutting holes in them for the eyes and mouth. We spent the afternoon dressed up as Steinberg creatures in these paper bags, playing.

That summer, Lucy and I boarded an airplane by ourselves to Chicago—the first time that we ever traveled alone—and then piled into a green station wagon driven by my uncle George. We drove across the country, my sister reading Jane Austen and writing in neat girl's handwriting in a diary as we crossed the Badlands while I fought with my youngest cousin in the way back of the station wagon. We spent two weeks on a Wyoming "dude ranch," well-to-do city slickers riding around on horses with Western saddles through the most beautiful countryside in the world—the vast plain near Jackson Hole with the Grand Teton mountains towering over us. My mother joined us there by plane in order to avoid the wear and tear of the long cross-country trip.

We rode twice a day. My mother had never ridden before and must have been feeling rather delicate physically after her breast operation. She was given a horse to ride named Highball, which seemed oddly appropriate for my cocktail-drinking mother. While we cantered and galloped along with the fearlessness of youth, my mother plodded along on the "slow ride," on this old nag whom she had been given, in all likelihood, because it was the slowest and tamest horse on the ranch, a step or two from the glue factory. My mother, a stylish city girl, looked decidedly out of place and somewhat comical, dressed in dungarees, sitting on top of a horse. "Highball!" we yelled with mocking laughs of delight. I doubt she much wanted to be doing this, but she took the indignity of being an awkward middle-aged equestrian novice on a broken-down horse with good-natured grace. She and my aunt and uncle smuggled in bottles of whiskey and vodka and had their evening cocktails on the porch of one of our little cabins. My sister, in full adolescence, fell in love with one of the "wranglers," the cowboys who led the rides and took care of the horses.

There was a single gentleman at the dude ranch named Mr. Polk who seemed to show some interest in my mother. I recall half hoping that they might take up with each other. He seemed less interesting than my father, but perhaps he would be easier for my mother to live with, I thought. But nothing came of it.

The enduring image of my mother from that trip is that of the fiery end of a lit cigarette shining in the darkness as she sat by herself on the porch of our cabin smoking and thinking: smoldering alone in the dark, contemplating in the quiet night the state and future of her life.

I remember being out at a restaurant in San Francisco later on our trip when my mother suddenly and rather abruptly had to leave the table. "She's bleeding," Lucy said, which sounded dire and scary—I don't think I knew anything about menstruation at the time. My sister later explained to me that my mother was undergoing menopause at the time—which, coming right after her breast cancer operation, must have seemed a confirmation of her sense that her life as a woman was over. During this trip, her body gave one final, unexpected cry—her youth's last roar.

My mother, normally so voluble, confiding, and indiscreet, never talked with me about any of this, about what must have been one of the great crises of her life. I was impressed by her stoicism. She handled it by keeping up a strong front for me and continuing to behave like my mother. But evidently this wasn't my sister's experience. After the operation, when Lucy was in earshot, my mother would phone her friends and rage about her new condition: "I've been mutilated! I look like a freak! My life is over!" Forced into the role of adult before her time, my sister had to whip my mother into shape like a strict parent. "You put down that phone, right now! Stop speaking that way. Pull yourself together immediately!"

2.

My father, I think, was on good behavior for a while after my mother's operation. It must have been a scare for him, too. My mother told a close friend of hers that my father had done "the gallant thing" by making love to her after she recovered from her operation. But I suspect that that was a rare event and that there was not a lot more of that in her remaining twenty-six years of life. "I remember Misha took her out to dinner and gave her some jewelry, trying to make things romantic," Lucy recalled. After the fear that my mother might die passed, my father reverted to his usual behavior, and in late 1967 my mother went to see a lawyer about a divorce, as we know from a letter from my grandmother to my mother, dated January 5, 1968.

Darling Liz,

Am distressed to hear that you are feeling badly physically, nervously, and emotionally. It is not hard to account for, surely. Surely, somehow a halt must be called to this hectic living, this killing pace, else there will be no Elizabeth.

So your consultation with a lawyer is on the whole welcome news. And I say this with some sadness on account of Michael. He is a victim of his early environment and it could hardly have been worse, I would infer. But that is no reason for your carrying the environment on, to ruin your life and your children's. Do keep in touch with us. If money is a problem, call us collect, preferably in the low rate hours, but any time, if it is urgent. Keep us informed as to your lawyer's advice, and let us know what we can do to help, if anything.

I think this was the time my father asked my sister, Lucy, to intervene. "You've got to talk her out of it!" he said. Economic considerations were also a factor. "I consulted a couple of lawyers," my mother told me. "I wouldn't have gotten much. So I stuck it out."

That same year, 1968, Lucy applied to college, and the two places she was seriously considering were Cornell (which my mother and so many other Bogerts had attended) and the University of Colorado, where her cowboy boyfriend was going to school. When she went to visit Cornell, my mother got the idea that Lucy should look up Clinton Rossiter, her old beau, who was now one of the university's most distinguished professors. Rossiter was delighted, showed my sister around the campus, and was extremely gracious and encouraging to her. As it turned out, my sister chose Colorado and the boyfriend—a somewhat rebellious move, taking her far from my parents and further from their New York intellectual milieu. But her visit to Cornell briefly revived my mother's relationship with Rossiter.

A good friend of my mother's, Alice Wohl, claims that the two of them actually arranged a meeting somewhere. Both, for quite different reasons, were groping for a way out of their current lives. My mother never told me about their meeting, but I do recall her telling me (years after the fact) that Rossiter had proposed that they run off together. She says she didn't take the idea seriously: after nearly thirty years it seemed like a desperate fantasy.

The following year, black students at Cornell occupied one of the main buildings on campus, Straight Hall, protesting the treatment of blacks at the university and, in particular, disciplinary action taken against three black students in an earlier protest. The students had guns, and there was a tense two-day standoff in which police surrounded the building and the university deliberated what it should do. At first the faculty voted by a wide margin that Cornell should not accede to the students' demands because of the threat of violence. But when the black protesters refused to lay down their arms and thousands of other students staged a peaceful protest in support of the occupation, the university was faced with the prospect of an extremely bloody shoot-out; the faculty suddenly reversed its position. The Cornell protest—unprecedented because of students' taking up arms—was big news all around the country. *The New York Times* offered daily reports, which my mother read with special interest. The day the protest ended, the *Times* featured a photograph of a black student leader exiting Straight Hall triumphantly carrying a gun.

The history and government department, of which Rossiter was perhaps the most prominent member, played a crucial role in the struggle. First, he had been among forty members of the department faculty who threatened to resign if the university gave in to the students' demands, and he was quoted in *The New York Times* saying "There is nothing reasonable about a gun." But his sudden reversal, just a day later, helped sway the Cornell faculty to change its vote, leading to a peaceful resolution of the crisis but one many of his friends and colleagues denounced as "abject capitulation." "Do we leave this hall as free men or as cowards?" another said.

The *New York Times* article stressed Rossiter's pivotal role in the stand-off as well as criticism from some of his close colleagues, who termed the faculty's reversal "nothing short of 'surrender to intimidation.'" A number of Cornell faculty resigned over the university's handling of the crisis, seeing it as the equivalent of the appeasement of the Nazis at Munich. Some of Rossiter's closest friends and colleagues stopped speaking to him and refused to shake his hand.

The following year, my mother picked up her morning *New York Times* and read the news that Clinton Rossiter had been found dead in his basement, an apparent suicide. Many attributed Rossiter's suicide to emotional fallout from the Cornell protest standoff. Rossiter was greatly pained by the ruptured friendships and acrimony his role in the crisis had caused. Some friends felt that Rossiter had come to despair in the American constitutional system that he loved and had written so much about: a system that seemed so supple and adaptable to change now appeared to be in crisis from the increasingly radical and even violent demands of the growing protest movement.

Some thirty years later, several years after my mother's death, Rossiter's middle son, Caleb, published a very different account of his father's death. He, too, had thought that the 1960s and the Cornell crisis had done his father in, with the added sense of guilt that his and his two brothers' personal and political rebellion had helped push their father over the edge. David, Rossiter's oldest son, had dropped out of Yale to cut cane in Castro's Cuba, while Caleb's high school yearbook photograph had been a picture of himself holding aloft a rifle, in clear imitation of the black students who had occupied Cornell's Straight Hall. Against his father's wishes, Caleb had refused an academic referral to avoid the draft, insisting on open resistance. He had, in fact, put in an advertisement in *The Ithaca Journal*, stating in bold letters: "SONS OF AMERICA, DON'T ACCEPT THEIR LIES!!" When his father saw the ad, he told his wife, "I don't see how I can live in the same town as Caleb." Three weeks later, Rossiter took a massive overdose of barbiturates. Caleb was convinced that "by disappointing my father I had forced him to kill himself."

Twenty years later, Caleb learned that his father's inner turmoil had little to do with the troubling events of the 1960s or with his sons' private and political revolt.

Finally talking about her husband's death, his mother revealed that Rossiter had fought a long and terrible battle for more than twenty years with what would certainly be diagnosed today as clinical depression. Too proud to seek help, Rossiter had begun medicating himself with barbiturates in order to combat his insomnia. Addicted to the barbiturates, he began drinking to help him try to wean himself from them and suffered through fierce bouts of depression and alcohol and substance abuse.

Up in the attic of his parents' home, Caleb found his father's private diary, which traced battles with depression but offered no evidence for the theory that Rossiter had been especially shaken by the political stand-off at Cornell in 1969. The considerable achievements of Rossiter's life seem all the more remarkable in light of the other things he was struggling with.

Twenty years after his death (perhaps because of shame over suicide), Rossiter's wife finally revealed that her husband had left a note before killing himself:

> The hell was private, very private. There should be no grief, guilt, feeling of responsibility, etc., on anyone's part, above all MCR [Rossiter's wife]. I have had the death wish for years—and were there hope I would go on suppressing it. There is no hope, I am of no value.

"There was no causal 'why' for my father's death outside of his illness, a true killer of a disease known generally as clinical depression," Caleb Rossiter wrote. "The real mystery was not why he died so soon, but how he managed to live so long with this tremendous burden, which was all the heavier because he carried it in secret."

Rossiter's death had nothing to do with the sixties, with the Cornell crisis, with his political battles with his sons, and, least of all, with my mother and her refusal to take seriously his suggestion that they run off together. But my mother did not know that. I don't think she blamed herself; I think she saw his reaching out to her as a symptom of his final despair rather than a cause, but his suicide remained a troubling mystery that obviously struck her. The yellowed clipping of his death notice in

The New York Times was among the twenty or so pieces of paper she had bothered to keep in her bedside table at the time of her death, together with the list Rossiter had drawn up of my mother's faults and virtues about thirty-five years earlier. Rossiter's death was clearly the end of something, the definitive end of the world of her youth. He had represented the road not taken, and now that road had closed.

3.

In 1970, after my sister had gone away to college and I went off to boarding school, my mother finally made a serious attempt to leave my father. She called her friend Alice Wohl up in Stockbridge, Massachusetts, where we had begun to spend time, announced she was leaving my father, and asked whether she could come and stay for a while. Almost as soon as she arrived, my mother asked Alice if she could use the phone: "I have to call Misha to tell him where I am, otherwise he will be worried." "Right away," Alice said, "I knew your mother wasn't really leaving."

Friendship

I.

A woman trapped in an unhappy marriage tries to leave her husband and fails. The onset of middle age, a brutal operation that leaves her badly scarred, the fear of remaining alone, all cause her to lose her nerve. There were all the elements of tragedy, albeit a minor, everyday sort of tragedy. The script appeared to be written for the sad final act: a gradual, inexorable descent into bitterness, regret, alcoholism, and death.

Fortunately, life is more complicated than that.

Abandoning once and for all the idea of leaving my father meant, in effect, giving up on the great quest for romantic happiness that had dominated her adult life up to that point. Men—the frantic, anxious, desperate pursuit of love—had been at the center of her life since she was a teenager. The failure to find marital happiness with either of her two husbands had led to much grief, aggravated by the itching dissatisfaction that it might still be found out there with someone else. Ironically, my mother had focused on the thing she was perhaps least good at: love and marriage, which her early life had set her up to fail at. Giving it up, I expect, must have felt like a great weight falling from her shoulders.

Rather than leave my father, she did something that actually made more sense: she pursued a life of much greater independence in which her relationship with my father mattered less and therefore bothered her less. She focused in the last third of her life on the things she did best, on the aspects of her life that gave her the most satisfaction—friendship, her children, her siblings and their children, work and her colleagues at work—in a life that was much of her own making.

Crucial to her new, much more autonomous life was buying a house. Rather luckily, in 1970, right around the time that my mother was struggling with the question of what to do next, she inherited some money from an aunt. This was Lotta Jean Bogert, her father's sister, who had never married and had no children. Aunt Jean (as we knew her) had worked very successfully as a chemist and author on chemistry and nutrition and died a fairly prosperous woman. She left most of her money to my aunt Ginny, with whom she was genuinely close, but she also left something to my mother and her brother. I believe it was about thirty thousand dollars, not a fortune but a tidy sum at the time, enough to make a down payment on a house in the country with some money to fix it up.

Mom concentrated her search in Berkshire County, Massachusetts, where she already had a couple of friends. It was closer and more affordable than Cape Cod. We had already been renting in the area and looking for houses even before my mother inherited the money from Aunt Jean. It was less than three hours' drive from New York and only two hours' drive from her office in Westchester, where she had begun working at the time cutting books for *Reader's Digest*. She made an arrangement with the *Digest* requiring her to be in the office only three days a week, editing at home the other two days, so she could, if she wanted, spent three or four nights a week in the Berkshires and about the same amount in New York.

She found the house under peculiar circumstances. Unable to buy anything quickly, my mother had decided to rent a house there so that she could keep looking. On Easter Sunday morning in 1971, my mother walked down the main street of Stockbridge to buy *The New York Times* when she saw a huge crowd gathered around a car that had smashed into the fountain in the middle of town. Dead inside was George Klein, the man whose house my mother had arranged to rent; he had suffered a massive heart attack and lost control of his car. The Kleins obviously were not going to Europe for the summer as planned, and my mother no longer had a house to rent. Klein's widow, Bessie, asked my mother if she would drive her to pick up her daughter at college, in Connecticut, so that she could bring her home for the funeral. My mother agreed. In the middle of this chaotic day, my mother's real estate agent called and said, "I have a house I think you might be interested in." Squeezing it in between one thing and another, my mother took a quick look around and, in her extremely decisive fashion, told the broker, "Okay, I'll take it." Two years of looking ended with a ten-minute visit.

That summer, my mother, I think, found what perhaps could have been her true calling: fixing up and decorating houses.

She had always put an enormous amount of herself into the houses she made. They all had an incredible aura about them. They were a pure expression of herself: a very personal mixture of things, a certain Bauhaus spareness combined with a totally undogmatic, imaginatively eclectic taste. Everywhere she lived she managed to transform into a place that was extremely appealing, not in a showy or expensive way, but in a way that attracted you, that both managed to be aesthetically elegant and made you feel comfortable and welcome. My parents knew a number of famous people in the art world, and some of their houses—remarkably beautiful and innovative—wound up in books and articles on architecture and design. But the houses my mother created were, in my opinion as a child, just as attractive and generally much more comfortable and livable. Marcel Breuer's house on Cape Cod was stunning and filled with furniture that he himself had designed, but it looked better than it felt. It seemed more like a museum of design than a home: you were never quite sure where you were supposed to sit, and were afraid of breaking something or of moving something out of its proper place.

My mother's "masterpiece" (too grand a term), if we can call it that, was our house in Great Barrington. She had never owned anything before, and so she had merely decorated various apartments without changing their structure. The house in the Berkshires she transformed. She had the talent that a good architect or designer has: being able to look beyond the actual state of a house and to see what it might become. The house she had bought was unimpressive, a somewhat dark, run-down farmhouse with some charming elements on a nice piece of land.

My mother set to work with remarkable clarity and decisiveness, tearing down walls and moving things around with great ease and without a moment of second-guessing or regret. Cutting down old trees is generally taboo, but Mom walked around the house, said it was too dark, and immediately had a couple of trees near the house cut down—and suddenly the house was light. She discovered that inside the attic were the original floorboards—big thick oak boards, each plank more than a foot wide—and she had a carpenter rip up the attic floor and use the wood to make three pieces of furniture in the living room. She ripped out a large, imposing white brick mantelpiece that was something of an eyesore and created a mantelpiece out of the old wood, which suddenly looked as if it had been there since the time the house was built.

My mother had an incredible knack for making something out of nothing or out of something else. She found the bottom of what had probably been a child's desk drawer, with wooden slots for pens and inkwells. She put it up on the wall and it looked like a Louise Nevelson sculpture. She bought the bottom of an old cast-iron stove, placed a marble top on it, and turned it into a table. I realized, watching her work on the house, that one needed to be ruthless and unsentimental to be a good designer. One day she took a perfectly attractive and useful dining table, cut off its legs, and turned it into a coffee table. When I looked horrified and asked her why, she simply said, "I don't need a dining table, I need a coffee table." And that was that. (But then she took the sawed-off table legs, which had been molded by a lathe, and turned them upside down, and they became sculptures, which she placed on a bookcase.)

We had a set of carpenters and workmen basically living with us from eight-thirty till four-thirty each day. And my mother dragooned my sister and me into forced labor in order to add to her pool of available workers, ripping out wallpaper and shrubs, removing varnish, stripping and repainting chairs, planting trees, and digging a vegetable garden.

My father was conspicuously absent during that summer while the work was being done. He came up the next fall to inspect his new property. I think he was amazed that he was the owner of any property. He was, after all, a wandering Jew, who had been a renter all his life. He was a lifelong city dweller—Moscow, Rome, New York—and had never learned to drive a car, and I expect that the idea of owning a house in the country seemed as unlikely to him as becoming an astronaut. He arrived in his city clothes, his black business shoes, and his thick black glasses and walked around peering at everything with a mixture of suspicion and incomprehension. It was the height of fall; the trees were a riot of yellow, orange, red—tourists drive hours to the area for the leaves in fall. My father, suddenly noticing the leaves, turned to my mother and said, "*Eleezabet*, what have you done? The trees are dying!" Evidently he had reached his early fifties without knowing anything about the seasons, about evergreen and deciduous trees.

Among other things, having her own life up in the Berkshires changed the balance of power in my mother's marriage, which my mother seems to have understood at the time. In a letter she wrote to Lucy, who was then back at college, she said:

Misha came up last week—and full of piss and vinegar, but I was in such high spirits and feeling so independent that everything nasty just rolled over me. I was patient but very firm and unmoved. Pleasant and not upset. He was very impressed by the progress of the house and garden and even more, I think, by my behavior. He behaved with some of his usual ridiculousness and fatuousness—simply not knowing how to act—but he was smart enough to see it himself. Sandro turned on him and was very nasty but I stayed out of it. Anyhow I told him that I was going to change my life—spend more time here—be more flexible and, by implication, not put up anymore with all the chaos and disagreeableness. For once I seem to have made a big impression. A new respect and carefulness and affection has crept in. He sees I've got something going here—that I did it alone—and he wants part of it.

My father had no idea of what to do with himself in the country, since working on the house or even taking a walk was an incomprehensibly foreign idea to him. Instead, he transferred one of his great city passions—building a library and ordering his books—to the country. To give him his own country activity, my mother began including massive numbers of bookshelves in her ongoing renovation project, and my father would bring boxes or suitcases full of books with him when he came. He developed a filing system unknown to the creators of the Dewey decimal system, dividing books into "country" and "city." "I think this would be a good country book, don't you think?" he would say. He had refined ideas about the kinds of books—biographies, novels, works of belles lettres, detective stories, works of narrative nonfiction, lighter and more entertaining works of history, certain kinds of illustrated books—that he felt were "country books," the kind you might ideally want to sink into a comfortable chair by the fire with and read. My father didn't drive, and so my mother would have to drive him up there with his box of books so that he could spend a weekend puttering around the house ordering and reordering the books. He tried to match subject matter and genre, so that a shelf of detective novels or a string of books about chess ("excellent country books") would be matched with aesthetic considerations—putting together the books of a particular Oxford series that looked especially

good when stacked up in a row. "What your mother has never realized—
with all her complaining about the number of books—is books are *beau-
ti-ful*. It is the books that make the house." My mother accommodated
him, adding bookshelves to almost every available wall or surface—as
long as it was consistent with other aesthetic considerations and didn't
create a distressing sense of clutter.

Despite coming only occasionally, he knew where absolutely every
book in the house was. He was unhappy even when one of us would take
a book off the shelf and read it without taking it out of the house. Once,
to avoid his wrath, Sarah, my first wife, tried to fool him by removing an
Edith Wharton anthology from the bookshelf, removing the dust jacket,
and carefully putting it back in place so that it was almost impossible to
tell anything was missing. "Where's the Wharton!?" my father yelled
within twenty-four hours. "Where's the Wharton?"

Since he couldn't drive, my father hated riding in a car and took to
actually flying up to the Berkshires for weekends. Thus my parents worked
out an insane arrangement, where sometimes my mother might drive up
on a Friday afternoon while my father would fly up on Saturday and then
fly back the following day. For a time, there was a rinky-dink airline that
flew between LaGuardia Airport in New York and Pittsfield, which is
about half an hour's drive from our house. So my father would take a cab
to the airport (half an hour) in order to check in and wait around (another half an hour to an hour) in order to fly for half an hour in order to
reach Pittsfield, where my mother would pick him up and drive him another half an hour back to our house. At the most, flying might have
saved him half an hour; more likely, flying took the same amount of time
as driving. But my father liked flying and he didn't like driving, and flying up and having my mother move heaven and earth on his behalf made
him feel properly fussed over, not simply an extra piece of baggage in the
car. (Once, he claimed, when he was standing at the Pittsfield airport,
someone asked him if he was the actor Robert Redford—a less likely
mistake you cannot imagine, other than their both being short. But my
father was obviously flattered—that wasn't an experience he was going
to get in a car.) Of course, the thought of making my mother drive an
extra hour to and from the airport after having driven for nearly three
hours the previous day did not trouble him at all. These were the prerogatives of the lord of the manor. And my mother (while it seemed like
madness to the rest of us) found that treating my father like the lord of

the manor once every couple of months was a more than acceptable price for her independence, for winning his support and giving him a stake in the new life she was setting up for herself. The reality is that in Great Barrington, she was the boss; he was, however, helping considerably to make it all possible by writing substantial checks for her various renovation projects. The occasional extra trip to Pittsfield, to keep him happily on board, seemed like a small price to pay.

My father often felt stranded in the country. There was only so much time he could spend ordering, reordering, and keeping vigil over the books. Occasionally, he would grow restless and would begin pestering one of the rest of us to take him shopping, a bit like a petulant teenager lobbying her parents to take her to the mall. Along with "country books," my father also had a separate sartorial category for country attire, even though he virtually never ventured out of doors. His favorite haunt was Jack's Country Squire, where he stocked up on various windbreakers, corduroy pants, and flannel shirts that almost never saw their way out of a drawer or a closet again but kept him occupied on dull country weekends.

For my mother, the house was a constant, unending work in progress. Spending time there, she would brood over what the house still needed, what was missing, what didn't quite work. Gradually, things would appear: a footstool in front of a certain chair, the right table for a cup of coffee, a better light for reading next to a particular couch, something rearranged to give you a view out of a particular window. Her houses were meant to be lived in, places where people could enjoy themselves, together or in solitude. The chairs and mattresses were comfortable; there was always plenty of closet space. When you lived in the rooms of the house, you realized that all the things you suddenly needed had already been thought of. You almost had the feeling of being attended to silently by the house's creator.

After getting the house in basic good order, my mother then began attacking the outdoors, mining a set of old stone walls up in the woods (left there by farmers in the nineteenth century who fled and went west when much more fertile, flat land became available in the Midwest—land without all those darn rocks) to build a stone wall in our back garden. She created a swimming pond in our backyard, fed by a stream running through the woods, which cleaned itself naturally as water flowed in and out constantly. My father would sometimes swim. He was so nearsighted that he never swam without his glasses, although he might change his thick black glasses for an identical pair of thick black sunglasses with dark green prescription lenses. He never put his head underwater. He would swim the crawl with short, choppy, inexpert strokes, his head visible above the water, jerking a bit from side to side as he swam, the way a turtle's head moves about when it peers out from within its shell. And when he emerged from the water, his white, flabby body, so seemingly out of place in nature, looked poignantly vulnerable, like the body of a turtle without its shell.

At a certain point, my mother suddenly decided to undertake a major expansion. It seemed pure madness. Never mind that there were already four bedrooms and that the house was underutilized. Along with adding two bedrooms, my mother decided to enlarge the living room, which seemed an even crazier extravagance. The living room is a perfectly good-size room, I argued, and besides, people rarely spend time there; they usually congregate in the kitchen. That's exactly the point, my mother said: the living room doesn't have the right feel; it's too narrow. And so she knocked down the wall and expanded the room out toward the garden, opening it up and giving it a very different feel. Some architects have studied things like the dimensions of rooms and come up with theories—like those of Pythagoras, who believed that there were divinely ordained relations between numbers—about people's positive or negative responses to the positioning and proportions of rooms. My mother appeared to have understood this intuitively, and she was absolutely right about the living room.

I always felt that she had missed her real calling in life. Why don't you do this for a living? I asked her. She dismissed the idea with a wave of her hand: "It doesn't interest me unless it's somewhere that I am going to live." And she was probably right; it was the intense personal interest—living with and knowing a space—that made her houses what they were.

And yet there was also something restless about my mother's constant fixing and decorating. She rarely seemed capable of sitting still and enjoying what she had created. It was a pleasure to see her reading a book on the chaise longue on the screened porch she had created or playing a long game of Scrabble with Lucy on a languid afternoon. But for the most part, no sooner had she finished one project than she cooked up another. If she was done with the indoors, she attacked the garden. If the garden didn't need anything, she would invent something to do in the woods.

Not surprisingly, she was the patron saint of contractors and merchants, of whom she asked only: "How much do I owe you?" She might occasionally get taken advantage of, but more often than not she brought out the best in workmen, making them partners in her various projects, discussing and admiring their skills. She would hound our auto mechanic to make sure he sent her his bills, chiding him that he would land himself in the poorhouse if he didn't improve his bookkeeping. Part of this stemmed from a fear of confrontation and a desire to be liked, but at the same time, she was genuinely interested in the lives of Armenian carpenters and Polish handymen, of a young boy who lived in an abandoned school bus and came for a time to prune bushes.*

2.

The house worked for my mother on many levels. It gave her breathing room in her relationship with my father; a place to go when he was behaving impossibly, which reduced the wear and tear of their marriage. But, more important, it was an independent power base, where they

---

*Nearly thirty years after my parents moved away from Greenwich Village, I found myself back in our old neighborhood around dusk, feeling terribly nostalgic. I was walking on Sixth Avenue and paused in front of Jefferson Market, a wonderful food shop, with superb meat and fish and Italian specialty items, decades before words like "prosciutto" and "pesto" entered mainstream American vernacular. In fact, the legendary American cook and food writer James Beard used to shop there when we lived downtown. It was a smallish neighborhood store during my childhood. In the gourmet food boom, it had grown significantly, taking over space on either side of its original store, and become one of New York's major luxury food emporia. I decided to poke my head in to see what, if anything, of the original store remained. To my great surprise, I saw Bill, the butcher, still at his post, but behind a very grand, shiny meat counter, looking just as fat and round with his large, bulbous red nose redder and more bulbous than ever. There was Angelo, the half-witted cousin whom the family employed to deliver the groceries, still standing in front of his cart. I watched for a long time, debating whether to speak to Bill, feeling like Odysseus after he has snuck back into Ithaca, wondering whether he will be recognized by his shepherd or his childhood nurse. Finally, I went up to Bill and explained who I was, fearful he wouldn't remember us at all. "Mrs. Stille! Of course, she was a terrific lady. I was so sorry when she moved uptown!"

would meet now more as equals, since they both knew that she would come and go as she pleased. It also gave her a place in which to receive her friends and relatives without needing to consult my father.

My mother's buying the house in Great Barrington coincided roughly with my grandparents' decision to sell their farm in Michigan and to retire permanently to Florida. The decision was prompted, in part, by my grandmother's increasingly evident Alzheimer's (although that term wasn't used at the time). It was obvious that she could no longer run a farm, let alone maintain two households at a distance apart of two thousand miles. After what was euphemistically referred to as a "cerebral accident," her descent into dementia was swift and inexorable. Her transformation from mother and grandmother into a mere patient and dependent was shockingly quick. The whole equilibrium of the family had been thrown out of whack. My grandmother had been the emotional center—and the center of information—that had held together that part of the family. And their farm had been the physical location where my mother and her siblings congregated. Now those emotional and geographic centers were gone and everyone was on their own. My mother used the house in Great Barrington, in part, to fill that void and to create a new center. One of the only benefits of my grandmother's illness was that it brought my mother and her siblings together more. It was so depressing to see my grandmother gradually turn into a complete stranger who failed to recognize her own children (my mother would invariably get sick for a week after each visit) that they arranged always to go in the company of another sibling. If nothing else, my mother, her brother, and her sister, all of whom had been busy raising their own families for many years, met again and formed new adult friendships, which were in many ways stronger and more satisfying than their childhood bonds.

In this new configuration, my mother, as the eldest, took on something of a role of family matriarch and used the house in Great Barrington to give the family a new place to get together. She hosted her brother and sister frequently, and, as several of their children had come east to attend college, she took to inviting them each year at Thanksgiving, since it was too long and expensive a trip back to the Midwest for just four or five days. Some of the children remained in the east, and my mother kept up this Thanksgiving tradition throughout her life, enjoying her role as "hostess with the mostest," starting a local tradition of a post-Thanksgiving Saturday party, combining our relatives with my mother's growing cast of local friends—dinners of twenty-five or thirty people, after which everyone played charades.

She formed deep and long-lasting relationships with more than a few of her nieces and nephews, for whom she became an important figure. Both her brother and her sister maintained much of their midwestern reserve, and often their kids didn't feel they could talk about important emotional issues with their parents. My mother was far more direct and would come right out and ask, "So, tell me, what's going on in your life?" When she didn't get a convincing answer, she would continue, "No, I mean what's *really* going on in your life?" As an adult and a close relative who was not their parent, my mother became a person they could confide in and open up to. She could also be brutally honest in ways that her brother and sister were much too polite to be. She didn't hesitate to upbraid her nieces and nephews when she thought they were behaving badly or going wrong. My mother could sometimes be excessively judgmental and too free with her advice, a fault that was mitigated by the fact that she genuinely listened. Her nieces and nephews had a lasting and deep respect and affection for her. Some of them consulted her often on the important choices in their lives, knowing that they could count on honest, occasionally tough, but loving advice.

She also used the house to maintain and develop friendships new and old. She still occasionally rented a place for a month on the Cape to see her old friends from her Bauhaus days in Chicago, and now she was able to invite them to come see her in Great Barrington. She could see her friends for longer, more relaxed stretches and didn't have to worry about my father objecting or creating a disturbance.

"Elizabeth made an art of friendship," Katharine Kuh said. "That was her art: being a friend. Funnily enough, I think she was more interested in her women friends than in men—men were interested in her. She was the best friend you can imagine having. She was totally honest and yet incredibly kind. She was incredibly thoughtful and generous. I remember after I broke off my relationship with Dan Rich, back in the 1950s, she brought me with her to Cape Cod because she thought I needed a change of scene. She introduced me to the Cape and to that whole world. She remained incredibly attractive to people until the end of her life. I mean people were literally attracted to her. Every time I introduced her to a friend, she mesmerized them, and I'll tell you why. Because when she talked to a person, she was totally yours. She wasn't wandering around, looking elsewhere, fidgeting; she would sit there and really talk to you. She was wonderfully companionable. It was just really fun to go places and do things with her. She was incredibly strong. She never complained in all her years of cancer operations and illness. And she was a great relative. She became the rock of her family."

She was one of the relatively few people of her generation whose friendships I understood and even envied. She continued making friends up until the very end of her life. She made friends with women her own age and women thirty or forty years younger than herself. She had a directness, a curiosity, a desire and ability to cut through formalities and form a genuine human bond, but she did so in a way that was gentle and caring rather than brutal or intrusive.

My aunt Lally once said to me, "I adored your father, but you know, in a certain way he lacked a strong moral compass. He never really took a stand. This served him very well in his work, where he managed to see all sides of a problem, but in his life he was missing something. My mother had a moral center. And Elizabeth had a strong moral center." Interestingly, a first cousin of mine, who was another person for whom my mother was an extremely important figure, said almost the exact same thing in almost the exact same language. "Your mother had a real strong moral code, a right way of behaving toward people that she stuck to and expected other people to stick to," she said.

When faced with choices about a generous or mean and selfish thing to do—whether to include a kindly but boring person in some occasion, whether to give someone something that the other person needed more than we did—Mom could be counted on to do the right thing. At times, I felt she had a pathological need to always be liked by everyone and a repression of her own ego. My father would say my mother needed to develop more "healthy selfishness," a quality he possessed to an unhealthy degree. And yet it was not only a need to please; there were times, as with my cousin, when she could be very confrontational when someone violated her moral code. I remember a couple of incidents from my childhood. One day when I must have been very small, she and I were walking down Eleventh Street and when we reached Sixth Avenue, we stopped in front of a run-down apartment building where we knew a family of Italian immigrants. The father was out on the sidewalk, beating his older son, whom he always seemed to pick on. Beating him right on the open street, as if this were an entirely normal thing to do. My mother turned on him in a fury and began yelling at him: "You take your hands off that child right now! How dare you? You aren't fit to be a parent!" She laced into him until he stopped what he was doing and meekly returned home, a thoroughly defeated man.

My mother could be narrow-minded in some of her views but was remarkably open-minded and generous with people. She became good friends with an older woman named Gabriella Sedgwick, a relative of her friend Alice Wohl. Gabriella was a mystic who practiced yoga—sometimes nude on the lawn in the early morning dew before everyone woke—long before there was a single yoga studio in western Massachusetts. She drove a small motorbike, wearing a helmet and a leopard-print biking jacket, even though she was a woman in her sixties, and she always carried a sleeping bag in case the desire to sleep under the stars took her. "I feel sure we've met in another life," she told my mother, who was much more practical and clear-eyed and unmystical. But my mother could see the kindness and generosity in Gabriella (she was always creating enormous problems as well as unexpected interesting situations through random acts of kindness to perfect strangers), and the fact that Gabriella lived a life of imagination with a sense of whimsy and poetry that made everything she did special. She came to visit my mother on Cape Cod one summer when we rented a house there, and Gabriella had my mother standing on her head and walking to the beach before dawn so that they could watch the sun rise over the ocean.

Gabriella could not have been more different from her friend Bessie Klein, with whom my mother became fast friends after buying our house. Having just lost her husband, Bessie was open to an important new friendship, as was my mother, having just moved to a new place, and they had fun scouring junkyards and antique shops to furnish the house. An extremely gifted artist who painted under her maiden name, Bessie Boris, she gave my mother a large painting to put over the mantelpiece. The child of Jewish immigrants from Russia, Bessie had the pessimism and self-deprecating humor of Eastern European Jewry. If you asked Bessie how she was, she would usually respond with a weary, fatalistic shrug of her shoulders. Admitting to happiness was an invitation to bad luck. At her funeral a close friend observed that Bessie firmly believed in life, liberty, and the pursuit of unhappiness. But Bessie was smart, perceptive, a great storyteller, and deeply kind, and could be wickedly funny. Occasionally, my mother would convince Bessie to go clothes shopping, and the two were something of an odd couple, my mother an elegant, free-spending Wasp and Bessie with the frugality of her immigrant roots and a utilitarian attitude toward things like clothing. My mother represented a bit of the pleasure principle for Bessie and generally succeeded in pushing Bessie into stretching both her budget and her taste: buying something more daring and more expensive than she would ever have done on her own. The outing would always result in funny stories, told with Bessie's self-deprecating humor, about how absurd she looked in this or that outfit, but you could tell she was secretly pleased with the final results.

3.

It would be inaccurate to say that my mother had suddenly solved all her problems by buying a second home and creating an independent life for herself. In other ways, she found it hard to change. Despite her breast cancer operation—followed by operations years later for bladder and lung cancer—my mother continued smoking two packs of cigarettes a day. She continued, whether in the city battling with my father or in the country having dinner with friends, to drink steadily every evening. She was not a fall-down drunk, but she was deeply dependent on alcohol. I would be surprised if there was a night in her adult life she didn't have a drink, except perhaps when she was in the hospital. She was part of a generation of drinkers—like many of her friends and relatives—for whom the arrival of evening was simply synonymous with cocktails. Some evenings she stopped after two or three and you didn't notice much, and other evenings she drank more and was visibly tipsy. She often became gloomy and lugubrious when she drank and sometimes cantankerous, expressing herself more strongly and with greater personal animus. My mother was something of a case of Dr. Jekyll and Mr. Hyde: extremely agreeable, easygoing, and fair-minded during the daytime; rather dark and even aggressive during the evenings. (If I had something important to talk to my mother about I avoided doing it in the evening.) I have often thought that women of my mother's generation, who had been trained to place their own needs and wants after those of their husband and children and had embraced a long-suffering life of self-sacrifice, had a very hard time acknowledging the normal selfish and aggressive impulses that everyone has; as a result, those impulses would come out in strange, backhanded, sometimes passive-aggressive ways. In my mother's case, I think she drank in part to let the more aggressive side of her personality—the pent-up anger built throughout her marriage—enjoy a few hours out of the cage. My father, who had no trouble expressing his aggressive or selfish side during daylight hours, had a very different relationship to drink. He normally didn't drink much, and when he did, he tended to be gregarious and sentimental, sides of his personality he didn't always express.

The contrast between my mother's morning and evening identities was dramatic. In the morning she radiated a wonderful optimism and energy. She made her lists and was full of projects and ideas. She would phone (and generally wake) Lucy and me to tell us of her latest scheme. Being with her was like taking a stroll on a spring day. But I found her evening presence often heavy and depressing. When she drank more than usual, her face would get rather puffy and she would lean her elbows on the dining table and prop her face up with her hands, as if the effort of holding up her head was too much for her. She looked like someone who had been beaten by life. (How could all the energy of morning have so completely vanished?) And her conversation often became a monologue of victimization: "What you kids don't realize is how hard it is to live with someone like Misha . . ."

While the problems with my father improved slightly and mattered a bit less than before, when they were together their marriage was not fundamentally different. "He was brutal to her," Katharine Kuh said. "Whenever Elizabeth would be talking intelligently about something, your father would shut her up, saying, 'Oh, you don't really know anything about this,' which was not good for her. Whereas she was very intelligent—and she had her own ideas—he always said she didn't know what she was talking about. But I think as the years went on, it got a little better. But he once almost broke my arm, did you know that? He yelled at me and he grabbed me. I thought he'd broken my arm! So we all went home . . . But I'm sure your mother could have left if she wanted to."

It was difficult not to see her addiction to smoking as deeply self-destructive. I remember when she had her first lung cancer operation, I went to see her in the recovery room the evening of the surgery. At the time, these operations were rather crude and brutal and involved literally sawing open the rib cage in order to remove the affected areas. That night my mother looked more dead than alive; she lay unconscious from the sedation, her face drained of any blood and seemingly of any life except for light breathing. Her body looked kind of broken and caved in, as if it had been in a terrible car crash. But when I visited the next day in her hospital room, she was sitting up in her bed, smoking. "You have got to be kidding!" I said. She looked slightly sheepish but perhaps even a little proud at having successfully smuggled a stash of cigarettes into a cancer ward. It was hard not to see something like this as a death wish.

4·

My mother was not as fulfilled in her work as she might have been. After the closing of *The Reporter*, she did a certain amount of freelance editing. She did a book for the anthropologist Oscar Lewis, which she enjoyed very much. But she needed something more regular that paid better, and she took a more or less full-time job at the book division of *Reader's Digest*, where she remained for about fifteen years. She was embarrassed to work for the *Digest*, that symbol of middlebrow culture, not to mention that its founder, DeWitt Wallace, was a staunch Republican and received the Presidential Medal of Freedom from my mother's bête noire Richard Nixon in 1972, not long after she began working there. It was something of a comedown in the world for her after working at places like *PM*, *Partisan Review*, *The New York Review of Books*, and *The Reporter*, but, as she used to say, it paid the bills and gave her and my father excellent health insurance. Truth be told, if you questioned her closely, she also took some pride in her work there and in her cutting skills, which were greatly prized. She would insist to anyone who accused her of desecrating some of the world's great books that she had improved them. "Believe me, there are plenty of dull stretches in there," she would say about having cut Boswell's *Life of Samuel Johnson*, and she very much believed that she greatly improved the world's most famous book in creating *The Reader's Digest Bible*. "Trust me," she said, "you don't need all those 'begots' and 'begats'—it's much better without them."

The Return of Michele Kamenetzki

While my mother was remaking her life up in Great Barrington, my father remained deeply tied to his old routines. He, too, bought a house, but not in order to change his life—on the contrary: in order not to change it. My parents had already been forced to move once, after our neighbor and landlord Abe Ellstein—the Irving Berlin of Second Avenue—dropped dead of a heart attack while his wife, Sylvia was at the hairdresser. Now that she was alone, Sylvia decided to sell the building. My parents moved to an apartment on Sixty-First Street, but several years later our landlord there announced that he was selling the apartment and told my father he could either buy it or move out. In order to avoid moving, my father went against his immigrant, renting mentality and bought the apartment. As it turned out, it was a great deal. New York real estate was at an all-time low, and for my father, who was a money-under-the-mattress type, this was the only intelligent investment he ever made. But the motivation was not to change.

My father in his fifties and sixties followed the same routine he had followed in his thirties and forties. He worked at home in his pajamas. Read the newspapers while lying on the couch and drinking little demitasse cups of black unsweetened espresso. He had given up cigarettes but now smoked a pipe. He would pass the day reading books, talking on the phone, clipping newspapers in his office and then eventually rouse himself and write his story. Even after the advent of new technologies like the fax machine and the personal computer, my father always worked on his old Royal typewriter and then read his pieces over the phone to a news clerk in Milan. His attachment to this old system of transmission led to the legend at the paper that my father didn't actually write down his pieces, but improvised them while dictating them over the phone. Given the clarity and orderliness of my father's pieces, this contributed to making him something of a mythic figure at the paper.

Although he was, in many ways, an extremely industrious and hardworking man, there was something extremely immobile about him: the working at home, the pajamas, the couch, a kind of repetition-compulsion in the stories he did. He spent his entire adult life after the war—forty-nine years—working for the same newspaper, almost all of it in the same job. While other journalists at the paper moved around, seeking glamorous foreign postings in places like Paris, London, Berlin, and Moscow, or changing papers and returning at a higher salary or with greater freedom, my father stayed in the same job, in his same routine, preferring to stay put. He spoke about writing books, and people of all kinds offered him every encouragement. Publishers who had never read a word he had written, based on his brilliant conversation and his overall reputation, offered him contracts and peppered him with book ideas. His thinking had so much more depth than that of most journalists—even those writing for major papers—and so much of what he said could never find its way into newspaper columns that it seemed only natural that he would turn to books. A couple of publishing houses even offered him generous advances, one of which he actually pocketed while never delivering the book. He seemed frozen. He was too much a creature of habit, and a book meant a change from his well-established, familiar routine. My father wrote a couple of pieces for *The New York Review of Books*, but he struggled mightily at it. I don't think it was writing in English—his English was excellent—but the sheer variation from his routine, writing at a different length with a different tone, without an office in Milan calling him every half hour to prod him.

He seemed in some ways a blocked man. I think he went through a couple of periods of depression and crisis about his work—although he would never have used that sort of language about himself. There were a few years in the 1970s when his productivity fell off markedly and he found it difficult to get off the couch, march upstairs, and write his story. "All this nonsense bores me terribly!" he would say, speaking of the political scene as a kind of fair of vanities. "I would much rather read a good book." From time to time, the paper would threaten to send over a second correspondent or a writer to do a series on America, and my father would suddenly switch gears and enter a period of frantic activity, writing two or three stories a day to convince the paper that sending someone else was a waste of time and money. Both his activity and his immobility sprang from the same source: a fear of change. I suspect (although I never dared speak with him about it) that his never entertaining the idea of divorce and always trying to talk my mother out of it had a similar origin: a desire that everything should remain the same.

Like his life itself—bifurcated between his American family life and his Italian professional life—my father's work method had a kind of emotional economy to it. My father banished emotion and personal passion from his work. He had been an enthusiastic Democrat in his early years in America but stopped voting in the 1970s. He was skeptical of political rhetoric and of political change and decided, I think, that having a political position would get in the way of his work, which was to analyze and explain a political phenomenon whether he agreed with it or not. Passion—with my mother as exhibit A of this approach—only clouded the judgment.

Thus my father could write appreciatively of Ronald Reagan, whose technical skill as a politician in setting and accomplishing an agenda, changing the mood and direction of the country, my father admired. Objectively speaking, my father would reason, Reagan is very good at what he does, and whether you like it or not is a matter of opinion. My mother, on the other hand, deplored everything that Reagan did and stood for: he played on not-so-hidden white resentment against blacks by talking about "welfare queens" driving Cadillacs; gutted environmental regulations; put homeless people out on the street by cutting the housing budget; broke unions; cut taxes for the wealthy; celebrated a culture of wealth and greed, etcetera, etcetera. For my mother, you could not separate politics from moral judgments, which to her were clear: "Let's face it: you and Reagan are with the Wall Street fat cats!" my mother would tell my father.

I could not help thinking that there was a strange inverse relationship between the chaos, furious emotion, and irrationality of my father's private life—the blizzard of paper, the screaming fits, the anxieties—and the clarity and order of the world of his articles. He would have a violent argument with my mother over a pile of newspapers he claimed she had thrown out—seeming like a man possessed—and then go upstairs and write his story: from his old, broken typewriter would appear this crystalline analysis written with a tone of Olympian detachment which would fit perfectly in a line of type in the august pages of the *Corriere della Sera*. My father was very fond of using numbers in his stories to summarize his key points. "There are five points to keep in mind when considering current American foreign policy vis-à-vis Russia." Or: "There are three reasons why the American Congress is unlikely to do [such and such]." Of course, it was hard, objectively, to see why the points should have been five (rather than four or six) and the reasons three (rather than four or two), but lining up his points numerically seemed to bring comfort to both writer and reader that order had been brought to bear on a messy and dangerous world—just as Spinoza, whom my father admired, used the formula of the geometric axiom to prove unprovable things like the existence of God. For my father, work was a sanctuary of order and reason in a life of disorder and unreason.

I suspect that to have written books, or books of a certain depth and complexity, my father would have had to draw on other parts of his own personality—the realm of passions, emotions, opinions—that he kept carefully walled up and separate from his work and that, if turned loose and allowed free rein, might have run amok and overwhelmed the carefully constructed and remarkably well-defended and highly successful edifice he had created.

Along with fear and neurosis, there was, however, also an element of wise passivity in my father's approach to life. He may have known, instinctively, that he would not have been at his best in the long form—the vast majority of journalistic books are mediocre, and only a few are genuinely good. As an old friend of my parents once said: "One of your father's greatest strengths is his laziness; it keeps him from making so many stupid mistakes."

He used to speak to me with enormous admiration of the figure of General Kutuzov, who is depicted in Tolstoy's *War and Peace*. Everyone criticized Kutuzov because he kept retreating in the face of Napoléon's conquering army. Napoléon represented the overweening pride of modern man, believing that his destiny depended merely on his own individual will. Kutuzov had the wisdom to understand that larger forces in the world shape history. Kutuzov kept retreating and retreating until Napoléon was eventually engulfed by the Russian winter and the frozen expanses of the Russian steppe. My father used to tell me about this with enormous relish, and, although he didn't say so, he clearly identified with the old Russian general. Indeed, he applied the Kutuzov strategy to almost everything: procrastination was almost his second profession. No decision was too important to be put off—when he was offered a promotion he asked for more time to make up his mind. (That his teeth didn't need to be removed after forty years of putting off going to see a dentist indicated, in his view, that his strategy of avoidance had been sound.)

He believed that if you did what you wanted and were good at it, the rest of life would take care of itself. One of the striking things to me about my father's life is that all of the biggest breaks in his career were a series of happy accidents, which he had the ability to take full advantage of. He fell into journalism almost by chance through his boyhood friendships. His forced immigration to the United States placed him in a perfect position to begin work as a foreign correspondent. At a certain point, in 1980, my father was heavily courted by a rival newspaper, *La Repubblica*, which had started just a few years earlier and was challenging his employer, the *Corriere della Sera*, for its place as Italy's top newspaper. In order to steal away one of the competition's stars, *La Repubblica* offered him a plum deal: he would be a kind of planetary correspondent with the ability to report from anywhere in Europe and the United States, maximum freedom, and a lot of money. He negotiated and signed the contract, but when *La Repubblica* asked for it back, he said he needed a few more days to think things over. He spent the next two weeks wandering around Rome and Milan in a state of high anxiety and psychological paralysis. He would ask everyone he met what he should do, listing the pros and cons of taking the job. He dithered and delayed so long that he gave time to a group of journalists within his own paper to organize a counteroffer that more or less matched *La Repubblica*'s, without the part about being planetary correspondent, which may have meant much more movement than my father in his heart of hearts was ready for. The editor of *La Repubblica* was furious, convinced that my father had used him in a perfectly calibrated effort to get a raise from the *Corriere* without any real intention of moving—but he didn't know that what appeared to him as shrewd calculation had been massive indecision and the deep immobility in the marrow of my father's bones: he wanted to move; he simply couldn't.

It struck me as a sign of my father's fear of change, and I regretted that he had been unable to take a new opportunity that might have stretched him. He was talking excitedly about reporting from places like Paris and Russia, but truth be told he was happy to stay in his pajamas. And yet he may have known something about himself. *La Repubblica* was more a journal of opinion whose left-of-center leanings were evident throughout the paper. My father's great strength—which Italians readers often called his "Anglo-Saxon" type of journalism—his cool, detached, analytical style, fit better with the *Corriere*'s stodgier tone, centrist politics, and reputation for being the more authoritative newspaper. As some of the paper's most established journalists left for *La Repubblica* or other papers, retired, or died, my father, already extremely well-known and respected, one of the last of a series of great journalists to emerge after World War II, began to be seen increasingly as one of the pillars—indeed, a symbol—of the paper's best traditions, a name that induced automatic recognition and respect.

In fact, when the paper, in the midst of a serious crisis, changed editors in 1984, the management offered him the position of editor in chief of the *Corriere*. Although it was perhaps the most sought-after job in Italian journalism, he hesitated. He was afraid that it might jeopardize his American citizenship. Italian law requires that the editor of a newspaper be an Italian citizen; the editor's official title is *direttore responsabile*, meaning that the editor is legally responsible for all that appears in the paper. At the time, the U.S. government looked askance at dual citizenship, and for my father, twice a refugee, his American passport had been the life raft that he had clung to during the storm of World War II. Forty years had passed and Italy was a well-established democracy, and the chances of the American government actually revoking his citizenship were remotely small (under the rules, in order to lose your citizenship, you had to declare your loyalty to another state and vote in another country's elections). But my father was in no way ready to take even the slightest risk and place himself at the mercy of Italian law again. For him the years of the racial laws, in which they had suddenly been deprived of all their rights, in which they had waited and waited for their American visa while Hitler conquered country after country, the visa always about to arrive but then suddenly out of their grasp—and the memory of the poor Hungarian gentleman who was turned back at Portuguese passport control to almost certain death—it was all too much for my father. He didn't take the job.

When he turned down the offer, I felt a bit disappointed, as if my father, when finally offered the opportunity of a lifetime, had allowed his own private demons, his own neuroses, to paralyze him, as if when the brass ring came around he could not lift his arm to seize it. I found myself thinking of Dante's famous phrase "*Colui che fece per viltade il gran rifiuto*," "He who out of cowardice made the big refusal," referring to the medieval pope Celestine V, who had abdicated the papacy in order to retire to a monastery and allow the powerful political schemer who became Boniface VIII to ascend the throne of Saint Peter's, with (in Dante's view) disastrous results for Italy. But for my father, once again, the wisest policy was doing nothing.

To my and most people's surprise, it proved to be the right thing. Three years later, they offered him the position again, and he accepted. This time he felt that the paper really wanted him, and, most important, the American government had changed its position on dual citizenship. Still, my father fretted, delayed, and hesitated. "Listen," I told him, "if it took this country thirty years to deport Ivan Demjanjuk, the Butcher of Treblinka, I don't think they are going to deport you." He snarled at the comparison but accepted my point. "But what if they don't give me my Italian citizenship back?" he asked. He had been away from Italy too long. "Powerful interests want you to take this job, so it will be resolved very easily." And, sure enough, an Italian judge simply ruled that since the laws depriving him of his Italian citizenship had long since been abrogated, he had always been an Italian citizen in the eyes of the Italian law. They handed him a crisp new Italian passport—but with the name Michele Kamenetzki. Whereas in the United States, you can be whoever you say you are, in Italy, you are not allowed to change your name.

Thus, rather happily, toward the end of his life, the halves of his life—or perhaps two important different parts of his life, which had been kept separate—came together. It was as if he was reconciling with the life and name he had left behind.

He also regained friendships from his youth that had seemed lost. After World War II, geography and political differences had separated him from most of the close circle of friends he had shared with Giaime, many of whom were deeply committed Communists. At the height of the Cold War, Lucio Lombardo Radice, Pietro Ingrao, Antonello Trombadori, Aldo and Ugo Natoli, and Giaime's younger brother, Luigi, turned their backs on my father, regarding him—since he worked for the *Corriere della Sera*, the ultimate bourgeois newspaper—as aiding and abetting the enemy. Italian Communist culture of the 1940s, 1950s, and 1960s was exceptionally doctrinaire. Its leaders often insisted on taking their vacations in places like Bulgaria and refused on principle to travel to the United States—although, in fairness, the United States routinely denied access to known Communist Party members. My father, although he rarely spoke of it, was deeply hurt that his close childhood friends did not hesitate to throw over their friendship in the name of ideology. This gradually changed during the 1970s, when the Italian Communists became much more openly critical of the Soviet Union and more appreciative of the imperfect virtues of liberal bourgeois democracy. They were genuinely glad when their old friend was named the head of the country's largest paper, and many of them sent congratulations and reestablished contact. "Tell your father he is a bourgeois reactionary!" Giancarlo Pajetta, a well-known Italian Communist leader, told me jokingly when I met him in the late 1980s. They could now joke about the rift that separated them, but Pajetta was repeating something he might have said in all seriousness ten or twenty years earlier.

When an editor takes over at a newspaper in Italy it is common to write a front-page editorial piece introducing himself (or herself) to readers. These are usually pro forma commitments to journalistic integrity and respect for readers, and vows to follow a paper's best traditions while blazing new paths, etcetera. My father's piece had some of this (it was entitled "A Modern Newspaper for a Country That Is Changing"), but it also introduced a personal element that was entirely new to my father's work.

> This return to the country in which I was raised and in which I was formed culturally and psychologically represents for me, on a personal level, a moment of intense emotion, and has the significance of completing a cycle that the tragic years of the racial persecutions seemed to have broken.
>
> During my long stay in America, the *Corriere della Sera* constituted my constant tie to Italy, and the decision to accept the editorship today reflects and confirms this truth.

It was the first time that my father sounded such a personal note in his work, and it was certainly the first time he had ever made mention of being Jewish or acknowledged the existence of the racial laws. I felt proud that he had mentioned his Jewishness in such a public forum; it seemed an act of courage for a man who had sometimes hidden or lied about this part of his life. And it seemed a sign of strength and health that he could refer to the time of the racial laws—a painful and traumatic event in his life.

Even so, he retained many of the deep, instinctive fears of the refugee. When he would travel back to the United States, he would not even bring his Italian passport, stashing it at the house of a good friend in Milan, for fear U.S. Customs would find it. "I left my Italian passport with Valeria," he would say in a conspiratorial whisper, as if some government eavesdropping device might be listening. Obviously, he had a kind of nightmare fantasy that upon entering the United States he would be strip-searched by border guards. They would find his Italian passport and suddenly deport him or take away his American citizenship. At some level, he remained the refugee who stood in the passport lines in Madrid and Lisbon and New York, terrified to see who would be admitted and who would be turned back.

As a family, we were rather surprised by this unexpected development in my father's (and our own) life. How would this man who worked alone in his pajamas and did not seem to have control over the piles of newspapers in his bedroom office suddenly manage hundreds of people and run one of Europe's largest and most important newspapers? It seemed bizarre to pick a sixty-seven-year-old man with a bad heart who had never worked as an editor, had never worked inside the paper, and had left Italy forty-six years earlier.

But there were good reasons for the choice, which was a kind of vindication of my father's Kutuzov strategy. Italian journalism at the time was (once again) in a moment of intense political struggle, and there had been a ferocious battle on the part of various forces to take control of Italy's largest paper. Most of the people who had been working inside the Italian context were associated with this or that group—had, indeed, cultivated relations with a particular power axis—and were therefore feared and bitterly opposed by other factions. My father was friendly with everyone but not compromised with any single group. Having been outside the country for his entire career at the *Corriere* made him a neutral candidate who was above the fray. His natural caution—and his refusal to take a clear political position—had kept him from becoming too closely associated with any faction. His natural curiosity, one of his best qualities, meant that he could talk with any faction; he loved talking to people he found *simpatici* or intelligent, whether they were Communists or right-wing conservatives. His strategy of concentrating on his work and letting the rest take care of itself had worked: there was no one at the

paper who did not have great respect for the quality of his work. His fear
of change worked in his favor. He had been at the *Corriere* for forty-one
straight years and was by now synonymous with the paper itself, the only
figure who brought together the warring factions within.

He was not the typical newspaper editor. He was, in fact, already a
rather sick man when he took the job—something, of course, he did not
share with the paper. He had had a heart attack three years earlier, and he
had two leaky heart valves. Often he would sleep until eleven, would
miss the paper's morning story meeting and wander into the office around
lunchtime. He left most of the day-to-day editing of the paper to two
strong deputy editors. But he still managed to be a surprisingly effective
editor, giving a definite tone and direction to the paper.

Not long after he took over as editor, national elections were called in
Italy and he received a call from the head of the paper's Rome office:
"What line should we take?" the man asked. "What do you mean?" my
father asked, genuinely confused. "What political line are we supposed
to take during the elections?" he explained. "There is no line, just tell us
what's happening." That simple direction, which would seem to be basic
to good journalism—"there is no line, just tell us what's happening"—
was a radical change in the Italian context. While extremely insecure in
his personal life, my father was remarkably free of insecurity in his professional world: he was not threatened by other intelligent people and
was keen to hire the best journalists he could find. He was able to woo
back to the paper a number of first-rate reporters who had left during the
ideological battles of the previous decade—conservatives who had left in
the late 1970s, when the paper had swerved sharply to the left, and left-
wing journalists who had left when the direction of the paper had been
taken over by a right-wing cabal. He hired a number of smart young
journalists who injected new energy into the paper.

Early on, he was able to win an important battle with the newspaper
union: getting it to drop a long-standing rule that would have prevented
him from rejecting an article on the basis of its poor quality. This would
seem an elementary principle of a good newspaper, but the rule had been
adopted during the ideological civil war to prevent whoever was in power
from boycotting the pieces of those out of favor. My father's professional
credibility convinced the union to overcome its resistance.

In a sense, my father applied the Kutuzov strategy to the *Corriere*. At
the time, the paper had been overtaken by *La Repubblica*, which had

thrived because of its quickness in spotting trends, banner headlines, polemical style, and ability to create controversy. Going against common wisdom, my father did not try to compete by matching *La Repubblica* blow for blow, scoop for scoop. "We shouldn't try to be first," he said; "the *Corriere* should be a slow newspaper." He felt the *Corriere* should wait a day or two for an event to settle before coming out with a major editorial. He understood that as an old, established paper, the *Corriere*'s strength lay in its credibility and its European reputation as the most authoritative paper in Italy. Gradually, many readers began to find *La Repubblica* too partisan and political, and the *Corriere* regained the terrain it had lost.

On a personal level, he was extremely well liked. Although he was often rude and overbearing in his private life, he had a strange lack of arrogance in his professional demeanor. He was free of a quality that Italians call *prepotenza*, a great word that has no exact equivalent in English but that means something like "the arrogance of power." In Italy *prepotenza* seems endemic to high places; it is what people who climb to the top seem to live for: yelling at and mistreating subordinates, keeping visitors waiting and waiting in order to impress them with your importance; the envious use of perquisites that distinguish you from others. A previous editor of the *Corriere* had forbidden his company driver from listening to the radio while he was waiting (for hours) in the car for the editor to eat his dinner. My father became very popular with the typesetters and the workers at the paper because he often ate at the paper's cafeteria rather than using the special VIP dining room, where the top editors normally ate. While I'm sure my father didn't do this as a populist move—I expect he simply found the cheap and greasy food tasty and convenient—it is also true that it never entered his head that he needed to exercise privileges to set himself apart. The secretaries, drivers, and company staff loved him because he genuinely liked them and did not consider them less interesting or worthy than the paper's top journalists—some of whom he found puffed up, vain, and silly. He had a jaundiced, skeptical view of people and told very funny stories that mocked the self-importance of some of the paper's leading peacocks as well as of some of Italy's leading politicians.

If he was free of *prepotenza* at work, my father fully enjoyed his apotheosis—remarking with pleasure on how people now stopped him in the street or in stores—and talked about his new status with a kind of naive vanity that was almost touching in his candid, unabashed pleasure.

"I feel like a rock star," he said. At another point, he said, "It's all like a movie. I have a part to play and I play it pretty well."

To the surprise of many, my mother accompanied my father to Milan, effectively moving there more or less full-time with him. When I asked her why she had supported my father's decision to take the job and followed him to Milan, she said, "Well, I didn't want to spend the last years of my life arguing with Misha over what kind of tuna fish to buy at the supermarket." She finally set about learning Italian, something she had taken a few ineffectual stabs at over the years. At sixty-seven, she found this was a doomed uphill struggle, but she made a pretty valiant go at it. "She's the first lady of Milan!" my father said, glad to be able to confer some of his newfound status and fame on her.

My father became a highly desirable guest at the fashionable *salotti* of Milan's rich and famous. My mother had relatively little interest in this but went along to be a good sport. After one particularly glamorous event, a friend asked my mother how she had liked it: "It was about as interesting as being trapped in the powder room of the Chicago train station." When telling me about her new life there, she said, "You have no idea how tiring it is spending an evening exercising your facial muscles trying not to look stupid by pretending that you know what is going on."

For the first months, my parents lived in a fancy hotel in Milan. They had two adjacent rooms, but, for the first time in decades, they actually shared a bed. "We are so exhausted all we want to do is sleep and stay in bed," my father said, as if they were enjoying a kind of late-in-life second honeymoon. Eventually, the paper rented a gorgeous apartment in walking distance of the paper, in one of Milan's nicest neighborhoods. My mother got to fix up another apartment, which she did flawlessly, and my father continued his life as a "rock star."

In status-conscious Milan, my mother did not appear particularly cowed by the fancy people she met, and many of them found her straightforward lack of pretense refreshing and even a bit disarming. At one party, when she was introduced to Leopoldo Pirelli, the head of the Pirelli tire company, one of Italy's richest and most powerful men, my mother politely asked him if he, too, was a journalist. "I believe my name is well-known even in the United States!" he replied huffily. But when my mother didn't flinch and continued her conversation with him unruffled, he—used to being treated with greater deference—seemed impressed and a bit sheepish; he was very attentive to her the rest of the evening and gave her a ride home in his bulletproof limousine.

Despite age and illness (breast and bladder cancer, followed by two lung cancer operations), she remained extremely attractive and young-looking. Even after sixty years of smoking, her skin was remarkably fresh, and her legs were shapely and she dressed with a very elegant, understated style. "Look how pretty!" my father said in a rare moment of affection. "You have no idea how lovely she was when we met—a dream, a dream, and she's very pretty, feel that skin," he would say, touching her cheek with his hand—the only form of physical affection I ever saw between my parents. "Oh, I'm just an old bag," my mother would say, demonstrating impatience and embarrassment while being, I suspect, secretly pleased at the unexpected compliment.

Endgame

I.

My parents' Italian idyll was brought to a close by illness. In 1990, my
mother was diagnosed with a second lung cancer, and the doctor announced after the surgery that he was afraid there were still microscopic
amounts of cancer left, which would present themselves again sooner or
later. My father's heart continued to deteriorate. He spent longer and longer hours in bed and spent more time moaning and groaning about his
health. "I think my pulse is strange," he would say. "*Eleezabet*, do you
think my pulse is strange?" The move to Milan hardly changed the basic
dynamic between my parents. Their marriage was still rather brutal and
had its ugly moments. At first my father treated my mother with greater
care, visibly grateful for the effort she was making on his behalf to adapt
to a new country. But after some months, he lapsed into his usual behavior and would make fun of her Italian, even though she was making a
rather gallant (if only minimally successful) effort in that regard.

Suspecting that she didn't have very long to live, my mother began
spending more time in the States during the last two years of their time in
Milan, so that she could see more of the people she cared most about: my
sister, Lucy, and other relatives and friends. (I was living in Rome at the
time.)

In early 1992, my mother seemed to slow down, complained of frequent dizziness, and had trouble walking more than a very short distance. We were rather impatient with her until she was diagnosed with
six inoperable brain tumors. Livia M., one of my mother's younger Italian friends, came to see her when she got back from the doctor's office,
having received what was essentially a death sentence. When my father,
who knew the news, came in, he sprawled out on the couch and said, "I'm

exhausted! *Eleezabet*, where's my dinner?" My mother could barely walk, and so Livia prepared a simple supper, appalled by my father's selfishness and apparent lack of concern for his dying wife.

The Italians told me that her case was hopeless and that she would last only a matter of weeks. I flew up to Milan from Rome, to take her back to New York to see if doctors there felt that anything could be done and, if not, to let her die at home. At the airport we had a wheelchair waiting for my mother, and we were taken up in a special truck with a hydraulic lift to bring her wheelchair right up to the entrance of the plane.

We had a good chance to talk during the flight. (I was struggling between the vague desire to watch the crummy movies they were showing and the desire to take advantage of the opportunity to talk to my mother. No matter what the circumstances, one never ceases to be trivial.) At a certain point my mother said to me, "You know, I think at some level I've known for months. All during the fall I've been having very strange dreams. Dreams about setting right certain things I've done wrong in my life, trivial little things, about someone I was rude to when I was sixteen . . . I can't even remember the contents exactly but it was as if I was reviewing all sorts of things in my life . . ."

At another point she said, "I was never really scared with my past operations. I somehow always knew I would be all right. They just cut me open, removed what they had to, and sewed me back. This is the first time I've really thought I might die."

"You're kidding me," I said. "You had four extremely serious cancer operations; didn't you ever consider what the stakes were? Obviously you didn't, given that you continued smoking all this time. I have been worried that you might die from the time I was ten—after all, you've had friends who died of breast cancer. I'm amazed it's taken you this long."

We got home and Lucy arrived soon after us. We had a simple dinner of spaghetti with pesto sauce, and Mom was having real trouble eating the spaghetti with her fork. Strands of spaghetti kept slipping off and into her lap. She was wearing a blue cashmere scarf around her neck, and at a certain point the end of the scarf with the tassels fell onto her plate. "I'm sorry for making such a mess," Mom said apologetically. Perhaps because of the fatigue of the trip, the tension of the situation, and the desire to break it, I started joking around: "Don't worry about it, Mom," I said, "just make sure you don't eat the tassels of your scarf."

Lucy, who lived in Los Angeles, was able to stay only a few days because her son, Lucas, was just a few years old at the time. My wife, Sarah, joined me for a couple of weeks, and although Mom began radiation treatments, she seemed to get weaker and weaker. We had to help her brush her teeth and go to the bathroom. She looked like death—or like a concentration camp inmate—emaciated, rail-thin, her flesh consumed by cancer, her head shorn by radiation, wobbling unsteadily on her toothpick legs, the tumors pressing on her brain and impairing her balance and her sight. She didn't even have the strength to lift herself off one of those raised toilet seats. Seeing her so badly reduced—needing help from her son and daughter to get off the toilet—was a vision of death in all its humiliating squalor.

She was given massive doses of cortisone to relieve the swelling of the tumors that were pressing on her brain and making her lose her balance. Cortisone, like drink, accentuated the Jekyll-Hyde aspect of her personality.

"You're not on my wavelength!" she would yell at me. As she began losing her hair, she insisted we get her several turbans of different colors from Bloomingdale's—her fastidiousness and her instance on maintaining appearances (several colors, not one) never abandoned her, even though she could barely move. Because of the cortisone she had trouble sleeping and would often be up half the night, thinking and smoking. We gave her a loud little bell so that she could call us with minimal effort. Sometimes she would wake us up in the middle of the night with some bizarre idea or other. "We need to call someone to fix the roof! It needs to be done!" "Mom, we have a lot of bigger problems right now, let's wait until you're better," I would say. "Shut up, you're not on my wavelength! Somebody has to keep this house going." She was down to about eighty pounds, and what little flesh she had hung flaccidly on her stick-like legs as she tried to hobble, like someone walking on stilts, toward the bathroom. At a certain point, she rang her little bell furiously and announced: "I've got it! The whole history of the Kennedy administration is going to have to be rewritten. I have to call Arthur Schlesinger [the former Kennedy aide and biographer] right away! I now totally understand the Cuban Missile Crisis. It's cortisone! Kennedy was on cortisone because of his bad back. It totally explains the Cuban Missile Crisis!" I managed to keep her from calling Arthur Schlesinger with her cortisone view of history. "I've never been so brilliant—or so crazy," she said at one point. "Well, Mom, you've got that half right anyway," I said.

The cortisone worked something like a truth serum, and my mother began settling scores with various people in her life about things that had been bothering her for some time.

When her friend Bessie called to find out how she was and asked about my father in Italy, my mother stopped in her tracks. "Bessie, I hate the way you say that. It's not 'It-ly,' it's Italy, It-a-lee, three syllables, not two!" When my uncle George telephoned, my mother decided to give him a lesson on women and sex; apparently, in a previous conversation, my uncle had mentioned being bothered by the fact that one of his daughters had used the word "horny." "George, you are just going to have to face the facts. Women get horny, too, that's all there is to it!" When another friend called, my mother began doling out advice about what the friend should do about her adolescent daughter's appearance. "Listen, Sylvia, you have to accept that Kira's bottom is way, way too big. There's no way she's going to find a man or have a normal life with an ass that big. We're not talking diet here, we're talking major surgery!"

While I was there we began taping interviews about her life, which seemed to me a strategy for talking about things we wanted to talk about in what appeared to be our last time together while avoiding the appearance of some kind of final deathbed confession. I left after about six weeks in New York. Meanwhile, my father's health had deteriorated dramatically. He had what we thought was a minor hernia operation, but then suddenly when I spoke with him on the phone while I was with my mother in New York he showed signs of losing his mind. He couldn't remember his own phone number. He stayed in bed for weeks, telling the paper each day that he would be back in the office after a few days. His Italian doctors insisted that he needed a heart valve replacement operation. The only way we could manage these joint medical disasters, as a family, was to have our two parents in the same place, and we also did not feel comfortable subjecting my father to such a major operation in Italy, where care was often spotty. Lucy and I decided that we needed to get my father back to New York, where he could have the heart valve operation. My father, although confused and disoriented, retained a wily and shrewd sense of self-preservation: for at least six weeks, he had managed to keep the management of his newspaper in the dark about what was the matter with him. Italy was in the midst of a major political crisis (again?) as the huge financial scandal known as *Tangentopoli* (Bribe City) was unfolding, and the nation's largest newspaper effectively had no editor.

My father sensed instinctively that if the paper knew how sick he was, he would lose his position. When I arrived in Milan, close personal friends communicated to me that the publisher of the newspaper wanted to see me to find out what was going on. Without telling my father, I went with very mixed feelings. On the one hand, I knew that this was the one way to convince my father to return to New York and have the heart operation; on the other, I felt as if I was betraying my father, since telling the publisher about his medical situation would almost certainly bring to a close my father's happy idyll as editor. But in truth, there wasn't any choice. My father, in his current state, could not be the editor of anything. He could barely get out of bed, he didn't know what time of day it was, and the leakage of liquid from his heart valve was so bad that his ankles were the width of tree trunks and his testicles the size of tennis balls. He would die if he didn't get help soon. I begged the publisher to tell my father in the strongest possible terms that he should return to New York and take care of his medical problems. Luckily, my father was lucid enough to take his advice. Lucy flew to New York and oversaw his operation. When a heart surgeon examined him, he didn't even let him return home to get a pair of pajamas and a toothbrush; they replaced one of his heart valves with a pig's heart valve, repaired the other valve, and performed a quadruple heart bypass. My father was so feeble that the operation nearly killed him, and Lucy remained for two weeks while he was in intensive care, hanging by a thread.

So it looked in early 1992 as though we were going to lose both our parents, but it didn't happen. My mother, to the astonishment of everyone, in particular her own doctors, rallied and made a miraculous recovery. I had left New York expecting that I would never see her again, but then on the phone she would keep saying, "Well, I feel a little stronger today," and the next thing I knew she was out of bed, walking around, running errands on her own and even driving. The six brain tumors that were pressing against her brain and had made it almost impossible for her to walk had vanished from the CAT scans and MRIs. My mother's doctors began to speak about her as a subject of great interest. There were very few patients in medical literature who had effectively survived four different primary cancers. Over a period of more than twenty years, she had gotten and beaten cancers of the breast, bladder, and lung, none of which had returned. Her second lung cancer was entirely unrelated to the first (it was in the other lung), and now she appeared to be winning against brain tumors. She was extremely vulnerable to cancer—a life-time of smoking didn't help—but also seemed to possess extraordinary powers of recuperation.

Luckily, the rhythms of my parents' illnesses were different enough that they were actually able to help each other a bit and ease the strain on Lucy and me, who were reeling from this double parental disaster. My parents passed a rather nice period together when they were both conva-lescing, and their illnesses suddenly gave my aunt Lally a new role in life. "Florence Nightingale is coming over," my mother would tell me ironi-cally when we spoke on the phone. My father had generally avoided my aunt during the previous forty years, but now he needed her, and she was thrilled to be needed and to have an important role in her beloved brother's life.

When my mother was well enough to drive again, my parents took a trip up to our house in Great Barrington, and they took with them a nurse named Lillian, who had been helping take care of them. Lillian lived in the Bronx and had spent very little time in the country. She was fasci-nated to hear about and mildly worried about all the animals that lived in the woods nearby. She didn't quite believe that there were really deer liv-ing there and was anxious to see for herself. One day when my mother and Lillian were off getting groceries, my father suddenly heard the clat-tering of hooves and a great commotion in the kitchen. A young, con-fused deer had broken through the screen door to the kitchen and couldn't figure out how to leave. My father called Lucy in California and asked what he should do. She suggested first closing the door leading from the kitchen to the dining room, so the deer couldn't get into the rest of the house, and then opening the outside kitchen door so he could leave. My father closed the internal door but decided not to let the deer out of the kitchen, so that Lillian could see it. When Lillian and my mother returned, they were presented with the curious spectacle of a deer in the kitchen.

I returned home that summer and saw my mother for what turned out to be the last time. She remained in remission for more than a year, but the tumors returned in the early spring of 1993. "I don't want to put all of you through this again," she said, contemplating the possibility of not treating the tumors. But the doctors explained that without radiation her death would be very difficult and painful; she would gradually go blind as the tumors pressed tighter on her brain. My mother, never fond of pain and a great believer in the miracles of modern medicine, decided to go ahead with the treatment. Once again, to our amazement, she began to get better. Having seen her rise like Lazarus from the dead, we somehow believed that she would beat this as well, but at a certain point her body just couldn't take the beating that both the disease and the treatment were giving her. Doctors suspended treatment in late April, because she had become too weak and her white blood cell count too low, but neither Lucy nor I grasped that she was near the end. My father didn't want to believe that she was dying either, and we learned only later that she was now spending most of her days sleeping. She didn't urge either of us to come see her—perhaps she, too, didn't want to face that the end was near. Denial in her past illnesses had served her well. Also, to give her credit, she genuinely didn't want to bother us. The only one who seemed to know what was going on was Lillian, who had seen many others die before. She sensed my mother was near the end and decided to sleep at my parents' apartment on the night of May 7–8. She tried to make herself comfortable on a chaise longue in my mother's bedroom. My mother woke at one point and was surprised to find Lillian still there. She said, "What are you doing here, Toots? You should get some sleep, go into the other room and lie down." I found it extremely touching that her last words—spoken when she could barely move—were full of both playful good humor and concern for someone else.

When my father called to tell me the news of my mother's death, I was surprised that he sounded remarkably strong, calm, and rational. But then toward the end of the conversation I sensed something else: he started complaining about the fact that my mother's doctor was going to Philadelphia instead of coming to the funeral home where my mother's body had been taken. "We need him to sign the death certificate, now he can't sign the death certificate until Monday," my father said. "What do we care about a death certificate at this point?" I asked, wondering why my father was worrying about this bureaucratic detail. "Well, maybe she's not dead," he said. "There have been cases like that, you know." He sounded strong because he was in a state of total denial. When we spoke a few hours later, it had begun to sink in. "Oh, I feel terrible. I don't think I can live. To think I will never see that pretty face again. You know, even when she was dead she looked so pretty . . . Poor thing, she didn't have an easy life . . . and I made things so much harder for her."

2.

My father outlived my mother by about two years, and I remember those years as a rather sweet time of our life together.

Sad to say, it was always easier to deal with him by himself than with my mother around. It was the sorry paradox of their marriage: both were extremely charming and engaging people by themselves, but there was something toxic about the two of them together that ended up souring if not ruining most of the times I saw them both. Also, my father, perhaps because of physical frailty and sheer need, mellowed with age. He didn't have the energy and stamina to yell and argue the way he had as a young man. Now that he tasted mortality, had achieved what he was going to achieve, he suddenly became much more family-oriented. "The only people I feel like seeing are my family. The rest of the world bores me stiff," he would say.

He would call Lucy for cooking advice as he began to try to fend for himself in the kitchen, or just to chat. Since I was living across town, he called me three or four times a day on matters small and large. And we saw each other often. The conversations, which I often jotted down in my journal, often had a kind of Beckettian quality that reminded me of *Waiting for Godot* and *Endgame*.

> MISHA: I'm a dead man. (*Pause.*) Well, aren't you going to say anything?
> ME: Yes, I did think you looked pretty awful the other day.
> MISHA: What are you talking about? I look perfectly well. I don't have any strength. Not always. I wrote a story the other day. People in Milan called me to say it was excellent.
> ME: Well, you may be dead, but your ego is still alive and pretty healthy.

The next day:

> MISHA: Aren't you going to ask about my health? Yesterday I said I was dying.
> ME: I can tell from your chipper voice that you're not dead.

December 20, 1994:

> MISHA: I am close to death . . . Nothing works. My joints ache. I
> don't feel like getting dressed, I don't feel like going out. With
> great effort, I made myself some lamb chops. I am on my last
> legs. Actually, that's not true.

December 22, 1994:

> MISHA: I think my time is up. I have done all I can. I've probably
> reached the top of my career, so I might as well die now. What
> do you think?
> ME: I think you are a good violin player. You come in, play your
> violin, win everyone's sympathy, and then you'll probably
> outlive the rest of us.
> MISHA: I can't find an article I wrote on the American economy
> during the Truman administration; it was excellent . . . as
> always.
> ME: You don't need a fan club, you provide your own.
> MISHA: Well, I know my good points and I know my bad points.

My father led a simpler life, cutting back on his old busy social life and
staying home a lot. During his last two years, his sister, my aunt Lally,
came over almost every evening for supper. Neither of them was much in
the cooking department, and Lally would often go fetch some prepared
food for the two of them. My father was now grateful for his sister's help.
"I was too hard on her. She's very sweet in her own way," he would say.
My aunt, who adored my father, could not have been happier: for the first
time since their childhood, she was playing a central role in his life. It
was funny to see them together, the two Kamenetzkis, brother and sister,
united again. They looked a lot alike—the same long, sharp pointy nose,
the big ears, the same Russian pallor. And as they began to shrink with
age, they looked like a pair of children. "The two of you are like the
Katzenjammer Kids," I said, kidding my father, referring to a comic strip
from the early twentieth century featuring a pair of inseparable little
children. My father had enough of a sense of humor that he could both
take a joke and make one at his own expense. When I asked him what he
was doing one day, he replied, "Well, Katzenjammer is coming over."

Sometimes Sarah and I drove with him for the weekend to our house in Massachusetts. There was one particularly funny trip during which we stopped on the way for gas and my father disappeared to go to the bathroom. At a certain point, a young boy came up to our car and, pointing to my father, who was walking from behind the gas station toward the car, asked us, "Do you know that man?" "I'm afraid we do," I answered. "He just peed in the parking lot behind the gas station," the boy said. It turned out that my father couldn't figure out how to open the men's room door, which required a key from the gas station attendant, and had simply pissed en plein air. "You're lucky they didn't arrest you for exposing yourself to a minor!" I said. And for the rest of the trip, we kept repeating: "Do you know that man?" Yet it was clear he was very fragile. At another point during the weekend, when we went out to eat, his feet suddenly seemed to give out underneath him, he lost his balance, and his feet did some bizarre pretzel-like contortion. It almost looked as if he was a teenager doing break dancing. Luckily, he righted himself just before falling over. "No more break dancing!" I told him when we were walking around.

My father developed a kind of world-weary philosophical attitude toward life, in which his traditional pessimism was leavened with a bit of humor and a certain amount of dramatic posing. "*Siamo nati per soffrire,*" he would say. "We are born to suffer."

He repeated a funny Italian couplet:

Sia che vado sia che vengo
Stronzi lascio e stronzi trovo.

Whether I stay or whether I go
Shits I leave behind and shits I find.

During what turned out to be the last summer of my father's life, Lucy, her husband, David, and their son, Lucas, came east and rented a house with some friends on Long Island. My father, Sarah, and I decided, as a result, to rent something nearby so that we could see them. It was perhaps the best holiday with my father I can recall. He was so relaxed and happy that he actually allowed me for the first time to interview him with a tape recorder about his life. He wasn't very forthcoming, but I still learned a good number of things. Large parts of the interview consisted of exchanges such as the following:

ME: What was so-and-so like?

MISHA: What do you mean, what was he was like? How can I answer a question like that?

ME: You could try.

MISHA: He was how he was.

But on other subjects he was loquacious and funny. He tended to stay away from the more serious, emotional topics and steered toward amusing anecdotes.

In the afternoons, we would meet Lucy and her family at the beach. My father had a huge, thick pink scar across his chest from his heart operation—it looked like a large pink snake. He had been told that the best thing for the scar was salt water, and so he was determined at all costs to get into the ocean every day. The surf was often strong enough to knock a fit younger man off his feet, let alone a sick man of seventy-four, who looked at least ten years older. We had to take him in—usually two of us—each holding one of his scrawny white arms and slowly maneuvering him in above his waist so that he could simply lean back for a moment and plunge his body into the cold ocean water. He stood unsteadily on his thin, spindly legs, but there was something extremely poignant about this frail old man's desire to make it into the ocean. The rest of the time, we lay on the beach and chatted and watched the seagulls that soared and circled and cavorted above us. My father had had so little exposure to nature that he found the simple presence of wild birds exhilarating. "Look, look at him!" he would say as a bird did some interesting diving maneuver. "*Gabbiano! Gabbianuccio!*" ("Seagull! Little seagull!") he would say to them in Italian. He enjoyed the first and only grandchild he had during his lifetime, Lucy and David's son, Lucas. Like his Russian-Italian grandfather, Lucas has an excellent memory and, although only about five years old, had memorized the names and numbers of all the American presidents, which my father also knew. So my father would test him: Okay, who's the nineteenth president? Rutherford Hayes. Who's the ninth president? William Henry Harrison. It must have brought back the days when my father recited the names of all the popes and the kings of France.

My father continued to be my father in his more annoying ways. Spending a full week with him was a housekeeping challenge. Living with him was like living with Hansel from the fairy tale "Hansel and Gretel": my father left a trail of crumbs (as well as dirty dishes, half-eaten pieces of food) behind him wherever he went. He would stand in the middle of the kitchen eating without a plate while reading the newspaper, smacking his lips and getting crumbs all over the floor without the least concern as to who would have to clean up behind him. But by this point, I knew my father and didn't expect anything different, and when he was in a good mood, he could be a lot of fun to be around.

Toward the end of our stay, we went to the movies a couple of times. My father had not been to the movies much at all in the past several years, and so for him it was like entering a world of magic. He saw two moderately good movies, but he was simply awestruck by how good the performances were and how much fun they were. The second movie ended with some samba music playing as the credits rolled, and my father did the samba as we walked out of the theater. He had looked like a frail man of ninety when we left for this brief vacation, and he looked fifteen years younger, fitter and stronger by the time we left.

My father could still be enormously difficult. He almost undid a great deal of the goodwill he had created shortly afterward. Sarah, a friend, and I were having dinner one evening with my father, and at a certain point in the discussion, Sarah, who was thirty-two and had almost completed her PhD in art history, said, "Well, as an art historian, I tend to think—" My father interrupted her and said something like: "Do you really consider yourself an art historian? I think of people like Rudolf Wittkower and Ernst Gombrich as art historians, not someone who hasn't even finished her PhD." Sarah burst into tears and stormed away from the table, rather violently bumping my father's chair as she ran to the ladies' room. "Why is she so touchy?" my father asked, looking bewildered. Sarah was so furious that she told me that if my father didn't apologize to her, she was going to have nothing more to do with him—ever. "You tell that old man that I am not going to lift a finger for him anymore unless he tells me in person that he is sorry." I explained everything to my father and told him he needed to apologize. Perhaps because he was old and realized that he was very needy, he apologized.

Now that my mother was no longer alive and Lucy was in Los Angeles, we decided to spend Christmas with Sarah's family in New Jersey. We persuaded my father to come down with us for Christmas Eve, my father complaining the whole way. "I should have stayed at home. I was so warm in my bed."

On the way we visited a local clothes store in Princeton, Landau's, to look for a winter coat for me, which was going to be Sarah's combination Christmas-birthday present. Misha was enchanted with the store, attracted by the reasonable country prices. "This is a great store," he said, insisting on trying on various Icelandic sweaters that he didn't need and would never wear, and that looked terrible on him. "Don't be ridiculous, they look excellent on me!" I was looking to buy a simple duffel coat, which they had on sale for $195. But we were all taken with a very handsome lined gray Austrian loden coat. Unfortunately, it was $490, considerably more than I wanted Sarah to spend. After we left, my father said to me, "If Landau's had been open another hour I would have bought you that coat." "What would it matter how long the store was open? If you had wanted to buy the coat you could have gotten it when we were there," I said, somewhat annoyed. "You don't understand anything about life," he said. I had failed evidently to factor in the Kutuzov principle: that one needed to gradually evolve toward that kind of decision. It seemed to me an excuse.

But the next day when we took him to the train (we were staying on for a couple more days), he took Sarah aside and said, "I've decided to get Sandro that coat. Can you buy it without his knowing it and I'll pay you back?" When Sarah told me (I needed to know, since I was still thinking of getting one of the two coats), I was genuinely touched.

"I have realized recently how much, now that Mom is dead, I have come to depend on having him around," I wrote in my journal. "I am no longer irritated by having him telephone three or four times a day. There is a great deal of easy intimacy in our conversations. I can joke and banter with him. I don't open myself up that way with that many people."

Then there was an incident that made me feel that he was losing control.

January 29, 1995

The other day I got several calls from my father. He wasn't feeling well, he had diarrhea and the timer clock on the stove was ringing incessantly and couldn't be turned off. We needed to do something on the East Side together. When I saw him he didn't look well, he was very pale, thin and he walked very slowly. I decided to walk him home and cook him some dinner.

The house, which was so beautiful when my mother was alive, looks like a bomb hit it. Newspapers and magazines are taking over like tropical vegetation. There are stacks of magazines on the couch, piles of newspapers on the dining table so that there are not even two places free to eat dinner at. The timer in the kitchen is screaming at full throttle. By simply turning it, I get it to stop, although it goes back on about every fifteen minutes. One of the knobs on the stove is missing. Two of the handles of the kitchen cabinets have broken off. Paint is chipping and the entire place needs painting.

"Dinner is ready," I said. I had made a chicken soup with carrots. "I just want a clear broth, this soup is too heavy." "When somebody does a favor for you, don't complain," I said. "I'm sure it's good, you've been very sweet."

. . .

He told me that the people at Harper & Row had called him to ask about the book he had contracted to do with them eight years ago and had never produced. He had taken a $30,000 advance and hoped they would simply go away, which they appeared to have done before yesterday. "What should I do?" he asked. "If I were you, I would buy a fake mustache, dye my hair, and quietly slip out of town."

But after this visit, I began to fear that he might not be able to live on his own. My father was fiercely independent and bristled angrily whenever I suggested that he might consider living with Sarah and me. People die as they live, I thought. My mother slipped out quietly so as to cause the least disturbance possible, all of her errands crossed off on her list. My father's death was going to be a mess.

It didn't exactly turn out that way.

June 2, 1995

My father died early this morning. At about eight o'clock last evening I got a call from Lally, who was worried because she had been trying to reach him and he had not answered the phone. She couldn't get into the apartment because he had locked the upper lock of his door, which none of us had keys to. The newspapers were still outside indicating he had never gone out.

He had been declining noticeably in recent weeks, looking particularly sallow and weak and showing some signs of disorientation. Sarah called him yesterday morning about sending him a Polish cleaning lady, he had been a bit rude, saying: "I don't want to talk about that now." She had been irritated. I called him at about 10:30, he had sounded fairly normal, but he had not wanted to talk for long and said I'm feeling a little woozy. I should have known something was wrong. I worked all day and called him at around 5:30 in the afternoon. No one answered. I thought he had gone out to do a little shopping as he often did in the late afternoon. I made a mental note to call back in an hour to check on him, but forgot. I rode the stationary bicycle and was preparing for the arrival of two dinner guests when Lally called.

When I arrived the police and the Emergency Medical people were crowded around in front of the house. They then took a sledgehammer and broke the upper part of the doorframe. I let the police go upstairs first, expecting them to find him cold and dead. "He's all right," they called out. They found him in my mother's old room lying in his pajamas in a strange position on his bed. He had his slippered feet on the floor as if he had been sitting on the side of the bed about to get up but had lain backwards. He was conscious but immobile and strangely disoriented. When the police asked him how he was he said he was fine, but he could not tell them what day or month it was. He had pissed on himself as he had been lying there all day. He was looking up more curious and baffled than frightened, his myopic eyes without glasses squinting a bit. His left arm was twitching slightly.

They put an oxygen mask over his mouth, gave him an IV, and placed electrodes on his body that were hooked up to an EKG machine. It wasn't immediately clear what had happened. His heart seems all right, they said. He might have had a little stroke; it's hard to tell. The officers were talking and joking among themselves as Misha lay there breathing. I suppose it's only natural when this sort of thing becomes a routine business that you can't take it all to heart. "Michael, how are you doing?" "Fine," he said from underneath the oxygen mask. "Michael, do you know what day it is?" He nodded. "What day is it, Michael?" He was silent. "Do you know what month it is?" Same reply. He fidgeted with the wires and tubes on his body. "Misha, leave them alone. They're uncomfortable but they're necessary."

Lally and I scurried around, pulling together a few things to take to the hospital, trying to give ourselves something practical to do while we waited for them to get ready to move him to the ambulance. When I went into the bathroom of my mother's room, I saw all the Xeroxes of his old articles that he was going through for the collection of his pieces spread out all over the bathroom counters. The jungle of newsprint had already engulfed almost every other possible surface in the house—tables, beds, couches, and chairs—but the bathroom was an alarming new development. A sign of the Kamenetzki disease run out of control, the last frontier of disorder.

Lally was scurrying around the apartment getting a night bag for him. Do you think this pair of pajamas is all right? Do you think this robe is all right? she asked, glad to be busy with this task rather than watching her brother under the oxygen mask, looking about the room in confusion and fear. "I am so glad he's alive," she said. "I was afraid we would find him dead."

. . .

They carried him downstairs and wheeled him to the ambulance. There was a large urine stain on the bed where he had been lying in a semicircle. I lifted up the sheet to air it out and wondered whether the mattress would be badly damaged. When I went down to the street, the cops and the EMS men were flirting with a young woman wearing shorts and a halter-top. She was out walking her dog. Inside the van, Misha continued to agitate about the wires and tubes, trying to remove the oxygen tube from his nostrils. He would stop when I told him to, but then would start again a minute or two later. His right hand groped along the wall, trying to grab on to something, and his left arm twitched strangely. "Michael, do you know what day it is?"

We took him to Mount Sinai hospital. "This is where it all begins and where it all ends," I said to Sarah when she arrived later. I was born and dropped on my head at Mount Sinai, my mother had a few of her operations there. Lally had been operated on there. And now here was Misha.

He was taken into the emergency room and he seemed to respond gradually to the intake of oxygen and fluids. He had not eaten or drunk all day and he seemed to revive in the emergency room. He was attended to by a handsome Indian physician who looked like a young Raja. The doctor appeared baffled by what exactly had happened to Misha. There were not evident signs of heart failure. We watched his heart beat regular as clockwork on the EKG. I sent Sarah and Lally home to get his drugs so the doctor could see what doses of medicine he was on. Maybe he had been taking the wrong amounts of the drugs. "How are you feeling?" the doctor asked him. Fine, he said. "One thing you need to know about this patient," I said, "is that he lies like a bandit to all doctors. He always says he's fine." When the doctor asked for the name of his insurance company, he answered correctly and responded with a series of numbers when asked for his social security number, but then stopped after six or seven, fading off into a confused silence. I tried to start up the motor of memory by repeating the first few numbers he had given and he responded, giving several more, but when he gave eleven or twelve numerals, it was clear he had gotten it wrong. "Do you know who the president of the United States is?" the doctor asked him. "Yes," he said. "Who is it?" the doctor asked. Silence. "The president of the United States?" he asked. Silence. "Who is the president of the United States?" he asked, like an exacting schoolmaster. "Gronchi," my father said, referring to an Italian president of the Republic of the 1950s. "Who is the greatest Italian movie actor?" the doctor asked, smiling. I didn't like that. It seemed as if he were making fun of Misha. "That's a difficult question," Misha answered. It seemed so sad that a man who knew more American history than I will probably ever know, and had actually met several American presidents, could no longer remember the name of the president of the United States. He seemed to understand quite well, but he could not come up with names. His mind was like a telephone that could receive calls, but from which you could not call out. After the doctor left, I asked him, "Did you see that President Clinton has said he is prepared to send ground troops to

Bosnia?" My father answered: "He says that, but, in the end, he won't." In fact, this is exactly what happened. So that even though he could not come up with the president's name, he still seemed to have a subtle understanding of things.

At around eleven at night, to my surprise, they decided to release him from the emergency room and send him up to a normal hospital room for the night. There were no rooms available in the fancy new wing of Mount Sinai, so we followed him up on his stretcher bed through elevators and corridors to the old Klingenstein wing. Most of the rooms were empty and a group of nurses were sitting around the nurses' station chatting. We got Misha comfortable in his bed. There was not even a heart monitor in the room, just an IV and a tube feeding oxygen into his nose. There was a big fat black nurse who must have weighed 250 pounds, who called him "Papa." "Now move your leg, Papa. Sit back, Papa." Misha wanted to know where his glasses were. In all the excitement of the evening we had forgotten them. I knew there was something different about the way Misha looked but I hadn't thought what it was. Without the protective barrier/mediating filter of his glasses, his naked eyes looked larger than usual, more curious, baffled and vulnerable. It was perhaps the first time in nearly seventy years he had spent a night without his glasses. Where are my glasses?

He hadn't eaten all day, so I went off to find a vending machine, where I bought a yogurt and juice. I found my way through the labyrinthine belly of Mount Sinai back to Misha's room. He drank the juice and ate the yogurt with relish. He sat up in bed as I fed him the yogurt. He responded every time I told him to take another spoonful. I felt glad that I could do something to take care of him. He seemed like a little bird being fed worms by its mother. The wheel of life comes full circle and the children are feeding the parents. The wheel of life turns, crushing all of us.

On at least two occasions, Misha looked up at me and said, "Povero Sandro." (Poor Sandro.) I found this enormously moving. In the last two years, Misha had often complained about his own lot in life, saying with a sigh, "Povero Misha . . . povero Misha." But now, in this moment in which he was really in deep trouble, he was thinking not about himself, but about me: "Povero

Sandro." Probably he didn't think he was going to die that night, and perhaps he was only feeling bad that we had all passed a long, difficult evening—it was now past midnight and none of us had eaten dinner—but I could not help thinking that he felt sorry for me because he knew he was leaving me alone in the world.

After he had eaten, he said he was tired and ready to sleep. He wanted to go to the bathroom before sleeping. We found a urinal bottle for him to piss into. Sarah and Lally left the room. I did not want to have to do this and imagined this as the first of many horrible, humiliating tasks (for both of us). Luckily he was able to handle his penis and direct it into the hole of the urinal I was holding. Nothing happened and the big black nurse came in. "Come on, Papa." I asked her to hold the bottle while I got a bowl of hot water. He put his other hand into the hot water in order to help the urination. But nothing happened. This is what life comes down to: pissing into a cup, or not being able to piss into a cup. Still I was glad to be able to do something concrete and practical for the person who had given me life. Still, nothing. We gave up and got ready to leave.

Sarah and Lally came in to say good night. He asked Lally what slippers she had brought. Sarah put another blanket on him. "Thank you, I was cold," he said. Those were possibly his last words. We said good night and left.

What to Keep and What to Throw Out

I.

My very early life seems like a parody of a Freudian Oedipal case study: I tried to kill my father and marry my mother.

I can recall very distinctly standing in the door frame of our kitchen on Eleventh Street; my father had his back to me, rummaging through the refrigerator after finishing a story. I had a ball in my hand and calculated the angle it would take to hit him in the head. I must have been very small, perhaps four, for my father, not a tall man, seemed two or three times my size and very, very far away. I threw the ball and, to my amazement, it hit my father right in the head. He wheeled around and understood instinctively the homicidal nature of this premeditated, unprovoked attack. I bolted out of the room and ran for the stairs with him hot after me. I had almost made the crucial turn up the stairs to safety when he caught me and gave me a spanking.

I also remember sitting on my mother's bed after she had retreated to her bedroom after some huge blowup with my father. They often fought during dinner, and if it was particularly bad, my mother would bring her food upstairs on a brown tray. After the shouting and the tears ended, a strange calm prevailed. "Let's leave here right away," I would say. "Why don't we run off somewhere and you can marry me?" My mother laughed.

My parents always had separate bedrooms. Partly, it was a European thing. Plus, they kept different hours: my mother liked to go to bed and wake up early. My father worked until late at night, clipping newspapers and writing stories with the radio on. And then, there was the mess factor: my mother wanted to confine my father's mess to his own room. Of course, the separate bedrooms reflected the considerable distance between them. As a result, I remember feeling shocked and horrified when, every once in a while, I would find my father asleep in my mother's bed when I came into her room in the morning. What was this large hairy interloper doing snoring in *my* mother's bed? The fact that he didn't normally sleep there made it seem particularly monstrous and out of place.

My father was a figure of fascination, admiration, and horror to me. Everything about him seemed Rabelaisian and larger than life. Everything he did, he did to excess. He could work for twelve hours straight or spend all day lounging on the couch; work all day, then attend a string of parties and come home at three. He played poker games that ended at dawn and at which he always seemed to either win or lose large sums of money. No other person I knew stayed in his pajamas until four in the afternoon.

He could be good-natured and funny and affectionate, but his temper was volcanic and when he lost it, the whole house seemed to shake. When he screamed, he screamed louder than anyone else I had ever heard.

For many years he smoked six packs of cigarettes a day, an almost unheard of amount. I wouldn't have believed it had I not heard him tell a doctor who was taking his medical history after he'd been hospitalized for heart failure. "Did I hear you say you smoked six packs a day?" I asked after the doctor left. Yes, my father said nonchalantly, as if this was nothing out of the ordinary. Doing a little arithmetic in my head: at six minutes a cigarette and 120 cigarettes a day, my father would have had to smoke twelve hours a day. But, in fact, this fit with the memories of childhood. For him smoking and breathing were actually the same thing. First thing in the morning, he would light a cigarette and would literally puff and breathe at the same time, the cigarette bobbing up and down in this mouth as ashes curled and fell down the front of his pajamas or on the newspaper he was reading. And when it wore down, he would light a new cigarette from the stub of the last one. When anyone asked him a question or tried to speak with him at that hour he would yell, "Let me breathe! Let me breathe!"

His eating habits were equally extreme. In the morning and early afternoon, he would drink at least a couple of large pots of espresso—black with no sugar—while he smoked and read. (He used these funny Neapolitan coffeemakers that you placed upside down on the flame and then had to skillfully turn right side up when boiling water came dripping out of a hole in the pot, sizzling into the flame of the gas stove.) He would barely eat all day, maintaining his own peculiar kind of ascetic discipline, a prolonged fast fueled by massive doses of caffeine and nicotine, until he had written his daily story. Then he would come downstairs from his room and gorge himself, raiding the refrigerator like a bear pawing his way through a campsite eating everything he could get his hands on. He would slather huge amounts of butter and marmalade onto a large slice of Italian bread—sometimes an entire loaf—and would sit on the couch lustily smacking his lips and spilling crumbs down his front as he read the Italian papers, which were delivered in the afternoon.

His intake of newspapers and the mess in his room were not ordinary. It was unlike any casual disorder I found in the houses of my schoolmates. It was mess on an epic scale with lofty ambitions run amok. It was out of all proportion with what an individual could read and keep up with, and it piled up with alarming speed. And yet my father's efforts to stay on top of it and make order of the growing chaos around him were somehow heroic, if ultimately doomed. On evenings when he was at home he would clip and file articles, and he had a personal archive that was almost on a scale with the archive of *Newsweek*, where I later worked, which was maintained by a staff of several people.

His fingers, like his teeth, were brown from nicotine, and when he drank alcohol, he drank lustily and to excess and could hold prodigious amounts. He could crank out stories in enormous quantities, alternating between the extremes of complete immobility and bursts of activity when he would file two or three stories in a day.

His personal hygiene was also unique. Believe it or not, a game I played with my childhood friend Andew Suhl was a kind of endurance contest to see how long each of us could stand to smell one of my father's shoes, which gave off an unspeakable stench. It was our own private version of rodeo riding, in which the cowboy is timed for how long he can stay atop a wild bull or a bucking bronco. We would time each other while sticking our nose into one of the shoes along the long row of old shoes in my father's closet.

He was ruder than anyone I knew and seemed more brilliant than anyone I knew. These qualities sometimes went together. I can recall watching with a mixture of embarrassment and horror mingled with pride as he skillfully picked apart and dismantled some poor guest of ours with the bullying style of a debating champion: "Let's examine the premise of your argument. If you believe this, then you must also believe that— and yet you say you don't. What are you saying has no logical foundation."

I remember seeing him do this to Marcel Breuer, the great architect and designer. "Don't bring that little man with the dirty fingernails around anymore," Breuer once told his wife apropos of my father (according to my mother), although they continued to be close family friends.

And yet the excess that made the greatest impression on me as a child was his screaming and verbal abuse of my mother. "Shut up, you fool. Spare me your silly nonsense. You have nothing to contribute to this conversation. You understand nothing. You are an idiot!" As a child, I saw their relationship in black-and-white terms and accepted more or less uncritically my mother's version of things, in which she painted herself as an entirely blameless victim and my father as a loathsome villain. I remember walking around as a child repeating to myself: "I will never be like him. I will never be like him. I will never be like him!"

As I matured I gradually saw things in a more complex way. I did not excuse my father's behavior, which was in fact impossible, but I saw my parents as locked into a relationship that was mutual and in some way reciprocal. My mother, staying in her marriage for more than forty years, clearly got something out of it, perhaps even out of the fighting, if only the meager consolation prize of being a victim.

When I was twelve or thirteen my parents' marriage went through the lowest point I can recall. Lucy had left for college that fall, leaving me without a crucial ally and protector. It also altered the already shaky equilibrium in our household. Now that she was gone, my parents fought relentlessly. And without my sister, the family lawyer and diplomat, I was more likely to intervene and, instead of negotiating, end up fighting with my father. In eighth-grade French class, they assigned us Jean-Paul Sartre's *No Exit* (curiously enough, introductory French literature classes at the time routinely assigned very dark existentialist works, because the language was fairly simple), and I remember lingering over the phrase "Hell is other people." I knew exactly what that meant: it described my parents' marriage—at least to me at that time. When I got ready to leave for boarding school, I told my mother point blank, "If you want to leave, go right ahead." From the time I was a small child, my mother asked us if she should leave my father. Even though I hated my father, I also loved him, and I always told her no. Children rarely want their parents to divorce. As a result, my mother always insisted that she couldn't leave my father "because of the children." "Don't use me as an alibi any longer," I said; "if you want to leave, leave." Of course, she did try to leave that year but was back a couple of months later. Lucy recalls that my mother was keen for me to leave home as well, because she thought I needed "positive male role models."

It is not good to go through life hating your father (or wanting to marry your mother), and so I think I felt instinctively the need to redress the imbalance and find ways to love my father without excusing his bad behavior. My father was affectionate; he enjoyed bouncing us on his knee when we were small, but he mostly lost interest in us from about the time we went to school to the time we had reached the age of reason. When we began reading adult books and could discuss them with him, his interest would temporarily reemerge. When my sister changed high schools and needed to be ready for a second-year Latin class, my father rose to the occasion and tutored her. Everything in between—school, friends, playground fights, baseball games, school plays, doctor's visits, dinosaurs, Dr. Seuss, and Winnie-the-Pooh—didn't interest him at all. (Lucy claims that he made my mother hire a babysitter if she needed to go out, even if he was planning on being home alone.)

In my last year of boarding school they suddenly offered an intensive introductory Italian course. I signed up, curious to finally learn a language I had heard my whole life but never understood. I dropped it when I got to university and forgot most of what I knew, but then when I was twenty and in my third year of college, I went to Italy, almost as an afterthought when a trip to England went awry. I asked my father if he knew anyone I could stay with in Rome. He told me to call back the next day and when I did he said he'd found the perfect person: Miriam Chiaromonte, an American woman who was the widow of my father's old friend Nicola Chiaromonte, a brilliant critic and writer who been an anti-Fascist exile first in Paris and then in New York.

2.

There in Italy I was introduced to the world of Italian anti-Fascism, the world my father had grown up in. The Chiaromontes were wonderful people, so decent and self-effacing that it took me years of knowing them well to piece together scraps of their story.

Nicola had left Italy in the early 1930s, as a young man, because he could not abide Fascism and could not stand living in a country where he could not say and write as he pleased. He went to Paris, which was a center of anti-Fascist groups. He briefly joined Giustizia e Libertà (Justice and Liberty), which was the strongest non-Marxist left-of-center anti-Fascist group. Nicola became good friends with André Malraux and other leading French writers and intellectuals. He went to Spain to fight Fascism, served in Malraux's air regiment, and was immortalized in Malraux's novel *L'Espoir*. Back in France, he married a woman of Austrian Jewish origin, Annie Pohl. On the fall of France to Hitler in 1940, her parents committed suicide. Then, during Nicola and Annie's flight to the south, she herself died of tuberculosis and Chiaromonte was forced to bury her with his own hands before making his escape to Algeria. There he met the young Albert Camus, who would become a close friend and ideological soul mate. After Algeria, Nicola went to New York, where he met Miriam in 1941, as well as my father.

Back in Rome, Nicola's parents, brother, and sister had hidden a family of Jews during the German occupation (the family of a friend of my father's, as a matter of fact) but never mentioned it, considering it a normal and unremarkable thing that any decent people would do under the circumstances.

But Miriam did tell me—because it reflected well on my father and not merely on Nicola—that after Nicola's death, my father called Miriam and recited to her a terzet of Dante's that he associated with Nicola:

Facesti come quei che va di notte,
Che porta il lume dietro e sé non giova,
Ma dopo sé fa le persone dotte ...

You were like one who travels by night
and carries behind himself a lantern that, no good to himself,
lights the path for those behind.

Many of the protagonists of that world were now dead—Chiaromonte, Silone, Camus, Malraux—but a good number of their widows were still around, and I met many of them, including Darina Silone, Francine Camus, and Natalia Ginzburg, the novelist, whose husband, Leone Ginzburg, had been tortured and killed by the Nazis. So the world I had read about began to merge with the one I was actually living in.

When I was in Rome I went to visit the painting studio of Carlo Levi, a good friend of my father's who had died recently. Levi had also been a member of Giustizia e Libertà and had been arrested and sentenced for anti-Fascist activity. Rather than sending them to prison, Fascists sent many of their political enemies into a kind of "internal exile," in small towns in southern Italy, where they lived in isolation, having to report to the local police each day. Levi, who had trained as a medical doctor but had become a painter, was sentenced to live in a tiny village in Lucania, in the region of Basilicata. Levi's beautiful memoir of life in Lucania took its name, *Christ Stopped at Eboli*, from a local expression, which meant that the mercy of the Christian redeemer had never reached their remote area but had stopped farther north, in the town of Eboli. It was one of the few Italian books I had read at that point, and I knew Levi had painted many of the people he described in the book. I managed, with Miriam's help, to visit his studio. There was Levi's work, covering the walls but mostly stacked up on racks or against the walls. I was able to pick through the stacks and look at his pictures of the characters of *Christ Stopped at Eboli*, such as the woman who the villagers were convinced was really a wolf. Levi's longtime companion, Linuccia Saba (daughter of the poet Umberto Saba), turned up while I was there. She was by then a very old, rail-thin woman. When I asked her if she knew my father, she answered, "*E come!*" ("And how!")

I had discovered a world that was extraordinarily rich and appealing, the world that had been my father's growing up, where he continued to be loved and admired. Having discovered it, I wondered why my father had excluded us from it.

My experience of Italy, as that of thousands or millions of tourists setting foot in Italy for the first time, was in many ways classic Henry James: that love-at-first-sight sense of being overcome by the beauty of everything. In my case, there was also a strange sense of familiarity, the sense in Rome of walking around what had been my father's and grandparents' world.

3.

That trip changed my life. And I vowed to myself that I would go back and become fluent in the language. After graduating from college, I returned to New York and spent a year living with my parents, working in book publishing, which I quickly realized was not for me. I decided, since I didn't know what to do with my life, that I was better off being lost and directionless in Italy than in New York. At least I would learn another language and get to know better this country I had been so struck by. I began meeting every week with my aunt Lally and reading Italian books very consistently and seriously.

So in early 1980, I went to live in Milan for two years. Very few Italians at that time spoke fluent English, and I lived and worked in an entirely Italian environment. Everything I did from the time I woke till the time I went to bed I did in Italian. I was also living in the city that published my father's paper, so I got to know the world of his work quite well. Knowing relatively few people in Milan, I filled the void by voraciously reading four or five Italian newspapers a day, becoming obsessed with the country's politics. I entered my father's world rather deeply, and we suddenly had many more things to talk about than in the past.

My contact with Italy also helped me resolve another crucial part of my life. It was during those two years that I decided to become a journalist. Of course, any dime-store psychologist could see that this was a form of identification with my father: coming to love Italy had given me ways of loving my father and allowed me to pick a profession that was almost synonymous for me with my father. But it was slightly more complicated than that.

The move toward journalism was one that I had long resisted and one that my family never encouraged. I had always felt, instinctively, that journalism was off-limits. I had always avoided writing for the school newspaper, both in high school and at college, regarding those who did with a mixture of envy and condescension. To volunteer for the paper always seemed like a confession of personal ambition that was taboo or shameful, as if I was invading my father's turf. Instead, I carved out a different sphere for myself. My interests were more literary and less journalistic than my father's, and, for several years, I thought I wanted to write fiction. Perhaps out of reaction, I regarded journalism as a lower form of literary activity, too bogged down in the grubby world of literal fact. But my budding career as a fiction writer hit a point of crisis by the time I was finishing college. I had written a series of short stories that, like much of the work of young writers, had a strong autobiographical component—even though most of the events and plots of the stories were invented. But since my well of experience was rather shallow, I felt by the time I was twenty-one that I had nothing more to say, that I was washed up. I would, I decided, have to do something else.

In my time in Italy, I became entirely absorbed by contemporary events. Italy, at that moment, was in the grip of political violence. Hardly a day went by when someone wasn't shot or killed. There were left-wing kidnappings, kneecappings, and assassinations, right-wing bombs and aborted coup plots, and the government seemed to fall every three to six months. There was a vicious mafia war in Sicily—or was it in fact another form of terrorism? The five-starred emblem of the Red Brigades could be found ominously on the walls of most Italian cities. I met people with bodyguards and bulletproof cars, people whose mothers had been kidnapped, whose older brothers had disappeared into the netherworld of underground revolutionary groups. Making sense of all this became an all-consuming challenge. Reading the newspapers, one would have thought that Italy was on the verge of collapse. And yet as I got to know the country better, I could see quite well that this was clearly not the case. The country was richer than it had ever been, and Italian society was surprisingly stable, even immobile. Governments rose and fell, but the same groups were in power the whole time. Making sense of this strange and violent world, finding some connection between the surface violence and the underlying stability, seemed a fascinating semiotic problem to solve. In helping me grapple with this confusing reality, literature came to the rescue. The theater of Pirandello and the novels of Leonardo Sciascia and Tommasi di Lampedusa made more sense to me than most of the journalism I read. Suddenly I seemed to find a way of combining two important parts of my life, a way to reintegrate my love of fiction and narrative with my new interest in Italy and contemporary politics. The realization that I could practice journalism without abandoning my love of fiction and narrative offered a way out of the dead end I seemed to have reached when I finished college. I had felt that, having exhausted my limited store of life experience, I could no longer go on. Now I realized that I could write about anything that interested me, that I need not worry about running out of material; the world was all before me, endlessly variable and endlessly interesting, and could be written about with the same mind-set and satisfactions of novel writing. I felt as if I had squared my own particular circle.

It wasn't until I realized that I was free to handle factual events with the eye of a novelist—to engage in a different kind of journalism, different from my father's and more in tune with my own temperament—that I decided to go into the field. I did not feel entirely that I was taking the natural step of joining the family business—nor was my decision greeted by either of my parents with enthusiasm. "I don't really think you have the right makeup for it," my mother said. "You struggle too much when you write. You are too reflective. I'm not sure you are cut out to bang out stories on deadline."

My father and I were very different temperamentally. He had not had the luxury, perhaps, of introspection: in order to keep moving forward, he avoided either looking back or looking inside. He felt I was, by contrast, too brooding and introspective for my own good. "You take your temperature too much!" he liked to say. He saw me, I think, as engaged in a lot of Hamletizing, consumed and paralyzed by doubt and self-doubt. "You can't live if you're always taking your temperature," he said, watching me scribbling in my journal late into the night and pursuing readings that he considered excessively detached from the world. He saw me as something of an idle dreamer caught up in chimerical literary fancies without having my feet firmly planted on the ground. One evening, my father saw me lying on the couch spending hours poring over Kafka's "Letter to His Father," a powerful document of Oedipal indictment and filial animus against an overbearing father. "Listen, I know that you tend to get caught up in the things you read," he said to me with a rare delicacy, "and take it for reality. But don't get carried away: our relationship is not like that," he said, pointing to the Kafka book.

Nonetheless, my professional choice did undoubtedly represent some form of identification with my father. Going to Italy and writing about Italy, I was searching for ways in which I could incorporate the things I found appealing about my father into my life. At the same time, I would like to think that my going to Italy and immersing myself in that world helped to some degree to reintegrate my father's life with Italy. In the first decades after the war, he went to Italy infrequently, every two or three years, in part because transatlantic air travel was still new and expensive. He came several times during the two years I lived in Milan. Partly this was because transatlantic travel had become easier and cheaper, but it was also because he had a son living there. I had become good friends with many of his closest friends in Milan, and they became an integral part of our family life.

4.

There was one negative result of my immersion in things Italian. It created something of an asymmetry within our family: I now knew Italian, but my sister did not. My entrance into my father's world accentuated her feeling of being left out and neglected by my father. She had never been to Italy until she was about twenty-nine, when she came to visit me while I was living in Milan. I remember one particularly painful moment when we met up with my father and went to visit some friend of his. My father launched into an involved discussion with his friends in Italian and made no effort whatsoever to include or involve Lucy, not even stopping to translate or explain what he or anyone else was saying. I saw tears welling up in her eyes, and then she lost her composure. My father, of course, was completely oblivious and surprised and annoyed by my sister's sudden explosion of hurt and anger. There was another (in)famous incident when my father and Lucy came to Rome together. She had rather heroically organized the trip because I was dangerously ill in a Rome hospital. She would be staying at my apartment, while my father had arranged to stay with some wealthy friends with a beautiful terrace overlooking the Spanish Steps. On the way in from the airport, Lucy dropped my father off at his friends' house before going on to my apartment. When the door opened and my father's friends greeted them at the door, my father's first words were "Don't worry, she's not staying." My sister was deeply offended, as if she was being treated as some piece of unwanted baggage.

If my father was not particularly encouraging when I decided to go into journalism, he was perhaps even less enthusiastic about my sister's choices. After working in theater administration for a few years (which my parents weren't crazy about), she landed a good job as a literary agent and came to dinner at my parents' house, excited to tell them the news. "Why do you want to be an agent?" my father said. "Agents are whores." Lucy understandably burst into tears and rushed upstairs. "Why is she so upset?" my father asked me. "Why is she so touchy?" "Do you have any idea what you just said? She changes careers and you tell her that her new chosen field is no better than prostitution." "So? I think most journalists are whores," he said. Notice he said most, not all.

Lucy and I chose different ways of dealing with our family legacy. She was equally close to my parents but chose to put a certain distance between herself and them. She moved to Los Angeles in order to marry a man she had fallen in love with and transferred her skills as a book agent to the film business. She not only left New York but abandoned the literary-journalistic world of my parents for the glamorous and more lucrative world of Hollywood, breaking a certain family taboo. My parents could be extremely narrow-minded and judgmental and my sister felt, with some justification, that they never fully embraced or accepted her choices. Being farther away geographically and in a field they didn't really understand, she felt she got less attention and approval than I did. This was very painful to her. But distance had its advantages, too. And Lucy, to her credit, made her choices work very well. Not only did she build a highly successful career as a respected agent, but she also managed what—given our family background—would have to qualify as a genuine miracle: she made a successful marriage. Against all odds, she found a man who resembled my father in various ways but without any of his worst qualities. He was short, dark, intense, myopic, and Jewish, a very successful journalist with a large, charismatic personality and a big nose, but, unlike my father, he was kind, considerate, loving, generous, and extremely romantic. My sister may have lost some things by moving away from my parents, but she gained a lot, too.

5.

Remaining in my parents' world worked for me professionally, but that closeness may have exacted its price in my personal life. Against all my best intentions, I had helped create a relationship with Sarah that had (even if in a less dramatic fashion) something in common with my parents' marriage, and yet I felt compelled somehow to continue in it.

One day, as I thrashed around on the psychotherapist's couch, trying to figure out whether or not to marry, I called up the images of my forebears and thought of the generations of marital unhappiness in my family. I thought of Ilya and Sara Kamenetzki and their loveless marriage bed, from which my grandmother had expelled my grandfather when he began cheating on her. I thought of George and Lolita Bogert, frequently at odds with each other, each interested in other people but unable or unwilling to act on that interest. Then there were my parents, locked in their own version of Sartre's *No Exit*, tearing at each other's throats. So much unhappiness transmitted from generation to generation, so much unfulfilled longing and desire. Am I going, if I move ahead with this marriage, to take my place in this chain of misery and carry it forward another generation? Put in these terms, my choice seemed obvious, and yet this history was deep and powerful and I felt it like a swimmer swimming against the tide, with the massive swell of the ocean current carrying me farther out to sea as I struggled to reach the shore.

My parents had been, I felt, swept along by similar currents—my father had been tossed about by history from revolution to revolution, country to country, which left him deeply insecure and anxious. My mother's early life with her own father had predisposed her to be with someone as difficult and demanding as my father. And now I felt the force of things heavy on me, generations of unhappiness weighing like a boulder on my chest, making it difficult to breathe and impossible for me to move.

Finding the courage—several years later—to break things off was a crucial turning point in my life. And in Sarah's as well, I hope. Although I had been functioning quite successfully in my professional life for nearly twenty years, I felt that leaving my first marriage was the first truly adult act of my life, albeit at the age of forty.

When I came to marry again a few years later, I did so in an entirely different spirit. I was lucky enough to meet someone whom I wanted unambiguously. Our relationship was remarkably harmonious and unproblematic. Lexi died suddenly and unexpectedly at the age of thirty-two, after we had been married about a year and a half and just three months after our son was born—but that is another story.

Despite the loss of her, I felt I had pretty much banished the demons of my past, and that my relationship with Lexi bore no resemblance to my parents' marriage. The well-being I felt with her, despite the pain of her loss, has carried over into my life after her death, so that I feel far happier now than I think I ever felt in my twenties or thirties.

Casting out the demons of my childhood did not, I think, mean rejecting my parents and cutting all ties with my past. Quite the contrary: over many years I had gathered information and material about my parents, out of simple filial curiosity as well as a vague, unarticulated sense that there was something important and valuable there for me to understand. Sorting through the complicated mess of their lives, understanding what drove them, grasping the force of things, helped me step outside the stream of their lives and into my own life and also gave me greater compassion for their mistakes and excesses.

6.

A couple of years after Lexi's death, I was still in the New York apartment where I had been living for fourteen years. I had moved there from Italy with Sarah in 1993, soon after my mother's death. We had furnished the apartment largely with things we had gotten from my parents—the sofa, the dining table, the elegant glass coffee table they had had in Milan, the rugs on the floor. The art on the walls was theirs, much of it done by my parents' friends, Tino Nivola, György Kepes, Bessie Boris. For two or three years after my father's death, I had been unable to part with any of his vast library of about ten thousand books. I put all the books that Lucy didn't take back to Los Angeles into storage and for years paid monthly storage fees for books I had no practical way of keeping. I built bookcases from floor to ceiling on all four sides of our dining room and on virtually every other surface that wasn't needed to put my parents' pictures on. The object I had most coveted from their New York apartment, the contents of which Lucy and I divvied up after my father's death, was a large, handsome revolving bookcase that had been perhaps my father's most prized piece of furniture. He didn't care much about things like that, but this was a bookcase, one that managed to hold a wall's worth of books but was well made enough to swivel slowly and elegantly. Now it sat proudly in my living room. Of course, as a writer and journalist I was always accumulating books and papers of my own. We lived in an old, generously proportioned pre–World War II Upper West Side apartment, with twelve-foot-high ceilings, nice architectural detail, and large closets. These apartments were somehow well suited to the kind of people who lived on the Upper West Side, many of whom were Jewish refugees and pack rats (like my aunt). Our apartment contained an incredible amount of stuff. With each passing year, I was reduced to putting books on top of the bookcases, cramming paperbacks sideways into the spaces between the top of the books and the shelves. The closets were jammed with papers, boxes, old curtains, spare blankets, clothes we never wore. On top of my parents' things and my things, some kept from my marriage with Sarah, we now added Lexi's things, which I could not bring myself to part with even a few years after her death.

The apartment, even when cleaned, had assumed a somewhat oppressive feel, crammed to the gills, as if things were going, at any moment, to tumble off the shelves and fall on top of us. I knew that if there was suddenly 20 or 30 percent less stuff in the apartment, everything would feel vastly lighter and better, but it never occurred to me that I could simply get rid of furniture or books that had belonged to my parents, let alone my own or Lexi's papers and books. And yet I began to feel that I was living in something of a mausoleum, an unchanging museum of an apartment where I was hemmed in and oppressed by the accumulation of stuff. The material objects were, of course, a metaphor for something more important.

These particular walls had seen too much of my life: two marriages, two serious illnesses, the death of my father, the death of Sarah's stepfather, one divorce, two books, my second bachelorhood, my courtship with Lexi, Sam's birth—his bris took place on the dining table—Lexi's death, my third bachelorhood, my fourth book. Lexi's clothes were still in the closets and her photographs and jewelry still around the apartment. "It looks as if your wife has gone around the corner to run an errand, not as if she is dead," one woman I dated politely observed.

My father's child, I had a hard time with change and a difficult time throwing things out. But I realized that if I stayed in this same apartment, in five or ten years, I was going to feel very stuck, and that if my life was to move forward, I would need to move. I owed it to myself and to my little two-year-old son not to live in a household that felt stuck in the past.

As circumstances would have it, Columbia University, where I had begun teaching, offered me a three-bedroom apartment that was radically different from anywhere I had lived before. The apartment was in a massive, ultra-modern high-rise tower. It was on the forty-fourth floor of a fifty-story skyscraper. The building had no charm or character, but being on the forty-fourth floor, our apartment was full of light and had spectacular views of New York from every room. I had grown up in a nineteenth-century brownstone and had been living in an early-twentieth-century apartment building that was full of architectural detail and character but, like many of the buildings of that era, a bit run-down. This skyscraper was clean and modern with a certain hard, minimalist aesthetic, a kind of sleek beauty—perhaps it would do. I quickly realized that if I moved there, I could not live in the same way as before. My old apartment, with its high ceilings and shabby gentility, was tolerant of clutter and a certain amount of disorder. This modernist, minimalist building wanted clean and uncluttered spaces and surfaces; it could not have been more hostile to the Kamenetzki aesthetic. To live here, I realized, I was going to have to become a different person.

"I don't think you can bring all your books here," Vicki, Lexi's mother, gently suggested. "It's going to overwhelm the apartment." The new apartment had large, wide windows, a whole wall of windows in the living room to take advantage of the spectacular view; this meant, of course, also less wall space for books. She tactfully indicated that she didn't think there was a good space for the beautiful but large revolving bookcase that had been my father's prized possession. I resisted at first but had to concede the point. There was no reason to move into a place like this if I was simply going to reproduce my former apartment. Part of the point was accepting, even embracing change. As a compromise, she offered to drive the bookcase up to Great Barrington, where Lucy and I still kept my parents' old country house. In fact, I had kept it almost unchanged since the time of my parents' death.

With great pain, I realized that, even though the new apartment was slightly larger than my old one, I would need to get rid of about 20 to 30 percent of my books to live comfortably in the new space (as well as about 20 to 30 percent of everything else). Throwing out a book, according to the Talmud, is strictly forbidden, and I felt both my father's spirit and this atavistic prohibition rising up inside myself as I prepared boxes of books either to sell at the Strand used bookshop or to leave out on the street.

I brought cases of books up to the country and then realized that in order not to pollute that house, I needed to do a major culling there, where another four or five thousand family books resided. The closets of the house were (are) full of books that I had saved from my father's old library. But I realized that there were hundreds of books in the house that I realistically would never read: copies of Virgil's *Aeneid* in Latin; Pleiade editions of Karl Marx in French; a French book on the Jewish scholar Maimonides and the tradition of Jewish mysticism. It was painful to think of getting rid of these books, fruits and examples of my father's extraordinary broad and eclectic erudition. I remembered the days of my father's last summer, which Sarah and I spent with him out on Long Island. Sarah had reconstructed the contents of the personal library of the great Italian sculptor Gianlorenzo Bernini, full of long-forgotten seventeenth-century and Renaissance books, many of which had not been reprinted in centuries. Sarah would read off the titles, and to her and my amazement my father could actually identify most of the books and knew what they were. Getting rid of these books felt a bit as if I was trampling on my father's grave (which in fact was just up the hill), but I knew it had to be done. At another level, it felt good to make my life lighter. Having moved, I suddenly realized that I was not obliged to continue acting as the custodian of my parents' stuff forever. I could, if I wanted, replace furniture of theirs with things I liked better. There was nothing wrong with buying new furniture that fit my new apartment and getting rid of pieces of theirs that didn't seem to fit or that I was simply tired of. I was free to live as I chose and not be a slave to objects, even if some of those objects were books, which I had always held as sacred. And yet I still felt guilty getting rid of books: to relieve my guilty conscience I made a list of some of the more notable titles.

Ernst Kantorowicz's *Les Deux Corps du Roi*, Gallimard and his biography of Frederic II. Edmund Husserl's *Cartesian Meditations* (in French).
François Furet's dictionary of the French revolution
an Italian edition of Jan Huizinga's *The Waning of the Middle Ages* . . .

Having avoided this task for so many years, I now attacked it with a sense of mission and zeal. I worked with great determination but in a highly emotional state, not with the tranquil mind of someone accomplishing a useful task but in the feverish state of someone performing a kind of exorcism, doing something psychologically necessary but painful, feeling alternately relief and sorrow.

I was aware, of course, that there was something ridiculous about making a drama of what for most people is a normal part of life: moving. There was a particularly comic moment when I tried to move my father's revolving bookcase up to the house in Great Barrington. The bookcase was too big to get through the door to my father's room. I had to take the hinges off the door (a major project for someone as unskilled as myself), and when I finally got it in there, it looked all wrong. It seemed to swallow up the room and block out all the sunlight. The revolving bookshelf that had been in my father's room was out of proportion with the living room and didn't work there. It was much too big to get upstairs. So we had lugged this massive piece of furniture up to the country and suddenly had nowhere to put it. The only possible remaining room was my mother's bedroom. My mother had gone to great trouble to create a room with a wonderful sense of ease, in part by its being clear and open. Suddenly, with this substantial piece of furniture in it, the room took on a slight feeling of Kamenetzki clutter. I had polluted my mother's inner sanctum with my father's unmistakable touch. Looking at this large, handsome, but dark and somewhat cumbersome piece of furniture in my mother's light, clean, uncluttered room was a bit like watching my mother and father glaring at each other across the room while conducting an argument. The whole business of moving, of sifting through all my possessions, shifting back and forth between the desire to keep things and the aesthetic desire to keep things clear and simple, had cast some kind of spell: as if my mother and father had risen up from the dead and were warring for my soul.

The process of sorting out things—what to keep and what to throw out—brought about by moving was really a metaphor for growing up. What do we incorporate from our early lives; what do we keep of the psychological baggage handed down to us from our parents? And what part of their ways of doing things do we cast off as being unnecessary, unproductive, or even harmful? Disposing of their stuff was the final act in this process of deciding which parts of my parents' lives to incorporate into my own and which to leave behind.

Perhaps not coincidentally, I was undergoing this move at the same time as I was working on this memoir. Both were a sorting through of my parents' lives: picking my way through the letters, interviews, quotes, and episodes was not unlike the process of examining an article of clothing in a closet or dusting off a book in my father's library and deciding whether to keep it or throw it away. To some degree, my ability to get rid of my parents' material legacy—literally their things—was made easier by the fact that I was trying to distill what was most important about them to me into verbal form. I scanned documents and photographs, transcribed letters, dated, organized, and inventoried them, photographed my father's articles from Italian libraries, created a personal archive in which the rich and messy complexity of their lives was reduced to a few gigabytes of digital data and kept neatly inside my hard drive, as memories of them were in my heart and mind. As I tried, however imperfectly, to give shape and meaning to their lives (as I understand them), to restore texture and color to their fading memories, it seemed natural that their legacy should move from the material plane to the immaterial one, that they did not need to exist in physical form but only as memory and words.

Coda: A Counter-Narrative, or the Man Under the Rug

The week I handed in the manuscript of this book I had a terrible nightmare: a dead body turned up unexpectedly in my hotel room. "I didn't kill this person," I thought, "but everyone will think I did." I went outside to clear my head and when I came back the body was gone. I breathed a huge sigh of relief and went about my business as if nothing had happened. But a little knot in my stomach remained, as if to say, this can't be the end of the story; dead bodies don't just appear and disappear. Then, as I was packing up to leave, I couldn't find my camera and, looking around, noticed a lump in the rug. Thinking the camera might have somehow ended up under the carpet, I lifted it to find a man's head, or rather the front third of a man's head, sawed off from the rest, like a bloody mask. I put the rug back down in horror. "Now they are definitely going to think I killed this person," I thought. "What am I going to do?" Perhaps I could just leave it under the rug and hope that no one would notice. After a moment, I realized that this was ridiculous: the hotel cleaning staff would find it as soon as they vacuumed the room. What if I put it in a plastic bag and threw it out in the garbage somewhere? It might never be found. But then I would be actually committing a crime, destroying evidence, and if it were traced to me I would look even guiltier. Perhaps that's what whoever put it there wanted me to do. Either way, I was sunk. At that point I woke up.

I recognized the face of the man whose bloody head was hidden under the rug, but he was someone I barely knew, a friend of a friend. His presence seemed quite random until I suddenly remembered something: the man's wife was an author who had written a book based on his family and his father, who had committed suicide. Then, not long after the wife's novel appeared, his mother committed suicide. My dream was clearly a dream of guilt and anxiety about writing a family memoir, guilt about pillaging the lives of the dead and anxiety about harming the living. After all, in writing about my parents, wasn't I something of a body snatcher? I hadn't killed them, it's true, but wasn't I, to some degree, trafficking among the dead? The relief and apparent ease after the disappearance of the body felt a bit like my state of mind while working on the book: since the book remained unpublished, I worked calmly, but with a hint of anxiety, knowing that a day of reckoning was somewhere ahead. I felt I had treated my parents as fairly as I could, but would my parents' friends and relatives feel that I had betrayed their memories? Certainly I had portrayed them differently than they would have portrayed themselves. But my parents were dead and their story was also mine.

My greatest concern was for my aunt Lally, my father's sister, who was very much alive and could well be hurt. Her apartment, which I described, was obviously a source of great shame. "Maybe she'll never read it," various friends said. This struck me as akin to the absurd moment in the dream when I briefly imagined I could hide the bloody face under the rug and no one would notice. "Of course she'll read it," I said. "There is no way I can publish a book about her family in which she is a character without her knowing about it!"

For a time, it seemed as if my nightmare was coming true.

I decided that the best policy would be to give the manuscript to my aunt to read before publishing it and give her a chance to comment. Months went by. "I'm afraid to read it," she told my sister. "Look, if you don't want to read it, that's okay," I said, "but then you can't complain afterward. If you want to comment you have to read it relatively soon." Four or five more months went by, and I decided to give her an ultimatum. "I've been busy, doing my taxes," she said. "Let's see, Lally, August, September, October, November, December, January, February, March, April, and May. I would think ten months would be enough for you to do your taxes and read this manuscript. I am giving you one more week."

Finally, she read it, and she was livid, so angry she would barely speak to me. "It's all wrong, it's terrible. I want you to remove me from the book entirely!" Interestingly, she was not upset by the things I would have expected her to react most strongly to: the description of her apartment and her compulsive hoarding. "That's all true," she said with a wave of her hand. She was upset by a series of other things, which I considered relatively minor—and potentially fixable—but which were not minor to her.

She was much more upset by how I had described her parents' apartment than her own apartment.

"It's not true that our apartment was dark or poorly kept, that the beds were left unmade," she said.

"That's what Lucy and I remember," I said.

"It was kept in perfect order. We had a cleaning lady. You were small children. Are you going to trust Lucy's memory from when she was nine or me?"

"Your credibility when it comes to housekeeping is not great."

"And it's not true that Mumi was ugly," she said.

"I never wrote that she was ugly, I said she was 'plain' and 'matronly,' which was true," I said, "I remember her and I've seen the photographs of when she was younger."

"She was attractive and beautiful as a young woman," my aunt said. "She wasn't thin, but she had a wonderful profile. And she had lots of men courting her. Everything you write is negative. It's disgusting.

"Everyone who knew Mumi agreed on one thing: she was a truly uncommon woman, she was exceptionally cultivated, kind, and a real Signora."

"But I wrote all of that," I said.

"It's not just the facts, it's the spirit that's all wrong, all negative," she said. "Everything you wrote about Father is negative. You might have written about him in a humorous way. Probably your views were poisoned by your mother's. When you and Lucy were born he opened a savings account for both of you, and although he didn't have much money, he put money into it. Nobody else did that, but he did.

"You make it seem like I have had a sad and empty life. I don't feel that way. It's not true. You obviously don't know me very well. You weren't interested." What was undeniably true was that she had had a long life—a couple of different lives—before I had really gotten to know her. I had begun to spend time with her when she was in her late fifties when she was living alone in her apartment filled with stuff. She had worked after World War II for an Italian pharmaceutical company, a job of responsibility and prestige, which she had greatly enjoyed. "I was the head of the Carlo Erba office here in the States," she said. "I managed $1.8 million in Marshall Plan money, buying drugs for Carlo Erba. I flew here and there signing contracts and making deals, first class. If I didn't finish university, it was because I chose to work instead. You write that

Misha gave us money to help us live. It's not true. He never gave us a dime until Father died. Misha paid for the funeral and he paid for Mumi's hospital care, but that's it. For years, I made more money than Misha."*

"You make it seem like I am some kind of poor, lonely spinster. If I didn't marry, it was my choice. I wasn't cut out for marriage.

"In your account of things, I do everything wrong. The only thing I did right was teach you Italian. I gave you the wrong Christmas presents and I didn't know how to knit. The little white jacket with a hood I knit for Lucy was perfect—perfect—and she wore it a lot!

"According to you, I am some boring old woman, who talks on and on about her silly dog. Ciao was not silly, she was extremely intelligent. One Christmas I had gotten a *panettone* that I was going to give to a friend and had placed it on top of the refrigerator to keep it safe. Ciao managed to move a chair over to the refrigerator, climb up on the chair, and get the *panettone*. She replaced the chair and took the *panettone* over to another part of the apartment. I was angry at first when I saw the *panettone* gone, but when I saw the incredible intelligence with which she had gotten it . . ."

But along with the factual disagreements, my aunt had a much deeper point, which was highly insightful and deeply touching. "The person you describe is not someone a person could love—only pity. And I don't want to be pitied by you or by anyone else! You don't really know me."

My aunt's objections—most of them quite reasonable and all of them entirely comprehensible—cut deeper, to the heart of the whole enterprise of writing a family memoir. The writer is taking something that belongs to several people, appropriating it for himself, and turning it into something that inevitably feels alien and wrong to those who have lived some of those events, but from inside another skin, and who have equal rights to the same material.

I had not treated my aunt as a human being, something of infinite

---

*The only documentation for my grandparents' finances was a "family budget" that had been prepared toward the end of my grandparents' life, which reported their monthly household income as being $328, $178 of it from Social Security and $150 from my father. It also mentioned another $115 as coming from my aunt. But I have no idea whether this document represents the real state of their finances or was prepared for some public purpose, to qualify for some kind of health insurance.

complexity and, in effect, unknowable; I had turned her into a character in a book. I had mostly focused on one aspect of my aunt's life—her apartment and her inability to throw things away—making her into something of a tragicomic figure in a story about my parents and the family as a whole. The apartment was an important motif in the book—both as the terminus of the Kamenetzki line, where all my grandparents' stuff and papers wound up, and as a kind of metaphor for a certain refugee mentality shared by my father and his sister. I had my good reasons for using the material as I did—and including everything she wanted me to include would have turned the book into something quite different: a biography of her, not the book I wanted to write. But, quite understandably, she did not want to be a character or a metaphor in someone else's book; she wanted to be, as she saw herself, the protagonist in her own story.

By the time I showed the book to my aunt, I had gradually become aware of how difficult a process this was as I consulted with various family members in the course of working on the book. Few of my relatives reacted positively to it. While I had been most concerned that they would object to the way I had characterized my parents, the thing that seemed to upset them the most was that their own experience had been minimized and marginalized. "I guess I wasn't that important to your mother," one of them said. "You have erased me from the historical record," said another.

I gradually began to understand that there was a common denominator to these different reactions, that the very act of my writing about our family, which was of course also *their* family, was deeply destabilizing in and of itself. It went much deeper than wounded narcissism. The psychology of it was far more complex. What my aunt—and my other relatives—were reacting to was something else. I had taken pieces of Lally's own life and put them into a narrative entirely different from what she would have written, so that they were now in fact deeply alien, in ways that made them almost unrecognizable to her. All of us, after all, develop a conception of the world and our place in it, work out a narrative of our lives, and these are things we need vitally to live. This narrative in our head is as basic as feeling the earth beneath your feet, and having someone else come along with his own narrative—especially if it is published and becomes a kind of official version—is deeply destabilizing, like having the ground start to shift underneath you and become unstable. After all, I was asking her to read about a piece of her own life—or rather her parents' lives—but placed in another context, the context of my parents' lives rather than her own, and told in my voice, not her own. Moreover, for reasons of literary economy, I had eliminated masses of detail, greatly foreshortened various characters' roles, like her own, in order to focus on what was, for me, the main story: my parents and their marriage. (It must have been like seeing someone else wearing your favorite coat: it would look instantly recognizable, but totally different—and totally wrong.)

During the months of my wrangling with Aunt Lally about the book, she turned up one day with a spiral notebook that contained a forty-page account of her life, written carefully in page after page of neat handwriting, all in the third person so that it could simply be inserted into my book. "Here's what you need to put into the third chapter," she said.

It was, in effect, a counter-narrative, written from her own point of view, albeit in the third person.

She began reading it aloud: "It's really ironic that Lally, who did not want to come to the U.S. and hoped that she would not be able to go, achieved a success in the U.S. in business and in her private life beyond any expectation, greater than she would have ever achieved in Italy."

The central episode in her narrative was her years running the New York office of Carlo Erba, which was started in order to take advantage of funds made available through the Marshall Plan. It was the high point of her career and a period of her life of which she was especially proud. Although she was a young woman in her mid-twenties without a college degree, they entrusted her with considerable responsibility, which she evidently carried out with great dedication. When the need to send signed contracts back and forth between the United States and Italy gummed up the works, the Americans suggested that Carlo Erba give Lally power of attorney, which the "*consligere delegato*" of Carlo Erba agreed to do. She wrote, "He had met Lally and was very well impressed, considering her very capable and trustworthy. So Lally handled the entire operation from A to Z with great success."

Lally's great point of pride was that working with the Marshall Plan required a high degree of planning and expertise: "Orders had to be placed at the beginning of the year and if you had estimated costs inaccurately you risked losing some of the Marshall Plan money, which was left unspent. Lally knew the exact cost of everything and estimated the costs of freight and shipping and insurance so precisely that she guessed almost exactly right, leaving a surplus of only $200." There are not a few elements of touching vanity in the document, about how fussed-over she was in her new status as business VIP.

One of my favorite passages is her description of a trip she took to Italy for Carlo Erba.

In December of 1950, Lally came back to Italy. She flew Pan American first class VIP treatment—Pan Am was her favorite airline. When she arrived at the airport she was the last passenger of the 1st class and was walking towards the plane. Three attendants came to her one carrying flowers, one a big box of chocolates one with a telegram. She felt and looked like a movie star elegant in a blue wool skirt, ¾ top lined with gray astrakhan fur, the lapels were also grey astrakhan as well as the cuffs, and with this send off she boarded the plane . . .

At the purchasing Department they knew that I was an Italian Jew that had left because of the racial laws and considering my work thought that I was a woman in her forties with Jewish features. Imagine their shock when they saw a good-looking blond girl in her late twenties, smiling and elegant. They told me that. They were all very friendly and took me out to dinner and to the theater . . .

She was also anxious to defend her reputation as a knitter, which she felt I had maligned, and wanted to emphasize that for many years she had showered my family with beautiful presents: "Lucy came home from the Presbyterian Hospital with the outfit I knitted her in yellow because we did not know the sex of the baby . . . with little yellow boots, yellow bonnet, adorable coat with white pearl buttons. I also gave Lucy Xmas a white knitted cap and gloves." Lally, in effect, wanted to substitute her own narrative for mine—entirely understandable but impossible.

After months of discussions and disagreements, I wrote Lally a long letter listing the things I was prepared to change and the things I was not prepared to change—and why. Perhaps more important, I explained why I had wanted to write the book—something she genuinely didn't understand. Afterward, she said quite simply, "As long as you write that before you knew me I had a successful career working for the Carlo Erba pharmaceutical company, you can leave in all the rest." This was an extraordinarily gracious and magnanimous position to take. She had understood that this was my book, told from my point of view, and that it didn't presume to be a complete record of her life. But that is not an easy position to arrive at and demonstrated a considerable largeness of soul, for I knew that she was never going to be truly happy with the book. She died a few months later. She refused all medical help and insisted she wanted to be left alone in her apartment to die with the same fierce independence with which she had lived. I was glad that we had come to some resolution with the book—even if it had taken a year.

The conflict at the heart of memoir is inevitable and fundamentally tragic. Not tragic in the sense that it must lead to broken relationships and enduring ill will—it is possible for family members, outside of the frame of the book, to minimize the damage. I changed things when I felt they were right, adding things or making cuts that I felt would genuinely improve the book, rather than water down or weaken it. But I knew that I could never fully satisfy them because it would still be my book, told in my voice, not theirs. For even when I try to give Lally's side of the story—as in this counter-narrative (she hated that, too!)—although I quoted her objections at length, they are nonetheless folded into a narrative of mine. I, of course, could not help plucking out her spirited and lengthy defense of her dead dog, Ciao, to help build my version of her character. And so she once again found herself trapped as a character in my story—a tragicomic character, something quite understandably she did not see herself as.

Within this kind of work there is inherent conflict—a kind of head-on collision. The reasons of life and the reasons of literature are not—and cannot be—the same, no matter how truthful or "lifelike" we make them. Life is infinitely complex and messy, and literature works the opposite way: through the distilling and fixing of things into a limited number of words and pages that then (one hopes) takes on a life and meaning of its own. We do, in effect, kill off the people we write about in order to turn them into characters in a book, characters who draw their life from those real people like vampires feeding on the blood of the living. And it is entirely natural and appropriate for others to react and defend their own conception of things as if they are fighting for their lives.

I did kill the man under the rug.

Acknowledgments

This project has received help of various kinds from different quarters. I owe an extraordinary debt to my late aunt Myra (Lally) Kamenetzki, whom I interviewed dozens of times and whose outstanding memory and recall of fact and detail greatly enriched this book, as did the large trove of documents she jealously kept in her apartment. My uncle George Bogert and aunt Virginia (Ginny) Sample were also exceedingly kind and generous with their time and passed along many stories and family documents that were invaluable in filling out the picture of the Bogert family.

Dana Prescott, director of the Civitella Ranieri Foundation, gave me a chance to begin work on this book—a precious and greatly appreciated opportunity. I am very grateful for the support of the Solomon R. Guggenheim Foundation for a yearlong fellowship, without which it would have been extremely difficult to make significant progress. The American Academy in Rome generously offered me a period of residence during my Guggenheim fellowship, which allowed me to consult local archives and provided me with an exceptionally beautiful and serene place in which to write. The Academy's president, Adele Chatfield-Taylor; its then-director, Carmela Vircillo Franklin; and the assistant director, Pina Pasquantonio, were unfailingly kind and supportive, as was the Academy community as a whole.

Because of the highly personal nature of this book, I made much greater use of outside readers than usual. In dealing with matters so close to the heart, self-critical faculties may abandon one, and outside eyes are crucial for avoiding (or minimizing) false notes and rhetorical missteps and for maintaining the right tone and proportion. Among the many who gave essential assistance of this kind, I would like to thank Polly Weissman, Suzanne Bocanegra, Louis and Anka Begley, Joan and Jay Wickersham, Donna Masini, Carroll Bogert, Lucy Stille, Erika Fry,

Alice Wohl, Claire Nivola, Suzanne Daley, and Amy Bagan. Rob Maass generously helped me by reshooting many old family photographs for use in the book. Mary Streezel and Francesca Trianni contributed valuable research.

I would also like to thank those at The Wylie Agency—Sarah Chalfant, Scott Moyers, and Andrew Wylie himself—who helped me think through the conception and publication of the book. Jonathan Galassi at Farrar, Straus and Giroux is a remarkable editor and a close reader with a terrific ear and a sensitive touch. Jesse Coleman performed all the important work at FSG of moving from manuscript to printed book. Lisa Silverman did a super job as the book's copy editor, as did production editor Mareike Grover.